# The Tennessee
VOLUME TWO

---

Southern Classics Series

M. E. Bradford, Editor

# Southern Classics Series
## M. E. Bradford, Series Editor

| | |
|---|---|
| *Donald Davidson* | The Tennessee, Volume I |
| *Donald Davidson* | The Tennessee, Volume II |
| *Caroline Gordon* | Green Centuries |
| *Caroline Gordon* | Penhally |
| *Augustus Baldwin Longstreet* | Georgia Scenes |
| *Andrew Nelson Lytle* | Bedford Forrest and His Critter Company |
| *Thomas Nelson Page* | In Ole Virginia |
| *William Pratt, Editor* | The Fugitive Poets |
| *Elizabeth Madox Roberts* | The Great Meadow |
| *Allen Tate* | Stonewall Jackson |

# The Tennessee

VOLUME TWO

## The New River: Civil War to TVA

DONALD DAVIDSON

Illustrated by
Theresa Sherrer Davidson

with a preface by
Russell Kirk

J. S. Sanders & Company
NASHVILLE

Copyright 1948 by Donald Davidson,
Copyright 1992 by Mrs. Eric Davidson Bell.

Preface to this edition © copyright 1992
by J. S. Sanders & Company

All rights reserved. No part of this publication may be reproduced or transmitted in any form or by any means, electronic or mechanical, including photocopy, recording, or any information storage and retrieval system now known or to be invented, without permission in writing from the publisher, except written for inclusion in a magazine, newspaper, or broadcast.

*Library of Congress Catalog Card Number:*
91-62454

ISBN: 978-1-879941-08-3

Published in the United States by
J. S. Sanders & Company
P. O. Box 50331
Nashville, Tennessee 37205

Distributed to the trade by
National Book Network
4720-A Boston Way
Lanham, Maryland 20706

1992 printing
Manufactured in the United States of America

# Contents

| | | |
|---|---|---|
| | PREFACE BY RUSSELL KIRK | vii |
| I. | AMPHIBIOUS WARFARE: PADUCAH TO FORT HENRY | 5 |
| II. | THE BATTLE OF SHILOH | 25 |
| III. | THE STRATEGIC IMPORTANCE OF MUSCLE SHOALS | 40 |
| IV. | CHICKAMAUGA AND ITS SEQUEL | 51 |
| V. | GUERRILLAS VERSUS GUNBOATS | 77 |
| VI. | FORREST WREAKS HAVOC AMONG THE GUNBOATS | 91 |
| VII. | THE COST OF CIVIL WAR | 107 |
| VIII. | PARSON BROWNLOW AND THE KU KLUX KLAN | 118 |
| IX. | KINGDOM COMING | 137 |
| X. | THE LAST GREAT DAYS OF THE STEAMBOATS | 156 |
| XI. | THE UNEASY REIGN OF KING KILOWATT I | 176 |
| XII. | TRIALS BY JURY AND OTHERWISE | 195 |
| XIII. | AT LAST! THE KINGDOM REALLY COMES! | 213 |
| XIV. | THE TVA MAKES A NEW RIVER | 226 |
| XV. | THE WORKINGS OF TVA | 251 |

|       |                                                                                          |     |
|-------|------------------------------------------------------------------------------------------|-----|
| XVI.  | NAVIGATION, NEW STYLE                                                                    | 272 |
| XVII. | GREEN LANDS AND GREAT WATERS                                                             | 289 |
| XVIII.| THE BATTLES OF TVA                                                                       | 306 |
| XIX.  | JOURNAL OF A VOYAGE FROM CHATTANOOGA TO PADUCAH ON THE GOOD STEAMBOAT *GORDON C. GREENE* | 334 |
|       | ACKNOWLEDGMENTS                                                                          | 362 |
|       | BIBLIOGRAPHY                                                                             | 364 |
|       | INDEX                                                                                    | 371 |

# Preface

We have it on the high authority of Richard Weaver that Middle Tennessee is the most Southern part of the South—culturally, that is. Near the town of Pulaski, in Middle Tennessee, Donald Davidson, the most Southern of twentieth-century Southern writers, was born in 1893. Yet by 1948, when the first edition of Volume II of *The Tennessee* was published, Professor Davidson found himself very nearly a prophet without honor in his own land, where the molders of popular opinion were concerned.

To Allen Tate he wrote, on 24 February, "Vol. II has been favorably received *outside* the South, but nearly all the Nashville, Chattanooga, Knoxville, Memphis reviews have sneered at my 'prejudices' and done their best to injure me. They hate me because in Vol. II I do something they can't endure—i. e., tell the plain, true story of Civil War, Reconstruction, later agitations, and TVA."[1]

Doubtless a good many Tennessee journalists, by the middle of the twentieth century, disliked Mr. Davidson because he was unreconstructed. New York City he abominated. On his annual expeditions from Nashville to the Bread Loaf School of English at Middlebury College in Vermont, Davidson took pains to avoid passing through Gotham. For nearly three decades, by 1948, Davidson had been a leading light of the Fugitives and the Agrarians, who stood high in American thought and letters during the 'Twenties, 'Thirties, and 'Forties. Some of those Southern writers and scholars fell silent or fell away during the era of Franklin Roosevelt; but Davidson still labored undiminished to the end of his life.

PREFACE

The Agrarians, and the Fugitives too, were genuine conservatives in a time of vertiginous change; so, despite the attention these writers obtained nationally, it was not easy for them to get their writings published—or, once published, to be kept in print. Nevertheless, their high talents gave them a degree of ascendancy over humane letters in America, even in Manhattan, until recent years—when the literary oligarchs of the publishing trade and of *The New York Review of Books* sneered away the remnant of the Agrarians' influence upon the *cognoscenti*.

Agrarians and Fugitives illustrated wondrously well Lionel Trilling's observation that the twentieth-century writers possessed of imagination distinctly were not liberals.[2] Allen Tate was so bold as to publish his *Reactionary Essays*; all the Agrarians reacted against modernist materialism.

In 1927, Davidson had published *The Tall Men*, some of the better verse in a decade of many good poets. The Tall Men are the heroes of old Tennessee. That book's prologue was entitled "The Long Street"—that thoroughfare the symbol of modern industrial existence, sterile and stifling, in opposition to the agrarian freedom of which Davidson was the most consistent and persistent defender. The Long Street is the urban desolation of an iron age of "dead men under a pall, nameless and choked."

Thirty-five years later, in his *Poems, 1922–1961*, Davidson would return to the charge, undismayed although beaten in many a fight for the good old cause, speaking

> *For us, deliberate exiles, whose dry sod*
> *Blossoms athwart the Long Street's servile rage . . .*

After Davidson's death in 1968, the South's pace of change would be more rapid and more overwhelming than even the gloomiest of the original twelve Agrarians had predicted in their collection *I'll Take My Stand*. Old Nashville would be thoroughly "urban renewed" and uglified, Strickland's Capitol on its hill beset by the arrogant office towers of state bureaucracies. Davidson lamented to this writer in 1955 that the Vanderbilt

PREFACE ix

campus had been converted into metered parking lots. Much else would go by the board, once Davidson was gone.

I first discovered Donald Davidson in 1938, when his polemical book *The Attack on Leviathan* was published by the University of North Carolina Press; a copy appeared on the new-book shelves of Michigan State College's library. It was an eloquent denunciation of political and cultural centralizing: strongly impressed, I took it that Davidson's readers must be numbered in the hundreds of thousands. Actually, I was one of the very few readers of the first edition. In the 'Fifties, I would name *The Attack on Leviathan*, in the pages of *The American Scholar*, as the most deserving neglected book of recent decades. A second edition, brought out by Peter Smith, would appear in 1962; and in 1991 I would bring out a third edition, with my introduction, through Transaction Books (the subtitle, *Regionalism and Nationalism in the United States*, being substituted for the original title).

When Donald Davidson and I first met, in the 'Fifties, Davidson would marvel that I had come upon *The Attack on Leviathan* at all; in a letter to me dated June 10, 1955, he would explain why few copies of his book existed:

> I now own the copyright; it was assigned to me by the University of North Carolina Press, just a few years ago, after Lambert Davis came in as editor of the Press—and after I had a terrific row with him. I was assured by my lawyer that I had grounds for a suit against the Press, but I did not have the money to carry the suit through. When Bill Couch [editor of that Press in 1938] printed the book, he left some hundreds of copies in sheets, to be bound up as demand might occur. During the interim, after Couch left and before Davis came in, a man named Wilson filled in as editor. He undertook to 'clear the stock room', and since the *Leviathan* had not been selling in quantity, he 'pulped' the stock of my book that was in sheets, and so, in effect, put the book out of print, since only a few bound copies remained. But he did not notify me before taking this action and give me the opportunity to buy the

stock, as the contract required the publisher to do. Furthermore, I discovered that the Press was withholding from me fees for reprint permission—and I had to come down hard on them to get the money that was due me. It was obvious to me that the book was being in effect "suppressed", and though Lambert Davis, Wilson's successor, protested that it was not so, I knew very well that if the book had been "liberal" or "radical", rather than "conservative", it would have been kept in print, or would have been reprinted, for it was continually being cited and was in some demand. Davis, by the way, in an interview he had with me in Nashville, had the gall to explain to me that he was a "Christian Socialist."[3]

Despite such encounters, Davidson was a polite and good-natured gentleman. His students and disciples invariably referred to him, even posthumously, as *Mr*. Davidson. He had an erect military carriage. Andrew Lytle was uneasy with his friend Davidson's Puritanism: once Lytle was shown a photograph of the extended family of the Davidsons, and none of them was smiling. Yet Davidson was a lovable man, warm-hearted. In Burke's aphorism, "They will never love where they ought to love who do not hate where they ought to hate."

In this volume about the New River, the second volume of *The Tennessee*, Davidson employs his narrative talents to describe the several stages of the defeat of the old society of the Tennessee valley by modernity: by war, by courts of law, by electrical technology and dam-builders, by grand-scale social planning. By the things technological and the things political that were done to the land and to the people who cultivated the rich soil along the river, more than the valley and more than the states of the Old South were altered almost out of recognition.

Here, as in his earlier writings, Davidson rowed against the tide of opinion among America's intellectuals—against that intolerant liberalism which had brought about the suppression of the first edition of *The Attack on Leviathan*. His Old River volume had been accepted and praised by reviewers, for substance and style, because it did not touch immediately upon subjects controversial about the middle of the twentieth century. But the New River volume was a challenge to liberals' dogmata concerning the Civil War, the Scopes trial, the Scottsboro case, the Tennessee Valley Authority, and much besides.

Davidson knew his adversaries for the intellectual heirs of Ralph Waldo Emerson. Nowadays the Tennessee Valley is forgiven by the North for its stubborn guerrillas during the Civil War only because it has been wholly subjugated by TVA and can be pitied as a part of an "Appalachia" presumably depressed and backward.

Davidson's second volume of *The Tennessee* is political as well as historical. But Davidson never divorced politics from religion or from imaginative literature, or tradition, or history. He knew that the greater works of politics have been poetic, from Plato onward. He was aware all too well of the huge blunders in public policy during the twentieth century: one finds in this volume subtitled *The New River: Civil War to TVA* three chapters exposing the failures of that enormous undertaking the Tennessee Valley Authority—so warmly commended by the liberal press, that TVA, and eventually by most Tennessee politicians, too. Donald Davidson, professor of literature, perceived the great flaws that engineers and sociologists preferred to ignore.

On the original board of directors of the Tennessee Valley Authority, the youngest member of that triumvirate (which pretended to establish a new form of democracy in the valley of the Tennessee!) was David Lilienthal. In this present volume (page 223) Davidson takes Lilienthal's measure:

> Of the three men, Lilienthal was farthest removed from the ancient, indigenous life of the valley; in fact, in comparison with the other two men, he seemed more definitely an "outsider." But Lilienthal was suave, as the two Morgans were not; he had obvious gifts of personal attraction that bound followers to him. He was essentially an advocate, and a skillful one, full of passionate conviction about the benefits of electric power and the great possibilities of TVA.

Davidson was not enraptured with Lilienthal. He comments (pp. 326–327) on that eminent administrator as chairman of TVA:

> Mr. Lilienthal was urbane and friendly. He could explain everything down to the last acre-foot, ton-mile, and kilowatt-hour, and was not bashful about doing so. In 1944 he published a little book, *TVA: Democracy on the March*, in which he gathered up all his explanations and restated them with his usual success. Reading it, you were bound to feel that everything was hunkydory in the Tennessee Valley. Tramp, tramp, tramp the boys were marching, although not to the old tune or in the same uniforms. All over the country people said what a wonderful thing it was that Mr. Lilienthal was doing for those poor fellows in Tennessee and Alabama.

Two decades after Lilienthal wrote his little book, this present writer appeared on television with David Lilienthal (Eric Sevareid's network discussion-program). Mr. Lilienthal still was urbane and friendly. He was then engaged in vast "development" schemes for the Shah of Iran, financed in large part by American money.[4] During the 1970s, as matters would turn out, the consequences of such developments would fetch the Shah down to his ruin; but meanwhile Mr. Lilienthal and his development firm would do very well indeed out of the Iranian equivalent of TVA. Our television discussion, with Mr. Sevareid as moderator, turned to the question of liberty. Was liberty diminishing in our time? Not at all, Mr. Lilienthal instructed us: for liberty, he said, is the ability to make choices. Because of the growth of wealth, far more liberty has come to pass, he went on, more choices thus having become available to Everyman. Riches, in short, equal freedom. This sophistry might not have gone down well with the Tennessee farmers dispossessed of their ancestral land, nor with their Persian-gardener counterparts. Davidson was quite right when he discerned in Lilienthal the archetype of the "futurist" promoters he detested.

Davidson's chapters on the blunders and misconceptions of the TVA could not undo that gigantic scheme, of course—although

PREFACE                                                              xiii

his earnest words may have done something to avert the creation of similar undertakings on other great rivers of the United States. Davidson was aware that he spoke for a lean and almost proscribed minority, even in Tennessee.

"Living in Nashville and teaching at Vanderbilt University," he wrote to me on August 31, 1954, "is very hard on a Southern Agrarian, I can assure you. It is, in fact, nothing but warfare, and we can't survive very long without some place to lick our wounds for a while." (He was then writing from Ripton, Vermont.)[5]

Vanderbilt University's administration disparaged Davidson and the other Agrarians; and in effect for a time would not accept as a gift Davidson's or Tate's papers. Only when New York City paid attention to Tate, Warren, Ransom, Lytle, Davidson, and other Southern writers did the South prick up its ears. As that seventeenth-century "Person of No Quality" had put it,

> *Seven cities now contend for Homer dead,*
> *Through which the living Homer begged his bread.*

Christian humanism, stern criticism of the industrial mass-society, detestation of Communism, attachment to the ways of the Old South in valor and in manners—these were the principles joining the twelve Southern Agrarians who took their stand in Dixieland in 1930, Donald Davidson eminent among them. Their book *I'll Take My Stand* has been discussed ever since. Tide what may betide, the Southern Agrarians loom large in American thought and letters. With liberalism in America now adrift, some of the rising generation are finding in Donald Davidson's prose and verse, and in the writings of other Agrarians, an understanding of personal and social order far removed from the desiccated liberal attitudes of 1992.

"Worn out with abstraction and novelty, plagued with divided counsels, some Americans have said: 'I will believe the old folks at home, who have kept alive through many treacherous outmodings some good secret of life.' So Davidson wrote in his chapter "The Diversity of America" in *The Attack on Leviathan*. "Such moderns prefer to grasp the particular," he continued. "They

want something to engage both their reason and their love. ...
They are learning how to meet the subtlest and most dangerous
foe of humanity—the tyranny that wears the mask of humanitarianism and benevolence."[6]

Poet, critic, folklorist, ballad-collector, social thinker, eloquent polemicist, Donald Davidson was wondrously humane and emphatically no humanitarian. In death, he has not been silenced.

*Mecosta, Michigan*                                                   RUSSELL KIRK

1. John Tyree Fain and Thomas Daniel Young (eds.), *The Literary Correspondence of Donald Davidson and Allen Tate* (Athens: University of Georgia Press, 1974), p. 348.
2. See Trilling, Preface, *The Liberal Imagination: Essays on Literature and Society* (New York: Macmillan, 1950), pp. ix–xv.
3. This and some twenty-five other letters of Donald Davidson to Russell Kirk are in the Kirk Papers, Clarke Historical Library, Central Michigan University, Mount Pleasant, Michigan.
4. For Lilienthal's ruinous developments in Iran, see Grace Goodell, *The Elementary Structures of Political Life: Rural Development in Pahlevi Iran* (New York: Oxford University Press, 1986). In her concluding comment on his undertakings there, she writes, much in the spirit and style of Donald Davidson (p. 341): "Mr. Lilienthal 'prophesied and promised' that the world would be watching his transformation of the Dez. Would that in *that* prophecy he had been correct! The Dez will not see him or Mr. Ebtehaj again, the founder of one more dynasty's Imperial Plan. But many other northern Khuzestans across the world will, as we continue to send out myriad visionaries like them to transform the 'nothingness' wherever they can find it: with the same self-serving vision; the same certainty of engineers, economists, and bankers that 'the majesty of man' will 'master this behemoth' by building 'things'; the same blindness to the landscape; the same grandiose schemes that we can construct 'the everlasting' in it—the same confidence in developing others through the fiat of centralized rule over them from on high."
5. Kirk Papers, Clarke Historical Library, *op. cit.*
6. Donald Davidson, *Regionalism and Nationalism in the United States* (original title, *The Attack on Leviathan*) (New Brunswick, New Jersey: Transaction Publishers, 1991), pp. 11–12.

# The Tennessee
VOLUME TWO

CHAPTER I

# Amphibious Warfare: Paducah to Fort Henry

A<small>T HALF PAST EIGHT</small> on the morning of September 6, 1861, three steamboats loaded with Federal soldiers came up the Ohio and drew close to the landing at Paducah, Kentucky. Two gunboats, black and ugly-looking, covered the landing, and threw a few shells at a Confederate flag that flew high and brave near the waterfront. But there was no resistance. The flag vanished before the troops disembarked. A small force of Kentucky state troops, commanded by Lloyd C. Tilghman, then Colonel Tilghman, a native Paducahan, withdrew as the Federals entered. Later, more Federal troops came across from the north bank of the Ohio by a hastily improvised bridge, in which flatboats served for pontoons. The Federal commander read a brief proclamation. The mouth of the Tennessee was in possession of the northern armies.

It was Mrs. Emily Jarrett that took down the Confederate flag. When the guns started shooting, she sent a little Negro boy to climb the flagstaff. He was scared by the shells, but he was still more scared of Miss Emily, and so he climbed up and climbed down, and, ashen-faced and trembling, brought her the flag. She decided to take it down because she wanted to put it away in a safe place against the time, which she felt certain would arrive, when Confederate troops would re-enter Paducah in triumph. A squad of soldiers came to search her house, but they did not find the flag. More than thirty years later it was draped on her funeral casket and was buried with her. Except for a few brief hours in the spring of 1864, when Forrest's bold cavalry rode into town, Confederate forces did not re-enter Paducah during the war.

The commanding officer of the Federal expedition was a stocky quiet man who smoked a great deal and said little. He had a queer way of delaying answers to questions. If he kept on striking matches without being able to light his pipe or cigar, that meant he was excited, or puzzled, or perhaps embarrassed, or perhaps that he was just turning the question over carefully in his mind. As soon as he had the answer, the tobacco became magically ignited, and he spoke his mind between puffs. He was a man little known to Paducahans and to the world—Brigadier General Ulysses Simpson Grant, with headquarters at Cairo. Prevented from earlier movement by the necessity of observing the neutrality of Kentucky, he had really intended to occupy a seemingly more important position at Columbus, on the east bank of the Mississippi. But Bishop Polk, who was the Confederate general in command in the territory just east of the Mississippi, had moved his forces from their position south of the Tennessee line (where he, too, had been observing Kentucky's neutrality up to a certain point) and seized Columbus two days before. Grant took Paducah, then, as second-best, but as things turned out, it was really first choice. While he was about it, he occupied Smithland, not many miles above Paducah, and thus the mouths of the Tennessee and the Cumberland were blocked to the Confederacy.

Grant had begun the first effective invasion of southern soil. He had taken the first step toward the series of great battles that were to lead up the Tennessee and then on to Vicksburg, to Chattanooga, to Sherman's March Through Georgia. In its ultimate consequences, Grant's seizure of Paducah was decisive and far-reaching. It was a more fatal day for the Confederacy than the day of Lee's repulse at Gettysburg.

When Grant, in the late winter of 1862, moved upriver with his gunboats and transports, a new commanding officer took charge at Paducah, now a Federal base teeming with activity. The new man was red-bearded and redheaded, with sharp flashing eyes and a sharp rapid tongue. He was slender and quick. He dressed carelessly, and, like Grant, he smoked unceasingly. He was as talkative as Grant was silent, but his quick flow of words had tang and bite. This was General William Tecumseh Sherman, an officer of demonic energy, but, so far as he was publicly known at this time, he was in disrepute. A report had gone out that Sherman was crazy, for he had openly said that it would take tremendous numbers of men and tremendous quantities of munitions to defeat the Confederacy in the West.

Destiny was at hand. Stocky, silent Grant and wiry, red-bearded Sherman were beginning their careers as famous generals. On the banks of the Tennessee, to which their invading armies brought war and destruction, they would win the victories that brought them at last to high command and military greatness. The banks of the Tennessee and the fields and woods beyond it were the school in which Grant and Sherman, still relatively green apprentices, practiced their strategy and learned the art of war in the only way it can be learned—from having to face brave, resourceful, and dauntless opponents.

While these invaders were making their preparations, the scattered and inadequate forces of the Confederacy were striving to get their defenses in order. Committed by Jefferson Davis's policy to a scheme of territorial defense, they were deployed here and there in a tenuous "line" that stretched from Columbus through Bowling Green to eastern Kentucky. Already the dear cost of Kentucky's "neutrality" and Tennessee's late secession was evident, for they were far behind in all their preparations. The prime importance of the Tennessee and the Cumberland was early apparent to them, but their river defenses, at Fort Henry on the Tennessee and Fort Donelson on the Cumberland, just south of the Tennessee-Kentucky boundary, were located more out of respect to Kentucky's neutrality than with regard for strategic considerations. The forts were too near the east-west railroad, from Memphis to Bowling Green to Louisville, that they were in part designed to protect. And in the fall of 1861 they were far from being finished and manned.

Nevertheless, Confederates of the West took great comfort in the appointment of General Albert Sidney Johnston to command their armies. They also rejoiced in the presence of General Beauregard, the hero of Fort Sumter and Bull Run, as department commander and general military adviser. Johnston was a gallant and noble figure; he knew how to lead men, and the Confederates of the West responded to him. And Beauregard had a fine military mind and had already proved his worth. Surely, with such leaders, directing such fighting men as they were assembling, they could defend their home ground and repel the invader.

But neither they nor their generals fully realized the handicaps they were under or the nature of the attack about to be launched. In the fall of 1861 the chief danger seemed to be from Buell's army, which, under Lincoln's specific orders, was turned toward a political objective: the "rescue" of the Union population of East Kentucky and East Tennessee. But the real danger was not there. It was at Paducah. When the blow came from that direction, Johnston did not concentrate to meet it as he could easily have done. The result was Grant's victories at Fort Henry and Fort Donelson, and the loss of Kentucky and most of Tennessee to the Confederacy. Johnston should not be too harshly blamed. Events were already far advanced when he took command. And even the Federal leaders themselves cannot be credited with overmuch discernment and design. They took their opportunities and made the most of them, but they did not altogether understand the reasons for their success.

For that matter, it has not been well understood to this day. Military historians have been fully three-quarters of a century in deciding that the ultimate victory of the North came from the conquering sweep of the Federal armies in the West, which split up the western South and used up Confederate men and resources while it eventually threatened Lee's Army of Northern Virginia from the rear. This theory has been well stated and documented by such British military critics as General J. F. C. Fuller and Liddell Hart. Southern historians of our generation, too—Lytle, in his *Bedford Forrest,* Horn in his *The Army of Tennessee,* Henry in his *"First with the Most" Forrest,* have been sharp in their criticisms of Jefferson Davis and the Richmond strategists who magnified the importance of Virginia as a theater of operations and neglected the West.

But even these illuminating afterviews do not fully explain the true nature of Federal operations along the Tennessee. The sweep of the fighting—the grand "wheel" of the Federal right wing—followed the line of the river. Federal possession of the Lower Tennessee, after the fall of Fort Henry and Fort Donelson and the Battle of Shiloh, made Confederate positions on the Mississippi untenable as far south as Memphis, and cleared the way for the Vicksburg campaign. Later, Bragg's defeat at Chattanooga opened Georgia to Sherman's advance. That much is easy to see. But that is not all.

On the Tennessee, the Federal armies first practiced the tactics of what is now known as amphibious warfare. There it was demonstrated, in terms of strategy and logistics, what it means to have command of the inland waters; or, contrarily, for the Confederacy, how tragic it is not to have that command.

This is the supreme fact that military historians ignore, or dismiss with a side glance. The course of the war would have been very different if the Confederates had held the mouth of the Tennessee, or if they had been able to maintain a strong fortress at the point, near Gilbertsville, Kentucky, where the Tennessee and the Cumberland almost come together, or even if they had kept Fort Henry and Fort Donelson. If they had had river shipping in quantity, both gunboats and steamboats, their military position would have been much stronger, and the Tennessee would have served them well. They could achieve neither of these ends, and so their own river became their foe and aided their enemies.

The map tells the tale. The Tennessee is shaped like a fishhook. The shaft is the Lower Tennessee, which for two hundred miles parallels the Mississippi. The Great Bend is the hook, with its barb in the mountainous region of Chattanooga. An invader who could use the shaft as his approach could turn any Confederate positions on the Mississippi. He could also come into the flank and rear of the defenses of Middle Kentucky and Middle Tennessee. Furthermore, the Tennessee crossed perpendicularly the one important railroad connecting Memphis with Bowling Green and Louisville. Possession of the Lower Tennessee up to Eastport would bring the invader within easy reach of the Memphis & Charleston Railroad. A strong move up the Tennessee would therefore cut east and west connections in a large part of the western South. If the invader also controlled the Cumberland—as he inevitably would if he controlled the Lower Tennessee—he would have two roadways into the heart of the Confederacy and could move his great amphibious expeditions rapidly to the attack and afterwards supply his advanced bases for further drives.

That is what happened. And that is why Johnston and Beauregard, after the fall of Fort Henry and Fort Donelson, had to retire and reorganize at Corinth, south and a little west of the Great Bend. That is why, too, the Confederate defense of the Mississippi above Memphis collapsed almost as quickly as their line of defense in Kentucky and Tennessee.

The evidence shows that the Confederates were early alive to these possibilities, but for several reasons they were slow in taking the proper defensive—or, for that matter, offensive—steps. The neutrality of Kentucky and the late secession of Tennessee delayed preparations, as has been indicated. But even if the Confederates had closed the mouths of both the Tennessee and the Cumberland, they probably would not have been able to make use of the rivers as the Federal forces did. In that sphere, the North had tremendous advantages.

At the beginning of the war, the Lower Tennessee was served mainly by the packets of northern-owned lines, which operated out of St. Louis and the great Ohio ports. When war broke out, these steamers returned to their home landings. The Lower Tennessee—and the Tennessee as a whole—was left short of river shipping, while on the Ohio and the Upper Mississippi there was a vast surplus of shipping ready to be converted to war use. Furthermore, the North, and especially the Ohio Valley, had facilities for building, manning, and maintaining river shipping that were sadly lacking on the Tennessee and not bounteously available anywhere in the South, except perhaps on the Lower Mississippi. The Ohio Valley had skilled pilots—a first necessity. Although not prepared, as Federal naval officers soon discovered, for servicing warships, the Ohio Valley and the Upper Mississippi had the facilities out of which naval yards could quickly be improvised: boatyards, marine ways, repair shops, and supplies. The North could build gunboats and steamboats, manufacture engines and armor plate, and furnish guns. It had everything, and the Tennessee had little.

True, there had been some building of steamboats on the Tennessee before the war. But the machinery had to come from the North. The great majority of the Tennessee boats that were southern-owned were northern-built. There would have been more if it had not been for the old barrier, Muscle Shoals. If the southern states, with or without Federal aid, could have constructed a satisfactory canal around Muscle Shoals they might have had many steamboats and local facilities to serve them when the war came.

The Confederates bravely attempted to "make-do" with what little they had. When Grant's Fort Henry campaign opened, the *Eastport,* one of the finest and speediest of river steamers, was in process of conversion to a gunboat near Cerro Gordo on the Lower Tennessee. The work was in charge of Lieutenant I. N. Brown, who had resigned his commission in the United States Navy to go with the Confederacy. Other Lower Tennessee boats were armed, or were pressed into service as transports and supply boats. All but one of these were lost in the quick Federal advance. The *Dunbar* alone escaped, and with the *Paint Rock,* the *James Glover,* and a scattered few other Upper Tennessee boats, served the Confederacy above Muscle Shoals until late in the war.

On the Ohio and Upper Mississippi, the picture was entirely different. Before the first Battle of Bull Run had been fought, the Federal navy sent one of its ablest officers, Commander John Rodgers, to start construction of a gunboat fleet on the western waters. There was some notion in the West that the salt-water navy could not possibly understand the problems of the western rivers, and for this reason Rodgers was under the command of the army. Although rather poorly supported, Rodgers made rapid progress. By August, 1861, he had purchased at Cincinnati three powerful steamboats and converted them into gunboats. Rodgers cut down their superstructures, lowered the boilers into the hold, provided bulwarks of oak, and fitted them with guns which he himself selected from the ordnance works at Erie, Pennsylvania. Delayed in coming down the Ohio by the low stage of the river, Rodgers was forced to dally for a long while at Louisville, but the gunboats were ready for service and went into action in September of 1861. These were the "old wooden gunboats" of later fame: *Conestoga, Tyler,* and *Lexington*. They were not plated with iron, and were therefore too vulnerable for heavy fighting, but they did the Federal cause excellent service on reconnaissance, patrol, and escort duty.

Meanwhile James Eads was building on the Upper Mississippi the formidable ironclads that came into service late in 1861 and early in 1862: *Baron de Kalb* (first known as the *St. Louis*), *Carondelet, Cincinnati, Louisville, Mound City, Cairo, Pittsburgh, Essex,* and *Benton.* It was a considerable feat, all things considered, to build these boats and equip them for service in the late winter and early spring of 1862. The Confederacy had nothing to meet them on the Tennessee, and not until Columbus and Island No. 10 had been taken were they able to challenge this great array on the Mississippi.

The ironclads, though formidable, had their defects as fighting craft. Since they were expected to fight bow-on, their two and a half inches of armor covered only the more vulnerable parts, the forward portion, the boilers and wheel, the pilothouse; and even two and a half inches of armor were not a protection against heavy rifled cannon. Therefore they were exposed to the worst of all mishaps for steam vessels: explosion of the boiler. Furthermore, they drew six feet of water, and were therefore unsuitable for use on the Tennessee, except when the river was high. The need of fast, light-draft gunboats was evident, but this building program did not get under way until after the Battle of Shiloh.

The indefatigable Rodgers, after building the nucleus of the Western Flotilla—later called the Mississippi Squadron —was denied the privilege of commanding it. He was returned to eastern service and in his place came Captain A. H. Foote, a boyhood friend of Secretary Gideon Welles. Foote arrived barely in time for the occupation of Paducah. At once he took firm hold, and energetically rushed the building of the gunboat fleet. His gunboat commanders were all able and daring men: Henry Walke, Roger Stembel,

W. D. Porter, and others like Gwin, Shirk, Paulding, Winslow. There was some difficulty in recruiting crews and gunners. The Great Lakes furnished some men; others were old "man-of-war" seamen from the East; some, in desperation, were recruited from army ranks. There was also trouble in enlisting pilots, partly because the army under whose command Foote had to operate, would not meet the civilian rates of pay and partly because the pilot's job on a gunboat was all too clearly a more exposed and unsatisfactory kind of piloting than any Ohio or Mississippi pilot had ever contemplated. Commander W. D. Porter, sent to recruit pilots, offered a savage recommendation that all licensed pilots at St. Louis be compelled to report to the office of the provost marshal.

Those old river men knew, all too well, that the Confederates were handy with rifles. And who wanted to stand at the wheel when not only rifles but cannon were banging away? Furthermore, if the gunboat grounded on a sand bar or reef, the pilot would be blamed, and his loyalty might be questioned. Lieutenant Shirk, commanding the *Lexington*, reported in January, 1862, that his boat "was run upon a rock by a person who represented himself as a Tennessee river pilot." The angry Shirk confined the pilot in double irons, but finally released him after becoming convinced that his action was not deliberate. Well might a pilot ask himself whether these fussy and dictatorial naval officers would understand the usage of the rivers, where the pilot is king in all matters of navigation, or whether, indeed, a deep-sea sailor could begin to comprehend the tricky ways of a great river. Nevertheless, Foote got his pilots, and, in the end, enough of everything; if not enough to please him, abundantly more than the struggling Confederates.

With such a fleet, well manned, well officered, and powerfully armed, the Federals possessed enormous advantages for warfare along the rivers, particularly the Tennessee. From the base at Cairo, gunboats could move quickly to the strategic points: down the Mississippi to attack forts and escort transports; or up the Ohio and around the corner into the Tennessee and the Cumberland. They could afford to be more venturesome on the Tennessee than on the Mississippi, for on the Tennessee they were moving upstream, and a disabled boat had only to drift to safety with the current until temporary repairs could be made or a tug or a sister boat could take hold. If the boat needed to be laid up for general repairs, it dropped back to the convenient docks at Mound City, Cairo, or St. Louis.

But gunboat commanders drove their craft to the limit, and would not be put on the ways unless it was absolutely necessary. As long as their boats were anywhere near being riverworthy, they steamed up and down on an unceasing round of miscellaneous duties, though their New England and Great Lakes crews withered in the southern heat and fell sick in scores from malaria. During the campaign of 1862, one of their chief duties was reconnaissance. Back and forth they cruised, spotting Confederate positions and picking up news of troop movements. Upon occasion, as at Fort Henry, they led the attack—though this might be costly, as Foote learned at Fort Donelson.

Normally, they convoyed troop movements and protected landings and embarkations. Sometimes these were the vast movements of whole armies. Sometimes they were special expeditions, like Colonel Abel D. Streight's cavalry raid across North Alabama in 1863. When the Confederates learned, as they quickly did, that the river was serving their enemy as a supply route, and began to harry the freight steamers, the gunboats had to convoy all supply movements, as oceangoing supply fleets are convoyed in our time. The gunboats also acted as blockaders. They stopped and examined suspicious boats and checked the movements of southern cotton, in which a large illicit trade developed during the war. They broke up cross-river communication whenever they could, by confiscating or burning ferryboats, flatboats, and small craft. They rushed help to Federal detachments that got into trouble. In the later, grimmer years of the war they became marauders, harrying the population along the riverbanks and delivering punitive blows at towns and houses. They carried off fugitive slaves and transported contingents of Union sympathizers away from the wrath of their Confederate neighbors. They sometimes ferried large bodies of Federal troops across the river.

One could argue, not without plausibility, that the decisive factor in the western campaigns was, in the last analysis, the Federal naval force. Certainly the river fleet was an indispensable element in all the major campaigns in the West. With excellent reason one of the principal Federal armies in the West took its name from the river and was called the Army of the Tennessee, while its valiant opponent, the Army of Tennessee, took the name of the state. The Federal command based its operations on the rivers and named its armies for rivers. The Confederate army was a land army, committed to the defense of territory and confined to railroads and highways for its movements.

The western campaign of 1862 was the only extensive campaign of the war that was deliberately planned and carried through under winter conditions. Like Caesar's legions in Gaul, the armies of the Civil War generally subsided into winter quarters when cold weather came on, because roads became impassable for large troop movements. But Grant needed high water for the gunboats and transports. Therefore he came upriver in February, during the winter rise of the Tennessee. Handily and quickly, Grant put his striking force exactly at the point where the blow must fall, while Johnston and his armies, hastening to adjust their deployment to an unorthodox situation, struggled through snow, ice, and mud.

The Tennessee state government was fully aroused to the danger of a movement up the river, and Governor Isham

G. Harris, in September, 1861, sent Captain Jesse Taylor, an ex-naval officer and an experienced artillerist, to examine the defenses of Fort Henry. Taylor noted at once, with dismay, that the fort was placed in a river bottom, and was commanded on east and west by lofty ridges, spurs of the highland that borders the Tennessee at this point. Still worse, he found watermarks on trees above and below the fort and concluded that "we had a more dangerous foe to contend with than the Federals—the river itself." When the February rise came, he estimated that there would be two feet of water in the fort.

Taylor did what he could to persuade state authorities to improve the defenses, but the state troops were in process of being taken over by the Confederacy, and he found himself being referred to Polk, who in turn referred him to Johnston. Johnston sent his engineer officer, Major Jeremy F. Gilmer, to make improvements, and Gilmer at once decided to fortify an additional position, a bluff on the Kentucky, or west, bank, just across from Fort Henry. Much time had been lost, and this position, known as Fort Heiman, was not completed or armed before the attack came. At Fort Henry the armament, though powerful, was not as strong as the importance of the place demanded. There was one excellent six-inch rifled gun, and one huge Columbiad; the rest, all smooth-bore guns, were not good enough to meet gunboat fire.

The gunboats were already showing up. From time to time they appeared on reconnaissance and shelled the fort in an effort to draw fire and discover gun positions.

In the autobiography of Lew Wallace, author of *Ben Hur*, we are told exactly what such reconnaissances were like. Wallace, a newly made brigadier general, was stationed at Paducah, and he was the guest of Lieutenant Phelps, on the *Conestoga*, during one of the last reconnaissances before the attack. This was in January, 1862. Wallace was impressed by the broad, black, low-lying *Conestoga*, by her great bow gun, the scrubbed whiteness of the deck, the silent stealth of her cruising, the snappiness of the crew, and the white napkins and tablecloths of the officers' mess. On both sides the country seemed closed up, unpeopled. Nobody came to look at them from the shut houses. Late in the January afternoon they heard the yelp of hounds. Presently a Negro "contraband" came running toward the river and made for the willows on the bank near the gunboat. Men on horseback and dogs were after him, and he was escaping to the "Linkum gunboat," or so Wallace and his companions thought. Phelps called for rifles. They fired at the men on horseback, and sent a yawl to pick up the Negro. The mounted men withdrew, but the dogs came on, and were snapping at the Negro's dangling heels when the yawl reached him among the willows. His tale was that he had tried to escape, and had been discovered and pursued. Now here he was, panting and ashen, telling the story that he knew the Linkum gunboat expected to hear.

Next morning they uncovered the bow gun and posted two sentries to gaze into the water. They were "in the torpedo zone," and were going slow. Cavalry videttes raced along the bank to warn the fort of their approach. Phelps put the *Conestoga* into the western channel at Panther Island, rounded it, and moved, bow-on, toward the fort. There it was: a flagstaff with some dim flag drooping; low bastions, hardly discernible above the riverbank; the noses of three heavy guns at their embrasures; the roofs of barracks and sheds. They came up and stopped, at a distance. While they looked, an officer stepped to the parapet and quietly looked back at them. Later, Wallace found out that this officer was General Lloyd Tilghman. Through his glasses Phelps checked the guns. One big new gun had been mounted since his last reconnaissance. He signaled the pilothouse, and the gunboat turned downstream. On the way back, Phelps wrote a report for Grant: "Fort Henry I have examined, and the work is formidable. There are a thousand rumors, but I conclude that the batteries upon both sides, the character and location of the obstructions, may be considered as known. It is now too late to move against the works on either river, except with a powerful naval force."

On February 4, 1862, Grant moved upriver. It was one of those warmish seasons, characteristic of Tennessee winters, when a deceptive feeling of spring is in the air. The river was at flood stage, and still rising. The three wooden gunboats—*Tyler, Lexington, Conestoga*—and four ironclads —*Cincinnati* (Foote's flagship), *Essex, Carondelet,* and *St. Louis*—convoyed a great procession of steamboats. Grant's seventeen thousand troops crowded the decks. Bands played, flags waved, as the convoy left Paducah. For miles along the river the black smoke gushed from the stacks as the convoy bucked the strong current.

Late in the afternoon of February 4 the expedition stopped six miles below Fort Henry. Next morning, while the ironclads went up to reconnoiter, other gunboats shelled the landing at Bailey's Ferry, three miles below Fort Henry, and the troops began to disembark. Grant's plan called for a division of his army, and a simultaneous attack on both sides of the river, under cover of fire from the gunboats. The veteran, white-mustached General C. F. Smith would attack Fort Heiman, while Grant with the other troops would move on Fort Henry. But the high water, excellent for gunboats, was bad for marching troops that had to struggle over miry roads, through flooded fields and roaring creeks.

During the night of February 5, the gunboats could hardly stay anchored in the swift current, and crews had to work constantly to fend off floating trees, driftwood, lumber, and fences. At early dawn they saw "a large number of white objects, which looked like polar bears, coming down the stream." These were Confederate torpedoes, which the flood, luckily for the Federals, had torn from their moorings.

At 11:35 A.M., when the gunboats moved to the attack, a light breeze came across river. More luck—it would blow the smoke away and help the gunners. The gunboats passed Panther Island and formed in two divisions as Foote had ordered: the ironclads, four abreast, in front; the three wooden gunboats keeping far back, where they would not be under heavy fire. Foote had a total of fifty-four guns. The fort could bring twelve to bear. Grant's army, far behind schedule, was splashing slowly through the bottoms.

For no good apparent reason, General Lloyd Tilghman, commanding at Fort Henry, was twelve miles away at Fort Donelson when news came that Grant was landing troops at Bailey's Ferry. He returned to Fort Henry, none too quickly, with a decision to fight a delaying action only. Out of the garrison, Tilghman retained only an artillery company of about sixty men, to man the guns. The remainder of the garrison of something over two thousand was ordered to be in readiness to retreat to Fort Donelson.

The gunboats opened fire at a range of 1,700 yards, as soon as they cleared Panther Island. The fort replied, at first with great effectiveness. Captain Taylor had "assigned to each gun a particular vessel, to which it was to pay its compliments." Taylor himself supervised the rifled gun. For a while the action seemed to favor the defenders. A Confederate shot passed through the middle boiler of the *Essex*, filling the entire vessel with scalding steam. William D. Porter, the commander, was seriously wounded, and thirty-one others were either killed or wounded. The pilot was found standing at the wheel, literally cooked to death in an instant. Men jumped overboard as the *Essex* drifted downstream and out of action. The Confederate fire was telling on the other gunboats. The heavy shot, Walke said later, "broke and scattered our ironplating as if it had been putty." His own boat, the *Carondelet*, was hit thirty times. Nevertheless, the gunboats came steadily upriver, closing the range, as Foote had ordered, from 1,700 to 600 yards.

Presently their boldness began to count. Their shot penetrated the earthworks easily, knocking out guns and killing guncrews. And the Confederates were having bad luck. The rifled gun burst, with havoc to all around it. The Columbiad was spiked by its own priming wire and could not be repaired in the heat of action. Foote, noticing that the Confederate fire was slackening, closed in and pounded harder.

At the end of about an hour's fighting, the fort had only four guns in action. Resistance could not be maintained much longer, but Tilghman would not give up as yet. Finding that the guns were short of crews to fire them, he threw off his coat and sprang to the nearest gun himself. Meanwhile he ordered fifty soldiers from Colonel Heiman's command to be brought in to help. But at 1:50 P.M., after consultation with his officers, Tilghman decided to surrender. The troops of the garrison were already moving out toward the Donelson road as Tilghman attempted to show a flag of truce. The dense smoke obscured it, and firing continued for a little while.

Tilghman now ordered Captain Taylor to lower the Confederate flag. This was a ticklish and dangerous assignment, for the flag mast had been struck, and the halliards cut. With a sergeant—an "old man-of-war's man"—Taylor mounted the lower rigging of the flag mast to the crosstrees, and from that lofty perch began to lower the flag. To the north he could see Grant's lines, now belatedly approaching after their struggle with the backwater, and, on the west bank, the troops of General Smith, moving on Fort Heiman. The bluecoats crowded the vantage points, interested spectators of the combat on the river. To the east Taylor caught glimpses of the retiring garrison of Fort Henry. Below him lay the broad river at floodtide. It covered the bottoms and lapped at the breastworks as at a levee. When Commander Stembel came in a small boat to receive the surrender for Foote, his cutter pulled into the sally port of Fort Henry, and the Federal officers stepped directly from their boat into the fort. A sheet of water a quarter of a mile wide and "running like a millrace" was inundating the low ground where Fort Henry's supporting infantry would have been. "If the attack had been delayed forty-eight hours," wrote Taylor in later years, "there would hardly have been a hostile shot fired; the Tennessee would have accomplished the work by drowning the magazine."

But the attack had not waited. A strongly fortified and courageously defended position was surrendered to Federal naval officers before the laboring infantry and artillery could come up. The Federal river fleet, which up to this time had done no real fighting—for Grant's previous excursion to Belmont was not, for the gunboats, a real fight—had met its first test and proved its power.

Grant now occupied the two forts—Fort Heiman had not been defended—and moved his main force against Fort Donelson, twelve miles away, across the neck of wooded highland between the Tennessee and the Cumberland. The ironclads turned downstream again. Their next engagement would be at Fort Donelson.

The wooden gunboats had other work to do. By the time the surrender was completed, the *Conestoga*, *Tyler*, and *Lexington* were dashing up the Tennessee according to plan. At nightfall of that day, February 6, they reached the bridge of the Memphis-Louisville Railroad, which crossed the Tennessee at Danville, twenty-five miles above Fort Henry. The draw of the bridge had been closed and disabled, but they soon repaired it. Gwin was left with the *Tyler* to cut the railroad, while Phelps with the other two boats pushed on in hot pursuit of the Confederate steamers that had been lying at Fort Henry. In five hours, Phelps began to catch up. The Confederates were forced to abandon and burn three of their boats: the *Appleton Belle*, *Lynn Boyd*, and *Samuel Orr* (an Evansville mail steamer seized by the Confederates in August, 1861, in reprisal for Federal seizure of the *W. B. Terry* at Paducah). Two of these exploded, with some danger to Phelps's gunboats. The *R. M. Patton,* a hospital boat, also was captured.

On the night of February 7, Phelps's gunboats reached Cerro Gordo, and there captured the *Eastport,* a real prize. The work of converting the *Eastport* to a gunboat was only about half completed. The Confederates, aware of their peril, had made plans to scuttle her. A lookout had been posted on the bluff, with orders to fire a warning signal when gunboats came in sight. He did so, and the gunboats answered him with shell fire. The axmen heard the noise and began to chop holes in the bottom of the *Eastport,* but they did not linger to make a good job of scuttling. Phelps stopped the leaks and got the *Eastport* ready to go downriver, together with the lumber and equipment that the Confederates had on hand.

By daylight of February 8, Phelps passed the town of Eastport. Near Chickasaw, Alabama, he seized two more steamers, the *Sallie Wood* and *Muscle.* Soon afterwards he arrived at Florence and found three steamers burning. Citizens approached him and anxiously beseeched him not to destroy their railroad bridge. Phelps let the bridge stand, but seized quantities of military stores. He could not get over Muscle Shoals, and so he turned back, after doing some vain searching for the *Dunbar* and the *Robb,* which he felt sure must be hidden up some bush-fringed creek. He was right; they were concealed in Cypress Creek, two miles below Florence. The Federals would get the *Robb* later, after the Battle of Shiloh, but not the *Dunbar.*

Returning, Phelps burned the mill which had sawed the lumber for the *Eastport* and landed a party at Savannah to investigate a small Confederate encampment, where a regiment had been recruiting. The Confederates were not there, and he went back to Paducah with his booty and his prizes. To his superiors, Phelps reported that he had received "gratifying proofs of loyalty" from citizens crowding the banks; but others—"whole communities"—had fled at the approach of his gunboats. In later years, neither Phelps nor other commanders would be able to report much in the way of gratifying proofs of loyalty. Instead, it would be "guerrillas."

Five days after the fall of Fort Henry, Grant was attacking Fort Donelson, and again gunboats were there to help him and transports brought up reinforcements. Five days was a longer interval than Grant intended—long enough, indeed, for Johnston, if he chose, to concentrate and fight on the Cumberland. The roads were bad, and Grant took five days to move twelve miles and make other preparations. In the snowy, freezing weather that followed the false spring, there came the unconditional surrender at Fort Donelson, after a fine defensive fight by the Confederate troops, who deserved much better generalship than they got from Floyd, Pillow, and Buckner. One Confederate officer declined to surrender, and took his cavalry out through the icy backwaters. This was Lieutenant Colonel Nathan Bedford Forrest. Earlier, Forrest and his men had met the *Conestoga,* on the Cumberland, and had driven her off by aiming sharp rifle fire at her portholes. Forrest had also been an interested witness of the attack of Foote's gunboats at Donelson and had observed the devastating effect of Confederate artillery fire on the Federal fleet. Then and there he may have decided that gunboats were not as formidable as they looked.

CHAPTER II

# The Battle of Shiloh

AFTER the fall of Fort Donelson, Grant's army was free to move swiftly up the Tennessee. If such an advance had been made immediately, and if Buell had simultaneously moved south from Kentucky, the Confederate defense in the West might have been broken early in 1862. Grant, with the mobility allowed him by the use of gunboats and transports, could have struck at North Alabama and Mississippi, cut the Memphis & Charleston Railroad, and interposed his army between the dispersed portions of the Confederate forces. Buell, very likely, could have taken Chattanooga.

Instead, Halleck, in supreme command at St. Louis, held his generals in check and prepared for a slow and cautious advance. Querulously finding fault with Grant for making an unexplained trip to Nashville, Halleck removed him from command, and made Grant feel that he was practically under arrest. Lincoln saved Grant by promoting him to a major-generalship, but that did not greatly improve the situation for the time being. There is no indication that the Federal leaders recognized what an advantage they possessed in their ability to transport large striking forces by the river route. At any rate, they did not immediately use their advantage. When they did, the Confederates were no longer scattered.

Johnston and Beauregard saw that the Tennessee was like a dagger pointed at their undefended parts, and between them worked out a sound and realistic strategy. No longer would they attempt to hold a "line." They would concentrate a real striking force at Corinth to meet the inevitable Federal advance, even if, in order to do so, they had to give up Tennessee and Kentucky and weaken their defenses of the Mississippi.

So, while the Federal commanders were dillydallying and politicking, Johnston's army withdrew from Bowling Green to Nashville, and thence to North Alabama and Corinth. The march of Hardee's brigades from Bowling Green to Nashville, made in harsh wintry weather, brought heavy losses from exposure and illness. But Johnston's retreat and his movement to Corinth, by the long way around, stand in bright contrast to Buell's plodding advance and the slothful refusal of the Army of the Tennessee to use its transportation facilities. To Corinth, too, came ten thousand well-trained troops from Florida, under Bragg. Polk withdrew from Columbus. The surviving fragments of the Fort Donelson garrison were gathered up. Van Dorn's Arkansas army was ordered up, but it did not arrive in time for the Battle of Shiloh, largely because Governor Moore of Louisiana refused Beauregard's request for New Orleans steamboats to ferry them up the Mississippi.

Not until March 10, nearly a month after the surrender of Fort Donelson, was the Federal advance up the Tennessee resumed, with Sherman, this time, in the vanguard, and General C. F. Smith in command. Before the advance started, the *Tyler* and *Lexington* were busily reconnoitering. They examined the river from Savannah to Chickasaw, and brought back reports of the Confederate concentration at Corinth. Early in March the gunboats skirmished with Confederate troops at Pittsburg Landing. This was the point at which Corinth received freight that came by way of the Tennessee River. It was an ordinary steamboat landing, identified with a settler named Pitts, whose "burg" consisted of a store and two or three houses. Lieutenant Gwin found a Confederate

battery in position there, shelled it, landed troops to develop the Federal strength, and burned a house. Nobody dreamed that this brief skirmish was the forerunner of a great battle.

The Federal advance, when it finally began, was spectacular to the last degree. Nothing like it had ever been seen on the American continent before. Nothing like it, for magnitude, has been seen since, except in the great transoceanic expeditions of World War I and World War II. It was a river-borne expedition. The Federal command assembled 173 steamboats for use as transports, and these were convoyed by a dozen or more gunboats. Among the steamers was the *Tigress,* a small, fast side-wheeler that Grant afterwards used as a flagship. General Lew Wallace came upriver on the *John J. Roe,* a Mississippi boat on which Mark Twain had served as pilot. The list of boats included the *Bostona I,* a fast steamer on the New Orleans-Louisville run, and several boats of the "Railroad Line": the *Imperial,* the *City of Memphis,* the *New Uncle Sam;* and there were other well-remembered boats, the *Telegraph III,* the *Rocket,* and many more.

The transports did not proceed in one great convoy, of course, but in divisions, as the troops embarked from the advanced base at Fort Henry, or from Paducah and other points. Undoubtedly, too, there was some shuttling back and forth. In the *Official Records* one reads of the arrival of the first contingent of troops at Savannah, on sixty-three transports; and on another day, of forty transports. It was a considerable feat to have all these steamers at the right place at the right time, but we do not know who should have the credit for it. Sherman, who was in charge at Paducah during late February and early March, surely had a hand; but probably the major part of the credit should go to Foote and his naval officers, especially to A. M. Pennock, who was fleet captain at the Cairo base.

## THE BATTLE OF SHILOH 29

In his autobiography Lew Wallace has left a stirring record of the departure from Fort Henry:

> I can give but a faint idea of the spectacle of the embarkation. One must think of thirty thousand uniformed men in array on the river-bank, drums going, arms glistening, and nearly seventy steamboats with smoking funnels at anchor ready to haul in and take their assignments aboard. He must think, too, of the excitement that prevailed, of the cheering, and braying of bands, and the waving of flags; for this, it is to be remembered, was a victorious army that knew its strength and rejoiced in it. . . . And when the procession was formed and all in motion, the Tennessee River, always beautiful, was never more so.
>
> I can see the boats now, crowded below and above with their precious humanity; I can see them now in graceful onward sweep, some in dangerous tilt, churning in the sparkling flood with their huge wheels, and loading the scurrying winds and pearl-blue sky with clouds of sulphurous smoke, yet gay with flower-like colors of streaming flags. I can hear the hoarse coughing of the pipes, the cheering, the music, and the boisterous echoes hurtled back upon us from rocky bluff and wooded shore. . . .
>
> My feeling all the time was that there should be somebody somewhere on the shores to enjoy the wonderful spectacle we were offering—somebody to look at us if not signal a friendly welcome. But no. The houses and cabins here and there were in their accustomed places, and the landings were as of yore, and the dingy towns reminded us of society and trade and peace; but as a rule desertion was over them all; and if now and then a hat was waved or a handkerchief shaken out in cheer, something in the environment always showed itself to whisper of war as a recognized condition.

Once more it was a season of heavy rains and floods, excellent for river transport, depressing for men, mules, and horses that had to thread the fog-hung woods and ford the swollen creeks.

Despite its formidable power, the great Federal army was under restraining orders from Halleck: "Avoid any general engagements with strong forces . . . It will be better to retreat than to risk a general battle." The Federal plan was limited to driving against communications. On March 15, therefore, General Smith sent Sherman upriver with orders to land at Eastport and cut the Memphis & Charleston Railroad. The *Tyler* led Sherman's convoy of nineteen transport steamers. As the expedition passed Pittsburg Landing, Lieutenant Gwin pointed out to Sherman the bluffs where he had skirmished with the Confederates. Sherman looked at the high forested banks and scribbled a dispatch, to be sent back to Smith: Pittsburg Landing, he suggested, was a good point to post supporting troops.

Sherman found Eastport and Chickasaw occupied, and dropped back down the river to Yellow Creek. There, in a hard rain, he disembarked his troops. Within a few hours his forward movement was stopped by rising waters, some of his men were drowned, and he had to hurry back to avoid being caught by the floods. At Pittsburg Landing, he found Hurlbut's division waiting on steamboats, and presently there came an order from Smith for both Sherman and Hurlbut to take position where they were, and so to dispose their troops as to leave room for the whole army. On the wooded plateau, between Owl and Snake Creeks on one side and Lick Creek on the other, there was indeed room for an army and a good defensive position if they wanted to think of it in such terms. On the Corinth road Sherman found a little log church—Shiloh Church—which he used as headquarters. Thus, unwittingly, the field of battle was chosen.

Meanwhile, General Lew Wallace's division had come up and was on its transports, opposite Savannah. On the evening of Wallace's arrival General Smith crossed the river in a yawl to visit Wallace and explain his plans. He spread out a map and pointed to the railroad lines north and east of Corinth. Sherman, he said, must cut the eastern line (the Memphis & Charleston); Wallace, after occupying Crump's Landing, would move against the northern one (the Mobile & Ohio). It was dark when Smith said good night. As he stepped into the waiting yawl, he missed his footing and raked his shin against the sharp edge of a seat. The skin was scraped off from knee to ankle. Smith refused Wallace's offer of help and went back to Savannah. The injured leg became infected, and soon the general was mortally ill. The command passed again to Grant. Within a few days Grant too was almost out of action. His horse slipped in the mire at Pittsburg Landing and fell on Grant's leg. During the Battle of Shiloh, Grant was on crutches.

The yellow tide of the Tennessee, full to overflowing, ran below the bluff at Savannah where the windows of the Cherry House, Grant's headquarters, looked toward the west. The gunboats were there, the steamboats were there, and Grant had power to move his army anywhere along the river. But Grant did not move. He simply let the army stay where it was. Wallace was posted at Crump's Landing. The other divisions, with Sherman as a kind of acting commander on the field, were dispersed in a sprawling, unfortified encampment in the woods between Shiloh Church and Pittsburg Landing. Both Sherman and Grant thought it unlikely that the Confederates would leave their excellent base at Corinth and come forth to the attack. The cavalry screen flung out by Johnston and Beauregard checked every Federal attempt to reconnoiter toward Corinth.

But Beauregard and Johnston knew precisely what Grant was doing. He was waiting for Buell to join him by overland marches, from Nashville, and they determined to strike him in his camps before Buell could arrive. They were fully informed of Buell's progress by Forrest's cavalry, a detachment of which was posted at Marr's Landing. On the night of April 2—the very day when Sherman and his gunboat escort were shelling the empty woods, during a second reconnaissance at Eastport and Chickasaw—Johnston made his decision and gave the order to advance against Grant. As yet the Confederate army was neither well drilled nor well equipped, and it had been hastily reorganized during the concentration at Corinth. Van Dorn had not arrived. There was reason to wonder, too, whether the intended surprise attack really could be carried out. Nevertheless, the spirit of the army was excellent, and Johnston was determined to put into effect his well-conceived plan of battle—in the words of his son, Colonel William Preston Johnston, "to interpose his whole force in front of the Great Bend of the Tennessee, the natural base of the Federal army: this effected, to crush Grant in battle before the arrival of Buell."

Early on Sunday morning, April 6, Johnston's forty thousand Confederates struck the Union camp. It was a surprise, although the Confederates, delayed by bad roads and inexperienced commanders, had not arrived for the attack as soon as they intended, and had bivouacked, the night before, almost within shot of the Federal lines.

Restless Sherman, up early, was inspecting his lines when the Confederate advance rolled back the Federal pickets. Aware that something unusual was afoot, he began to get his troops into line of battle, but he was not convinced of the seriousness of his situation until he found himself in the midst of heavy firing. His orderly was killed at his side. He saw the glitter of Confederate bayonets in his front and, to his left, masses of gray warriors passing toward his flank. It was the real thing—not a Bull Run, not a Fort Donelson, but a full-scale battle which would make the earlier fights look like skirmishes. Sherman rode energetically to and fro, seeking to keep his untried regiments under control. But as he rode and looked, some of them dissolved before his eyes in the fury of the Confederate attack. Regiment confusedly merged with regiment, and organization almost disappeared as he sought to establish a new line nearer the river.

Grant was having breakfast at the Cherry House when the sound of cannon, followed by the sustained crackle of musketry, came to his ears. He set down his cup of coffee and grabbed his crutches. Steaming, on the *Tigress*, toward the sound of the firing, he stopped at Crump's Landing, to order Wallace to hold his troops in readiness. At Pittsburg Landing, he found broken remnants of his army already crowding the riverside, panic stricken and clamorous. Ahead,

## THE BATTLE OF SHILOH

in the gloomy forests around Shiloh, the roar of battle, now almost continuous, told Grant that his men were still fighting; but the wild Confederate yell, rising above the din, told him they were losing. The Confederates were driving his men back, pushing his left toward the landing itself, crushing the whole Federal line into a rough crescent, and threatening to back them up against Owl and Snake Creeks and thus cut them off from their gunboats and steamboats.

It was a bad day for Grant. He was saved, it would now seem, not by his own dispositions and orders, but by the stubborn courage of his raw midwestern soldiers, who somehow kept on fighting, and by the energy of his subordinate commanders. Grant's own confusion of mind is clearly revealed by his failure to give unequivocal orders for the movement and disposition of his plentiful reserves. The case of Lew Wallace—long and bitterly argued—illustrates one such failure. Grant sent Wallace some kind of vague order to join him at Pittsburg Landing. But he did not give a clear order, and he trusted it, apparently in oral form, to messengers who garbled it still more. Wallace did not know where Grant's right was located, or by what road he should come, and therefore, after tedious marching and countermarching, he did not come up until the first day's fighting was over.

Nelson's division of Buell's army arrived at Savannah on April 5, the day before the battle. Grant kept these troops waiting at Savannah. "You cannot march through the swamps," he said. "Make the troops comfortable; I will send boats for you Monday or Tuesday, or some time early in the week. There will be no fight at Pittsburg Landing; we will have to go to Corinth, where the rebels are fortified. If they come to attack us, we can whip them, as I have more than twice as many troops as I had at Fort Donelson." When the noise of battle came down the river on Sunday morning, Nelson's men were preparing for a parade. In some indecision, they waited to see whether Grant would send steamboats for them. Finally they set out by a swampy road that led up the east bank of the Tennessee and arrived opposite Pittsburg Landing late in the afternoon. Then, and only then were they ferried across the river.

Meanwhile, on the Confederate side there was an inferior force, with bottomless roads in its rear; an army as raw as Grant's, more hastily organized, and badly disposed, tactically. And there were no gunboats and steamboats to help. But there was superior strategy and terrific driving force. Beauregard, keeping the rear at Shiloh Church, received reports and did the staff work. Johnston, with his own staff, rode from point to point of the attacking line, driving it forward by personal commands, inspiring it with his words and presence. Johnston has been criticized for exposing himself at the front, where, it is alleged, he could control only local actions. The criticism derives force largely from the fact that during the attack on the Hornet's Nest Johnston was struck in the thigh by a Minié ball, and, not having a surgeon in attendance, bled to death on the field. But Johnston was doing for his army only what Sherman was doing for Grant's: directing it in action and rendering it a coherent force. Sherman was wounded, too; it so happened, not mortally. It was a day when generals were killed or wounded on both sides. Possibly the old Confederates who argued, for years after the war, that through Johnston's death the Confederates lost, not only the chance of victory at Shiloh, but perhaps the war itself, came instinctively near the truth. When Johnston fell, the army lost a leader who in his person gave meaning to their cause.

At any rate, up to the moment of Johnston's death, all went well for the Confederate side, and the victory seemed theirs. Even after his death, the Confederate advance pressed on. By sundown the Confederate right wing rested on the Tennessee and was surging against the heavy guns posted just above the landing. One fresh contingent of reserves, or perhaps one more determined push, would have done the

## THE BATTLE OF SHILOH 35

work. Forrest, pushing hard with his own men on the Confederate right, gauged the situation and wanted the attack pressed, even after dark fell. But no order came, and the final push was not made.

At this point of the battle, when the Confederate right was within a few hundred yards of Pittsburg Landing, the Federal gunboats at last found something to do. Throughout the morning's fighting the *Tyler* remained about a mile above the landing, hearkening to the noise of battle, but not able to take part. The *Lexington* meanwhile stayed at Crump's Landing. Tired of inaction, Lieutenant Gwin shelled the woods during the afternoon, but without being able to observe results. Still impatient and anxious, Gwin asked Grant for orders, and got the reply "to use his own judgment in the matter." Accordingly, at four o'clock, Gwin brought both the *Tyler* and the *Lexington* a little above Pittsburg Landing and shelled the batteries posted on the Confederate right, near the river. Gwin reported afterwards that he silenced the batteries and drove them back in confusion; and in some accounts of the battle, the gunboats are credited with intervening successfully at the moment when the Confederates were about to attack Pittsburg Landing itself. Throughout the night the gunboats continued to throw shells, at ten- or fifteen-minute intervals, in the supposed direction of the Confederate line.

Undoubtedly the presence of gunboats in action gave moral support to Grant's disordered rear and to the harried battle line that was pressed close against the landing. But probably Gwin overestimated the effectiveness of his fire. The gunboats "sounded terribly and looked ugly and hurt but few," reported Colonel John D. Martin of the 2nd Confederate Infantry.

At this late hour, too, Nelson's division arrived after its difficult march from Savannah, and began to cross the river. In the *Official Records* Colonel Jacob Ammen, of Nelson's division, has left a vivid account of this episode:

The head of the column emerged from the dense forest into a field that bordered on the Tennessee River. Now at intervals the shouts of men could be heard, the steam-whistle, discharge of all kinds of arms—a confused noise. In we went to a point opposite the landing at Pittsburg. The pioneers were put to work to cut a road down the bank to enable men and horses to get on the boats. The northeast bank is low, the opposite bank is high—100 feet or more. The space between the top of the bank and the river, up and down half a mile or more was crowded with men; the river was full of boats with steam up, and these boats had many soldiers on them; men in uniform on the boats and under the river bank (10,000 to 15,000) demoralized. Signals urging us to hurry over, which I could not understand, as there were so many on the boats and under the bank not engaged of the reserve, as I supposed them. . . . On each side the boats were crowded with demoralized soldiers, so that only three or four companies could cross on a boat. On our passage over they said their regiments were cut to pieces, etc. The vagabonds under the bank told the same story, and yet my new troops pressed through the crowd without showing any signs of fear. In crossing the river some of my men called my attention to men with uniforms, even with shoulder-straps, making their way across the stream on logs, and wished to shoot the cowards. Such looks of terror, such confusion, I never saw before, and do not wish to see again.

At the end of the first day's fighting, Grant's army was used up, but with Buell's troops, arriving in strength during the night, and Lew Wallace's fresh division he had a new army for the next day. Victory was with the Confederates, but the moment of making that victory certain had passed. Although the Confederates attacked briskly the next morning and gave the new arrivals severe punishment, the Federal superiority in numbers was obvious, and Beauregard made an orderly withdrawal in the afternoon. There was no effective pursuit. Forrest's cavalry was covering the retreat, and for the first time Sherman, coming up to Monterey with two brigades of infantry and a regiment of cavalry, learned what a staggering blow Forrest's hard riders could deliver. In the sudden charge that smashed Sherman's

# THE BATTLE OF SHILOH 37

advance, Forrest himself was badly wounded, but Sherman's pursuit stopped right there.

When it was all over, the Confederates slowly retired to Corinth, where they had started, and the Federals, shaken but not dislodged, were back in their wrecked camps at Pittsburg Landing, amid the horrible debris of battle. It was one of the bloodiest and most savage conflicts in American history. Each side lost, in killed, wounded, and missing, about one-fourth of the numbers that it brought into action. In no other battles, except at Chickamauga or in some of the Wilderness fighting, were two great armies so closely interlocked, without power to maneuver, fighting breast to breast along the whole line of battle for two days. Each side now knew how grim the war would be. The North learned with what dash and consuming fury, with what passionate and bitter intensity, the Southerners of the West would fight. And the South learned how stubbornly brave, how coolly unyielding, were those men of the northern West: the regiments from Ohio, Indiana, Wisconsin, Michigan, and all the upper Mississippi Valley. At Shiloh the hot anger of the South against the invader poured itself out to the full; and the North, recovering after the first shock of surprise at finding its invasion so detested, reorganized and with methodical resolution began another campaign.

Grant's eyes were opened. In his *Personal Memoirs* he later wrote:

Up to the battle of Shiloh, I, as well as thousands of other citizens, believed that the rebellion against the Government would collapse suddenly and soon, if a decisive victory could be gained against any of its armies. Donelson and Henry were such victories. . . . But when Confederate armies were collected which not only attempted to hold a line farther south . . . but assumed the offensive and made such a gallant effort to regain what had been lost, then, indeed, I gave up all idea of saving the Union except by complete conquest.

Perhaps the war of devastation which the Federal armies began soon after Shiloh originated in such a realization as Grant at this moment had. A military victory would not suffice; it must be "conquest."

Whatever the judgment of historians, Shiloh ranks in southern folk memory as a victory. Some unknown songmaker of the countryside made a ballad about it, full of echoes of British military and naval ballads of centuries gone by, heedless of geography, wrenching the date to fit the meter, and yet sharply local in some stanzas. It goes to a stirring eighteenth century tune, with the lilt of bugle, fife, and drum in its measures.

## The Battle of Shiloh

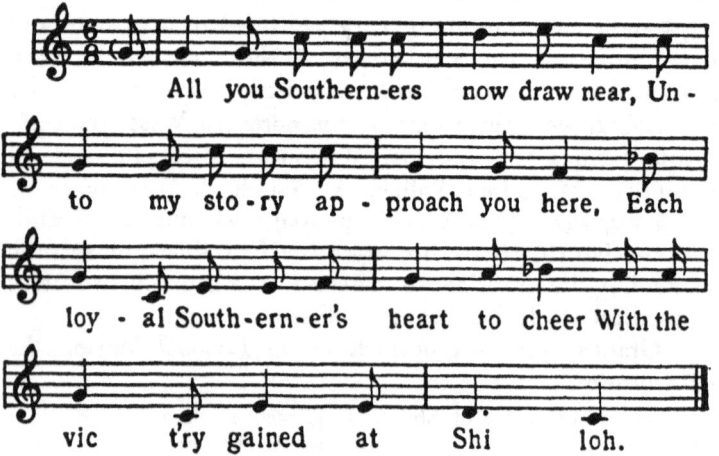

All you South-ern-ers now draw near, Unto my sto-ry ap-proach you here, Each loy-al South-ern-er's heart to cheer With the vic-t'ry gained at Shi-loh.

O it was on April the sixteenth day,
In spite of a long and muddy way,
We landed safe at Corinth Bay
All on our route to Shiloh.

That night we lay on the cold ground,
No tents and shelters could we find;
And in the rain we almost drowned
All on our way to Shiloh.

Next morning a burning sun did rise
Beneath the eastern cloudless sky,
And General Beauregard replied:
Prepare to march to Shiloh.

And when our Shiloh hove in view,
It would the bravest hearts subdue
To see the Yankee melody crew
That held the works at Shiloh.

For they were strongly fortified
With batteries on the river-side.
Our generals viewed the plains and cried:
We'll get hot work at Shiloh.

And when those batteries strove to gain,
The balls fell around us thick as rain,
And many a hero there was slain,
Upon the plains of Shiloh.

The thirty-third and the Zouaves,
They charged the batteries and gave three cheers,
And General Beauregard rang the airs
With Southern steel at Shiloh.

Their guns and knapsacks they threw down,
They ran like hares before the hounds.
The Yankee Dutch could not withstand
The Southern charge at Shiloh.

Now many a pretty maid did mourn
A lover who'll no more return;
The cruel war has from her torn;
His body lies at Shiloh.

CHAPTER III

# The Strategic Importance of Muscle Shoals

FROM the close of the Shiloh-Corinth campaign to the Battle of Missionary Ridge, Muscle Shoals was worth many divisions of troops and miles of fortifications to the Confederacy. The great natural obstacle closed the Tennessee at Florence and made it impossible for the Federals to send against Chattanooga such amphibious expeditions as had been launched at Fort Henry, Fort Donelson, and Shiloh, or as had carried Sherman's thirty thousand troops down the Mississippi for the first attack on Vicksburg. The gunboats could not in safety venture above the shoals, and where gunboats could not go, steamboats could not carry an army. Thus, while the Lower Tennessee quickly became a Federal highway, the Upper Tennessee and, more dubiously, the Great Bend, were on the Confederate side until Federal possession of Chattanooga at last was made secure by the Battle of Missionary Ridge. Since the Confederates had only the *Paint Rock* and the *Dunbar* and a few other steamboats above the shoals, and no gunboats at all, they could not make full use of their advantage; and there is no clear indication that the Confederate high command, which was not river-minded, understood exactly what the advantage was.

Historians of the Civil War have not understood it, either, but the advantage was there all the same. In the blockade set up by Muscle Shoals we may find an explanation of certain strange features of the western campaigns of late 1862 and of 1863. How did it happen that Grant, in his campaigns against Vicksburg, could strike deep into Southern territory, overcome strong opposition, and finally win victory, while simultaneously Bragg, with the Confederate Army of Tennessee, could move north, invade Kentucky, threaten the Ohio Valley, and subsequently reoccupy most of Middle Tennessee for a long period, despite the active presence in this area of the powerful Army of the Cumberland? In Grant's sector the fighting moved south. But east of the Great Bend it swung north and threatened to cancel Grant's efforts. Evidently Bragg had a power of maneuver which was denied the Confederate forces that faced Grant. And Grant had advantages not enjoyed by Buell and his successor, Rosecrans. The difference was that in Grant's field of operations the Federals had the use of the Lower Tennessee and most of the Mississippi. But for Bragg, Muscle Shoals was in effect a flank guard, as good as a mountain range, or better. East of Muscle Shoals Bragg could maneuver freely, secure in the knowledge that any army operating against him must move overland by road and rail, subject to the disadvantages of any land army invading a hostile country.

Bragg's elevation to command of the Army of Tennessee came on June 27, 1862, after Beauregard's skillful withdrawal from Corinth left the powerful Federal army, then under personal command of Halleck, free to achieve a barren victory. The high commands of North and South now acted with about equal stupidity. Halleck split up his great army into several commands; one, under Buell, was to move east, repairing the Memphis & Charleston Railroad as it went, and strike Chattanooga; another, under Grant, was to continue operations in Mississippi. Halleck returned to Washington. Meanwhile Jefferson Davis, with comparable blindness, rewarded the skillful Beauregard by removing him from command, made his own favorite, Braxton Bragg, a full general, and gave that ill-starred leader command of the Army of Tennessee.

Bragg, a North Carolinian, and a West Pointer, had already fought brilliantly as a subordinate commander. He was in fact an experienced and rather coldly efficient military man, extremely capable as a drillmaster and organizer, and not lacking in gifts as a strategist. If Bragg had also been a lucky general, all might have been well. But he seemed to attract ill luck, and became ultimately mistrustful both of his subordinates and of himself, with bad results for the Army of Tennessee.

Yet little of this appeared on the surface in the summer of 1862. Bragg's march into Kentucky, though it failed in its ultimate objective, was one of the most remarkable achievements of the Civil War. From Tupelo, Mississippi, Bragg sent his infantry by rail to Mobile, then, doubling back north, by rail to Chattanooga; artillery, cavalry, and wagons moved east by a more direct route. By July 24, 1862, his troops had already begun to arrive at Chattanooga. A month later his army was ready to begin its swift march across the Cumberland plateau and into Kentucky.

Meanwhile, the hapless Buell, protesting to Halleck, struggled vainly to repair the Memphis & Charleston Railroad and prepare his stroke against Chattanooga. The railroad was so exposed to Confederate attack as to make his repairs futile, and he soon changed his line of supply to the Nashville & Chattanooga Railroad. But this, too, was vulnerable. The swift raids of Morgan and Forrest caused Buell the greatest discomfort and apprehension—particularly the blows of Forrest, whose cavalry was Chattanooga's chief protection until Bragg's army came up. The result was much interruption to Buell's preparations and much diversion of troops for guard duty and pursuit. When Bragg finally moved into Kentucky, the annoyed and overcautious Buell found himself engaged in a life-and-death race for the Ohio, with Bragg's army ahead in the race. In all this, Muscle Shoals played its

## IMPORTANCE OF MUSCLE SHOALS 43

silent part. It was Buell's uneasy dependence upon railroads that encumbered his movements, and his successors, operating in the same area, were similarly encumbered. It was very hard on the Federals to have the river against them in North Alabama.

The details of Bragg's Kentucky campaign lie outside the scope of this narrative. It must suffice to say that, when Kentuckians failed to throng to the Confederate flag, as Bragg had hoped they would, he somehow lost heart, frittered away his chance of crushing Buell, wasted time in the empty gesture of inaugurating a Confederate state government in Kentucky, and then, after a bloody but minor conflict at Perryville, retired into Tennessee. Autumn of 1862 found Bragg's Army of Tennessee at Murfreesboro, toughened but not tired by its tremendous marches; and facing them, at Nashville, was the Army of the Cumberland under its new commander, General William S. Rosecrans. Early in January, 1863, Rosecrans undertook an offensive movement and Bragg met him in the savage, but indecisive Battle of Murfreesboro. The fierce Confederate onset did great damage to the Federal army, and at one time threatened to sweep it in disorder from the wintry field, but the Federals retrieved their disadvantage in the second day's fighting, and Bragg, taking the conservative course, withdrew to a strong position on the Shelbyville-Tullahoma line, which commanded the approaches to the broken escarpment of the plateau known as the Highland Rim.

There, throughout the remainder of that winter and the spring, Bragg's army lay unmolested, drilling, recuperating, watching. In his front, at Murfreesboro, Rosecrans's army remained quiescent, watched and checked by the magnificent Confederate cavalry under Forrest and others. And now Muscle Shoals guarded Bragg's flank and rear. Federal forces could, and did, come right up to Florence and Tuscumbia, but they never seriously endangered Bragg's communications during these months. Such raids as they could contrive were abortive. They could not get over Muscle Shoals, and they could not match the alert, hard-hitting Forrest.

One dashing attempt was made on the Federal side to emulate Forrest's methods, but it failed completely. This was the famous raid across North Alabama and into Georgia carried out by Colonel Abel W. Streight's "mule cavalry" in April, 1863.

Streight, an Indiana man, had the odd notion that it would be advisable to mount his raiders on mules, apparently on the theory that mules could negotiate the mountainous terrain of North Alabama and Georgia better than horses. He did not realize that the mule is primarily a draft animal and might have stubborn, temperamental objections to being ridden hard and continuously. With two thousand men, composed chiefly of infantry regiments from Indiana, Ohio, and Illinois, Streight came down the Cumberland by steamboat to Palmyra, Tennessee, and there disembarked among blackened ruins—for Palmyra had been burned by the Federals in retaliation for guerrilla attacks on gunboats. From Palmyra, Streight's expedition marched overland to Fort Henry on the Tennessee; en route they picked up, from the countryside, other mules and horses to add to the eight hundred quartermaster mules they had brought from Nashville. At Fort Henry they loaded up again on steamboats and came up the Tennessee to Eastport. There Streight disembarked again and joined Dodge's forces, which had come up from Corinth to screen his movement and to support him by creating a diversion in the Great Bend. At a suitable moment Streight slipped away for his eastward dash across the highlands of North Alabama toward his objective in Georgia, where he aimed to "cut the railroads which supply the rebel army by Chattanooga."

But Forrest, moving quickly south from Middle Tennessee, joined General Philip D. Roddey's forces, and, taking command, not only checked Dodge and kept him at bay, but with a portion of his cavalry came tearing after Streight. The Federal raiders already had a comfortable lead. In fancied security, they were riding on to glory, after mounting, by Day's Gap, to the piny plateau of Sand Mountain. There, as they reached the top of the climb at sunrise on April 30, Streight heard the sound of cannon in his rear. Forrest had caught up, and Streight, though he fought skillfully and rode hard, was doomed. After a five-day pursuit, and a series of sharp running fights, Forrest cut off Streight from Rome, Georgia, and with five hundred men wore out, intimidated, tricked, and captured Streight and his eighteen hundred survivors. As for the mules, they contributed to Streight's downfall. Roddey's men, creeping up in Indian style, stampeded four hundred mules at Eastport, and so delayed Streight's getaway. The mules' protesting brays from time to time gave away Streight's presence to Confederate scouts. The larger number broke down on the march, and Streight had to scour the country for horses to replace them.

Forrest's victory over Streight is only one of several episodes that reveal the superiority of the Confederates in rapid overland movements. Bragg could not make that superiority count for the long-suffering, far-marching Army of Tennessee, but Forrest, the master of swift attack, understood it and built victories upon it. Late in 1862, on his first raid into West Tennessee, Forrest tore Grant's supply system to pieces. His blows, coming in conjunction with Van Dorn's raid on Grant's base at Holly Springs, upset Grant's timetable and prevented him from delivering a land attack on Vicksburg to support Sherman's first approach by way of the Mississippi River.

Nothing could stop Forrest, even though, on this occasion as on others, he started with untried and half-armed forces, and recruited more men and armed them with captured weapons as he rode, while Federal commanders rushed troops hither and thither from every quarter of the compass in a fruitless effort to trap him. Nothing stopped him—not even the great river where the gunboats prowled. On this West Tennessee raid, Forrest sent carpenters ahead to Clifton, Tennessee, to make flatboats and conceal them in a slough. When Forrest arrived for the crossing, he flung out a line of pickets to watch for gunboats, ferried his men over during the rainy December night, and then sank the flatboats at a convenient spot, only to raise them and use them again, on his return after the battle of Parker's Cross Roads.

Rosecrans, meanwhile, was pleading with the government for more gunboats, and especially for gunboats capable of operating above Muscle Shoals. In January, 1863, when he was beginning to shape his plans for a move toward Chattanooga, he asked Halleck for "three or four small, light-draught, staunch-built powerful tugs and gunboats, capable of ascending the Tennessee above the Shoals." These boats, he argued, would save the government "millions in time and expense." "In moving this army," he continued, "these gunboats are of the utmost importance to guard the Tennessee, now masked by impassable roads and superior cavalry." But not until after Rosecrans had met disaster and Grant had taken over the command were such gunboats finally built above Muscle Shoals. By the time they were ready, the need for them had almost passed.

Meanwhile, too, Forrest was undoubtedly turning the gunboat problem over in his mind. Before the Battle of Chickamauga, Forrest, discontented with Bragg's conduct toward him, asked the Richmond government to permit him to raise an independent command with which he could operate against Federal supply lines on the Mississippi. It was a common-sense proposal for systematic action against the gunboat-transport menace. Jefferson Davis turned it down, and thereby lost a great opportunity. Bragg, with Davis concurring, insisted on retaining Forrest for orthodox cavalry service.

The long stalemate between Rosecrans and Bragg ended in late June, 1863, while Lee's army, in the east, was moving

## IMPORTANCE OF MUSCLE SHOALS 47

into Pennsylvania and, in the southwest, the fall of Vicksburg was imminent. With great adroitness, Rosecrans maneuvered Bragg out of his well-fortified positions without having to fight a real battle. His success was the more creditable —and the more surprising—in that the complex maneuvers took place during a season of drenching, steamy rains that made the Tennessee roads difficult and slowed the advance of his columns.

With Fabian caution, Bragg retired into Chattanooga and did not make a stand in the mountains. For good reasons, Rosecrans did not press closely after the retreating Confederates. The next stage of the campaign would involve the Army of the Cumberland in greater risks than any Federal army had yet taken. Rosecrans paused at the foot of the Cumberlands to prepare his next stroke. It was more than a month before he delivered it. The most significant feature of that period of waiting was the posting of Sheridan's division at Stevenson, Alabama, where the railroad turns east to cross the Tennessee River at nearby Bridgeport.

The farther Rosecrans's army advanced into the difficult mountain region stretching from the Great Bend to Chattanooga and beyond, the more risky its advance would inevitably become. All routes of advance would be dangerous, with a powerful opponent close by, and not least of the dangers was the mere operation of setting his large army with its supply trains across a major river. And really, no matter what other methods of approach might seem theoretically feasible, only one choice of routes promised anything like security. That is, he must necessarily advance by a route that would cover and secure the Nashville & Chattanooga Railroad, for that was the life line of his army. If the Tennessee River had been open to use above Florence—if Muscle Shoals had not existed or if it had been surmountable—he might have made a more direct approach from the north, or contrived an encirclement above and below Chattanooga. With only the railroad to supply him, he was bound to keep to the west and to cross his whole army below Chattanooga. Any other plan would have put the Army of the Cumberland far away from its communications, with mountain ranges between it and its life line. Even then, after crossing the Tennessee to the west, his supply line would be most vulnerable, especially if he proposed to occupy Chattanooga and use it as an advanced base.

In those days, as now, the Nashville & Chattanooga Railroad ran south to Stevenson and crossed the Tennessee at Bridgeport. Then, winding along the south bank of the river and threading the mountain ravines, it came past Wauhatchie and around the shoulder of Lookout Mountain into Chattanooga. Immediately north of the river there was no railroad east of Bridgeport. But the long valleys on that side funneled toward the southwest in such a way that Rosecrans's army, advancing on an extended front, could threaten Chattanooga from the north and shift behind a mountain screen for a crossing at Bridgeport. Once over the river at that point, however, the army must advance across a series of parallel ranges unless it followed a winding path with the railroad.

While Rosecrans rested and planned, Bragg begged for reinforcements. The Richmond government sent him a new corps commander, D. H. Hill, put Buckner's small East Tennessee force under his command, and ordered up nine thousand men from Johnston's command. After much discussion, Lee agreed late in August to send Longstreet with his corps —a move which Longstreet earlier had advocated—but by August Burnside's advance into East Tennessee had closed the nearer route, and Longstreet had to take a circuitous railroad journey to the south and around.

Rosecrans's movement began, August 16, on a majestic front of 150 miles. General Thomas L. Crittenden's Twenty-first Corps, feinting from the northeast, demonstrated along the Tennessee. The noisiest demonstration was made by Wilder's Mounted Brigade, which on August 21 appeared on

## IMPORTANCE OF MUSCLE SHOALS 49

the north bank and began to shell Chattanooga without warning. Two Confederate steamboats, *Paint Rock* and *Dunbar*, were tied up at the wharf. Wilder turned his guns on them and later reported exultantly that he had sunk one and severely damaged the other. It was a destruction that the Federals would later regret.

The Fourteenth Corps, under General George H. Thomas, moved south and crossed the Tennessee at Battle Creek and Shellmound, by flatboat, small boat, and raft, like the Tennessee pioneers of the Nickajack expedition. The Twentieth Corps, under A. M. McCook, hugged the railroad and began to cross at Bridgeport, where Sheridan's engineers had put up a patchwork trestle-and-pontoon bridge, and at Caperton's Ferry on a regular pontoon bridge. Meanwhile Crittenden shifted toward the same points. By September 4 Rosecrans's army, unmolested, was over the river, and Gordon Granger with the reserve corps was ready to cross.

All this time Bragg waited and watched, but was not completely inactive. He drew in Buckner from East Tennessee and pulled back Anderson's brigade from its position near Bridgeport as if deliberately to open that crossing. Apparently Bragg also considered striking Crittenden, north of the river, but he abandoned this idea as soon as he was sure of where Rosecrans was crossing the Tennessee. When Rosecrans, after crossing, sent Crittenden toward Chattanooga and pushed Thomas and McCook across the mountains to the south, with wide intervals between their corps, Bragg evacuated Chattanooga. As Crittenden came up, the Army of Tennessee disappeared to the south in the deep valleys of North Georgia.

Soon it was Rosecrans's turn to wonder where that army was lurking. But at first, inflated by the easy capture of Chattanooga and gulled by the tales of "deserters," some of whom were certainly sent by Bragg, Rosecrans believed what he hoped was true—that the Confederate army, demoralized, was gloomily retreating to Rome or Atlanta. The grand strategy of maneuver had apparently succeeded again. Chattanooga, the key to the Deep South, was in his hands without a battle. Exultantly he urged his columns forward. Let Thomas cross Lookout range and press toward Lafayette. Let McCook sweep much farther south toward Alpine. Let Crittenden, after leaving a small guard in Chattanooga, follow the railroad toward Ringgold and Dalton and try to make contact with the Confederates. The chase was on.

CHAPTER IV

# Chickamauga and Its Sequel

It was September 13—nine days after the crossing of the Tennessee—before Rosecrans completely realized in what grave peril his brilliant maneuvering had placed his great army. On that day he learned conclusively that his picture of a Confederate army in distant, perhaps hurried retreat to Rome was but a wild fantasy. For on that day Negley's division of Thomas's corps, after advancing as ordered into MacLemore's Cove, found the Confederates in heavy force in the valley and in the gaps of Pigeon Mountain beyond; and indeed, but for the blundering willfulness of Bragg's subordinates, Negley's division, and possibly Thomas's entire corps, might have been destroyed then and there. Knowledge of the near presence of Bragg's army, while his own was still scattered widely, afflicted Rosecrans with such tremors as, surely, are experienced only by commanding generals of great armies. He was from that time a desperate man, in truth, though the political and military necessities of that day and the processes of rationalization of later times have both conspired to obscure and somewhat glorify his plight. Rosecrans had walked into a trap. It partly closed upon his army at Chickamauga. Rosecrans himself never got out of it. Only Grant, in the end, was able, by an extremely narrow margin, to extricate the Federal army. Chickamauga and the siege and battles that followed, indeed, so shook up and checked the Federal army that, despite the access of powerful reinforcements which enabled Grant to raise the siege of Chattanooga, the Federals made no other effective forward move until May, 1864.

In degree of complexity—or, if one prefers, confusion—the Battle of Chickamauga itself is unique in Civil War history; and, furthermore, the movements of troops before and after the battle seem, like the intricate flow of the actual combat, a puzzle that cannot be mapped, or made completely understandable by any means known to man. But the salient features of Chickamauga stand out boldly enough today; and they appear in still greater clarity when all the events from September, 1863, to the winter of 1864 are regarded as in a single chain of cause and effect. All that happened after Rosecrans crossed the Tennessee and swept southeast was probably an inevitable result of his approach from Bridgeport by the route he chose, on a terrain most unfavorable to his scheme, in the near presence of the Confederate Army of Tennessee. The confusion of the battle was itself a product of these circumstances.

When Bragg moved south from Chattanooga on September 4, he did not follow the Western & Atlantic Railroad toward Dalton and Rome, as Rosecrans inferred, but marched toward La'fayette, Georgia, and kept his army well in hand, close to Lafayette and largely to the east of Pigeon Mountain, which, with other ridges, screened his lurking place. The southwest swing of Rosecrans's widely separated Twentieth and Fourteenth corps brought them, once they crossed the great range of Lookout Mountain, into a position where Bragg's whole army could assail and destroy either of these two corps before the other could be marched to its support. Or he could turn upon the Twenty-first Corps, under Crittenden, which, blithely engaged in a "pursuit" of an imaginary army, was marching down from the north, out of position either to give or to receive support. Bragg was, in short, opposite the center of the advancing Federal army, ready to take his choice of meat when the unwary victims descended the mountain.

But that was not all. Pigeon Mountain, projecting northward from Lookout Mountain, forms MacLemore's Cove, a long valley open to the northeast, but closed at the south by the curve of the ridge that joins it with Lookout. The west fork of Chickamauga Creek rises in this cove and flows northeast. Thomas's corps, the Fourteenth, was headed across Lookout into the cove, by Rosecrans's orders. Bragg had easy access to the cove by Bluebird, Dug, and Catlett Gaps in Pigeon Mountain, and could also move around the northern end of Pigeon Mountain. His orders and dispatches clearly indicate that it was his intention to strike Thomas's Corps in MacLemore's Cove, and, penning it there, destroy it; and seemingly, too, to trap and destroy there whatever forces Rosecrans might bring to Thomas's support, conceivably even the whole Federal army, if Rosecrans put it all there.

Rosecrans did put it there, or approximately there. And though it is fashionable among military historians to blame ill-starred Bragg for Rosecrans's ultimate escape, it seems much more sensible to attribute that escape to the valor of Rosecrans's fighting men and to God's infinite mercy.

In this September, instead of the steaming downpours that accompanied Rosecrans's June offensive, a drouthy season had set in. The great wooded ranges of North Georgia were parched. Water was very scarce. Heat and dust were supreme. Clouds of dust, rising about every troop movement, caked the uniforms and bodies of the marching columns and betrayed their positions to distant signal posts. It was a lonesome, uninviting country to the Federals, who had for so long luxuriated in the pleasant farming region of Middle Tennessee. It was not the South they might have pictured—this land of interminable lofty ridges, running northeast and southwest for tedious distances without a break except at the so-called "gaps," which were not real gaps but precipitous ravines where narrow, inconsequential roads mounted snake-like above deep hollows. It was a land of little habitation, even in the valleys from which the old Cherokee dwellers had been gone only a bare quarter of a century. The scrubby but persistent mountain woodland, largely oak and pine, only here and there opened into a brushy glade or some mountaineer's clearing. There was little forage; it was a poor land for corn; but there were numerous wild hogs like those which, back at Stevenson and Bridgeport, they had jokingly named "Alabama sunfish."

Federal reports, letters, reminiscences rarely fail to attest the extreme discomfort and fatigue of the troops who marched and countermarched on this campaign. The 21st Michigan Infantry, for example, when they reached the clear waters of Crawfish Spring on September 19, after crossing Lookout Mountain three times during McCook's movement forward and back, "broke like a flock of sheep, many of the men speechless, their parched tongues and lips covered with dust." Ignoring the crash of guns all around them, they plunged into the stream. Earlier, the members of an artillery unit, while crossing Raccoon Mountain, labored to fetch water up from the depths of an abandoned coal mine. Other units (both Federal and Confederate) went for twenty-four hours or more during the battle without water. Soldiers of either army would have envied the lucky Federal outfit that had time to pause at the falls of Little River to bathe and remove ticks; the tick, like the ubiquitous chigoe, was one of the nuisances of war. But nobody, on the other hand, could envy the luckless Federal infantrymen who were detailed to assist wagon trains up and down the mountain roads; that was terrible toil. And, for the Federal soldiers in particular, there was, worst of all, a foreboding notion, after a time, that all was not well, that some mischief was tracking them through this too-untenanted wilderness.

Such foreboding was mild suspicion compared to the horror that must have come over Rosecrans and his staff when Negley's report, combined with other trickles of information, told him that he, the hunter, had suddenly become the hunted, and that the tough Confederate army, swelling in numbers, was in position to devour his army piece by piece. From that moment, though he put up a brave front in dispatches and later reports, Rosecrans's whole endeavor was to pull together the scattered pieces of his army —to hurry back the puzzled McCook, from far over the mountain, sixty miles away; to pull close the fatuous Crittenden, who kept boasting about his capacity to whip all comers; and finally, and most desperately, to slide his line of battle, once it was consolidated, toward the left, toward Rossville Gap, lest the army be cut off from Chattanooga.

Meanwhile Bragg prepared stroke after stroke against the dispersed elements of the Federal army, only to see opportunities lost by the willfulness or mental paralysis of his subordinate commanders. To this day, nothing really explains why Hindman did not attack parts of Thomas's Corps in MacLemore's Cove, or why Polk did not, as ordered, fall on Crittenden; and nothing, at last, explains why Bragg, with his army assembled and ready, did not give battle between September 12 and 19, when Rosecrans was still not fully concentrated. The excuses of the various generals, Bragg included, make no sense in the end. Such things are among the mysteries of war.

After some sharp preliminary skirmishing, the battle proper opened on September 19. It was still Bragg's aim to envelop the Federal left and roll the enemy up into MacLemore's Cove, but the battle began, almost by accident, with the Confederate right temporarily on the defense. During the previous night Rosecrans had shifted Thomas's corps to his left, and closer to Rossville, so that it overlapped the attacking Confederate right. Thomas, acting on misinformation, sent troops to attack and cut off a Confederate "brigade" which was supposedly isolated west of the Chickamauga. He found his attack confronted and checked by the alert Forrest, who at once perceived that Bragg, thinking to outflank, was being outflanked. Forrest assumed command of the troops on the field, no matter whether he was entitled to it or not, and improvised a defense that gave Bragg time to adjust his battle line and that brought from Thomas the first of the loud cries for help which, in the end, contributed much to the Federal disaster. The fighting swelled and became more general, but the battle of the 19th was a welter of sharp, detached actions rather than an organized battle.

At the end of that first bloody day, the Federal army, shaken but unbudged, was busy all night with preparing makeshift breastworks and with the hazardous readjustment of lines toward the left, which had become an obsession with Rosecrans. The Confederates, bivouacked on the field, hearkened to the ring of Federal axes and the cries of the wounded. The smell of the burning woods mixed with the reek of powder and augmented the universal thirst. The September moonlight sifted through the forest and cast spectral shadows. But part of Longstreet's troops had already arrived and fought, and famous John Hood was leading them, his arm in a sling from his Gettysburg wound. And more were coming.

Longstreet himself arrived at Catoosa at eleven o'clock that night, with two brigades of the Virginia army. Bragg had sent no guide to meet him, and while riding with his staff in search of Confederate headquarters, Longstreet blundered into a Federal picket. In the uncertain moonlight he bluffed the picket into thinking them Federals, and rode off quickly, but it was a narrow escape. At midnight he found Bragg's headquarters and received from him the orders for the next day's battle and a map of the country. At "daydawn" Polk would begin the attack on the right, and successive units would attack, from right to left, as soon as his guns where heard. Furthermore, Bragg then and there divided his army: Polk to command the "right wing," Longstreet the "left wing." Although this action has been much criticized, nobody has explained what else Bragg could have done,

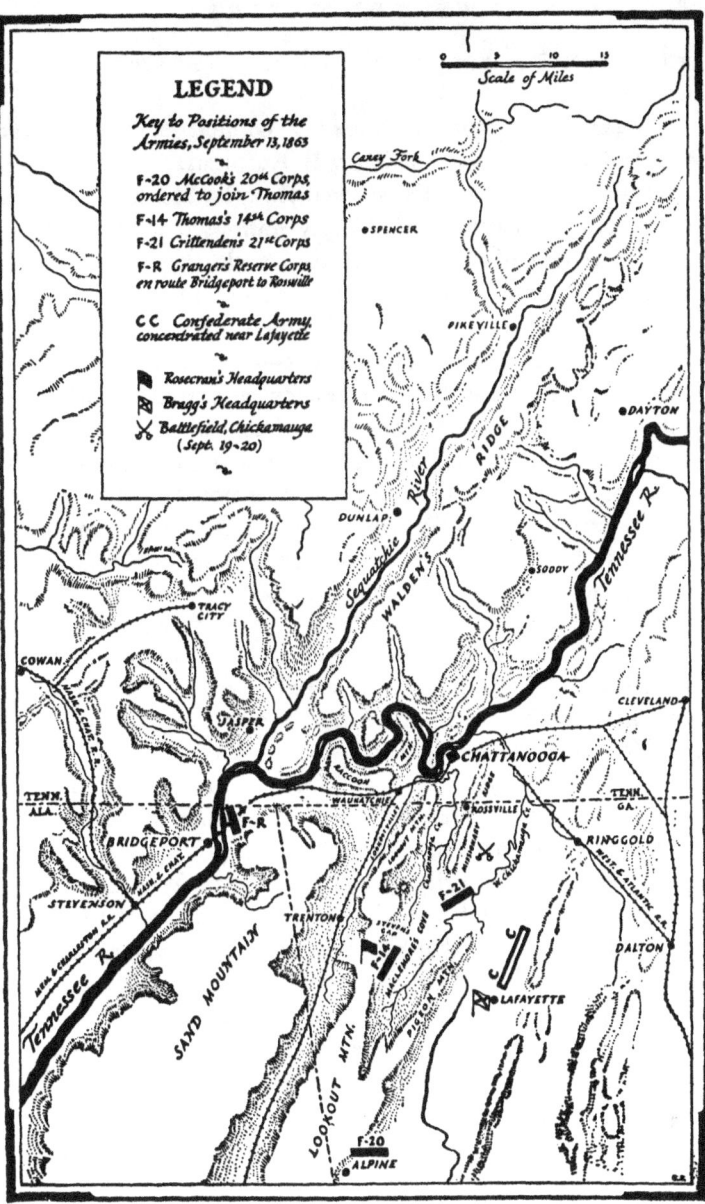

with a general of Longstreet's high rank and prestige on his hands.

Meanwhile gloom pervaded a council of war at the Widow Glenn's house, which was Rosecrans's headquarters. Rosecrans and his generals believed that the Federal army was now terribly outnumbered. Deeply impressed by the savageness and weight of the Confederate attack, they were close to a last-ditch mood, though determined not to budge. Charles A. Dana, who a little earlier had joined the army as a special observer for the War Department—"Stanton's spy," they felt—was present at this conference, and told, in his later reminiscences, how the exhausted Thomas kept dozing off in the midst of the deliberations. When asked a question, he would startle awake and, like the Dormouse, would always say the same thing: "Strengthen the left." Rosecrans's dispositions for the next day's battle were calculated to strengthen that left, with Thomas behind breastworks in a semicircular position east of the Lafayette-Rossville-Chattanooga road, and McCook closed up still more tightly on his right, and Crittenden in reserve. In the rear of Thomas's position was the cluster of hills later to become famous as the Horseshoe Ridge.

When day-dawn of September 20 came, Polk did not attack promptly, after all. It was another unaccountable delay, which infuriated and disheartened Bragg, and it has never been satisfactorily explained. When Polk finally attacked, the Federal left had been further strengthened, and the hard fighting of that morning only battered and did not dislodge or envelop Thomas's position. It did draw from him, however, more requests for reinforcements, and so, when Longstreet's powerful advance got under way about noon, it struck the Federal lines just at the moment when some rather frantic readjustments of position were being made in McCook's line. Longstreet's massive attack, made in column of brigades, hit the gap left by the displacement of Wood's division. Hood's Texans, and the divisions of Bushrod Johnson,

## CHICKAMAUGA AND ITS SEQUEL 59

Stewart, and Hindman, simply tore the Federal lines to pieces and hurled them back in disordered fragments. Longstreet, always at his best on the battlefield, took in the situation instantly. Ignoring Bragg's plan of battle, he bore to his own right and toward the rear of Thomas's position. The Federal army was broken in two by his drive. Some remnants of the beaten Federal right clung to the Horseshoe Ridge, and Thomas still held out. The remainder of McCook's corps, some units in orderly retreat, others confused and disordered, was borne back, and divisions and brigades disintegrated before the Confederate rush. Rosecrans's headquarters was overrun, and Rosecrans himself, with Garfield, his chief of staff, rode to Chattanooga to reorganize resistance, if possible, from that point. The two corps commanders, McCook and Crittenden, also went with the tide of retreat to Chattanooga.

Charles A. Dana saw the rout. He was awakened from a nap, he afterwards wrote, by "the most infernal noise I ever heard. I sat up on the grass, and the first thing I saw was General Rosecrans crossing himself. . . . 'Hello,' I said to myself, 'if the general is crossing himself we are in a desperate situation.' I had no sooner collected my thoughts and looked toward the front, where all the din came from, than I saw our lines break and melt away. . . . Then the headquarters around me disappeared. The graybacks came through with a rush, and soon the musket-balls and cannon-shot began to reach the place where we stood." Dana rode, hatless, to Chattanooga, and there sent Stanton a woeful dispatch, beginning: "My report today is of deplorable importance. Chickamauga is as fatal a name in our history as Bull Run."

Rosecrans, dismounting pale and shaken at Chattanooga, sent similar dispatches to Burnside and Halleck, and also, a little later, warned his commander at Bridgeport to be on the alert and save the bridges for a possible retreat. But he also returned Garfield to the battlefield, with orders to report the situation, and, as soon as he learned that Thomas still held his ground, ordered him to assume command of the troops on the field and to withdraw to Rossville and take "a threatening attitude."

Thomas, at first ignorant of the extent of the Federal disaster, did hold out against the unco-ordinated Confederate attacks of the afternoon. The fighting on the slopes of the Horseshoe Ridge was grim; indeed, at times it was hand to hand, with clubbed rifles or with bayonets. And Thomas's steadiness during this critical period no doubt rightfully won for him—or his troops did—his traditional title, the "Rock of Chickamauga." At the same time it must be remembered that Thomas was saved, at one critical moment, by the opportune arrival of Gordon Granger, with parts of the Reserve Corps and fresh ammunition. Likewise, it was the strengthening of Thomas that helped to weaken and disorder the Federal left.

Actually Thomas stood like a rock only through the morning and the first part of the afternoon. If he had stood thus much longer, his troops, now the merged fragments of all four corps, would have been cut off and surrounded by the powerful Confederate attack of the late afternoon which crossed and possessed the Lafayette-Rossville road, surged up and around the Horseshoe Ridge, and captured the regiments and parts of regiments left there. Thomas, upon receiving Rosecrans's order to withdraw, began the retreat at about 4:30 P.M., leading and directing it himself. His troops retired gradually, as best they could, through McFarland's Gap, for they could escape no other way. Even then some of them had to fight their way through the eager, encircling advance of the victorious, the fully victorious Confederate army. The "Rock of Chickamauga" was at that moment a rolling stone, firmly and wisely bent on getting the remnants of the army into a better defensive position. Thomas, too, was utterly and completely, though not disgracefully, defeated. And the two wings of the Confederate army, meeting at about sunset

## CHICKAMAUGA AND ITS SEQUEL 61

near the Horseshoe Ridge, gave a mighty Rebel yell, which passed from regiment to regiment until it resounded, over and over, from end to end of the triumphant Confederate battle line.

Critics say the pursuit should have been pressed, and blame Bragg, who in midafternoon had rather sulkily gone off to his headquarters at Reed's Bridge, and seemed, according to Longstreet and others, quite unconscious of having won a great, conclusive victory. Perhaps an immediate pursuit would have inflicted more disaster upon the weary Unionists; perhaps it would not, since they had made some preparations at Rossville against it. Critics seem to forget that in none of the great battles of the Civil War did the victor, whether Confederate or Federal, make an effective pursuit. Such great battles invariably left the victor as well as the defeated in disorder and confusion. Indeed, a battle itself is merely a noisy chaos to which generals can convey only a meager semblance of order. So it was at Chickamauga.

Though no estimate of effective strength is trustworthy, it is probable that Rosecrans put close to 60,000 men into action (about all he had available); of these, 16,550 were casualties—dead, wounded, or missing. But Bragg's force of possibly 50,000 counted 17,800 casualties, a third of the total. Many Confederate regiments, like the opposing Federal units, lost more than half their strength. Officer casualties were heavy, and they included generals; the hard-fighting Hood, already wounded in the arm, lost a leg at Chickamauga. Whether the word "Chickamauga" means, as legend says, River of Death, or as the scholar maintains, "Dwelling Place of the War Chief," its significance was grim, and its effect in terms of battle shock can hardly be overestimated. Some Confederate units did relatively little fighting and were "fresh," but it would have been no mean feat to locate them on the evening of September 20, to orient them, and to send them in a well-organized pursuit. Commands had been mixed, officers had been killed or separated from their commands, the whole army was sprawled in only vaguely identifiable or unknown positions among the dark woods and hills over a wide front. The wounded had to be sought out and cared for. Above all, there was exhaustion, hunger, thirst after two days of battle preceded by heavy marching and sharp skirmishing. The Confederates had paid a price for their great victory and their profuse capture of cannon, small arms, prisoners, and supplies. The military critics' remarks about pursuit may be disregarded as academic chirpings. The post-mortem remarks of Confederate officers about what might have been done may also be disregarded. The ragged and hungry Johnny Reb of those times was undoubtedly content, like any other soldier, to find himself miraculously preserved, to build a campfire once more, and then, sweet God, to sleep.

For the next day and later the criticisms may be in order. Bragg was undoubtedly slow to follow up and press the retreating Federal army, which soon busily began to fortify its positions at Chattanooga. Forrest, energetic as ever, pushed his cavalry toward Chattanooga early on September 21 and captured a Federal signal post from which high perch he could overlook Federal movements in the Chattanooga neighborhood. He then sent Bragg a dispatch, oft-quoted, in which he said, "I think they are evacuating as hard as they can go . . . I think we ought to press forward as rapidly as possible." Later, intensely stirred by Bragg's slowness to move, Forrest exclaimed, "What does he fight battles for?" This feeling was general in the army. The old distrust of Bragg returned, and was reinforced by the quarrels and recriminations between the surly Bragg and his generals. Nevertheless, Bragg did push the army forward, and seizing Lookout Mountain and Missionary Ridge, he shut up the defeated Federals in their Chattanooga defenses—all close to the river, and mostly on low ground, with the river at their back. There they had no egress, except across the river to the north.

## CHICKAMAUGA AND ITS SEQUEL 63

At first Rosecrans considered the possibility of a further retreat. And well he might, for he had evaded one trap, at great cost, only to fall into another which might be more disastrous still. Although the unfortunate Federal commander issued an inspiring proclamation, in which he congratulated his army on winning Chattanooga, "the objective point of the campaign," such bluster was merely a front. Longstreet's men on Lookout Mountain blocked the railroad between Chattanooga and Bridgeport, and his sharpshooters and pickets, there and on Raccoon Mountain, covered the river and the river road opposite. To bring supplies from the Bridgeport railhead, Rosecrans had only the dismally inadequate mountain road over Walden's Ridge—a sixty-mile stretch of torture for his exhausted and forageless wagon-teams. There had been no accumulation in Chattanooga of supplies of any sort, and much had been lost at Chickamauga. Rosecrans's army, hemmed up by the triumphant Confederates, would certainly starve, and that soon, unless the supply problem could be solved or a new army sent up to drive the Confederates away.

Bragg was certain that they would starve, and would be forced by starvation to surrender. This certainty may explain his delay in closing in. Why hurry, if your enemy is conveniently arranging his army to hold what you know to be only a trap? It also explains, possibly, his brushing aside of Longstreet's proposal for a movement north of Chattanooga, to Rosecrans's rear. There is much to justify Bragg's view. He was greatly at fault, however, in not perceiving that the Tennessee River would be the salvation of the Federals and in not taking stern, practical measures to cut them off from that last salvation. Apparently neither Bragg, the commanding general, nor the mighty Longstreet, who had the Federal life line in his grasp, ever thought of the river as something to carry steamboats; to them, it was just something to cross; they were land-minded. So, while the Confederate army lazed away the time on the pleasant, autumn-hued ridges around Chattanooga, and drilled impudently within plain sight of their foes, and while, also, their high-ranking generals engaged in unseemly quarrels, the ingenious Yankees, leaner now than Yankees commonly were, got desperately busy.

Rosecrans, assured of reinforcements, initiated some of the plans for salvation, but others carried them out. There was unseemly bickering among generals on the Federal side, too. But the Washington government soon gave Grant full command of its western armies, removed Rosecrans from the Army of the Cumberland, and put Thomas in temporary command at Chattanooga. Orders for Grant to take charge and for Sherman to hurry east with his troops had long since gone out. It was impossible to move the scared Burnside from East Tennessee, but "Fighting Joe" Hooker was dispatched by rail from the far east, with troops from the Army of the Potomac. It would take long for these additions to come up. Meanwhile, the army at Chattanooga was in the worst plight of any Federal army during the whole war. The grinning Confederate pickets, knowing this, flung the taunt across the lines: "Well, Yank, how do you like being in Vicksburg?"

The taunt hurt. The horrors of a siege were more deeply impressed upon the Federals in early October when Wheeler, by Bragg's orders combining with his own troops a portion of Forrest's hard-driven cavalry, crossed the Tennessee at Cottonport, above Chattanooga, despite the presence of opposing Federal cavalry, and rode southwest down the Sequatchie Valley to meet and destroy the Federal wagon trains coming from the railhead. Wheeler filled the valley for miles with dead mules and burned wagons, then, crossing the mountains and circling west, cut the railroad to the north, and recrossed the Tennessee at Muscle Shoals, after causing much anguish to Federal garrisons en route.

Soon four pieces of hard bread and a quarter of a pound of bacon were all the Federal soldier at Chattanooga had for a three-day ration. Mules and horses were dying by the hundreds for lack of food. There were no horses fit to pull artillery or loaded wagons. Fuel began to run short. The soldiers cut down forest trees to burn, then cut away the stumps, then dug up the roots. There were other demands for wood—pontoon boats were needed, and timber for a bridge. The forest trees supplied these needs, too, and the Chattanooga sawmills, which Bragg had left intact, were put into service. This ravaging of timber left the valley bare; it is almost completely bare in Civil War photographs of Chattanooga.

Among other shortages, there was a shortage of nails. The nails were needed for bridgework, but were not obtainable. A military bridge had to be built, then, and was finally built, without nails. There were no spikes for the pontoons. The spikes were brought up, in small lots, by the courier line over Walden's Ridge; every courier brought a small bag of spikes with his dispatches. The shortage of materials was, in fact, almost as grim an element as the shortage of food.

Since it was do or die, the Federals turned to the river and made it work for them. They had no steamboats above Muscle Shoals and, most regrettably, Wilder's guns had wrecked the *Paint Rock* and *Dunbar*. These could be raised and repaired, but the army might starve before they were ready. While the slow process of repair was under way, a steamboat service must be improvised. The improvised steamboat service was quickly named the Cracker Line by the hungry Federal soldiers. Its first boat, the *Chattanooga*, was hardly more than an ordinary flatboat with an engine, a boiler, and a stern wheel, and a minimum of superstructure. To the Confederates she became known as the "Chicken Thief."

The *Chattanooga* was built at Bridgeport by Captain Arthur Edwards, an assistant quartermaster, who used the services of a Lake Erie shipbuilder named Turner and whatever carpenters could be hastily assembled. William Le Duc, a quartermaster of Hooker's newly arrived corps, tells how he found Edwards and Turner in great distress. The Tennessee was rising, and they had set up the hull of the *Chattanooga* on blocks near the water's edge. Fearing their craft would float off on the rising tide, they had loaded the hull with pig iron. Le Duc pointed out that even if the pig iron kept the boat from being carried away, they could not do any calking until the hull had dried out, and by that time the Army of the Cumberland might have perished.

"I've done all I can," cried Edwards. "I don't know what the water wants to rise here for. It never rose this way where I was brought up."

Le Duc suggested putting the hull on pontoons, which the Army of the Cumberland was constructing for future operations. The pontoons, partly filled with water, were pushed under the hull. The water was then pumped out, pontoons and hull rose with the river, and all was safe. On the night of October 28 the *Chattanooga* made her first trip, towing flatboats loaded with thirty-four thousand rations. The bold navigators had much trouble with the swift current and the unfamiliar winding channel of the Narrows. Nevertheless, they got through to Rankin's Ferry, from which point the supplies were hauled to Chattanooga. The Confederate pickets and sharpshooters did not interfere, and though they later fired on the *Paint Rock*, they did nothing effective to interrupt the operations of the Cracker Line.

The *Paint Rock* came into operation soon after the *Chattanooga*. The *Dunbar*, more sadly battered, took longer to repair. Lieutenant Alfred Pirtle, of the 10th Ohio Infantry, left an account of how ingenious soldier mechanics salvaged the *Dunbar*.

Having pumped out her hull and patched up the breaks in it, the boat floated, but she was a sorry-looking craft. Fire had removed the cabin, pilot-house, wheel-houses, and thrown down the smokestacks and 'scape-pipes, but had not seriously damaged the machinery at the decks, as the burning wreck had sunk. Our men had repaired the machinery and put up the inside of the wheelhouse so as to keep the water off the decks. The pilot-wheel, placed upon a temporary platform, had a hemp rope rigged up which moved a temporary tiller; the old bells hung over the engines; one short and one long smokestack carried the smoke away from the patched-up furnace. But the boat moved obediently to the handling of the pilot, and the machinery did its duty amid the cheers of the crowd on the bank.

These boats, especially the *Chattanooga,* saved the Federal army. The stores they brought, insufficient though they were to an army's needs, provided just enough to permit survival and stave off surrender. Just that much, and no more. They could not supply the margin needed for powerful offensive operations, for they could not bring horses and mules to pull guns and wagons, or sufficient forage to supply animals, or other bulky supplies. They merely sustained the defense, and barely did that. But throughout the operations of the subsequent campaign, the Federals plugged away stubbornly to increase their margin of safety on the river. They recovered and put into service the old *Lookout.* They kept building new light-draft steamboats which could negotiate the shoals of the upper river. In addition to the boats already named, they put into service the *Chickamauga, Kingston, Bridgeport, Missionary, Wauhatchie, Resaca,* and *Stone River.* They also finally raised and put to use the *James Glover, Holston,* and *Tennessee,* which by Forrest's orders had been burned and scuttled when he left East Tennessee at the beginning of the Chickamauga campaign. During these days, also, Charles A. Dana, whose reports to Stanton had now become rather unjustifiably optimistic, urged the building of the gunboat squadron which Rosecrans had asked for the year before. These, too, were ultimately put on the ways at Bridgeport, which had become a center of boatbuilding operations. The four gunboats, constructed under the supervision of Lieutenant Le Roy Fitch, were the *General Burnside, General Thomas, General Grant, General Sherman.* Each of these mounted five guns. They were under the command of Lieutenant

Moreau Forrest, and they went into service in the summer of 1864.

While all this was going on, the Confederates did nothing but loll comfortably on the mountains around Chattanooga and indulge occasionally in futile long-range shelling of the Federal positions below, while, at the higher military levels, their generals quarreled sullenly with Bragg, whose weakness was more obvious than ever. Yet nobody blamed him or any other general for the critical defect—the failure to close the river or to do anything to hamper steamboat operations. The steamboats, unescorted as they were, could have been wrecked at any time by quick, determined raids. Their unloading points could have been kept under fire. The river itself could have been covered by gunfire, or its channel could have been blocked at any one of a number of places. A surprise blow at Bridgeport itself, if conducted by such a leader as Forrest, would have brought devastating results. Nothing of this sort was done, or attempted, or apparently even dreamed of.

And Longstreet's guard over the vital river segment of the Narrows—the weak link in the Federal supply system—was puny and slothful. When the Federals, seeking to shorten their supply line, sent a landing party in pontoon boats downriver by night to Brown's Ferry, they found only a weak Confederate picket to oppose them, and forthwith established a strong bridgehead on the south side of the river, convenient to Wauhatchie Valley. It had never dawned on Longstreet that that position was important. Next, when Hooker pushed his troops from Bridgeport and up Lookout Valley to Wauhatchie, to complete the Brown's Ferry link of supply, Longstreet's reaction was slow, halfhearted, weak. The night attack ordered by Bragg was poorly executed and failed. Afterwards, though Hooker was badly placed for a real fight, and could have been destroyed, neither Bragg nor Longstreet did anything more. They simply sat still and allowed the Federals to build up a better supply system. Even then, the system remained one of the most intricate and hazardous that ever supplied an army. Supplies came by steamboat to Kelley's Ferry at the foot of the Suck; thence by road to the new pontoon bridge at Brown's Ferry (a frail affair) and across to the north bank; thence around Moccasin Bend to a point opposite Chattanooga; thence across to the south bank again. The supply line therefore crossed the Tennessee three times between Bridgeport and Chattanooga. And Hooker's protecting corps—in which he himself had not too much confidence—was in isolation south of the river.

Never was Confederate army more badly handled than was the Army of Tennessee at this time. Its morale sank, and distrust of Bragg reached a climax. The higher officers were frankly rebellious. Forrest was already irritated by diversion of part of his troops to Wheeler for the Sequatchie Valley raid. A little later, when the inept Bragg ordered Forrest to turn over practically all of his cavalry to Wheeler—the troops Forrest himself had raised, trained, and armed—a black rage seized him. He wrote Bragg a letter in which he charged the commanding general with lying and double-dealing, and followed this up with a face-to-face denunciation. Dr. J. B. Cowan, Forrest's chief surgeon, witnessed the encounter and remembered Forrest's words.

"I have stood your meanness as long as I intend to," said Forrest, while Bragg sat at his field desk, blanched and inert. "You have played the part of a damned scoundrel, and if you were any part of a man I would slap your jaws and force you to resent it.

"You may as well not issue any more orders to me, for I will not obey them. And I will hold you personally responsible for any further indignities you try to inflict on me.

"You have threatened to arrest me for not obeying your orders promptly. I dare you to do it, and I say to you that if you ever again interfere with me or cross my path, it will be at peril of your life."

Bragg attempted no punitive measures. Presently, when Forrest applied for independent command, his request was approved, and he left for the west. Jefferson Davis, disturbed out of his abstraction by the quarrels of his officers, visited the Confederate army to investigate matters personally. Instead of removing Bragg, he made a characteristically unrealistic and futile effort to smooth out dissensions. Davis disliked the idea of replacing his favorite with Longstreet or some other eligible. It never occurred to him, or to anybody else at that time, that Forrest was the great genius of the western South as Lee was the genius of the eastern South. But who can now doubt that under Forrest the Army of Tennessee would have been to the West what Lee's army was to Virginia? Strangely enough, in 1865, when Jefferson Davis was fleeing from lost Virginia after Lee's surrender, his final, desperate hope was that he might reach Forrest in Mississippi, and with him rally new forces.

On the Federal side similar dissension existed, but it vanished when Grant came to Chattanooga and took personal command. Misfortune had again visited Grant. His horse had fallen, and he was injured and sick. His second visit to the banks of the Tennessee found him crippled as he had been at Shiloh. But his head was still working—and he brought along his luck.

One of Grant's first moves was to reconnoiter the ground in person. During this reconnaissance he came opposite a Confederate position on the south side of the river. Dismounting, he walked down to the bank for a good look across the water. On the other side, in plain view, was a Confederate picket of about twenty men. They did not fire at the party of Federal officers; they just gazed. One account of the incident holds that they saluted Grant. "I suppose," Grant wrote later, "they looked upon the garrison of Chattanooga as prisoners of war, feeding or starving themselves, and thought it would be inhuman to kill any of them except in self-defense."

The rescue of the Army of the Cumberland from the trap into which Rosecrans had led it was not, indeed, any simple and easy business. Hooker's arrival and the lodgment at Brown's Ferry shortened the line of supply, but it also unfortunately increased the number of troops to be supplied. The railroad from Chattanooga to Bridgeport to Nashville, overburdened and in bad repair, was subject to frequent interruption. Furthermore, it required considerable numbers of troops for guard duty. In late October, a month after Rosecrans had retreated into "the objective of the campaign," the Federal army was still in serious trouble.

In early November Bragg, yielding at last to Longstreet's repeated urgings, detached the old warhorse with fourteen thousand men to strike Burnside at Knoxville. This diversion of a part of the army at a time when Grant was gathering strength has been generally criticized as an error. It was, however, an entirely feasible movement if it had been carried out with speed—as it was not. Grant, if judged from his dispatches and plans, regarded it with apprehension. A quick defeat of Burnside and a Confederate repossession of East Tennessee would have complicated his problems enormously. His subsequent movements, including the Battle of Missionary Ridge, were intended as much to relieve pressure on Burnside and reopen connections with him as to raise the siege of Chattanooga.

Sherman, coming east from Memphis, was moving to Grant's support, but not nearly fast enough. Seemingly Sherman, ignorant of Muscle Shoals, supposed at first that he might use the Tennessee as a line of supply. He dallied at Eastport, where supplies could reach him by river, and called for gunboats and steamboats to ferry his army across. From this point he wrote Admiral Porter:

Boats cannot yet pass Colbert Shoals; so for the time we must foot it up to Florence and Tuscumbia, trusting in a short time to get a ferryboat up to Florence. We are much obliged to the Tennessee, which has favored us most opportunely, for I am never easy with a railroad which takes a whole army to guard, each foot of rail being essential to the whole; whereas they can't stop the Tennessee, and each boat can make its own game.

At this point, however, he received a brief telegram from Grant ordering him to stop his repair work on the railroad (the Memphis & Charleston), cross the Tennessee, and hurry to Bridgeport. The telegram was alarming enough, but the most puzzling thing was how it had come to him. It was brought by one Corporal Pike, "a dirty, black-haired individual with mixed dress and strange demeanor." Corporal Pike had come down the Tennessee in a canoe, past guerrillas, who fired at him, and over Muscle Shoals. It was a most desperately primitive way for the commanding general of the West to send an important message.

Sherman hurried his troops across, but soon, without a river to help him, was in more trouble. He wrote Porter again, in a different vein:

My movement carries me away from the river channels, near which I thought I should live out my 'three years.' . . . I found Elk River 200 yards wide, 4½ feet deep, and running a mill-tail. I was therefore forced to skirt up to this place [Fayetteville], where there is a fine stone bridge. . . . The roads up here are very rocky and hard on our men and horses used to a softer ground, but we can get used to anything. . . . It will be utterly impossible for me to use the Tennessee River from this quarter, and I fear we have made too extensive preparations.

The nearer Sherman marched to Chattanooga, plodding where poor Buell also had plodded a year and a half before, the more impressed he was with the difficulties of army operations away from a helpful river. Arriving in mid-November a little ahead of his troops, Sherman conferred with Grant at Chattanooga and with him viewed the scene: the Federal army cooped on the low ground and overlooked by the lofty circle of Confederate entrenchments and, lower down, the rifle pits pushed forward into Chattanooga Valley itself. It was a vast amphitheater in which the Confederates, occupying the choice seats, apparently watched to see what entertainment the Federals could stage.

"General Grant, you're besieged!" said Sherman.

"It's too true," said Grant.

But despite all difficulties on the Federal side, the game was now up for Bragg and the Confederates. There on the old Indian ground it had been a strange enchanted season, an Indian summer among misty peaks and deep woods, with the pygmy Federal camps spread before them, and the glint of the river beyond. Now that Indian summer was over, for with the fall of leaf Grant set afoot his elaborate battle plan, and the fierce victors of Chickamauga became spellbound men, wielding harmless, bemagicked weapons.

Even the Federal troops were somewhat bemagicked. In Grant's extraordinarily complex maneuvers hardly anything turned out according to plan. The Battle of Missionary Ridge was won by accidents and by vague impulses kindling impossible charges against orders rather than by Grant's strategy. The front of action was so wide and the mountain terrain so baffling that both Sherman and Hooker went astray. Sherman, charged with rolling up the Confederate right, made an ingenious concealed march north of the Tennessee, crossed the river on pontoons that had been cleverly hidden in North Chickamauga Creek, put up a pontoon bridge, and with the help of that bridge and the old *Dunbar* as a ferryboat, made good his lodgment on the south side. He then delivered a rousing attack—upon an empty hill! When Sherman located the true Confederate position and attacked on the next day, his veterans were roughly handled by Cleburne's men, and made slight progress.

At the other end of the line, Hooker's men struggled up the shoulder of Lookout Mountain through the fog that rose in early morning from the Tennessee. Walthall's thin brigade posted there could not hold back Hooker's masses and fought only a rear-guard action. Soon Hooker's men were raising the Stars and Stripes on the mountaintop, but their achievement was more a feat of mountain climbing than a battle. The fog, however, created the legend of "the Battle Above the Clouds," and to this day tourists gape at the cliffs, never knowing that the hardest fighting took place far away on the Confederate right, where Cleburne's men baffled red-bearded Sherman.

In the center, victory came to the Federals by a fluke—or, if one prefers, by an odd spontaneous impulse of Thomas's soldiers. Grant, worried by the failure of Sherman and Hooker to dent the main Confederate position, ordered Thomas to take the line of Confederate rifle pits on the lower slope and then halt to await orders. Thomas's men took the rifle pits. Then, possibly because they preferred to go forward into the "dead space" on the slope, where Confederate fire could not reach them, rather than stay and take the fire where they were, they kept going. They rushed spontaneously up the steep slope, and then on to the very crest, in full view of the surprised and almost angry commander in chief. The Confederates were equally surprised. Their resistance was ineffective. They broke—perhaps not only because of the stiff Federal attack, but simply because they were tired of fighting for Bragg. This break determined the battle, despite Sherman's failure on the right. Bragg withdrew the Confederate army to Dalton and there at long last asked to be relieved of command. His unlamented departure raised the spirits of the Army of Tennessee. It was, in truth, anything but a defeated army. It had been dislodged from Missionary Ridge only by a combination of two Federal armies directed by the combined genius of Grant, Sherman, Thomas, Sheridan, and Hooker. It took that much to drive the hardy Confederates

CHICKAMAUGA AND ITS SEQUEL    75

only as far as Dalton, Georgia. They were not pursued or in any way bothered for many months.

Meanwhile, Longstreet's drive against Knoxville, after almost frightening Burnside into abrupt retreat, had slowed down into another siege. The deliberateness of his investment of Knoxville, at a time when the needs of Bragg's army demanded that he deliver a swift blow and return, suggests Longstreet's lack of concern for the fate of that army. At all costs, he would not serve longer under Bragg. His investment, too, was not complete. If the reminiscences of the historian Ramsey are to be credited, Longstreet, mistaking the insignificant Little River for the French Broad, erroneously believed that the French Broad River flowed into the Tennessee *below* Knoxville, and stubbornly ignored the fact that Burnside was receiving supplies by way of the French Broad, from *above* Knoxville. Longstreet also, like Bragg, had trouble with his subordinates, and partly for that reason his attack on Fort Sanders, the strong point of the city's western defenses, turned into a fiasco.

Grant's first move after Missionary Ridge was to send a strong force under Sherman to the relief of Burnside. Sherman marched rapidly eastward. The steamboat *Chattanooga*, loaded with supplies, moved upriver with him. Longstreet withdrew farther east, into the Watauga country. After living off East Tennessee for a short while, Sherman hurried most of his troops back into winter quarters in North Alabama and went north for a vacation. He would not stay, he said, in "that cursed gorge at Chattanooga."

Throughout the following winter the Federal garrison of East Tennessee repeated the sufferings of Rosecrans's army at Chattanooga. Their thin trickle of supplies came mostly by steamboat from the meager store brought with difficulty to Chattanooga, and the supply line was always breaking down. The situation worried Grant exceedingly. The belligerent presence of Longstreet alarmed him. Federal commanders were slothful and undependable. The Federal army was weakened by the "veteranizing" process, under which units that re-enlisted as units were given a thirty-day furlough.

Longstreet argued that, if reinforced, he could drive into Kentucky and relieve pressure on other fronts. A strengthening of Longstreet and any sort of offensive campaign might, indeed, have affected Federal plans—might even have delayed Grant's 1864 campaign against Lee.

But Longstreet was ultimately withdrawn. Joseph E. Johnston was given command of the Army of Tennessee. By spring Grant was in Virginia and his drive against Lee coordinated with Sherman's drive into Georgia. Sherman's advanced base was now the Chattanooga area. It was well provided, and there were gunboats on the Upper Tennessee. His supply line, however, was a railroad, and it was vulnerable.

CHAPTER V

# Guerrillas versus Gunboats

THE ARRIVAL OF FEDERAL gunboats on the Tennessee and other western rivers furnished Henry C. Work a theme for his famous song, "Kingdom Coming," more commonly known as "The Year of Jubilo." The jubilating Negro of Work's song, set free by the "Linkum gunboats," clearly belongs in the blackface minstrel tradition, as does Work's treatment of the sprightly melody—a variant of a tune found in religious songbooks familiar to southern folk tradition and ultimately derived from an old Scottish melody, "The Boatie Rows." The panic of "de massa" is comically rendered; and de massa in sheer avoirdupois resembles the famous "thousand pound man" of West Tennessee, Miles Darden, who had to use a two-horse wagon to go about his duties as farmer.

But Work's song of course was caricature, not much nearer reality than the drawings of the period in *Harper's Weekly*, which with a perfectly uninhibited stretching of the imagination represented the inhabitants of Florence and other river towns as thronging to the riverside and giving the "Linkum gunboats" something very like the glad hand of welcome.

Certainly the gunboats created alarm on their first appearance, and it was no wonder that they did. But the tables were soon turned, and the commanders of gunboats and transports quickly found that they had better keep a wary eye upon the silent, seemingly deserted banks of the Tennessee. At any moment de massa or any one of thousands of his lean and earnest countrymen might squint a contemplative eye from behind a bush and bring a blue uniform or a luckless pilot into the sights of his excellent squirrel rifle.

The Confederate answer to the Linkum gunboats was guerrilla warfare, ceaseless, nagging, and occasionally capable of wholesale destruction. There could be no other answer, unless the Confederates would flatly submit or just pretend not to notice. After the campaign of 1862 the Confederates had no fortresses on the river, and no naval forces to speak of; and except for Forrest's operations in 1864 they were at no time able to strike at the Tennessee shipping with sizable bodies of troops.

It would be hard to say whether Confederate guerrilla attacks were part of a general strategy, duly authorized at headquarters, or whether they were just the spontaneous reaction of the invaded population and local military officers to a disagreeable intrusion. The records show that "Volunteer Companies" were authorized by the Confederate Congress, to be charged with local defense. As members of the Provisional Army of the Confederate States they would be entitled to status as prisoners of war, if captured. But there is little indication that such "Home Guards" were systematically organized to do guerrilla fighting on the rivers. Such units were too often only a means of evading the Confederate draft law. More likely, the Confederates simply did whatever they could, whenever and wherever they could. They handed out to the gunboats the old medicine they had learned from the Indians. There was no other medicine available.

Federal gunboat commanders, of course, used the term "guerrilla" in a highly derogatory sense. Anybody who fired at them from the bank, from any position not identified as a fort or a line of battle, was a guerrilla, whether he was in Confederate uniform or not. To them, guerrilla warfare was "barbarous" and "uncivilized," and they retaliated in kind. There were undoubtedly civilian attacks on Federal shipping;

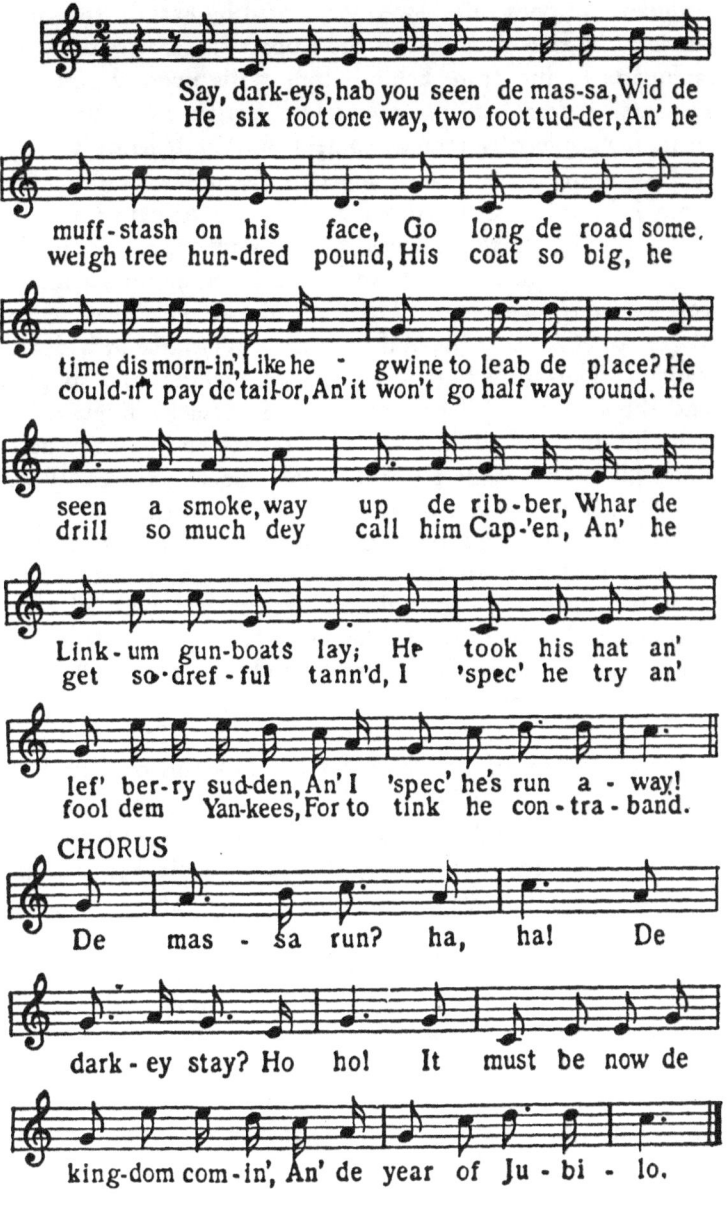

but these—if we except the genuine bushwhackers, who were a nuisance to both sides—were prompted by exactly the same patriotic impulse that caused the embattled farmers of Massachusetts to fire from behind stone walls upon the British redcoats. Federal reports themselves testify that the most formidable guerrilla attacks came from Confederate troops, in bodies up to the size of a regiment, and were generally from field artillery supported by infantry or cavalry.

Guerrilla attacks followed what is now considered, in the period of commandos and world wars, the approved model for harassing operations. The Confederate guerrillas strove always to effect surprise and to catch river traffic at a disadvantage. They aimed at destruction of facilities and supplies and the disruption of communications. Attacks of guerrillas were hit-and-run raids, intended to terrify and to intimidate. Guerrillas never made a stand against superior forces. When the gunboats landed troops, the guerrillas withdrew or dispersed, and hence gunboat commanders were always able to say that they had "driven off" or "broken up" guerrilla parties. If Confederate guerrilla operations had been directed systematically, by leaders like Forrest, the Federals would have been in great difficulty; they might have lost control of the rivers and the war.

Guerrilla warfare began on the Lower Tennessee soon after the Battle of Shiloh. Federal occupation of Tennessee and Kentucky only intensified it, and the countermeasures taken by the Federal commanders never had more than a local effect. Even late in the war, after the people had felt the full effect of the grim retaliations visited upon them, the guerrillas were striking as hard as ever. "An artillery company," wrote Admiral David D. Porter, speaking of this late period, "would sometimes travel for miles just for the pleasure of firing a few shots into a gunboat or transport."

In the summer of 1862, when Commodore C. H. Davis succeeded Foote in command of the western fleet, one of his first enterprises was to build a squadron of light-draft vessels specifically intended to guard shipping against guerrilla attacks on the Ohio and Tennessee rivers. Energetic Lieutenant Commander Le Roy Fitch was put in command of this squadron, which included the *St. Clair,* the *Brilliant,* the *Silver Lake,* and three boats captured from the Confederates, the *Robb,* the *Fairplay,* and the *Little Rebel.* These were the so-called "tinclads"—boats with light armor, proof against musket and rifle fire but not against cannon. They generally carried two rifled guns in the bows, and six or eight howitzers. Their draft did not exceed three feet, and they could, if necessary, crowd an infantry company or two on board in addition to their crews and gunners. Before another year was out, still more light-draft gunboats were needed, and guerrilla activity became so serious that Fitch was called to look after matters on the Cumberland, while Phelps replaced him on the Tennessee.

The anxiety of the Federals is clearly evident in the general orders, issued by Commodore Davis in the autumn of 1862, warning all vessels to take strict precautions against surprise. Boats were ordered not to "lie up to a bank at any time." Guns were to be kept loaded, and small arms were to be kept ready to repel boarders. At night the boats must be alert and ready for instant action, "guns pointed for the bank." "When any of our vessels are fired on," the order said, "it will be the duty of the commander to fire back with spirit, and to destroy everything in that neighborhood within reach of his guns. There is no impropriety in destroying houses supposed to be affording shelter to rebels, and it is the only way to stop guerrilla warfare. Should innocent persons suffer it will be their own fault— and teach others that it will be to their advantage to inform the Government authorities when guerrillas are about certain localities."

To increase their effectiveness, the light-draft squadron frequently carried contingents of troops, whose duty it was to pursue guerrilla parties inland and to inflict the punitive burnings and demolishments deemed necessary in retaliation for guerrilla attacks. Apparently these troops were generally borrowed from some local garrison, as convenience might allow. But since the garrison commander might not always see eye to eye with the naval officer, the arrangement was not altogether satisfactory. The Mississippi Marine Brigade, commanded by Brigadier General Alfred Ellet, and commonly known as Ellet's Marine Brigade, was organized to overcome this difficulty.

The Marine Brigade had its own fleet of seven steamers, fitted out so that each could carry 125 cavalrymen and their horses and 250 infantrymen. Field artillery was also provided. The whole force included about 1,000 infantry and 500 cavalry in addition to the boat crews. The Marines of this outfit were thus in part true "horse marines." The specially constructed boats could put out their landing stages in a hurry, and out would gallop cavalry and artillery, with infantry moving in close support. It was a good idea, but the personnel of the brigade were evidently a trifling and incompetent lot, and it soon became one of the most disreputable organizations in the Federal service. "A rotten concern . . . they do anything to make money," was one naval officer's comment on them. The Marines turned out to be a set of rather undisciplined rapscallions, who took advantage of their special opportunities for looting and pillaging. They were even accused of selling Federal stores to the Confederates. Grant was thoroughly disgusted with them, and tried, though without success, to have them removed from their special river service. In April, 1863, before their disrepute had become so great, the Marine Brigade did some practicing on the Lower Tennessee, but they achieved little or nothing. In their one recorded engagement, at Duck River Shoals, Fitch came up with his gunboats and helped them out of trouble with a Confederate battery which was shelling Ellet's boats.

One vastly important effect of the guerrilla attacks was the animus that they stirred up, particularly in Sherman's

mind. Possession and free use of the rivers, particularly the Mississippi, was a cardinal point in Sherman's war policy, and guerrilla attacks, to him, were on a par with Forrest's raids: he boiled at the thought of them and resolved upon the sternest retaliations. "Though to stand behind a big cottonwood and shoot at a passing boat is good sport, it may reach and kill their friends and families hundreds of miles off," he wrote to General Logan. Vindictively, he continued: "For every bullet shot at a steamboat, I would shoot a thousand 30-pounder Parrotts into even helpless towns . . . wherever a boat can float or soldier march." In fulfillment of this design, long before he began his March to the Sea, Sherman raided and sacked Meridian, Mississippi, and boasted that he had cut "a swath of destruction fifty miles wide across Mississippi which the present generation will not forget." To General Canby he gave orders to hold southern civilians responsible for guerrilla attacks, "for if they can fire on boats with women and children in them, we can fire and burn houses with women and children." Later, he issued an official letter or proclamation to be read to the civilians of North Alabama, in which he said:

> The United States have, in North Alabama, all the rights they choose to enforce in war—to take their lives, their homes, their lands, their everything, because they cannot deny that war exists here, and war is simply power unrestrained by constitution or compact. I know thousands of people who, at simple notice, would come to North Alabama and accept of the elegant houses and plantations there. . . .
> To those who submit to the rightful law and authority, all gentleness and forbearance, but to the petulant, and persistent, secessionists, why death is mercy, and the quicker he or she is disposed of the better. Satan and the rebellious spirits of heaven were allowed a continuance of existence in heaven merely to swell their just punishment in hell.

Although other considerations no doubt influenced Sherman's peculiarly modern conception of war, the guerrilla attacks were an effective cause in shaping his resolution to wage a war against the civilian population as well as the military; and his views and his orders had much to do with the gradually increasing savagery of the retaliations visited upon the Tennessee Valley.

From the Confederate point of view—which would have been Sherman's if Sherman had been a Confederate—all river traffic offered a completely legitimate target. The rivers were controlled by the Federals. To a Confederate, whether soldier or civilian, there was nothing innocent and nice about a steamboat, armed or not, on the Tennessee River. That boat was carrying either soldiers or supplies, and its presence meant war and death to the South. If women and children were on board, they were where they had no business to be; and of course their presence could not be detected in advance of an attack. Below Muscle Shoals, every boat on the Tennessee, after Shiloh, was a Federal boat—in one way or another a ship of war—and it ought to be stopped, captured, burned, or driven back. Therefore the Confederates, despite the utmost in the way of retaliation, continued to stand behind cottonwoods, or at any other convenient point, and to shoot at boats of all sorts.

But actually the guerrilla attacks were not so savage as Sherman wanted to think. For example, there was the transport *W. B. Terry*, a Confederate boat that the Federals captured at Paducah early in the war and put into their own service. In August, 1862, the *Terry* came up the Tennessee, bound for Hamburg with a load of coal for the gunboats. She could not get over Duck River Shoals, and at sundown Leonard G. Klinck, master of the boat, decided to turn back to Paducah. In turning he ran the *Terry* on a reef, and stuck there, helpless, under a bluff, twenty feet from shore, in less than two feet of water. Klinck knew that the *Terry* was now in fair shape to fall into Confederate hands, but he hoped that the *Des Moines City*, which was supposed to follow him, would arrive in time to pull her off.

The *Terry* was armed with two rifled Parrotts, but

these were all but useless underneath the bluff. She was also carrying ten riflemen from an Ohio regiment. Klinck sent out five riflemen as a picket, with instructions to slip back quietly and warn him if they saw signs of a guerrilla attack. The night passed without incident, but at dawn things began to happen.

"The first intimation we had of attack," wrote Klinck in his report, "was a discharge at daylight of about 200 guns into the broadside of the boat. Not a single stateroom escaped being pierced through. Our pickets had fired on their reconnoiterers and then ran. This precipitated an attack by their whole force, which took us by surprise. From what I afterwards saw I put their force at 200. . . . I was in the after cabin when the firing commenced, and went immediately through the cabin and down the forward gangway onto the lower deck to see about the cannon. Before reaching the after deck, where they were placed, both were discharged and deserted without spiking. I found every man lying down flat behind the icebox and coal pile. I do not accuse them of cowardice for this, because no set of men on earth could have loaded their guns amidst such a perfect hailstorm of bullets. . . . Their discharges were mingled with the wildest shouts I have ever heard. All of them were within 60 yards of the boat."

Klinck called out that he would surrender, but his cries were not heard in the din. He then put a sheet on a broom handle and waved it. Presently the firing ceased, and "Captains Napier and Algee came immediately on board and took formal possession in the name of the Confederate States of America."

The Confederates lightened the boat, got her off the rocks, used her to ferry troops across the river, and then stripped her of furniture and stores and burned her. Klinck and the *Terry*'s officers were allowed to construct a makeshift raft and drift down to Fort Henry. The passengers were paroled; the soldiers and the Negroes were made prisoners. In spite of all the shooting, none of the *Terry's* crew or guard were killed, but two of the pickets were missing. A lady passenger was wounded in the thigh, but not dangerously, and a gunner and a Negro were wounded. "With Captains Napier and Algee," wrote Klinck, "we have no fault to find while prisoners with them. They treated us gentlemanly, and respected our rights to private property of all kinds, but some of their men pilfered much of our clothing that was not under lock and key."

In his autobiography, *With Sabre and Scalpel*, Dr. John A. Wyeth, the great surgeon—and biographer of Forrest—tells about another kind of guerrilla attack in which he, as a boy, participated. General Ormsby Mitchel, Federal commander at Huntsville, attempted to make up for the lack of gunboats above Muscle Shoals by improvising a makeshift affair, which he called the *Tennessee*. Buell contemptuously described this craft as "an old flatboat in which he [Mitchel] had rigged the machinery of a saw-mill, incapable of harming anything or resisting anything." But at any rate, when the *Tennessee* appeared, there was plenty of excitement between Whitesburg and Guntersville.

Wyeth was just sixteen, and small of size, and therefore he had been bidden to stay at home and make a crop while his father went off to the war. The only day he missed working his crop was June 8, 1862, when the *Tennessee* came upriver. She was a slow boat, so slow that the sheriff of Marshall County said afterwards that "upstream it could run all day in the shade of a leaning sycamore, while going the other way the current went by so fast it made your head swim." So the news of her coming went around, long before the *Tennessee* reached Guntersville, and young Wyeth was as keen as anybody to join the gang of men and boys who were preparing to welcome the gunboat with a few well-aimed volleys. "As soon as I could unhitch my mule," Wyeth relates, "we rode toward home, and when near enough, not wishing to inform my mother, I slipped in through a back window, got my double-barrelled shotgun and ammunition, and was just making my exit through the same opening when I heard a familiar voice say, 'Hadn't you better go out through the door?' I saluted my commanding officer, my mother, and hurried out as directed. The truth is, if I hadn't come of my own accord she would have sent for me and handed me the gun and made me go."

Twenty in company, they reached the landing in time to see the *Tennessee* chug slowly past on the northern side. Mounting their mules and horses they rode upriver a few miles to a point where they knew the channel would bring the gunboat close to the south bank and within range of their weapons. Hidden in the cane, like Indians, they awaited the *Tennessee*. Presently here she came; unsuspecting blue-clad soldiers were lounging on the deck. The acting guerrilla captain shouted "Fire!" and the shotguns and rifles sent their volley, and every blue-clad soldier fell and vanished. But they had merely tumbled from surprise and gone below to man their guns. Now their shells and Minié balls came whistling into the cane thicket, and the guerrillas arose at once and fled. Their animals, frightened by the noise, were plunging and stampeding. Wyeth's mule, unable to break his tether, had run around and around the hitching tree until his head was so close to the bark that Wyeth could not untie the knot. In fear and haste, Wyeth proceeded to reverse the movement and unwind his mule. He caught up with his fellow guerrillas in time for a triumphal entry into Guntersville, where great tales were forthwith told among the cracker barrels. Wyeth's band, however, modestly declined to claim that they had killed all the Yankees; they compromised on one-half. Long after the war Wyeth discovered that actually only one Yankee had been hit, and he was only slightly wounded; but their volley had caused a "temporary panic."

This little "Battle of Law's Landing," however, had an aftermath. A woman spy across the river passed the word to the Federal commander at Huntsville, and soon the mem-

## GUERRILLAS VERSUS GUNBOATS 89

bers of the "guerrilla" band, learned that their names had been reported to the enemy and that, if they were caught, they would be hanged. This gave young Wyeth a good excuse to enlist, and when a detachment of Morgan's cavalry appeared at Guntersville that summer, he joined up.

Although the *Official Records* of both army and navy contain abundant and often plaintive reference to the operations of guerrilla bands, it is extremely difficult to identify the true guerrilla leaders. For obvious reasons they did not themselves court notoriety, and the Federal commanders, for their part, made no distinction between genuine partisan groups, on the one hand, and bushwhackers or criminal marauders, on the other hand. In the region of the Lower Tennessee, however, the groups led by Henon Cross, Duval McNairy, and James McLaughlin were evidently well organized and well directed. In Spence's history of Hickman County, Cross is identified as the son of "Professor Cross of Nashville." McNairy also was from Nashville, and McLaughlin was a Marylander. These leaders were evidently spirited young men who, after the fall of Nashville, "refugeed" in the wilds of Hickman County and there took up the old frontier type of fighting on behalf of the Confederacy. Another group, reputed to be stragglers from Forrest's command, apparently operated in the neighborhood of Newburg, Kentucky, and in the traditionally "rough" country "between the rivers" referred to by Robert Penn Warren in his "Ballad of Billy Potts." Frequently such Confederate groups found themselves challenged by groups of Union partisans, like the Perry County "Jayhawkers."

Old Man Jack Hinson, of Humphreys County, was quite a different kind of guerrilla. There may have been many more like him, unrecorded partisans, who waged an individual blood feud with the gunboats. Old Jack Hinson lived between the Tennessee and the Cumberland, with Johnsonville on one side of him and Fort Donelson on the other. His two sons were captured by Lowe's Cavalry, and were shot as bushwhackers. Hinson then took down his rifle and swore vengeance on anything that wore a blue uniform. When the river was low, and gunboats did not venture up, he shadowed the roads between the two rivers, picking off members of foraging parties and scouting patrols. When the river rose, he found himself a good place in the brush, where the channel would bring gunboats near the bank, and waited for his meat. Hinson paid no attention to transports, unless blue uniforms showed on board. He specialized in gunboats, and in officers and crew members of gunboats.

Hinson knew the country thoroughly, and every effort to trap and catch him failed. Since he watched the Federal troops and their shipping, he was able to furnish valuable information to Forrest, when the general came through on a raid. During Forrest's raid on Johnsonville, Old Jack Hinson inevitably turned up at Paris Landing, and later showed Forrest the road the guns should take through Cypress Creek Swamp to get a good position for the bombardment of Johnsonville. On this occasion Old Jack Hinson said to Major Charles W. Anderson, Forrest's adjutant general: "They murdered my boys, and may yet kill me, but the marks on the barrel of my gun will show that I am a long ways ahead in the game now and am not done yet."

When the war was over, Old Jack Hinson's rifle had thirty-six notches on its barrel.

CHAPTER VI

# Forrest Wreaks Havoc among the Gunboats

ALTHOUGH the guerrilla attacks were a great annoyance and danger, they did not stop river traffic. Probably the irritation that they caused Federal commanders only brought greater woe to the Confederacy in the end. Among Confederate commanders, only General Forrest saw clearly what needed to be done and had the genius and will to do it. Forrest knew that a mere nibbling, harassing policy would not get results. He believed that blows against Federal river power must be completely destructive and conclusive and, above all, that they should be a part of a wide-flung strategic design. Denied his opportunity to attack shipping on the Mississippi River, he had achieved tremendous results on land with limited means. Davis and the Confederate command underestimated him consistently, but not so the Federals. "Where is Forrest's headquarters?" queried Lincoln once, in apprehension. Sherman, in desperation, vowed to punish the people of the Confederacy for Forrest's audacity. In 1864 Sherman wrote to McPherson: "I wish to organize as large a force as possible at Memphis, with General A. J. Smith or Mower in command, to pursue Forrest on foot, devastating the land over which he has passed, or may pass, and to make the people of Tennessee and Mississippi feel that although a bold, daring, and successful leader, he will bring ruin and misery on any country where he may pass or tarry. If we do not punish Forrest and the people now, the whole effect of our vast conquest will be lost." Later, Sherman gave his subordinates stringent orders to destroy Forrest's command and kill Forrest himself. In fact, he offered Mower a promotion to the rank of major general if he would kill Forrest and notified Lincoln to this effect in the following letter:

> Sir,—I have ordered General A. J. Smith and General Mower from Memphis to pursue and kill Forrest, promising the latter, in case of success, my influence to promote him to a major-general. . . . Should accident befall me, I ask you to favor Mower, if he succeeds in disposing of Forrest.

Mower did not succeed, although he and others had every opportunity.

Forrest knew that Sherman's campaign in Georgia would fail if, while Sherman was still facing a resolute and powerful Confederate army, the long, exposed line of Federal communications and supplies was assailed far to the rear, as Forrest knew how to assail it. Jefferson Davis was slow to give consent to Forrest's plans. When he finally yielded, it was too late: the Army of Tennessee had been used up in Johnston's long retreat and in Hood's fierce lunges around Atlanta. Sherman's decision to make the March to the Sea, instead of following Hood north, was undoubtedly based in part on his knowledge that "that devil Forrest" was ripping his supply lines to pieces. It was really easier, and far more spectacular, to march through Georgia and the Carolinas, than to go back to Tennessee and deal with Forrest and Hood. Thus it happened that Forrest reached the critical field of action too late to accomplish decisive results. His blows along the Tennessee terrified the Federal command and disordered their defense, but Hood's army, despite its brilliant last fight in Tennessee, was not strong enough, or perhaps not lucky enough, to reap the fruits of Forrest's great efforts.

The first blow was Forrest's raid into Middle Tennessee in September, 1864. Guided by men who knew how to thread the shallows and avoid the holes, Forrest's command crossed the Tennessee at the lower end of Colbert Shoals. Within a few days, Forrest captured the garrison of Athens (Alabama) and began systematically to wreck the railroads, by tearing up rails and burning trestles. The system of Federal blockhouses, frequently garrisoned by Negro troops, was little hindrance to him. Within a short time Forrest was getting in position to cut Sherman's main supply artery, the Nashville & Chattanooga Railroad. Federal headquarters boiled with anxiety. Troops were moved against Forrest in large numbers from a wide circle of positions: from Nashville, from Chattanooga, even from Atlanta, and by river around from Memphis. "His cavalry will march one hundred miles in less time than ours will ten," wrote Sherman. "I can whip his infantry, but his cavalry is to be feared." Almost despairingly, Rousseau answered: "He is here to stay, unless driven back and routed by a superior cavalry force. Infantry can cause him to change camp, but cannot drive him out of the State. . . . This is much more than a raid; I regard it as a formidable invasion."

With the circle tightening around him, Forrest gave up his plan of cutting the Nashville & Chattanooga Railroad. Eluding his pursuers, he crossed the wooded uplands from Mt. Pleasant to Lawrenceburg to Florence, almost on the line of the old Natchez Trace. The Tennessee was swollen by rains and too deep to ford, and so, while Buford feinted toward Huntsville and some of Roddey's men held the Federals back at Shoal Creek, Forrest kept three ferryboats (probably flatboats) going night and day until most of his force had crossed. A thousand were left as the Federal pursuit pressed near. These Forrest led downriver to an island overgrown with cane thickets, oak, and hickory. Forrest loaded saddles, accouterments, and men on the ferryboats, and got them over to the south side of the island, where the cane hid them from view and the ferrying could be continued out of view of the Federal pursuers. The horses were pushed off the bluff and "swum across" to the cane thicket to await their turn on the ferryboats.

During the last trips, Forrest himself took a hand with the men at oars and poles. He saw a lieutenant standing in the bow and doing nothing. "Why don't you take hold of an oar or pole and help get this boat across?" Forrest asked him. The lieutenant indicated that he had not supposed officers were expected to do such work. Forrest, who was poling at the time, used his free hand to slap the lieutenant overboard. As the luckless officer crawled back dripping, Forrest said: "Now, damn you, get hold of the oars and go to work! If I knock you out of the boat again I'll let you drown."

Back at Corinth, Forrest counted results. Starting with about 3,500 men, he had killed or captured about that number of the enemy, and meanwhile had added to his own command, as he always did, numbers of recruits and discouraged stragglers from other units. He had brought back eight pieces of artillery, enormous quantities of small arms, medical stores, sugar, coffee, and other supplies. He had destroyed six large railroad bridges, various trestles, a hundred miles of railroad, and ten block houses. He had jolted Sherman and all other Federal commanders from Cairo to Atlanta into painful awareness of his hitting power. And all this—as was generally true of Forrest's raids—at small cost to his own soldiers' lives: 47 killed, 293 wounded.

As Forrest drew near Corinth, about three thousand troops, under the command of Washburn, came up the Tennessee with the design of landing at Eastport, cutting the railroad near Iuka, and delaying or stopping Forrest's retirement. Apparently they had the added objective of worrying Hood's advance, for he was at that moment moving north. Washburn's advance units, consisting of two Illinois regiments and some Negro troops, the whole under the command of Colonel George B. Hoge, reached Clifton on October 9.

But Forrest already had word of this threat, and on October 6 sent Colonel D. C. Kelley with five hundred men and Walton's section of Hudson's battery to take station at Eastport. Colonel Kelley put his troops and guns in ambush and waited.

On the afternoon of October 10, the flotilla came in sight: three transports, *City of Pekin, Aurora,* and *Kenton,* convoyed by two light-draft gunboats, the *Key West* and the *Undine,* which, as it turned out, were beginning a bad season on the Tennessee.

Kelley waited until Hoge's men began to disembark. The *Key West,* leading the flotilla, had just made signals: "Cannot be too cautious. Keep in close order." But the shore looked uninhabited and harmless. Lieutenant King, commanding the *Undine,* signaled the transports to land. A line of skirmishers went up the river bank. Still Kelley waited, holding his fire. The steamers tied up. The troops, unloading, began to form in line on the bank.

At this moment Kelley let go. His rifled guns, posted on a wooded hill, did heavy execution in a few brief moments. Artillery caissons on the transports were hit and exploded and the *Aurora* and *Kenton* caught fire. The soldiers on board began to jump into the water. The troops on the bank broke, without firing a shot, and ran down the riverside in panic. Colonel Hoge, who was in a gig, returning from a conference with Lieutenant King, lost control of the situation.

The gunboats tried to return the fire, but were helpless against Walton's accurate shooting. The *Key West,* hard hit, was almost out of control. The *Undine* was hit, too, but stayed in action. Despite shouted orders to the contrary, the excited masters of the transports cut their cables and drifted down with the current, leaving the troops on the bank. King withdrew the gunboats out of range. The *City of Pekin* gradually managed to pick up the soldiers floundering in the water and fleeing along the bank. Downriver, the badly rattled expedition got itself together, put out the fires on board the transports, and proceeded, in some fear, to Clifton.

Even Clifton was too close. Next day they went farther down, to Johnsonville.

This sharp little engagement was just a hint of what was to come. At Corinth, Forrest asked his superior, General Richard Taylor, for a month's leave, to get rest for himself and a period of recuperation for his command. The request was denied. Hood was already moving up to Tuscumbia, in preparation for his fierce sweep into Tennessee. Strategically, it might have been better for Forrest to join Hood immediately, so as to help speed his advance against the scattered Federal forces. Instead, it was decided that Forrest should first strike along the west bank of the Tennessee and carry out his old scheme of hitting Federal transport. Afterwards he would join Hood.

In 1863 and 1864 the Federals had extended the Nashville & Northwestern Railroad from its terminus, west of Nashville, to the Tennessee, and at that point had built up a great supply base, well equipped to handle the freight that came up the Tennessee by steamboat. This base was named Johnsonville, in honor of Andrew Johnson, military governor of Tennessee. The Nashville & Northwestern Railroad, the base and railhead at Johnsonville, and the Tennessee were three vital links in Sherman's supply system. Johnsonville was a weak link in the chain. It was guarded by a small fort, with a garrison of seven hundred troops of a new Wisconsin regiment, half a dozen 10-pounder Parrotts, and the usual contingent of Negro troops. The landing was always crowded with boats and army stores.

Forrest's main objective was Johnsonville. But first he went north, down the river, and set an ambush for gunboats and steamboats. General Buford, leading the advance with the Kentucky Brigade, quietly established himself at Paris Landing and at Fort Heiman, now no longer garrisoned by the Federals. At Paris Landing, Bell's Tennesseans and a section of Morton's battery commanded a mile-long section of the river. On the bluff at Fort Heiman, Buford had a division and two 22-pound Parrotts. The trap was set. Forrest had moved so quickly that the Federals did not dream he was in position on the Tennessee.

Empty transports came in sight, moving downstream. Buford restrained his gunners. "Keep quiet, men. Don't fire a gun. I want a loaded boat."

On the morning of October 29, the *Mazeppa* rounded the bend, puffing slowly up toward Johnsonville with two flatboats in tow. Here was the prize. The Confederates let her pass the lower battery. When she was trapped between the two batteries, they let her have it. Not a shot missed. The *Mazeppa*, unconvoyed, surprised, badly crippled, was beached on the east bank. All on board except her commander skedaddled for the bushes.

Private Clabe West volunteered to swim the river and secure the prize. Stripping almost naked, he paddled across on a slab of wood, his pistol tied around his neck. The captain of the *Mazeppa* helped him on board, then returned with him in the steamboat's yawl. The Confederates attached a hawser and pulled the *Mazeppa* across by hand. Immediately they began to unload the rich cargo, supplies richer than they had seen in many a day: more than enough shoes for everybody, blankets, flour, hardtack, axes. A soldier turned up with a demijohn of French brandy, but General Buford took it away from him. Gloating, Buford stood on the deck, tilting the brandy jug, while the soldiers pleaded: "General, save us some." "Plenty of meat, boys," he shouted back, "plenty of hardtack, shoes, and clothes—all for the boys, but just enough whisky for the general."

While they were unloading, three gunboats sallied up from below and began to shell them. The Confederate guns drove them back, but Buford thought it best to burn the *Mazeppa*. After setting the fires, they returned to ambush.

Perhaps the Federals thought it only another guerrilla attack. At any rate they kept steaming into the trap. Next morning the *Anna*, a speedy boat with a daring captain, ran the gantlet of the batteries and, though hit, was able to get away.

Next came the transport *Venus*, convoyed by the gunboat *Undine*, to try the same game. They ran the upper battery successfully, but the lower one stopped them, and they turned, to try to escape upriver. Colonel Rucker asked permission to move two guns nearer the boats, to get closer range. While this was going on, another steamer, the *J. W. Cheeseman*, came blithely into the trap from above. Disabled by batteries and raked by fire of small arms, the *Cheeseman* surrendered and was burned by the Confederates.

Midway between the batteries, the *Undine* and the *Venus* were bravely fighting it out, while Forrest's troops poured toward the bank from all points nearby, and opened fire with everything they had. In the rush, commands were improvised: "Halt! Dismount! Prepare, on foot, to fight gunboats!" After six hours of fighting, the two boats ran ashore on the east bank. The officers and crew of the *Undine* took to the bushes. The *Venus*, which had a detachment of infantry on board, surrendered to Colonel Kelley.

The year before these happenings, Admiral Porter wrote his friend, Gustavus V. Fox, assistant secretary of the navy: "I have a rumor that two of the light drafts have been worsted or destroyed by cavalry up the Cumberland River— I can hardly credit it, for I don't see how cavalry can take a gunboat." But Porter did not know much about cavalry, especially Forrest's cavalry. Forrest's cavalry had now taken a powerful boat, the *Undine*, armed with eight 24-pound howitzers. Not only that, the cavalry were going to man the boats and become floating cavalry.

It was Forrest, with his mind on Johnsonville, who had this idea. Forrest offered command of his newly acquired fleet to his brilliant chief of artillery, young Captain Morton, but Morton hastily declined the honor. Forrest's choice then fell on Colonel Dawson, whom he placed on the *Venus*, and on the *Undine* he put Captain Gracey, who had been a steamboat captain. Two guns from the land batteries were placed on the *Venus*, crews of volunteer "horse marines" were assembled, and Forrest's cavalry were ready to begin naval operations on their own native Tennessee waters, so long under the unchallenged sway of the invader.

"Commodore" Dawson protested a little, however.

"General," he said, "I will go with these boats wherever you order, but I tell you candidly I know very little about managing gunboats. You must promise me that if I lose the fleet you won't give me a cussing when I wade ashore and come back on foot."

Forrest laughed and told Dawson he could run the boats into the bank when he got into trouble. But he must set them afire, too.

Two days later they moved slowly upriver for Johnsonville, the captured boats keeping pace with the troops on the bank. The floating cavalry, affecting tearful sympathy, offered to carry the guns and forage sacks of the horse cavalry if the horse cavalry would wade out and hand the stuff on board. The horse cavalry, answering banter with banter, declined the favor on the ground that they needed their guns and sacks too much to risk them with landlubbers who would soon be sent to the bottom by Yankee gunboats.

On November 2, here came the gunboats. The floating cavalry, too brashly confident, forged ahead of their land support, and when Lieutenant King came around the bend from Johnsonville with the *Key West* and the *Tawah* and abruptly opened fire, the *Venus* was caught like a sitting duck. Captain Gracey put her into the bank, and the departing crew in their excitement forgot to set the *Venus* on fire. Then and there Forrest lost two guns and some supplies. Dawson, with the *Undine*, discreetly retired under the protection of the land batteries.

The next day the *Undine* went upriver and tried to lure the *Key West* and the *Tawah* into a fight with the land batteries. Lieutenant King was too clever, and turned back when he ran into rifle fire—"rebel sharpshooters," he reported, unsuspectingly. But the next day, despite a severe pounding from Forrest's guns, the *Key West* caught the *Undine* in a disadvantageous position at the island above Johnsonville, and Dawson thought it a good time to set her on fire and make his escape.

Meanwhile, a glimmer of what was happening began to penetrate at Paducah and Cairo and Nashville. The larger part of the Tennessee division of light-draft gunboats was trapped at Johnsonville by Forrest's blockade, and Fitch had to bring the Cumberland fleet around to help. But he found he could do little. While the *Key West* and the *Tawah* were engaging the *Undine*, Fitch came up with six gunboats, *Moose, Brilliant, Victory, Paw Paw, Fairy* and *Curlew*. From the foot of Reynoldsburg Island, Fitch saw the conflict and could even catch Lieutenant King's signals, but after studying the situation he decided not to run the gantlet of Forrest's batteries. To his superior, Rear Admiral S. P. Lee, he sent a sketch of the positions and reported: "I am confident not over two boats out of six would have got through, and they never could have got back again." After a still later reconnaissance, Fitch revised his estimate: he would have lost all his gunboats and all his men. Forrest's artillery was so cleverly located that the gunboats could not bring their firepower to bear on it. Fitch would have lost everything in the holocaust that Forrest was preparing. A master strategist and tactician, with the hardest-hitting soldiers in the Confederate armies of the West, was on the banks of the Tennessee at a vital point. Federal telegraph wires rippled with messages of dismay. That Hood was known already to be at Tuscumbia, and perhaps in the act of crossing the Tennessee, made the situation terrifying.

On the night of November 3 Forrest completed his arrangements for bombarding Johnsonville landing. On the west bank of the Tennessee he found a place where the ground sloped back from a slight crest near the river's edge.

Artillery in this position would be defiladed from gunboat fire, though not altogether protected from the guns of the fort above the landing. Forrest's guns were located with great care, embrasures were cut in the bank where they were needed, and the batteries were camouflaged ("masked" was the term used in those days) with hickory saplings woven into the trees and brush. Young Captain Morton was still not satisfied, and asked Forrest to let him post two guns at a point immediately opposite the landing, too lofty to be reached by gunboat fire and yet so close and so low that the guns of the fort could not be depressed sufficiently to fire on it. Forrest was reluctant, but Morton argued, and finally persuaded him. To reach the position, Morton had to work for two hours, making a roadway through the brush and fallen timber and dragging the guns through the sticky mud of the swamp. These preparations consumed all of the morning and part of the afternoon of November 4. The commanding officer at Johnsonville, though greatly alarmed, apparently did not suspect that Forrest's whole force, with a powerful array of artillery, was ensconced in the bushes that fringed the silent west bank.

About two o'clock in the afternoon the Federals began to wake up. Two gunboats, lashed together, crossed the river to reconnoiter. Forrest's batteries opened with a roar. A gunboat and the fort replied, but with little effect. In no time at all the orderly and peaceful stir of Johnsonville landing was turned to chaos.

At the third discharge from Morton's guns the boiler of one of the gunboats was struck and exploded, and the screams of the scalded arose. Within an hour two of the gunboats were on fire, and, drifting against the transports, set them aflame. A third gunboat, still fighting, was run to the landing, and its crew hopped off. Thrall's guns set two other steamers and their barges on fire. Lieutenant King, losing hope, set fire to his remaining gunboat and other vessels. In two hours' time all the shipping was ablaze.

Changing their aim, Forrest's men now dropped their shells on the warehouses, and on the stores spread out along the landing. Hay, piled up for Federal horses, caught on fire and spread the conflagration. Shells hit rows of barrels stacked under tarpaulins, and a flaming odorous liquid ran down to the river. "Yankee liquor," said the soldiers, as they sniffed the breeze, which also brought them mixed odors of burning bacon and coffee. The smells were inviting, but there was no chance to cross the river for salvage.

In the excitement Forrest himself came to the guns and began to point and fire one of the pieces. He posted an officer behind a tree to act as his artillery observer, and when a shot fell short, the general cried out, like a boy: "Rickety shay! a rickety shay! I'll hit her next time. Elevate the breech of that gun lower!"

After the war, Captain Morton met a young man from Illinois who said he had commanded the Negro troops in the Johnsonville fort. "Every time you would shoot from below," he told Morton, "my men would jump into the ditch above, and when you would shoot from above they'd jump into the ditch below, until they got so demoralized they ran out and never stopped until they got to Nashville."

At the end of the fight, Johnsonville was a wreck. The gunboats and the fort had fought back vigorously—so vigorously, Forrest reported, that "the rammers were shot from the hands of the cannoneers, and some of them were nearly buried amid the dirt which was thrown upon them by the storm of shell." But Forrest's fire was effective, and the Federal reply was not.

Three light-draft gunboats—*Key West, Tawah, Elfin* —were destroyed at Johnsonville. The *Undine* had been destroyed previously. That made four gunboats in all. Lieutenant Commander Shirk wrote plaintively to Rear Admiral Lee that only one good gunboat was left out of the Tennessee squadron. In addition, an unrecorded number of transports were destroyed—at least eight or ten, by Confederate accounts—and twelve or fifteen barges. The Confederates had made an end of everything within range of their guns. Forrest estimated the damage done to the enemy at six million dollars; the Federals put it lower—at $2,200,000.

At any rate Johnsonville was finished as railhead and supply base. The Federals did not complete the process of salvaging and cleaning up the remains until June, 1865. Forrest's loss during the entire expedition was two killed and nine wounded.

The alarm caused by Forrest's blows spread far and wide. The experienced Federal naval officers contemplated bringing up ironclads from the Mississippi to protect the injured supply line. Forrest was momentarily expected to arrive anywhere and everywhere in the West. From Chicago the provost marshal wired: "Forrest has been in disguise alternately in Chicago, Michigan City, and Canada, for two months; has fourteen thousand men, mostly from draft. On November seventh, at midnight, he will seize telegraph and rail at Chicago, release prisoners there, arm them, sack the city, shoot down all Federal soldiers, and urge concert of action with Southern sympathizers." At Nashville, Thomas, very greatly disturbed, actually got out an order for a whole corps of Federal troops to proceed to Johnsonville.

Earlier, Forrest had received an order from Beauregard to join Hood's army, which was moving toward the Great Bend and preparing to cross the river for a slashing attack against Sherman's communications at Bridgeport and the Federal forces scattered promiscuously about the region. Or such, at least, seems to have been Hood's original plan. But the order came to Forrest after he was already committed to the Johnsonville operations. When that business was finished, he turned away from the ruins and marched by difficult roads, through rain and deep mud, toward the junction with Hood. He would be somewhat late at the rendezvous. That could not be helped. To Captain Morton he said: "John, if they'd give you enough guns and me enough men, we could whip old Sherman off the face of the earth!" But it was not to be. Beauregard and Hood, not Forrest, had the guns and men; and Forrest had only the consolation prize. He was to be Hood's chief of cavalry, and would cover Hood's advance into Tennessee and the bitter retreat that came after the failure of Hood's last campaign.

By moving north, Hood apparently hoped to draw Sherman after him, to protect his threatened communications, and then, if a favorable opportunity offered, to launch another fierce attack, like those which had battered Sherman's army in the fighting around Atlanta. And for a while Sherman did follow Hood, cautiously, and at a respectful distance. When Sherman finally concluded that Hood was about to move into Tennessee, he turned back south, burned Atlanta, and cut loose from communications for the March to the Sea. It was, as Stanley Horn says, in *The Army of Tennessee* "a situation unique in military history: two opposing armies, theoretically campaigning to destroy each other, deliberately marching in opposite directions."

In the consultations between Hood and Beauregard Guntersville had been designated as the point where the army would cross the Tennessee. The immediate objective was Bridgeport, where the railroad bridge, now rebuilt by the Federals, was again to be destroyed. Wheeler's cavalry would remain on the south side to watch Sherman, and Forrest would give protection on the north. But Forrest's commitment in West Tennessee, and perhaps other considerations, including the presence of the new Federal gunboat squadron above Muscle Shoals, brought a change in Hood's plans. He sheered off from Guntersville; felt out Decatur, where a small but well-fortified Federal garrison and the gunboats *Stone River* and *General Thomas* resisted his advance detachments; then gave up the idea of crossing above Muscle Shoals and marched west to his new base at Tuscumbia. These delays, though not necessarily fatal, were harmful to Hood's campaign. Up to the 27th of October, the Tennessee was low, and Hood could easily have crossed. The gunboats were not really to be feared, for they had no armor and Hood's batteries could have knocked them to pieces; besides, the low stage of the river made it impossible, despite much urging from the higher Federal commanders, to assemble the whole gunboat squadron from the various posts assigned them. They "could not get over the bar," the helpless naval officers reported. Furthermore, the Federal forces defending Tennessee were at that time much more scattered than they were later.

When Hood finally began to cross the Tennessee, in the neighborhood of Florence, the early November rains had set in, the weather was very forbidding, the river had risen. It was a secure crossing, because the north bank was only lightly held; the barrier of Muscle Shoals prevented any rude incursions of gunboats from upriver; and downriver, Forrest's Johnsonville campaign had wiped out a considerable part of Federal gunboat strength, and put the fear of God into the rest, for the time being. The physical difficulties, however, were considerable. Pontoons were hard to manage in the swift current. At Florence itself, the engineers lashed the boats to the piers of the wrecked railroad bridge. Other forces crossed a few miles higher up, at Bainbridge.

With Forrest's cavalry leading, the Army of Tennessee marched through the scrub-oak country to Lawrenceburg and descended, amid the varied colors of autumn, into the fair lands of Middle Tennessee. They were in high spirits and were primed to fight. The country looked good to them, after so many months among the pines and red clay hills of Georgia, and it was their country.

At Springhill, Hood outmaneuvered Schofield—indeed had the Federal army cut off from Nashville, and all but trapped. It should have been a great Confederate victory. But nothing happened. There was some inexplainable failure by the generals. Then came the bloody and fruitless battle at Franklin, the "siege" of Nashville, the repulse and defeat of Hood, and the long retreat over icy roads, with Forrest commanding the rear guard and saving the harried Army of Tennessee from complete disintegration.

A fleet of gunboats, led by the powerful *Carondelet*, came up the Tennessee to cut Hood off at Florence, and transports brought twelve thousand troops to Eastport, while Thomas pressed the pursuit. The river fell, a January fog came down, and the gunboat pilots refused to attempt Little Muscle Shoals. Hood crossed on the pontoon bridge, unmolested. The thrifty Forrest not only held off the enemy, but brought off with him, and drove across the pontoon bridge, the cattle and hogs he had collected in Tennessee. Thus ended Forrest's last major campaign. He surrendered with his troops at Gainesville, Alabama, on May 9, 1865.

There was one more strange event on the Tennessee. About a month before Lee's surrender a 30-foot yawl was captured at Kingston. She was manned by nine picked men of the Confederate navy and was loaded with torpedoes and incendiary weapons which she had been specially built to carry. The yawl had been brought from Richmond to Bristol by rail, then overland to the Holston and launched on her career of intended destruction. The purpose, it was said, was to burn bridges and attack shipping and so to prepare for Lee's safe retreat into Georgia.

There was no more fighting, except by the persistent bushwhackers. The war was over in the Tennessee Valley.

CHAPTER VII

# The Cost of Civil War

AND NOW THE GREAT contestants could measure the results of their long strife. Grant and Sherman had evolved in the Tennessee Valley what is known today as total war. In that valley it was clearly evident at what expense their great fame had been bought.

From end to end the Tennessee Valley was a wasteland —a ruin cloaked only by the indomitable wilderness, which again put forth its seasonal green in the bitter spring of 1865 and advanced its fringe of sprouts and saplings a little farther over deserted farms and untilled fields. Even the wilderness was gashed where the hard fighting had been. Across the bruised earth, the track of the armies was plainly discernible. In future years it would be veiled, but never completely obliterated. On many a rocky hillside, cleared of trees to get an open field of fire, nothing but thin scrub and bramble would ever again spring up to check the wash of the rains. For three years war had been dominant, the armies had trampled back and forth, and the stern invader had had his way. No other part of the South had so long suffered from the continual presence of this invader and from the desperate efforts to repel him. Elsewhere, even in much-harried Virginia, there had been intervals of relief, or, as in the Shenandoah Valley, no real penetration until late in the war. In the Tennessee Valley occupation had been constant, and ravage had been heaped upon ravage. In comparison, Sherman's March to the Sea was relatively mild; for it came but once and was over. But in the Tennessee Valley the red hand of devastation visited again and again, bringing all conceivable forms of destruction. The enormous casual destruction of the ceaseless battles and skirmishes and raids and the repeated appropriations of supplies by quick-moving Confederate armies had to be added to the systematic devastations of the Federal troops, as calculated and relentless as were Sherman's in Georgia, and many times renewed.

By the end of the war Tennessee property, by one reliable estimate, was reduced fifty per cent in taxable value. But such an estimate was hardly a measure of the damage. Physical establishments of every kind, in country, town, and city, had suffered even where they had escaped gunfire or the torch. Homes had undergone the abuses of military residence or had deteriorated from vacancy or lack of repairs. School buildings, colleges, churches, courthouses, asylums had been wrecked or damaged by their appropriation for use as barracks and hospitals. Often they had been the center of hot fighting. Railroads were patched up, worn-out remainders except where they had been maintained by the Federal army for its own purposes. Turnpikes were battered, and highway bridges were gone. Mills and factories had been burned, or essential parts of their machinery had been destroyed or carried off. Fences had largely gone to make campfires or hasty breastworks.

The towns and lands of the Great Bend, in North Alabama, had suffered especially. There, at the close of the war, starvation was imminent. In the five counties immediately south of the Tennessee River, it was estimated that twenty thousand people were "in a condition of want bordering on starvation." The Freedmen's Bureau, which had been established to look after the Negroes, found that one of its first duties was to issue rations to the white population.

No part of the valley escaped. All cities, all towns, all homes counted their dead, their maimed, their missing, and all presented to the living a face of ruin. All, too, were embroiled in the raging animosities of the postwar years. There was animosity against the North for the ruin that it had brought in war and continued to bring in Reconstruction. But more bitter and deadly still was the animosity of neighbor against neighbor, and of locality against locality, that was bred in some parts of the valley by the fierce internal strife between Union and Confederate sympathizers. To make matters still worse, civil government had disappeared, and citizens were at the mercy of bandits and rapists.

Not since the Duke of Alva ravaged the Netherlands, or Cromwell (cited as a precedent by Sherman himself) harried Ireland, had a civilized country so felt the brunt of invasion.

Paducah, garrisoned by Federal troops since Grant's first occupation, might be counted as only war-worn. Yet even at Paducah, after Forrest's brief entry in 1864, sixty houses within range of the fort were burned by order of the Federal colonel in command. The reason he gave was that Forrest's sharpshooters used some houses near the fort for cover. During the same year, the Federal general, E. A. Paine, appointed to rule over the strongly pro-Confederate region of western Kentucky, promptly began what a Kentucky historian has termed "a fifty-one days' reign of violence, terror, rapine, extortion, and military murder." Paine levied extortionate taxes, confiscated property, arrested, banished, or executed Confederate sympathizers, and in general made himself thoroughly obnoxious. Upon McCracken County, of which Paducah is county seat, he imposed a fine of $95,000.

The Lower Tennessee, everywhere between Paducah and Florence, had suffered, especially from reprisals made by gunboats after guerrilla attacks. Savannah had escaped destruction, but Clifton had been burned, the newly built village of Johnsonville had been knocked about in a battle, and mills, gins, houses, and cabins all along the river had been harried freely. Farther inland, the Centerville courthouse, which Federals had converted into a fort, was burned by Confederate guerrillas under Captain Henon Cross, and later the town itself was burned by the Perry County Jayhawkers, a group of Unionist irregulars or bushwhackers.

Tuscumbia was all but destroyed. At Florence, Colonel Cornyn's 10th Missouri Cavalry, assisted by gunboats, burned an estimated two million dollars' worth of property in 1863. In fact, most of the towns of the Great Bend were destroyed during the war, either by shellfire or by deliberate burnings. Huntsville, which Federal General Ormsby Mitchel used as headquarters, suffered the wear and tear of long occupation. In addition, Mitchel destroyed the Huntsville shops of the Memphis & Charleston Railroad, together with much of its rolling stock, which had been assembled by the Confederates for removal after the Battle of Shiloh, and he wrecked the railroad itself. The destruction of the railroad ruined many prominent citizens of Madison County, who were large stockholders.

Guntersville was shelled in retaliation for an attack upon Federal forces by some Confederate scouts, and later was shelled again and burned. Athens was sacked and pillaged in the classic European manner, by order of the notorious Colonel Turchin (a Russian, whose real name was Ivan Vasilovitch Turchinoff). Upon complaint of General Buell, charges were finally brought against Turchin, but not until after he had been promoted. In Decatur, only three of the principal buildings were left standing.

Homes and farms throughout the beautiful countryside of the Great Bend were visited by the torch of the invader. A typical incident was the retaliatory burning inflicted after General Robert L. McCook was killed in a cavalry skirmish near Huntsville. For comfort in transportation, the general was riding in an ambulance wagon with a cavalry escort. The party was attacked by a detachment of the 4th Alabama Cavalry, under Captain Gurley. In the stampede along the road, the uniformed driver of the ambulance wagon refused to halt at Gurley's order, and Gurley, aiming at the driver, shot and mortally wounded McCook. The Federals claimed a violation of the rules of war. Whereupon "many of the soldiers spread themselves over the country and burned all the property of the rebels in the vicinity, and shot a rebel lieutenant who was on furlough."

The more general ravages inflicted by Federal armies were carried out on an enormous scale. In 1863 General G. M. Dodge boasted that he had carried off, in a single raid on the Town Creek neighborhood, "fifteen million bushels of corn, five hundred thousand pounds of bacon, quantities of wheat, rye, oats, and fodder, one thousand horses and mules, and an equal number of cattle, sheep, and hogs, besides the thousands that the army consumed in three weeks; we also brought out fifteen hundred negroes, destroyed five tanyards and six flourishing mills, and we left the country in such a devastated condition that no crop can be raised during the war." As General Dodge retreated from Town Creek to Tuscumbia, he illuminated his night march with the light of burning houses, granaries, stables, and fences.

Besides reverting to classic forms of sack and pillage, the Federal troops sometimes took hostages or, when occupying towns known to be strongly "secesh," singled out prominent citizens, generally men too old for Confederate military service, and sent them off to northern prisons. If "guerrillas" attacked their foraging parties, the neighborhood was subject to destructive reprisals or retaliatory levies. For example, at Mulberry, a small village in Lincoln County, Tennessee, a party of "guerrillas" fell upon a lagging wagon of a forage train and captured a lieutenant, two soldiers, the wagon-master, and the teamster. They took their captives to Elk River, tied their hands, lined them up, and shot four of them. The lieutenant ran for the river and managed to escape. One soldier, badly wounded, revived and swam off after being thrown into the river. For this attack General Thomas ordered that a $30,000 indemnity be collected from the citizens of the Mulberry community and sent north to be divided among the families of the three dead Federals. General H. W. Slocum, in obedience to this order, seized and sold at auction property (largely cotton) amounting to over $35,000. In his report General Slocum stated that he had intended to return the surplus $5,000, but guerrillas attacked the detail that was collecting the money and killed two more soldiers. He then divided the $5,000 between their bereaved families.

Federal occupation also meant, often enough, that commanding officers would invite denunciations of Confederate sympathizers by Unionist informers, forerunners of the quislings and fifth columnists of the modern era. At the same time, with a frequency that gave great concern to the higher Federal command, unscrupulous officers speculated in cotton on the side and enriched themselves through the illegal sale of goods confiscated in the name of the Lincoln government.

Commanding officers were by no means always thus harsh and dishonest. Confederate communities that had the good fortune to be occupied by a well-disciplined outfit, under a sensible and humane commander, often enough preferred such military rule to the chaos of war, since it meant that they would be protected from bushwhackers, and would in other ways be afforded at least temporary security. Some higher commanders, Buell among them, did what they could to check rape, arson, and pillage, or even torture, which subordinate commanders condoned or encouraged. But under Sherman's authority, ravage became an official Federal policy. During the later years of the war, therefore, the Federal invasion, especially in the Great Bend, could hardly be distinguished from the inroads of a Genghis Khan or an Attila. In April, 1864, Confederate General Clanton reported that "the Yankees spared neither age, sex, nor condition."

As a further refinement in the policy of destruction and humiliation, it became a Federal policy to quarter Negro troops at nearly every garrisoned point—a policy, of course,

## THE COST OF CIVIL WAR

which became one of the most repugnant features of the Reconstruction. But while the war still lasted, the Negro troops were more of an annoyance than a menace, since they were not particularly keen to face the cannon and rifle fire of their late masters, who might gallop up at any moment. Far different, and far worse, were the bushwhackers and other irregular bands, sometimes "tories" (Unionist sympathizers) from the hill country, sometimes mere bandits who took full advantage of the collapse of civil government under war conditions. Of such character were the "Destroying Angels," who made themselves feared in the Great Bend. Roddey, "the Defender of North Alabama," and other Confederate commanders did their best to hold down such terrorists and to check Federal depredations, but their forces were generally too small to be of much avail. By the end of the war, all of the Confederate population that could get away had "refugeed" farther south—only to be caught once more in the fearfully destructive raids of Wilson's cavalry. And the worst conceivable condition had been reached, for both sides stopped taking prisoners, except when real battles were fought. "When a man was caught," says the historian W. L. Fleming, "he was often strung up to a limb of the nearest tree, his captors waiting a few moments for their halters, and then passing on. The Confederate irregular cavalry became a terror even to the loyal Southern people. Stealing, robbery, and murder were common in the debatable land of North Alabama." But to the end the Confederate government steadily refused to allow Confederate troops to engage in systematic retaliations against the Unionist areas.

Young John Wyeth was captured during Wheeler's raid against Rosecrans's wagon trains in the Sequatchie Valley, and stayed in prison until the end of the war. He came home by a roundabout way, finally reaching Decatur by rail and journeying thence up the Tennessee River by boat to Guntersville. This is what he saw:

With the exception of half a dozen dwellings, which were spared because they sheltered the sick or wounded . . . the village had disappeared. Nothing but tumbledown walls and a mass of brick debris was left of our home. The nearest shelter which could be obtained was in a log house on Sand Mountain, five miles from town, and in this my parents found a temporary abode. We were not wholly unprepared for the scene of desolation about us. As we came west on the train nothing but lonesome-looking chimneys remained of the villages and farmhouses. They were suggestive of tombstones in a graveyard. Bridgeport, Stevenson, Bellefonte, Scottsboro, Larkinsville, Woodville, Paint Rock—in fact, every town in northern Alabama to and including Decatur (except Huntsville, which, being used as headquarters, had been spared)—had been wiped out by the war policy of starvation by fire. Farmhouses, gins, fences, and cattle were gone. From a hilltop in the farming district a few miles from New Market I counted the chimneys of six different houses which had been destroyed.

That was what a great many of the returning soldiers saw in the Tennessee Valley.

In East Tennessee it was the same story, with local variations. Chattanooga, then a town of about two thousand people, had been trampled and used up by both armies, but the Federal occupation inflicted the greater damage. The area near the river where the Federal army was held in siege had been denuded of trees; it was crisscrossed by fortifications; fields had been trampled and gullied; the inhabitants had largely fled; the place was an unpleasant gash among the still fair mountains. Knoxville had been battered by military occupation and siege. Up and down East Tennessee devastation had raged—more often, in this region, the result of raid and counterraid by local partisans than of earth-shaking battles between large armies. During the Confederate occupation, from 1861 to 1863, the more rabid Confederate partisans, along with the usual quota of ruffians who simply put on uniforms in order to accomplish outrage, harried their Unionist neighbors without mercy. When the tables were turned after Burnside's arrival, the rabid Unionists took their

revenge, and took it overplus as Confederate authority weakened and disappeared.

In this area the war was in bloody truth a civil war. Many a man used the war as an excuse for carrying out private vengeance. The historian Ramsey's fine home, Mecklenburg, was pillaged and burned during the Federal occupation of Knoxville. In his autobiography, written shortly after the war, Ramsey recorded his conviction that the ravaging of his home was instigated by one of his personal enemies. Whatever the reason, the manuscript of Ramsey's second volume of *The Annals of Tennessee* was irretrievably lost in this burning, together with his library and personal effects. Bloodier types of vengeance were carried out by such fabulous guerrillas as the Confederate Champ Ferguson, who, according to tradition but probably not in fact, swore to kill a hundred Federals in retaliation for an injury inflicted on his wife and daughter.

The East Tennesseeans resented, too, with an upsurge of almost forgotten wrath, the raids carried out from North Carolina by bands of their ancient foes, the Cherokee remnant of the Qualla Reservation. These, under their agent, Thomas, supported the Confederate side. To the East Tennesseans, the occasional appearance of the mounted Cherokees of Thomas's Legion in their valleys added insult to injury and seemed the acme of outrage.

On the other hand, nothing had been more disturbing than the conduct of their supposed deliverers, the Federal army. It was grief added to humiliation to discover, as Kentuckians had already discovered, that Federal occupation was as onerous, and almost as obnoxious, as Confederate occupation. Quite freely, the Federals requisitioned and took; often they did not requisition but just took; they were in fact very destructive. Federal headquarters in East Tennessee was flooded with anguished complaints from loyal Unionists. Surprisingly, the men in blue did not always seem able to distinguish Unionists from Confederates among the civil population. To a soldier from Wisconsin or Ohio, all Southerners looked alike and were to be treated with brusque suspicion. There were no subtle shadings. So in the end many East Tennessee Unionists rivaled the most bitter secessionists in their dislike for the Yankees. Since the East Tennesseans were also committed, on principle, to hating the Confederates, they were left without anybody to love, and their condition was most miserable.

As for the Tennessee River itself, it had returned, by the end of the war, to a natural condition. No bridges were left over the Tennessee, save only the rebuilt railroad bridge at Bridgeport, and two military bridges, both temporary affairs, at Knoxville and Chattanooga. Both of these latter went out in the record flood of 1867. The ferryboats were gone—captured or burned. The steamboats were gone, except for a few left by the Federal army above Muscle Shoals. The river was again almost as it had been in pioneer times, except for the sunken hulks left here and there, as at Johnsonville, where they were still visible at low water when the next century came with its new wars.

The wilderness, the fruitful soil, and the unbroken spirit of the people remained. Soil and people had lost much; the wilderness had gained. And so a strange thing happened. Brazelton, the historian of Hardin County, tells how in those days the wild game of the forest and river greatly multiplied, for in the four years when men were hunting each other, the wild game had not been hunted. In some parts of the Tennessee Valley the wild game supported the population until new crops could be raised and cattle, hogs, and poultry bred. Not since pioneer days had the folks of Hardin County, and many other counties, had such a feast of wild turkey, quail, deer, and fish of the river.

This is the only undebatably "good result" of the Civil War that any historian has recorded.

CHAPTER VIII

# Parson Brownlow and the Ku Klux Klan

IN JANUARY, 1865, over five hundred Unionist delegates met in convention at Nashville and took steps to improvise a civil government for Tennessee. A large number of them were Tennesseans who had fought on the Union side, and they came directly from Federal camps to the convention hall. As a body, they represented three different shades of native Unionist sentiment—extreme, moderate, and conservative—and they were therefore already torn by differences of opinion which would eventually destroy them as a political party.

But it was a moment of triumph for the Union cause. Hood's battered army had been recently thrown back from Nashville, and there were no Confederate forces of importance left in the state. In the exaltation of the moment the delegates subdued their differences long enough to nullify Tennessee's ordinance of secession, provide for the abolition of slavery, and arrange for two elections—one to ratify the acts of the convention, another to elect the ticket of state officers proposed by the convention.

The elections were held, and the vote was so light as to make them seem a farce, but they had the desired result. The acts of the convention were ratified, and Parson William G. Brownlow, the fanatical Whig leader, preacher, and editor of East Tennessee, was chosen governor. The authority of the

January convention was extremely doubtful. It was really a kind of coup d'état, and the legality of its acts was hotly questioned by some Unionists, many of whom, on that very account, boycotted the elections.

Nevertheless, this improvised government, unconstitutional though it might be, was all the civil government Tennessee had. There was nothing to withstand it, and it was acceptable to Andrew Johnson, who was anxious to quit his job as military governor. It was also acceptable, for the time being, to the Washington government, since it satisfied technically Lincoln's ten per cent plan for restoring government in the seceded states.

Thus before the Civil War itself was fairly over, Reconstruction was inaugurated in Tennessee under the auspices of its own citizens. In general, these citizens represented the dissident Unionist minority which had voted against secession in 1861. The large bloc of loyalists in East Tennessee was the main substance of their strength, but they also drew support from scattered localities in Middle and West Tennessee. Among the East Tennesseans were men who had fled before Confederate occupation or stayed to suffer under it. Some of the more prominent of them had languished in Confederate prisons. Numbers of them had served in the Federal army. Though some were conciliatory, the more extreme were in a bitterly vindictive mood. All felt, in one way or another, that their loyalty entitled them now to take the lead in restoring civil government. They might differ as to means and policies and in their attitudes toward the vanquished, but they did not differ otherwise. Back of them stood the armed, victorious power of the Federal government. Their man, Andrew Johnson, the Union Democrat from East Tennessee, had run on the ticket with Lincoln in 1864 and had been elected vice-president. Then in the swift and terrifying events of the spring of 1865, the assassination of Lincoln made Andrew Johnson president of the United States.

This remarkable chain of circumstances determined the

course of Reconstruction in Tennessee and made it distinct and unique. To the north Kentucky, which had never seceded, had nevertheless suffered, under Union occupation, many of the terrors of Reconstruction, and the reaction against misrule had made Kentucky more than ever an avowed champion of the South. Up there, extreme Unionists were soon having such a tough time that it was being said that Kentucky had waited until after the war to secede. To the south, Georgia, Alabama, and Mississippi, with other Confederate states, soon passed into the hands of carpetbagger and scalawag governments. The familiar ruling combination of carpetbagger and scalawag plus Negro, sustained by Federal troops of occupation, became the regular pattern for ten of the seceding states. But neither this pattern nor the Kentucky pattern prevailed in Tennessee. Tennessee escaped the military rule that was imposed elsewhere by the Radical Republicans who junked Lincoln's plan of Reconstruction. Furthermore, there were no important carpetbagger elements in the political framework of the Brownlow regime, and the Tennessee Unionists who came into power were not "scalawags" in the common southern meaning of the term. They were native citizens who, with varying degrees of fervor, had adhered to the Union cause through all the changes of fortune. They were a sizable and to a large degree a sincere and respectable minority.

If the war had not been so terrible and its aftermath so charged with vindictiveness, the native Unionist Reconstruction of Tennessee might have followed a milder course. The returning Confederates, now frankly willing to confess defeat and accept the results, would have met the moderate and conservative Unionists halfway. But under Brownlow as governor, no conciliation was possible. The years between 1865 and 1869 became a second stage of fierce civil war, and the terror of the times blotted out most other considerations for the people of the valley.

Before the war Parson Brownlow had achieved more

than local fame for his tremendous powers of vituperation. A Methodist preacher of the circuit-riding tradition, he was prone to refer to preachers of other sects as "pigpen orators and whiskyshop saints." An ardent Whig, he called Andrew Johnson, his hated Democratic rival, "an unmitigated liar and calumniator and a villainous coward." As editor of *Brownlow's Knoxville Whig*, he poured similar abuse upon all who differed with him. Earlier, Brownlow had been prosouthern and proslavery to the last degree, but as secession approached he became a fanatical Unionist leader. The Confederates, moving into East Tennessee, found him on hand, still agitating against them, and clapped him into jail; but the Confederate government, deciding finally that Brownlow in jail could do more harm than Brownlow out of jail, sent him through the lines as a gift to the North. Lionized by the eager North, Brownlow went about the country preaching vengeance and death. "This war," he said in a New York speech, "must be pursued with a vim and a vengeance until the rebellion is put down, if it exterminates from God's green earth every man, woman, and child south of Mason and Dixon's line."

Returning to Knoxville on the heels of Burnside's army, Brownlow re-established his paper as *Brownlow's Whig and Rebel Ventilator* and fomented violence toward all Confederate sympathizers and returning Confederate soldiers. "He encourages the people," wrote a diarist in late 1864, "to kill their rebel neighbors wherever they find them, to do it without noise, secretly, but do it, and bury them in the woods like brutes." As a result of this and other incitements, violence against Confederates became rampant in East Tennessee. The Confederate population, harried from their homes, fled to other parts.

After the election of 1865 Brownlow proceeded to entrench himself and his faction in power. Fearful that he might be unseated by an alliance of ex-Confederates and Conservative Unionists, he pushed through stringent laws that excluded Confederates from the franchise and that empowered him, as governor, to appoint and remove the commissioners of registration, who passed upon the qualifications of voters. This gave Brownlow absolute control of elections. At first, like most Tennessee Unionists, he opposed Negro suffrage, but that, too, became a political necessity, and in 1866 the Brownlow legislature enfranchised the Negro over the protests of Conservative Unionists. The legislature also authorized Brownlow to raise and equip militia companies which he used to police elections. In July, 1866, by violent and illegal measures, Brownlow forced a divided legislature to ratify the Fourteenth Amendment. As a result of this action Tennessee, the last of the states to secede, became the first to be readmitted to the Union. In general, Brownlow committed himself and his faction to a policy of dictatorship and proscription. He threw away all spirit of leniency and compromise and declared that the Confederates had "forfeited all rights to citizenship, and to life itself."

In the farcical election of 1867 the Negro freedmen, guarded by militia, marched to the polls in solid lines, anxiously clutching the election tickets shoved into their hands. The support of the Negroes, who had greeted the Day of Jubilo with understandable enthusiasm, since to them it meant not only an end to slavery but an end to work, was kept firm by the thoroughgoing indoctrination carried on by the Union League (also called the Loyal League) and by agents of the Freedmen's Bureau. Through these organizations the carpetbagger and scalawag elements, which were not official parts of the Brownlow government, made themselves felt in Tennessee. The intervention of these elements, combined with the frantic efforts of the Brownlow government to perpetuate itself, alienated the ex-slave from the ex-master and made it impossible for the time being to reach any true *modus vivendi* for the white and Negro races in Tennessee. The two organizations—one a government agency, the other unofficial but even more influential—taught the

Negro freedmen to suspect, fear, and hate their old masters and to look to the Radical party as their savior and guide. The Union League, furthermore, was a secret society with an elaborate initiation, impressive oaths of loyalty, and a carefully devised catechism. Negro members of the league often went armed to meetings, drilled and marched in formation, and practiced terrorist methods against both whites and hesitant Negroes.

While all this was developing, the ex-Confederates were not moping the time away among the ruins. They could hardly be thought of as a submissive kind of people, and it seems odd today that any politicians equipped with even crude intelligence could ever have dreamed that they could successfully impose upon a spirited majority of the population the measures attempted by the Brownlow regime. Disfranchised and disarmed, the Confederates waited, at first, to see whether the politics of Conservative Unionism would accomplish anything. During this period of waiting they offered no organized front of opposition, but violent local reactions burst out here and there. These were sporadic, and were generally brought about by the misconduct of Negro troops or the ebullience of Negro parades. Furthermore, such reactions were not confined to Confederate districts. In 1866 the East Tennesseans lynched, in front of Federal army headquarters in Knoxville, a Negro soldier who had shot and killed a white officer on a Knoxville street.

Organized opposition did not gather real force until Brownlow's new victory in 1867 made clear to all the impotence of the Conservative Unionists. But by that time the ex-Confederates were ready. They were ready to meet organization with organization, secret society with secret society, terror with terror, force with force; and to do so with a skill that showed the presence of high directing genius. Their success gave new courage to the ruined and beaten South. They had an answer to Brownlow—something that, in twentieth century terminology, could rightly be classified as "an underground movement" or a "resistance movement." It was not directed at the Negro as Negro; it was not an anti-Negro movement. It was aimed at the powers that corrupted and exploited the Negro—the Brownlow regime and its hangers-on. But it was above all a movement in protection and self-defense. It was the Ku Klux Klan.

No complete and authentic account of the origin and history of the Ku Klux Klan can ever be written. Its members were pledged to secrecy. Only a rare few of them in later life admitted membership or disclosed any of its mysteries. Even those who made revelations did so hesitantly and evasively, or in somewhat cryptic and doubtful terms. The Klan's documents, such as it may have had, and its famous emblems and habiliments were rather thoroughly destroyed when the Klan disbanded in the late sixties. A Congressional committee, appointed in 1872 to inquire into the Klan and similar secret organizations, emerged with thirteen enormous volumes of discussion and testimony; but these, though they describe the Klan's external activities, or activities attributed to it, and draw a vivid picture of the South under Reconstruction, leave the reader bewildered rather than instructed as to the exact nature of the Klan. Yet enough evidence survives for the historian to be definite on some points, and in its main outline the true story, as distinct from legend and hearsay, is capable of discovery.

The Klan originated at Pulaski, in Giles County, Tennessee, late in December, 1865. Its founders were six young Confederate veterans, all educated men of prominent Giles County families: Captain John C. Lester, Captain John B. Kennedy, Captain James R. Crowe, Frank O. McCord, Richard R. Reed, and J. Calvin Jones. The meeting at which their plan first took shape was at the law office of Calvin Jones's father, Judge Thomas M. Jones. Later they used the residence of Colonel Thomas Martin, which the colonel had asked young Kennedy to occupy, for purposes of security, during his absence in Mississippi. Still later, when the order had grown in size and scope, they met in a ruined house, once occupied by Dr. Benjamin Carter, on a hill just outside of the town. This eerie and desolate spot was peculiarly well suited to their enterprise.

At first these young men had no other idea than of forming a social club to while away the tedium of the first postwar winter. It was to be a prankish, somewhat boisterous secret society, no different from other harmless groups of the sort. The fun was in the secrecy, in the curiosity that it would arouse among their fellows, and in the pretended solemnity of the ritual of initiation, which wound up in horseplay and roars of laughter. It was also fun to devise a terminology—to call the meeting place a "Den," to give the officers such names as "Grand Cyclops," "Grand Magi," "Grand Turk" and, for lesser functionaries, "Night Hawks" and "Lictors." Nonofficeholding members were "Ghouls." Being brought up in the classic tradition, they sought to give their society a name with a Latin or Greek flavor. One member suggested the Greek word, *Kuklos,* meaning *circle.* Another said, "Why not 'Kuklos Klan?'" and presently somebody else suggested "Ku Klux Klan," and thus the famous name was born. Presently they began to make judiciously furtive appearances in weird costumes which provoked the curiosity of the uninitiated. Outside the gate of the deserted Carter house they posted a Lictor, clad in ghostly apparel. He guarded the entrance while within the dark ruins lights flickered mysteriously and shrieks of unearthly laughter resounded.

Such activities, at first carried out for the sheer pleasure of mystery and joke, had totally unexpected results. Negroes who saw the ghostly Lictor at the gate or strangely garbed horsemen galloping by became less prone to leave home at night. Rowdiness became suddenly less in the community. Pillage and theft decreased. And the attendance at Union League meetings fell off—especially at night meetings. The rumor spread, somehow, that the strange horsemen were ghosts of the Confederate dead. The young men noted these phenomena. So did other citizens who were interested in the public welfare. And so, by processes not clearly known, the "social club" was utilized for purposes not implied in its first origin. It enlarged its numbers, broadened and tightened its organization, passed under the direction of skillful leadership, and so became the historic Ku Klux Klan of the sixties.

Such, at any rate, is the story told by those who ought to know the true facts. It is the story told in a little book published in 1884 by Captain Lester and his coauthor D. L. Wilson, and it is accepted as authentic by Stanley F. Horn in his *Invisible Empire,* the only good modern historical account of the Klan. Yet it is significant, all the same, that the Klan originated in a strongly Confederate part of the Tennessee Valley, in the area which, with North Alabama just across the line, had been most harshly devastated during the war, and which was from the beginning a focus of opposition to the Brownlow regime and was under Brownlow's peculiar displeasure.

Whatever the circumstances of its development may have been, the nature of the Klan as it was ultimately shaped and the stages of its rise to power are plain enough. After the period of quick spontaneous growth in 1866, the wiser heads in the Klan perceived both its dangers and its possibilities. They determined to guide its future course. In answer to a summons from the Pulaski Den, delegates from various Dens gathered at the Maxwell House at Nashville, in April, 1867, and quietly laid plans to strengthen the organization of the Klan and to define and control its policy. Whether or not General Nathan Bedford Forrest was Grand Wizard—or chief executive—of the Klan at this time cannot be known; but there is little doubt that Forrest was the guiding genius of the Klan during the period of its most effective work.

A scant few copies of the "Prescript," or Constitution, of the Ku Klux Klan somehow escaped destruction, and from this Prescript—available in its day only to Klan members and never known to the general public—we may ascertain its purposes, laws, and organization, as conveyed to its membership. The drafting of the Prescript was the special charge of George W. Gordon of Pulaski, the youngest brigadier general in the Confederate army.

The revised and amended edition of the Prescript, issued in 1868, began with the following statement of principles:

This is an institution of Chivalry, Humanity, Mercy and Patriotism; embodying in its genius and its principles all that is chivalric in conduct, noble in sentiment, generous in manhood and patriotic in purpose; its peculiar objects being

First: To protect the weak, the innocent, and the defenseless from the indignities, wrongs and outrages of the lawless, the violent and the brutal; to relieve the injured and oppressed; to succor the suffering and unfortunate, and especially the widows and orphans of Confederate soldiers.

Second: To protect and defend the Constitution of the United States, and all laws passed in conformity thereto, and to protect the States and the people thereof from all invasion from any source whatever.

Third: To aid and assist in the execution of all constitutional laws, and to protect the people from unlawful seizure, and from trial except by their peers in conformity with the laws of the land.

At no point in the Prescript was the name of the organization given. Instead, at every point where the name would naturally appear, stars were inserted: Two stars * * in the first edition; three stars * * * in the second. The jurisdiction of the Klan, covering all the southern states, was divided into Realms, Dominions, Provinces, and Dens. The officers of the general organization were: Grand Wizard of the Empire; Grand Dragons for the Realms; Grand Titans for the Dominions; Grand Giants for the Provinces. Officers of the Dens continued under their old designations. Code words were prescribed for use in messages, to designate months, days, and hours. Thus, January, in Ku Klux language, would become "Dismal Month," and nine o'clock would be "Hideous Hour."

Such lurid language was intended for public notices, which were distributed as handbills or printed in newspapers —after being slipped under the door or mailed anonymously. They were deliberately couched in such terms as would both inform the Klan membership and overawe their enemies.

To its membership and to those whom it befriended the Klan was exactly what its Prescript said, a chivalric and humane institution, designed to protect those who in these terrible years of ruin and humiliation had at last no other recourse. Its banner, as authorized but seldom displayed, was a medieval pennon bearing the famous Christian motto: *Quod semper, quod ubique, quod ab omnibus* ("What always, what everywhere, what by all is held to be true"). Every page of the Prescript began and ended with some lofty sentiment from the Roman and Greek classics, like *Damnant quod non intelligunt* ("They condemn what they do not understand") on the title page, or *Ad unum omnes* ("All for one") on the last page. The Klan furthermore abandoned, except for special purposes, the spookish garb of its early days, and adopted uniforms generally of dark colors, which made the wearer resemble some Knight Templar of the Middle Ages rather than a spook. The dark disguise, also, was more practical for night operations, since it reduced visibility (and therefore vulnerability) while it still suggested mystery.

It should be noted that the reorganization of the Klan, its rise to power in Tennessee, and its vast growth elsewhere followed closely upon the passage by Congress of the Military Reconstruction Act of 1867, the rise of the Union Leagues, the rigged Tennessee election of 1867, and the Brownlow militia act which made the parson a despot. During the second half of 1867 and the first half of 1868 the Klan moved swiftly and skillfully into action.

Although the Klan did not hesitate to use force when force was needed, violent action was the exception rather than the rule in Tennessee. The Klan preferred, and consistently practiced, a war of nerves. The mysterious prospect of what the Klan *might* do was an even greater weapon than the deeds it actually performed. Purposefully, the Klan avoided direct conflict with the militia or with United States troops. There is no evidence whatever that it was, as the frightened Radicals immediately vowed, a second rebellion against the United States. Its members were sworn to uphold the Constitution and all constitutional laws. It soon abandoned, or relegated to minor use, the half-comical stunts of its early days; the sheeted horseman who lifted his head from his shoulders and offered it to the scared Negro to hold; the skeleton hand, extended from a white robe; the thirsty spirit who asked for water and, after downing a whole bucketful, remarked, in ghastly tones: "That's the first drink I've had since the Battle of Shiloh!"

Instead of these tricks, the Klan announced and held great public parades in important towns, its picturesque mounted columns marching and countermarching without word of command, moved by the shrilling of whistles only, under the flare of torches. Or its horsemen suddenly appeared, in plain daylight, at some point where bad doings were threatened or were in progress, and stood ready, in silent challenge.

Typical of Klan methods, both in Tennessee and in neighboring Alabama, was a spectacular appearance of the Ku Klux in October, 1868, at Huntsville, Alabama. A big rally of Negro voters was being held at the courthouse, and they were being harangued by one Sheets, a Republican firebrand. Sheets said that the Ku Klux had warned him at Florence, a few days previous, not to make any more incendiary speeches, but now, in Huntsville, where he had so many colored friends, he was not afraid. Thereupon he urged the Negroes to arm themselves and shoot down the Ku Klux wherever they appeared. The Negroes, thus aroused, began to boast of what they would do. When a rumor passed abroad that the Ku Klux would accept the challenge and come to Huntsville, a drunken carpetbagger cried, "If they come into town, shoot them down. Fire on them; kill them! Don't wait for them to come into town. Go out and meet them and waylay them." Bands of excited Negroes actually went out to set an ambush for the Ku Klux, but as the day wore on and no Ku Klux appeared, their courage ebbed away, and they returned to join the big celebration at the courthouse.

During the evening one hundred and fifty Ku Klux rode into the square. In complete silence they slowly and calmly encircled the courthouse, and then, with equal deliberation, they withdrew to the neighboring markethouse. There, in military formation, they quietly awaited the progress of events. No sooner had they withdrawn from the square than the crowd inside the courthouse stampeded to join the excited crowd of onlookers on the square itself. In the tumult somebody fired a gun, apparently from the courthouse yard, into the churning mob. This provoked a wild and indiscriminate outburst of firing from the crowd in the square, who apparently supposed the Ku Klux were beginning operations. In the absurd melee, two people were killed and five were wounded, and one of those killed, by sheer accident, was Judge Silas Thurlow, a Republican. All this while the Ku Klux stood silent, not breaking formation or making any hostile gesture. Presently the Cyclops blew his whistle, and they rode off into the darkness. General Ruger, commander of the Federal troops in Huntsville, witnessed the whole affair, but declined to interfere. There was a great furor afterwards, and the usual cry of "southern outrage" in northern newspapers, but nothing much came of all the stir. The bold, challenging presence of the Ku Klux, however, made a deep impression.

Such tactics played havoc with the ill-assorted elements that the Brownlow Reconstruction government had brought together. When just retribution threatens, men of uneasy conscience begin to quake. The Brownlow regime was full of

## PARSON BROWNLOW AND THE KLAN 131

men of uneasy conscience, whose sense of guilt magnified their fears. Northern agitators, troubled by ominous visitors and by forebodings of calamity, kept loaded guns under their pillows, lost sleep at night, and also found the Negroes less responsive to guidance. Brownlow's commissioners of registration could almost feel the coarse touch of hemp around their necks; they resigned, in some localities, so fast that Brownlow could hardly keep the office filled. The Negro freedmen, long gulled by wordy promises, became mistrustful of Radicals and missionaries. They felt an uneasy prickling in their scalps and a chill in the marrow of their bones. Brownlow, the big boy, was at the capitol, to be sure; the Brownlow militia, in rather shaky companies, were here and there; and the almighty Congress was at Washington. But the woods were full of Ku Klux, and with unerring accuracy those Ku Klux could call them by their first names and recite their misdeeds, open or secret. The Ku Klux knew them, and the plausible strangers of the bureau and the league did not—and were strangers. So it was not necessary for the Klan to put violent pressure upon them. A few shots ringing out here and there at night, the shrilling of distant whistles, the remorseless clatter of hoofbeats up and down the lane—that was enough.

Very likely both the strategy and the tactics of the Klan owed much to Forrest's direction. He was the great master of swift movement by mounted forces. Above all others, he knew how to deliver a telling blow, then vanish elusively. He was an artist at bluff and intimidation. He knew how to feed an enemy's guilty mind with products of the imagination and trick him into entangling himself. Forrest was also economical of means; he made a little go far. Though Forrest could strike with utter fierceness if fierceness was called for, it was his known principle to avoid unnecessary bloodshed. Above all, his name and presence attracted a perfect loyalty that no other name and presence could command. It was that indefinable loyalty and esprit, fused with a strong sense of imperative need and common purpose, that bound the Klan in an allegiance firmer than any oaths alone could establish. In the Klan was reborn, indeed, some of the old "clanship" of the frontier which brought the overmountainmen to the Revolutionary battlefields, and Sevier's mounted raiders to the long wars with Cherokee and Creek. On the other hand, the close organization and perfect discipline of the Klan were new elements, born of new need and late military experience. In the use of these elements, as in higher strategy and administration, it was plain at last that Forrest, who had been ignored when a commander was needed for the Confederate Army of Tennessee, was now able to conduct operations far more delicate and more sweeping than the Army of Tennessee ever had opportunity to engage in.

By June, 1868, Brownlow was in a panic. Calling the legislature into special session, he avowed that armed rebellion was imminent and in a wildly inflammatory message demanded a new levy of militia and legislation outlawing the Ku Klux and punishing Ku-Kluxism with death. About the same time he pleaded, but without success, for United States troops to be sent to Tennessee. The legislature did not instantly grant Brownlow's demands; the condition of the state's finances, made rickety by careless fulfillment of previous demands, raised a question as to how the militia would be paid.

In the uproarious excitement, which extended to neighboring states, thirteen prominent Tennesseans, all of whom, including Forrest, had been general officers in the Confederate army, filed a memorial of protest with the legislature. There was no need of armed force, they declared. In a conciliatory fashion, they pledged their efforts to maintain peace. There was no revolt against the government. Disorder would subside at once if the legislature would restore the vote to the disfranchised citizens. Forrest, arguing for the petition before a committee of the legislature, said: "Abolish the Loyal League and the Ku Klux Klan; let us come together and stand together." But later, elsewhere, to keep up the scare, he said: "If the Radical Legislature, with Governor Brownlow, arms the negroes and tells them to shoot down all Confederate soldiers, on the ground that they are members of this Kuklux Klan, as they call it, and outlaws, then, in my opinion, there will be civil war in Tennessee. . . . I don't want to see any more bloodshed, nor do I want to see negroes armed to shoot down white men. If they bring this war on us there is one thing that I will tell you—that I shall not shoot any negroes so long as I can see a white Radical to shoot, for it is the Radicals who will be to blame for bringing on this war."

Brownlow refused all peace offers. His partisan legislature gave him blanket authority to raise militia, declare martial law at discretion, and in general to do as he pleased. The election of 1868, which resulted in Grant's elevation to the presidency, was held under turbulent conditions in Tennessee, with Brownlow's militia again in action and United States troops, at last furnished by Andrew Johnson, on duty in some parts of Tennessee. It was another victory for the Radical group, but their margin of success in Middle and West Tennessee was ominously reduced, and the general results were not encouraging for them. In Middle Tennessee, where 30,959 votes had been cast for Brownlow the year before, only 17,122 were cast for Grant electors. In Giles County, where, in 1867, Brownlow had lined up 1,879 votes, the Grant ticket got only 561. Though other factors were beginning to operate, the Klan was the chief element in the decline of Radical strength.

It was clearly the beginning of the end. Perhaps foreseeing this, Brownlow had earlier, in 1867, had himself elected United States senator from Tennessee, not to occupy his seat, however, it so happened, until 1869. He was now both senator-elect and governor. As governor, he saved his grimmest inflictions for a farewell blow against the ex-Confederates. In January, 1869, Brownlow declared martial law in nine

Tennessee counties, including Giles and certain neighboring counties deemed to be the special seat of the Klan. To these counties he sent eighteen hundred newly assembled militia, five companies of which made Pulaski their headquarters. At the same time, determined to punish individual Ku Klux if possible, he hired a Cincinnati detective named Seymour Barmore, and brought him to Nashville, with promise of a large reward, as his special espionage agent.

The Ku Klux easily spotted Barmore upon his arrival at Nashville and set a watch upon his movements. He was a brave, but an entirely foolish man. His plan was to go to Pulaski and there, disguised as a Klansman, to enter the councils of the Pulaski Den, ferret out their secrets, take note of their membership, and expose them to Brownlow. The innocent man, self-advertised as "the greatest detective in the world," wore a velvet coat, plum-colored trousers, and a diamond pin in his shirt front. He also talked too freely.

Barmore took the train for Pulaski, as he had planned. But at Franklin, mysteriously enough, he got off the train and returned to Nashville. He did not explain why, but he must have realized that the Klan was already on his trail. The next day he took the train again. Near Columbia the train was stopped. A group of Klansmen escorted Barmore from the train into the nearby woods and there, after proper arraignment, admonished him severely, administered light punishment, and warned him that if he persisted he would certainly die. Then, after keeping him prisoner overnight, they allowed him to return to Nashville.

The redoubtable Barmore, not to be intimidated, took a freight train for Pulaski two days later, eluded the Klan's watchers, slipped into a meeting of the Pulaski Klan, and got clear away—or almost away—before his identity was discovered. It was, however, discovered. A warning flashed ahead. At Columbia, the train was held and guarded by two dozen Ku Klux, while Barmore was taken off. Nothing more was heard of him until, weeks later, on February 20, 1869, his body was found in Duck River. Barmore had been shot in the forehead. His diamond stickpin, his rings, his money were untouched. But the little book in which he undoubtedly had recorded some notes about the Pulaski Klan was not there.

This was Brownlow's last effort. On February 25, 1869, he resigned the governorship and soon departed for Washington. He was in feeble health, and his voice was completely used up. In the Senate he did little more than to write a few speeches and to act as claims agent for Tennessee Unionists who felt that the government had despoiled them.

Meanwhile, in Tennessee, DeWitt C. Senter, speaker of the State Senate, became governor in Brownlow's place. Senter was an East Tennessee Unionist who, like some other Unionist leaders, had spent part of the war in a Confederate prison, and had had various other harrowing experiences during the war. He was a Radical Republican, but now, like the Conservative and Moderate Unionists and even many Radicals, he had had enough of Brownlowism, which had indeed now fallen apart at its very core. Within a short time Senter ended martial law, and in general showed a disposition to conciliate the ex-Confederate majority. The Klan itself, meanwhile, diminished its activities and presently, by order of its leaders, ceased its demonstrations and disbanded. It had served its purpose. Already its disguises were being used, for private violence or simple crime, by unauthorized persons, including even Negroes. Such exploitation could not be condoned and must be stopped. Therefore, by order of the Grand Wizard, the Klan's organized existence was terminated—to quote the Lester and Wilson account—"as decisively and completely as General Lee's last order on the morning of the 10th of April [*sic*], 1865, disbanded the Army of Northern Virginia." By order, its paraphernalia and documents were burned. Thus the Ku Klux Klan of the sixties passed into history as far as Tennessee and the Tennessee Valley were concerned.

Whatever may have been Senter's motives, his conciliatory policy rendered impotent both the Radical Republican faction and the Republican party proper. A conservative legislature soon restored the franchise to the ex-Confederates and repealed much Radical legislation. It also provided for a constitutional convention. The convention, when it met, was dominated by ex-Confederates and Conservatives. It produced in 1870 a state constitution which in most respects returned to the old constitution of 1835. In particular it retained the exceedingly difficult process of amendment set up in that constitution. The result has been that, despite many earnest attempts, it has not yet been amended, and the state of Tennessee, in 1947, was still governed under the unamended constitution of 1870. Thus deeply and firmly did Reconstruction and the fight against Reconstruction set their mark upon the fundamental institutions of the state of Tennessee.

CHAPTER IX

# Kingdom Coming

**B**AD AS IT WAS, and long enduring in its evil effects, the Reconstruction period was not completely satanic. All the time, despite the misery and turmoil, the elements of a genuine reconstruction—a reconstruction with a little "r"— were present in Tennessee. When Radical misrule abated, these elements came forward, quickly and hopefully.

One remarkable indication of the willingness of Tennesseans to reconstruct themselves, if let alone, was the appearance in 1874, during the administration of Governor John C. Brown, of an extraordinary book entitled *Introduction to the Resources of Tennessee*. The thick, 1,193-page volume was published by the state of Tennessee. It was edited by James B. Killebrew, state secretary of agriculture, who had just served previously as assistant superintendent of public instruction. He was assisted by the learned state geologist, J. M. Safford, and other able gentlemen, and they all worked under the direction of the State Bureau of Agriculture. Officially, the book was a report from the Bureau of Agriculture. Really it was far more. It was what would be called in later times a "survey," or inventory, of all resources whatsoever. Now that battles and brawls presumably were over, these honest and realistic persons wanted to find out, and to be able to tell the world, what was left as the basis for an entirely fresh start at life.

The great emphasis in their formidable study was naturally on agriculture. Farm land was still the chief resource, and the people's hearts were with the land. True, it had been ravaged, beyond all imagining. Not until 1900, indeed, forty years after the election of Lincoln, would Tennessee farm land again reach or surpass even by a small fraction the total dollar value that it had in the great decade before the Civil War.

If the authors of *Resources of Tennessee* could have foreseen this discouraging prospect, they might have been less hopeful in 1874. But they believed in their land. It would retrieve them from ruin, if properly fostered. Proudly, yet not without a saving touch of realism, they displayed the land—its topography, climate, geology, soil types, first for the state as a whole, then by Grand Divisions, East, Middle, and West, and then, even more lovingly, county by county within the Grand Divisions, until the story and the prospects of each of the ninety-three counties of Tennessee were fully exhibited. But furthermore, with a range and catholicity not always found in modern surveys, they took notice of transportation facilities, mineral resources, education, occupational preferences; they went heavily into all kinds of statistics; and here and there they openly took account of such general political trends as might be dangerous to the well-being of Tennessee.

It was not exactly the kind of thing that might have been expected from Tennessee by a nation already weary with its turbulent misfortunes. It was not anything one would associate with the legendary South. Rather it was the kind of idea that clever Yankee heads were supposed to generate. The portly volume, indeed, had more than a faint boosterish flavor. It was partly for outside consumption. Frankly, it was wooing northern capital to a certain extent, and it was soliciting immigrants.

Anxiously the authors assured prospective immigrants that the Ku Klux Klan had gone out of style. Firmly they refuted the disagreeably prevalent but unjust notion "that a secret society, known as the Ku Klux, exists in the State and that persons who are obnoxious are maltreated and driven away by these secret emissaries." To the question, how would Tennesseans now receive northern men and women, they had a frank, not quite boosterish answer: "If they come to stir up strife between the races, they will not, and should not, be respected.... But if they come with earnest hearts, and willing hands, and cheerful voices, to help build up the prosperity of the State, be their politics what it may, their religion what it will, they will be received with all the heartiness and all the civility that it is possible for a gallant people to exercise."

With a similar mixture of frankness and high hope, Killebrew and his helpers surveyed the educational scene. Colleges were being both established and re-established. The University of the South, projected before the war, was now actually holding forth in its "Domain," on Sewanee Mountain. At Nashville the Methodist Church, South, had set up a new university, and named it Vanderbilt University in honor of Cornelius ("Commodore") Vanderbilt, who was providing a million dollars for buildings and endowment. There was also Cumberland University, as of old, at Lebanon, and there were other institutions including the "three so-called state universities."

At the common school level, private schools were starting again, and at last, after many disappointments and setbacks, a decent state system of public schools was being projected. The ingrained prejudice of Tennesseans against public schools was an obstacle to overcome, and furthermore it was easier to wring blood from a turnip than to get taxes for schools out of a moneyless population. The Peabody Fund, provided by George Peabody, a generous Northerner, was beginning to help some. But the great present danger, in 1874, was the prospect that Congress might pass the Civil Rights Bill, which would force the white public schools to receive Negro pupils. Such a law, said the Killebrew report, would end the biracial school system, to which even the Radical Republicans of Tennessee had adhered. Indeed, it would just end the public school system. It would be "a severer stroke to education than the war itself." Counties would not vote taxes for schools in which the two races were mingled, nor would the population approve or support them.

The application of force in this particular [said the report], under the color of securing rights, would be accompanied with evils so much greater than that intended to be corrected, that it would be like blotting out the sun in order that a tallow dip might send its feeble rays out over the world. . . . By keeping the schools separate, both races will be advanced, and a spirit of healthy emulation will spring up, and the very prejudice that exists may be made a powerful lever in forwarding the improvement of both races.

The new concern with public schools was one of the marks of new times coming on, though, in a sense, it resumed an interest that had begun to flourish during Andrew Johnson's governorship, before the war. War and Reconstruction had created an educational hiatus, more than a decade in length, during which schools had simply disappeared. The younger element of the population was, therefore, now more overwhelmingly illiterate than ever before. At the outset of the war, too, Governor Isham G. Harris had forced the Bank of Tennessee, where the state's "school fund" was deposited, to purchase state bonds which had been issued to finance war expenses. The defeat of the Confederacy made these bonds worthless, and with the failure of the Bank of Tennessee the "school fund" was irremediably gone. The Brownlow regime had made a futile effort to restore it, but finally, after years of quarreling, scandal, and litigation, the best the state could do was to establish a "Permanent School Fund" of two and a half million dollars as a legal fiction and pay interest of six per cent on this sum to establish an "Annual School Fund."

In addition, certain clauses of the state constitution of

1870 levied a poll tax on all male citizens of voting age, required evidence of poll tax payment to accompany exercise of suffrage, and specifically directed that all state moneys derived from poll taxes be devoted exclusively to the support of schools. The Brownlow regime had also made legislative provision for a good public school system, but the incompetence and general chicanery of those years, together with lack of funds, turned the fine plan into a mere paper gesture.

Yet the puniness of the public schools was still so obvious, and the general fear of Congressional interference was still so marked, that the old preference for private schools was whetted rather than diminished. The renaissance was led by a unique personality, a young Confederate soldier from North Carolina named William R. Webb, later known as "Sawney," or still more affectionately as "Old Sawney" Webb.

Webb had served in Lee's army, and had been severely wounded at Malvern Hill. During a period of invalidism he renewed his studies in Latin, Greek, and mathematics at the University of North Carolina, which had at that time only sixty-three students, most of them, like himself, temporarily unfit for war. In the latter days of the war he returned to service with Stuart's cavalry and was captured and sent to a New York prison three days before Lee's surrender. Webb escaped from the prison and, not knowing what to do next, wandered uncertainly around New York City. When asked who he was and what he was doing, he told the truth: "I am a Confederate soldier, just escaped from prison." The New Yorkers laughed derisively and refused to believe him. Deciding finally that he might be better off in prison than out of it, Webb contrived to loiter near the prison entrance in a suspicious way. The sentinel, taking him for a prisoner about to escape, promptly ordered him back into the enclosure.

Back in North Carolina finally, a veteran of twenty-three, Webb found the Reconstruction regime in the state not at all to his taste. Accordingly, in 1870 he chose to seek his fortune in Tennessee, where Reconstruction was apparently over and the climate was favorable to a young schoolteacher. At Culleoka, in the basement of a church, he established Webb School. With iron determination that made no compromise with frivolity, Webb decided that his school should be an institution of a strictly classical type: it would teach only a few subjects, those of basic importance; and it would have one major function—to prepare boys for entrance to college. No other school with such a function existed west of the mountains. Webb's resourcefulness and genius made his school not only the first boys' preparatory school of the region in point of time, but a progenitor and leader of a galaxy of boys' schools of varying types that profoundly influenced the South for the half century following.

In 1886 Webb moved his school from Culleoka to the little town of Bell Buckle. Meanwhile he had married, and he had been joined by his brother John, as great a teacher and scholar as William was great in directing genius. He had accumulated $12,000. With $2,200 of this capital he put up a simple wooden schoolhouse at Bell Buckle; alongside it, with $400, he erected a plain, one-room building—the library; and with $8,000 of that money he bought books—nothing but the best books. On catalogue and librarian he spent nothing at all! The library was wide open to whoever wanted to use it. It was run, like the school, on the honor system. There were no dormitories. The boys roomed and boarded in the town.

Webb School, always unique, always independent, could doubtless never have become what it was without the two men, "Old Sawney" and "Old Jack," the soon almost legendary personalities who shaped its character. But those two men, no less than the school, represented the tradition of antebellum days, altered only slightly by its hard encounter with war and Reconstruction. In a physical environment as plain as any old field school Old Sawney and Old Jack imparted to the sons of Confederate (or Union) soldiers the finest classical learning that the times afforded. They toadied to no educational fashion. Their staple diet was Greek, Latin, and mathematics, with some concessions to history and English. Out of the Spartan necessity enforced by the hard times they made a glory and a moral. The education of a young gentleman did not depend on physical appurtenances, nor did it have anything whatever to do with classes of society. What mattered was the inner being. What mattered was to know that Homer, Vergil, Cicero, Euclid and truth, honor, virtue, and religion were all one harmony, attainable by character and application, whether one was poor or rich, defeated or victorious. To know that was to know the essentials. But this gospel, so pertinent to the impoverished regime of the postwar days, was also the fundamental gospel of the older frontier society, which did not measure by externals and distrusted show. It was welcome gospel in Tennessee where now, at least for the time being, it was altogether disreputable to be rich.

What youngsters might not absorb from books, Old Sawney imparted in his exhortations. These, delivered in a drawling, rather melancholy tone of voice, which seemed often to deprecate the necessity of instructing or even talking, were really the dryly humorous homiletics of the frontier tradition: and Sawney was a master of the anecdote, the tale, the homely sally, and, when need was, of directly passionate utterance. Legend grew about his stocky, always somewhat unbuttoned, always informal yet traditional figure, with the black string tie generally a little askew under the gray beard, and the stiff-bosomed shirt perhaps a little stained with tobacco juice. His maxims were remembered, and they always meant business. "I'd rather hear a boy say *I seen* when he really saw something than to hear him say *I saw* if he didn't see anything." And there were stories, some true, some legendary, like the one about the cow that understood Greek and Latin. This was the cow that Sawney milked while small boys who had missed their paradigms came to his house to recite after school hours. Sawney milked while the boy who was made to stand at the cow's heels, conjugated *amo* or *tuptomai*. If the boy missed a form, the cow invariably kicked. (She always kicked when milked with one hand, but the boy didn't know that.) And all this, too, was in the frontier tradition. Boys who were thus educated at Webb School brought renown to the school and won honors for themselves at elegant Harvard or wherever they wished to study. And Old Sawney became, as Edd Winfield Parks has demonstrated in his historical sketch, an apotheosis of the schoolteacher; or more than that, a new kind of leader, respected and beloved in a region that had had many heroes but had lacked a schoolteacher hero.

This defiant rising from the ashes, which found Sawney Webb teaching boys in a church basement, and the secretary of agriculture wondering about the price of Tennessee land, had certain general features which should be noted. The mood of the times was to make no surrender, and frankly to assert no surrender, on such fundamental matters as the separation of the races; to submit to no more Brownlowism, no more bullying; and yet, while firmly holding that ground, to approach all questions in a conciliatory and practical way; to make great concessions, more sometimes than flesh or spirit was attuned to bear, if only peace could be obtained and life be decently begun again in Tennessee and the Tennessee Valley. With complete realism and sincerity, the Tennesseans and their neighbors were ready to make the new labor system work, if possible. On the farms, it had to be a sharecropping arrangement. There was no cash capital to draw on; wages could only come from crops, and then only at the end of the year when crops were sold. If the Negro would work under this arrangement, he was certainly welcome to his freedom. They were also ready to start educating the Negro at public expense and to allow him any reasonable opportunity to better his condition, but always on the principle of social separateness in clearly defined categories.

On these matters, there was no division of sentiment in the white population; they thought as one, whether they had been Confederate or Unionist in sympathy. At heart, the Unionists all along had been more hostile to the Negro than their Confederate opponents, and even after his enfranchisement had withheld him from officeholding. By a curious irony, the first Negro member of the legislature was elected *after* the collapse of the Radicals. He was elected in 1873 from Davidson County, an old center of secession, and was invited by Governor John C. Brown to attend a dinner given by the governor in honor of the members of the legislature.

Really, the ex-master was ready to concede the ex-slave his Day of Jubilo so far as it could be attained within the limits of economic ability and decent conduct. And truly both ex-master and ex-slave now knew that both were caught, and caught together, in the newer, vaguer bondage that was attached, almost as a penalty, to residence in a southern state. There would be no Day of Jubilo for anybody, any time, if that bondage were not lifted or circumvented. If each did what he could, in his own way, better times might come, and sometime, somehow there might be a Day of Jubilo for both. A mild optimism began to dawn. It received much stimulation, here and there, from the utopianism that had attended the process of Reconstruction itself, and that had healthy and amusing as well as tragic and disreputable phases.

Since the time of Christian Gottlieb Priber and his Cherokee "Kingdom of Paradise," the Tennessee country had attracted utopians from afar and quickened utopian dreams among valley dwellers themselves. In the Muscle Shoals country especially a man could hardly rest his head, even on something no better than a stone, without having a Jacob's vision of heaven descending to earth. Andrew Jackson, en route to the Creek Wars, had had such a vision at York's Bluff, later Sheffield. Even the surveys of the army engineers, resumed after the war, often broke away from sober calculation and made enthusiastic flights of rhetoric. Colonel W. B. Gaw, after his 1867 survey of the Tennessee River, had such a moment of exaltation: "To restore . . . vitality to a great section of the United States . . . is within the easy accomplishment of the engineer, and needs only a careful study of the Tennessee

River and the vast hydrographic system of which it is the trunk, to perceive the insignificance of the time and means required for this work when compared to the gigantic results to be achieved."

In the decades after the Civil War, the valley swarmed with utopians who would have agreed with Colonel Gaw although they knew nothing about engineering, civil or social. The carpetbaggers, Union Leaguers, and social missionaries of various sorts were utopians, sometimes sincere, sometimes not. The valley found their ministrations detestable, and the more detestable when offered, as they sometimes were, under the cloak of piety. Nothing hurt so much as the unctuous effort of northern churches, aided at certain points by the Brownlow administration in Tennessee and by the Reconstruction government of Alabama, to take over the property and administration of "disloyal" southern churches. It was hard to observe Christian forbearance toward preachers who enforced their texts at the point of the bayonet. It was difficult to be indulgent toward northern teachers who taught the ex-slave to hate the ex-master. Such busybodies soon checked and ended all willingness of the white Southerners to undertake, on their own responsibility, the teaching of the ex-slaves, as they had begun to do, at first, in various quarters. To teach a Negro school became, unfortunately, a sure proof of carpetbag or scalawag tendencies; soon, therefore, no white Southerner could afford to teach a Negro school.

But there were more subtle utopians, whom it was harder to resist. Among these were northern capitalists, who came bringing plentiful cash or credit and often enough large funds of honest good will. Their great armies had ruined the country, but now, come to think about it, they did not hate the southern people. Let the dead past bury its dead. They begged to be permitted to assist in the humane task of restoring the devastated regions. There was no reason why the valley should cut off its nose to spite its face, and therefore, while offering the genial right hand of fellowship and reconcilement, they thought it only common sense to point out that the rebuilding of railroads, the exploitation of mineral and timber rights, and the development of manufacturing might be so arranged as to confer mutual benefits. Before the nineteenth century was over, these plausible persons were met at least halfway by Henry Grady and the progressives of the New South school of thought, who had achieved an extraordinarily convenient formula. Under the New South formula one could, without turning a single southern hair, shower oratorical praise upon the footsore Confederate soldier returning to his ruined home and then, in the same tone of voice, eulogize the benevolent agents of Progress who cleaned up the ruins and provided a new home, in fashionable rococo gingerbread and golden oak, all for the trifling consideration of a 99-year lease and a majority of the preferred stock.

History was repeating itself, with an irony that may or may not have been justifiable. They who had invaded the old Indian lands had now in their turn been invaded and worsted. The Cherokees, who were soon in process of getting rich from Oklahoma oil, could exult over this if they happened to think about it. And as the men of Sevier's day had said to the Cherokees: "Come, let us fight no more, but be sensible and engage in trade," so the late warriors in blue said to the late warriors in gray, "Come, let us smoke a cigar and make a deal." And again, when the deal had been made, it might be discovered that the bargain had enriched the chiefs of the tribe, but not the tribe in general. By this simple, perhaps natural process vast resources in coal, iron, timber, and eventually power rights passed out of southern hands and into northern hands for little or nothing, and what revenues the people at large received were but a meager fraction of the wealth that went elsewhere, some of it forever.

Many a Northerner who used his capital, great or small, in the valley region, was a Federal soldier or officer who came back after the war to some attractive spot—a town by the river, a homestead on the mountain—that he had noted at the time when he marched with Sherman or Grant. So was it in the older wars, when the frontiersman burned Indian towns and made a mental note that here, right here, he would build a home someday. With such northern immigrants the bargain went rather well. Generally, the Federal soldier escaped the odium that attached to the carpetbagger and social crusader, and between Confederate veteran and Union veteran there was the respect, even the camaraderie, that one good fighting man feels for another. Furthermore, such Yankee settlers were not absentee landlords, but dwellers in the land, and shared the fate of the land. Presently when one of these married a girl of the valley, as often happened, he would be received into the tribe, like the old Indian countrymen among the Cherokees. Then the past would be indeed forgotten, and his children and his children's children would become more southern than the Southerners.

The other bargain, the bad bargain, when it was perceived, wrought division in the valley just as the treaties signed by the Little Carpenter and other "friends of the white man" wrought division among the Cherokees. Henry Grady was a kind of Little Carpenter, and his followers were the peace faction among the late Confederates. On the other side, less vocal by far, were the irreconcilables, ready to follow a Dragging Canoe if any such should arise, but on the whole without leadership. They had no Dragging Canoe. Even redoubtable Bedford Forrest, when reconstruction troubles subsided, went into railroad building, and spent his last years entangled in financial operations. And there were no Five Lower Towns to which to withdraw—though one might still move to Texas, or even to Brazil, as a few bitter souls did. All the irreconcilables could do was to doubt, and be stubborn, and stick it out where they were. Not until the agrarian crusade of the nineties would they again have a leadership.

People of the Kingdom Coming persuasion were always incredulous when they encountered such irreconcilables. In 1868, while the Brownlow regime was still riding high, a certain Hermann Bokum became commissioner of immigration for Tennessee, for Brownlow at that time was opposed to Negro suffrage, and he proposed to bring in immigrants to vote for him if he could get nobody else. Bokum drew up and published a small book entitled *The Tennessee Handbook and Immigrant's Guide,* in which he catalogued the undeveloped resources of the country and listed promising fields of endeavor for immigrants. During the course of his investigation he encountered a rebellious East Tennessean named Christian Carriger, an ancient citizen of Carter County and a member of the prewar legislature. Bokum recorded, though quite disapprovingly, Carriger's views on progress and civilization. Said Carriger, according to Bokum:

You know that I lived here when we went forty miles to mill with our oxen and wagon. I hunted deer; wife and daughters made all our clothing, the big wheel, the little wheel, the reel, and the cotton cards being all that was needed; we found dye-stuff in our woods, taking it from the bark of trees; we tanned the leather in a trough, and made shoes ourselves; wife could make a good thread button for the collar; vest striped up and down, made of cotton thread 1100 fine; buck-skin pants and hunting-shirt; straw hat in summer and woollen hat in winter; the wool we sheared from our lambs; good health, never sick; no law-suits, no churches, no schools, no money; we traded in bear skins, deer skins, muskrat skins; the smaller articles answering the purposes of change. Then came the merchant, and we all got into debt; the lawyer, and we all got at law; the doctor, and we all got sick; the preacher, and we all got religion.

The annoyed Bokum dismissed Carriger in a sentence: "It is plain that Christian Carriger did not understand the age in which he lived." But there were more Carrigers than Bokums in the Tennessee Valley. Many more.

The calamitous impact of war and reconstruction forced a heavy proportion of the citizenry to practice Carriger's self-sufficient philosophy, whether they liked it or not. The Tennessee country, just emerging from its pioneering in 1860, was "frozen" in its antebellum pattern, or in something still more primitive, if only from sheer inability to survive in any other way. So in 1874, for even such an advanced and formerly prosperous Middle Tennessee county as Marshall, the Killebrew report had to note that much homespun was still worn in the county; that women were still making jeans, linsey, blankets, and cotton cloth on hand looms. Plows, wagons, harness, saddles, shoes, furniture were still being made by local craftsmen at small village shops or in homes.

In the poorer or more ravaged counties conditions were even more primitive. Even where manufactures were restored they were often a return to the modest industries of antebellum days. As late as 1900, flour mills and gristmills, often turned by water power, were the leading industry; virtually every town or "settlement" milled its own grain. The country tended to stay fixed in the self-contained economy of other days.

In this respect, no part of the land was much different from any other. In later times, romantic and uninformed persons would attribute this famous "backwardness" to the mountain people in particular, and would write in nostalgic and patronizing tones about the quaint archaism of their ways. But such archaism prevailed in every locality where urban progress had not taken hold or sound agricultural prosperity intervened. It was a result of war and of continuous disadvantage extending over a long period, and not the result of inherent depravity or lack of education. It also represented, to some extent, a preference like Carriger's for a simple and independent life. Of the farmers of Claiborne County the Killebrew report said: "They are not ambitious of wealth or distinction, but make what they live upon and live upon what they make. . . . Life to them is a thing to be enjoyed, not merely to be endured."

On the other hand, many a citizen of the valley, no matter how unregenerate on the political side, could hardly be blamed for hearkening to the utopian promises that were in the air all around him. Before his eyes, presently, towns were growing into cities as boom followed boom. Chattanooga's population in 1870 was over six thousand—more than double what it had been before the war. By 1900 Chattanooga was a real city of 49,000 people. A like expansiveness appeared elsewhere. Knoxville, growing into a lusty wholesale center, the great market town for East Tennessee, with a developing marble industry close by, enlarged its area and influence. What had been Smith's Cross Roads, in Rhea

County, grew up quickly into Dayton. In the Great Bend, Sheffield sprang up out of nothing to become an ambitious mining town. Florence and Tuscumbia renewed their metropolitan dreams. But below Muscle Shoals there was somnolence except at the thriving river town Paducah.

Much of this expansion was due to northern capital, which was readily interested in the coal, iron, timber of the valley, and in textile manufacture and railroads. Much of it, too, like business enterprise everywhere at the time, was on a rather speculative basis, and the valley had much practice in inflating and deflating both its capital and its hopes.

Although there was always—necessarily it seemed—a destructive collapse between booms, there was frequently a residue of material gain after the collapse. The principle was illustrated in the case of Colonel J. C. Stanton, of Boston and New York, who arrived at Chattanooga in 1868 and brought to the city and to the neighboring states what has been called "the Stanton period." Stanton was described as "a hard-looking Scotchy fellow, a red-headed hustling rascal." He bought up some of the ruined and depreciated railroads and proceeded to combine them into a new line, the Alabama & Chattanooga Railroad. The pliable Reconstruction government of Alabama issued a charter which permitted the railroad to endorse bonds at the rate of $16,000 per mile for the first twenty miles. Before long the speculators had put on the market a huge quantity of bonds, underwritten by the state of Alabama. The bonds were sold, many of them in Europe, through New York companies, in disregard of legal requirements and sound finance. When the inevitable collapse came, $10,000,000 had vanished into the air, and the state of Alabama had on its hands a railroad worth hardly half that much money.

But the great speculator had been kinder to Chattanooga. There Stanton had built a railroad station, a freight depot, and a hundred thousand dollar hotel—the Stanton House—in which Chattanooga citizens had invested heavily.

These tangible assets remained, even though Chattanooga's money vanished with Stanton's in the bankruptcy brought on by the panics of 1869 and 1873.

But with Federal General John T. Wilder it was an entirely different story. In the Chickamauga campaign, Wilder's Mounted Infantry rode over the Cumberland ridges, turned their guns on Chattanooga, and fought the Confederates in the long valleys south of that city. Now the general returned to improve the very locality he had helped to devastate. In those great ridges there was, he knew, iron and coal in plenty. The Roane Iron Company, of which he became superintendent, soon brought in its great furnaces at Rockwood, on the edge of the Cumberland plateau between Chattanooga and Knoxville. These were the first furnaces in Tennessee to substitute coke for the familiar charcoal. Soon Wilder had a hand in other enterprises, business and civic, throughout East Tennessee. It was this development, along with the growth of the Knoxville Iron Company at Knoxville, that brought to Knoxville and Chattanooga, and even to smaller places, the dream of becoming "the Pittsburghs of the South." "Nothing is lacking," said the Killebrew report, in a burst of ecstasy, "to make it [the Chattanooga-Knoxville area] one of the most famous metallurgical centres in America, but facilities for transportation, capital, and enterprise. . . . A chain of fiery furnaces will be built that will illumine the whole eastern margin of the Cumberland Table-land."

It was the presence of iron and coal and its admirable location as a railroad center and river port that Chattanooga counted on for its future greatness. In 1875, the Southern States Coal, Iron & Land Company (soon absorbed by the Tennessee Coal & Iron Company) located their furnaces on the banks of the river at the old pioneer crossing below the mouth of Battle Creek, and in the afflatus of the moment, named the place South Pittsburg. But, alack for such dreams, the subsequent great development at Birmingham overshadowed all the Tennessee developments and they finally dwindled to relatively modest dimensions or passed out entirely. And Chattanooga, instead of mushrooming up into a southern Pittsburgh, became, by more gradual increase, a city of diversified industry, good enough in its way, but a mere industrial crossroads compared with the northern giants that it envied and imitated. Yet the meaning of such enterprises, whether they languished or succeeded, was, in the general opinion, that heavy industry would at some time sit down in the Tennessee Valley to stay. Whether the sitting down would be on the terms of an Indian trade, with the valley dwellers on the Indian side of the deal, the Henry Grady men and other utopians never thought to ask.

Yet all the trading was not of the Indian trade sort. In one notable instance it took a reverse course, and a young Southerner, coming north, bought a great northern institution from under the very noses of the Yankees, set the tottering thing on its feet, and proceeded to make it world-famous.

This was Adolph S. Ochs, a Chattanoogan, who at the age of thirty-eight bought and reformed the New York *Times*, which had fallen into difficulties. Ochs was the son of Julius Ochs, a Bavarian Jew who had settled in Knoxville before the Civil War and had become prominent in Knoxville affairs as merchant and teacher. The career of the son, Adolph, might have been used to bolster up the badly shaken southern legend that one Southerner could whip ten Yankees. In Ochs's case, Reconstruction backfired, and a miracle occurred.

He grew up in Knoxville in the hard time after the war, worked on the Knoxville *Journal*, and learned at first hand every department of journalism. When the Chattanooga *Times* needed a buyer, Ochs bought it; he paid $250 cash and assumed a $1,500 debt. Despite the bumps of deflation and the skyrocketings of inflation, Ochs held it steady and made it into a good newspaper. He learned how to win financial battles on a small margin, but above all he learned how good a newspaper might be if it could keep out of futile bickering and sensationalism. It seems entirely probable that Adolph Ochs brought to New York not only some of the utopianism of the seventies and eighties, but a profound desire born of the tragic conflicts of the Reconstruction years, to offer the nation something other than the bitter partisanship that had rent his native state. It was luck that made the New York *Times* a salable article just as Ochs was ripe to buy it. It was personal character and solid achievement that made it possible for Ochs to buy the *Times*, as Elmer Davis has noted, for his ability rather than his cash. But it was, surely, the old bitter years in Tennessee, it was everything from Parson Brownlow's ragings down to the uproars and scandals of the boom periods, it was a plain, almost countrified Tennessee wit that made Adolph S. Ochs print in a box on the front page of the New York *Times* the famous slogan, current to this day: ALL THE NEWS THAT'S FIT TO PRINT. Those words, so often puzzled over and joked at by New Yorkers, are in principle the Tennessee of Reconstruction in revulsion against Reconstruction. They could hardly seem queer to a Tennessean, emerging from the shadow of Brownlowism and Radicalism, who had seen, most certainly, and that too often, what was not fit to print.

CHAPTER X

# The Last Great Days of the Steamboats

Wʜɪʟᴇ all such postbellum troubles and fervors were running their course, other people, not utopians of any sort, turned quite simply to the things that must be done. The cotton and corn were presently growing again and must be hauled. People must go about the world somehow, to trade, to see kinfolks, even to move away from their troubles into Texas or California. So, as the farmer put his hand again to the plow, the old rivermen of the Tennessee, and many new ones with them, put their hands to the wheel and tried the river once more.

God knows how they managed it. They must have gone heavily into debt, or perhaps, in the course of the speculative expansion, they found sponsors willing to go into debt. At any rate, within ten or fifteen years after the close of the Civil War, steamboat traffic was thriving on the Tennessee, especially on the Upper Tennessee, as never before. The Muscle Shoals problem was still unsolved, and therefore any regular through traffic for large steamboats was out of the question. The rivermen countered by building their own steamboats and treating the Upper Tennessee as virtually a separate river.

In view of the relatively small amount of boat building before the war, the shift of emphasis was remarkable. Between 1865 and 1900 at least thirty-eight steamboats (and probably others, unrecorded) were built on the Upper Tennessee. Out of the fifty or more steamboats known to have operated on the upper river during this period, probably not more than a half dozen were "brought up," as of old, from such points as St. Louis, Evansville, Cincinnati, and Pittsburgh. At Chattanooga, at least sixteen boats were built in thirty-five years; at Kingston, nine; at Knoxville, seven. Others were built at Decatur, Loudon, Dandridge, and smaller places. Sometimes, of course, the building was a rebuilding of an old boat, which was made over and given a new name.

Two of the first boats to go into service after the Civil War were from the fleet left above Muscle Shoals by the Federal army, to be sold at auction. These were the *Resaca*, which was bought and refitted by Captain Doss, and the *Kingston*, which was rebuilt and named the *Emma*. Other boats that came into service during the hard years were: the *Alert*, a fast, light-draft western boat owned by W. L. Dugger; the *Cherokee*; the *Ida*, a fast boat with a texas deck that was brought over Muscle Shoals "without a line" in the record time of six hours and forty minutes; the *Last Chance*; *Lucy Coker*; *Mary Byrd*; *Minnie*; *R. P. Converse*.

In these difficult years the "store boat" supplemented the regular packets. The *J. B. Allison* and the *H. C. Murry*, boats of this class, called the "chicken wagons of the river," carried groceries and miscellaneous supplies to rural folks along the shores, and no doubt, like the country store, took produce in return. The *H. C. Murry* also had a gristmill on board.

The *Last Chance* originally an Upper Mississippi boat, had iron sheathing on her paddle wheel. In one unusually cold season when the river began to freeze above Chattanooga, Captain C. S. Peak turned the *Last Chance* around in midstream and backed up. The iron-sheathed paddle wheel smashed the ice, and Captain Peak backed on and on. Presently he passed the *Emma*, tied up to wait for a thaw. Captain W. O. Jones of the *Emma* saw what he thought was opportunity, cast off, and followed in the ice-free wake of the *Last Chance*. But he got little business because the *Last Chance* had had first go.

The *Cherokee* was christened at Chattanooga in 1866 by Mrs. Tom Cowart, a descendant of the Cherokees, and was put into service by Captain Woods Wilson and associates. Her hull and woodwork were built at Dayton, and her engines and boilers were installed at Chattanooga.

In March, 1867, the *Cherokee* did notable service during the great flood—the worst ever recorded on the Tennessee—when the rise in the Suck was reported to be seventy feet. As the flood was mounting to its height, Captain Wilson took the *Cherokee* upriver. Everything that would float was coming down. The *Cherokee* met—or avoided meeting—rafts, logs, small boats, ferryboats, whole haystacks, barns, dwelling houses, and flatboats loaded with refugees and their goods or drifting aimlessly down. At the farm of Dr. J. W. Wester, Captain Wilson found the river running between the doctor's barns and his house. As the *Cherokee* took this chute, the doctor shouted from his porch: "Come in, gentlemen. I am always happy to entertain my neighbors when they call."

After stopping for the night at Loudon, Captain Wilson decided to return to Chattanooga. On the way back he called at Washington by the simple process of steaming for a mile and a half up the road that led to the town from the submerged landing. He then tied up on the main street of the town, had breakfast, and gave some Washington folks a ride over their own submerged farm lands.

At Chattanooga he found the military bridge was gone and the city in need of rescue work. There were marooned travelers who urgently wanted to reach Decatur, and Captain Wilson agreed to risk the dangers of the Suck at extreme floodtide and make for Decatur.

To navigate the Suck and the rest of the Narrows under such conditions was much like shooting the chute on an Alpine torrent. All that Captain Wilson could do was to back on the wheel with all power and steer. The raging current did the rest. The passengers, unconscious of danger, stayed on deck to admire the view—the swollen creeks, the rivulets pitching from the cliffs, the torrent of the river dashing against rocks and bouncing off in magnificent waves. But the sweating officers and crew could hardly bear to look. The *Cherokee* rushed down "at almost railroad speed," and was all but out of control. At one point the current seemed about to drive her against a bluff. The pilot had "given her all the wheel," but the rudders had no effect. Fortunately a rebounding current turned away her head in time to avoid collision, and she shot past, safe by a margin of only a few feet. The *Cherokee* made the 60-mile trip from Chattanooga to Bridgeport in less than two hours, and later delivered her passengers at Decatur.

In time, the *Cherokee* was bought by Hugh Martin, who renovated her and gave her his own name. As the *Hugh Martin*, she had an unlucky career. In 1871 her captain, John Fritts, killed L. J. Coker, of the *Lucy Coker*, in a shooting affair. Soon afterward, Martin sold the boat to the Allison brothers, who had a contract to carry the mail. During a freshet, the *Hugh Martin* ran aground and could not be quickly got off. Since the mail had to be delivered, the Allisons made a quick trade with Captain Jacob Fritts and swapped the stranded *Hugh Martin* for the *Emory City*. In 1875, just as Captain Fritts was bringing the *Hugh Martin* into Washington Landing, the boiler exploded. Captain Fritts and two other persons were killed. The hulk of the *Hugh Martin* was left in the river, and still lies in the water near old Washington Landing.

The Allisons were one of several groups of brothers who followed the river. At Chattanooga the Kindrick brothers —J. P. and W. E.—built up a fleet that combined old-style packets and new-style towboats. The Kindricks acquired the *City of Knoxville* from the Nicholson brothers of Knoxville and added to their list the *R. M. Bishop* and the *J. T. Wilder*, the latter of which had carried pig iron for General Wilder's Roane Iron Company. The *J. T. Wilder*, in turn, was bought by the Gunter brothers—R. C., J. M., and Cue—who operated boats between Chattanooga and Decatur. They fitted her with a texas deck and renamed her *R. C. Gunter*.

In the eighteen-eighties the Kindricks rebuilt the *Bishop* and named her *W. L. Dugger*. The *Dugger* caught on fire at the Chattanooga wharf. T. J. Campbell, in *The Upper Tennessee*, relates that two rival fire companies answered the alarm. Neither had a hose long enough to reach the endangered steamboat, but the hose pipes of the two companies, if coupled, would have done the job. Instead of coupling, the rival companies argued. While they argued, the *W. L. Dugger* burned.

During the yellow fever epidemic of the eighteen-seventies some of these steamboats stood by and did valiant service for the stricken city of Chattanooga. While Adolph Ochs's newspaper, The Chattanooga *Times*, cheered the public by printing such sardonic quips as "The hospital is awful handy to the graveyard" or "11 deaths yesterday and more coming. Trot out your next funeral," the *R. M. Bishop* continued to bring mail and supplies to the quarantined and all but deserted city. Both the *Bishop* and the *Wilder*, at an earlier stage, carried refugees away to the mountains.

Although it was becoming evident that the towboat-and-barge combination might turn out to be the most practical solution of the problem of handling increased freight tonnage, the old-style packets continued to flourish. Their great days, on the Upper Tennessee, were in the two decades from 1880 to 1900, when packets enjoyed a Golden Era comparable, in a modest way, to the pre-Civil War period on the Ohio and Mississippi. The *Robert R. Anderson*, a packet of about 200 tons burden, built at Whitesburg, Alabama, was put into service at Chattanooga in 1879. She had twenty-four staterooms and accommodated 75 cabin and 50 deck passengers. The *J. C. Warner*, a packet of 347 tons, rebuilt from the old *City of Knoxville*, went into service in 1882 and became one of the most successful boats on the river. In the nineties several popular boats were named for Confederate heroes. The *N. B. Forrest*, a small, fast boat which came on the river in 1897, and the *Joe Wheeler*, which appeared in 1898 just as General Wheeler was making his second bid for fame, in the Spanish-American War, were owned by the Tennessee River Navigation Company. The *Joe Wheeler* ran for twenty-one years in the Chattanooga trade. The *N. B. Forrest* lasted until 1910, and then, transformed into the *James N. Trigg*, served into later times. There was also a *Sam Davis* which ran on the middle section of the river, and a *General Joe Wheeler*, an independent packet which operated out of Decatur for a short while.

The *J. C. Warner* is remembered on the Tennessee for her association with Captain W. C. Wilkey, one of the notable rivermen of the later days. Wilkey was a protégé of the old pioneer, Captain J. L. Doss. In the compass of their two lives these two men knew all there was to be known in a century of steamboating on the Upper Tennessee, from the days of the first *Knoxville* to the advent of the modern towboat. A raw country lad, Wilkey came to Captain Doss at Kingston Landing soon after the Civil War and asked for a job.

"What can you do?" asked Captain Doss.

"Anything," answered Wilkey. Then, seeing the roustabouts at their work, he added, "I can carry corn."

Captain Doss enrolled the boy as a deck hand and put him to work. From that beginning Wilkey went steadily up, all the degrees, from mate to pilot to master. At his death in 1918 he was manager of two lines of steamboats operating out of Chattanooga.

Not content with the regular runs between Chattanooga and Knoxville, and Chattanooga and Decatur, the men of the river began to develop segments of the local trade, as between Knoxville and Kingston, and to push light-draft boats up the shoal-infested tributaries of the Upper Tennessee. Earlier, old Captain Doss had navigated the Holston and once had taken the *Resaca* up the Little Tennessee almost to the North Carolina line, or so it was said. In the eighties and nineties steamboats ran regularly from Knoxville up the French Broad to Dandridge. In 1891 the *Lucille Borden* made ninety-six trips up the French Broad.

The name of Captain Ambrose B. Underwood of Knoxville, who was born on the French Broad River and remained in active service on the Upper Tennessee for more than fifty years, is associated with the *Lucille Borden*, and with the *Onega* (locally called the "O'Nigger"), *Flora Swann,* and other small, light-draft boats. Whoever navigated the Holston and French Broad, as Captain Underwood did, must know all the tricks of conquering shallow water. On the French Broad he had to deal with such obstacles as the shoals pertinently named Jumping Moses, Red Bank, The Gallops, Wild Bull, and Seven Islands. When steamboats could not run, he used the riverman's last reliance, the flatboat.

Captain Underwood brought up his two sons, Paul and Harris, to the life of the river. In the twentieth century, when the old river was changing into a new river, Paul and Harris Underwood, as Tennessee River pilots, had a background of experience that few could equal. With their father they had poled a flatboat *up* the French Broad, keelboat style. As deck hands they had jumped out to carry the warping line ahead, bounding through shallows and over rocks, and had toiled for hours to coax a steamboat a few hundred yards upstream against the swift currents of the Skillet or the Suck. They could even remember how their father carried an old horse on board the heavy flatboat of other days; and how Captain Underwood, when more locomotion was needed, would get that old horse out into the shallow water, hitch him to the boat, and whip him up to pull, as if the boat were a wagon, then load the horse again when they were over a shoal.

There was also Captain Ben Ferguson, who operated light-draft boats between Charleston, on the Hiwassee, and points on the Tennessee. The *City of Charleston* was one of the Ferguson boats. And meanwhile, in the Great Bend, Captain G. W. Swartz specialized in small boats that could go back and forth over Muscle Shoals. His boats were the *Clinton B. Fiske*, *W. J. Bryan*, and *Buck Lindsay*. The *Lindsay*, an exceptionally small boat of 14 tons burden, was an oil burner and used a caterpillar-wheel drive.

In 1898, faith in packets was so strong that the Chattanooga and Tennessee River Packet Company brought into service the *Avalon*, a large and unusually commodious steamboat, specially fitted for passenger and general service. She was the largest steamboat to operate with Chattanooga as home port during the later period, and her owners ambitiously attempted to use her on the through run to Ohio and Mississippi ports. The attempt was not a success, and the *Avalon* left the Tennessee for the Ohio trade.

The situation on the Upper Tennessee was becoming confused and uncertain by the turn of the century. Archaic forms of river transport still mixed with forms that were merely old-fashioned or that carried premonitions of changing times ahead. There were no longer any keelboats, but log rafts still came down the Clinch and other tributary rivers on the spring tide, the raftsmen shouting in wild competition as they rode the spate. And flatboats still tied up in great numbers at Chattanooga alongside handsome packets like the *Avalon*. But the towboat pushing its barges became a more common sight. At first it might be a boat like the *M. H. Clift*, operated by the Soddy Coal Company to carry the bulky product of its mines; or the twin towboats *Guntersville* and *Huntsville*, used by the N. C. & St. L. Railroad to ferry freight cars between Hobbs Island and Guntersville.

It may seem strange that steamboating prospered so mightily on the Tennessee during the very years of reconstruction and readjustment that were in general tragic for the valley. One possible reason for the prosperity of the steamboats was that they had little competition during this period from their later rivals, the railroads. It took a long time for the railroads to recover from the devastation of the Civil War. Long stretches of road had to be rebuilt entirely, and new rolling stock had to be acquired. The process of recovery, even when it got under way, was not always sound and steady. Furthermore, since the prewar railroads had been built in part to link with river traffic and supplement it, the first recovery was mainly a restoration of old, noncompetitive arrangements.

Even during the best period there was much difference between river traffic below and above Muscle Shoals. The Lower Tennessee was, as of old, the domain of the Ohio and Mississippi boats. In that stretch the St. Louis and Cincinnati interests competed for the trade, and locally owned boats were at a disadvantage. As late as 1900, when the great decline was already beginning above Muscle Shoals, thirty-six steamers were still plying between Florence and Paducah; in 1901 there were forty-nine. On the long, relatively unobstructed stretch of the Lower Tennessee, which could be navigated for most of the year, these boats could carry a large volume of freight with some passengers, and could maintain regular schedules. Even a decade later, people who traveled from Savannah or Clifton to points in Middle Tennessee customarily took the steamboat up to Johnsonville and there got the train for Nashville. Since steamboat and train schedules did not co-ordinate, this trip often involved a good deal of waiting at Johnsonville.

Since Colbert Shoals was a low-water obstruction of importance, it was still necessary, up to 1911, to make a transfer below Florence, for a through trip. Riverton, which had developed a railroad connection with the Memphis division of the Southern Railway (successor to the Memphis & Charleston), now took over the function formerly monopolized by Waterloo, and later invaded to some extent by

Eastport. Riverton now had its day as river terminal and transfer point. The *City of Florence* served as a shuttle boat in the later period, on this stretch where the *Muscle* and other boats once went, attended by their faithful keels.

Some of the boats using the Lower Tennessee around the turn of the century were: *City of Paducah, City of Sheffield, Edgar Cherry, Jack Frost, James Y. Lockwood, Josie, Louis Houck, Mary M. Michael, Mayflower, Tennessee.* A few of these were large, powerful boats. The *Mayflower* could carry 718 tons; the *Louis Houck*, 620; the *Clyde*, 335; the *Jack Frost*, 350. The *Clyde* and the *Tennessee* continued in operation until later decades.

In the memory of rivermen, the best boats of 1900 to 1910 and years following were: the *City of Clifton*, built in 1909; *City of Savannah; Saltillo*, built in 1906 by the Howard Shipyards. Captain Harry Crain was master of the *City of Clifton* and the *Saltillo*, but he had bad luck with these boats. The *City of Clifton* burned near her name-town, Clifton. The *Saltillo*, in a notable disaster, ran into a bluff on leaving St. Louis and sank with the loss of nine lives, among them persons prominent in Paducah and Nashville. For some strange reason wrecks were more frequent during this period of river improvement than in the old, haphazard, unimproved days of warps and keelboats. The shuttle boat, *City of Florence*, collided with the *Tommyhawk* and sank, a total loss, with two persons drowned. The *City of Nashville*, a St. Louis and Tennessee River Packet Company boat, burned near Birmingham, Kentucky; the mate threw a bale of cotton overboard, mounted on it, and floated ten miles before he was rescued. The *French* burned at the mouth of Big Sandy River. The *P. D. Staggs* struck Johnsonville bridge and sank, up to the boiler deck, and in that condition floated helpless down to Joppa, Illinois. The *Peter Hontz*, a towboat, blew up on July 1, 1901, with a loss of four lives. The *St. Louis* and the *Will J. Cummins* hit obstructions and sank.

But the *Alabama, Kentucky, Paducah, Tennessee Belle,* and *Tom Powell* escaped such disaster.

The old thorn, Muscle Shoals, still pricked. In fact it seemed more than ever a festering evil to river-minded people. At Chattanooga, particularly, there were people with heavy industrial goods to ship. They urgently wanted to send these, as cheaply as possible, to Ohio and Mississippi ports. Their want became the more urgent as Chattanooga grew and grew, and enlarged its industrial ambitions accordingly. Undoubtedly the new attack on the Muscle Shoals problem was prompted to a considerable degree by their solicitations, which joined insistently with the old perennial and always eloquent pleas of North Alabama.

And undoubtedly, too, their solicitations as to river improvements were not always completely disingenuous. A new motive had entered. They might ship their heavy goods by river, yes, if the river was improved; but then they might ship by rail if rail rates could be driven down. If the river were improved, steamboats could compete with the now growingly rambunctious railroads, which were becoming somewhat baronial as to rates. River improvements could be used to drive down freight rates. At government expense, too. It was being done everywhere. Why not in the Tennessee Valley?

The pressure became intense, and the result was that the second Muscle Shoals Canal was completed, after a long struggle, and was opened to use in 1890. Surveys by W. B. Gaw and by Major Walter McFarland prepared the way for this second great attempt to solve the Muscle Shoals problem. Finally, in 1875, nearly forty years after the abandonment of the old Muscle Shoals Canal, construction work began on the new one. The United States government, not the state of Alabama, was to pay the bill this time, and the army engineer officers were not "loaned" as of old but worked directly under federal authority. Yet such was the pace of engineering operations or the flow of appropriations from Congress that it took fifteen years to finish the job.

The new project in large measure was a restoration, an improvement, and an extension of the original Alabama canal, which had been rightly planned but incompletely executed. The old stonework, indeed, was still there, though obscured by siltage and tree growth.

The engineers widened and straightened the 14.5-mile length of the old canal and reduced the number of locks to nine. They dammed the creeks that emptied into the canal, and over the mouth of Shoal Creek, the worst offender, they provided an aqueduct, 900 feet long and 60 feet wide. A steamboat passing through this aqueduct gave, to an onlooker, the odd impression of a boat passing above the water by means of a bridge, for the aqueduct had wooden trestle work underneath. The engineers added a short canal, with two locks, at troublesome Elk River Shoals. Between Elk River Shoals and Muscle Shoals Canal they left the river open, but blasted a channel through Nance's Reef which would allow a low-water clearance of 2.5 feet. Although they recognized the need of a canal at Little Muscle Shoals too, and recommended one, this project was not carried out. They tried to make channel improvements do and were content with blasting the rocks and dredging. Alongside the canal they built a 14-mile railroad for construction operations, and then used it as a permanent towpath for the canal. The locomotives of this small railroad pulled steamboats through the winding reaches of the canal. When little boats appeared—canoes, yawls, skiffs—they hoisted these bodily upon flatcars and trundled them overland to avoid lockage. This arrangement gave old users of the river some novel sensations.

Various engineer officers contributed to this work. Much of it was under the general direction of Colonel J. W. Barlow, and some modifications were made on the basis of a report by Major W. R. King. But in its final stages the work acquired, in the light of subsequent history, an unusual notability, because it was in charge of a young engineer captain named George W. Goethals, later the builder of the Panama Canal.

In 1884, aging General William Tecumseh Sherman, then commander in chief, had noted the young West Pointer's work and had predicted for him a brilliant future. "The finest young officer on this coast," wrote Sherman to a friend, when Goethals was on duty in the Northwest. When work on the Muscle Shoals Canal dragged on endlessly and criticism began to boil up, the chief of engineers, General Thomas L. Casey, sent Goethals to the Tennessee River to hurry the job to completion. General Casey told Goethals that there had already been too many delays and postponements. A hearing on the rate case was about to come up at Chattanooga. It was important to finish the canal, declare it open, and put a loaded steamboat through it before the case was heard. The desired rate reduction depended upon proof that the canal was open to navigation. Captain Goethals took personal charge at once, organized day and night shifts, supervised the night shift himself, finished the canal, and got a St. Louis steamboat through to Chattanooga the day before the hearing was scheduled.

Goethals remained on his Tennessee River job for three years, and the stay was useful to him in his later work at Panama. The 14-mile railroad-towpath gave him experience in railroad building and management. In his subsequent work on the Riverton lock, which he designed and initiated, Goethals learned much about the shifty ways of quicksands and slides; he also determined, to his and others' satisfaction, the feasibility of a high-lift lock. At the Riverton lock, a part of a project planned for Colbert Shoals, it was first proposed to build two locks, each with a lift of 13 feet. Goethals designed a single lock with a lift of 26 feet—a higher lift than had been previously attempted in the United States. According to his biographers, Joseph Bucklin Bishop and Farnham

Bishop, the Riverton lock established a precedent. It "broke the trail for Gatun," in the Panama system.

The second Muscle Shoals Canal was a permanent improvement. It really worked, at least over the Big Muscle Shoals stretch and Elk River Shoals. There was an immediate increase in traffic. Very likely the prosperity of steamboat traffic on the Upper Tennessee during the nineties owed much to the canal.

Yet it was still not a complete solution of the Muscle Shoals problem. The numerous creeks that discharged into the canal kept the caretakers busy dredging out sediment and in flood seasons sometimes caused breaks in the canal walls. Hundreds of drift logs had to be taken out at every floodtide. Worst of all, the channel work at Nance's Reef proved to be insufficient, and at Little Muscle Shoals the crooked channel, the swift current, and the shallowness of the water above the rock bed still made navigation impracticable when the river was low.

Furthermore, while the canal-plus-channel-improvement system was helpful to packets, it did not provide safe navigating conditions for the new-style towboats with their strings of barges. The *City of Chattanooga*, a powerful towboat of over five hundred tons burden, owned by the Chattanooga Steamboat Company, was wrecked while pushing her barges through Little Muscle Shoals. She struck the rocks which the engineers had blasted out and piled near the channel, and sank at once, though her barges remained afloat. Her owners hastened to the scene, raised the *City of Chattanooga*, took her to the canal harbor, repaired her, and sent her through again. Again the *City of Chattanooga* struck the rocks, and once more she sank. The owners raised her one more time and kept her afloat long enough to sell her to an Ohio company. Then the Chattanooga Steamboat Company suspended operations.

Yet although this important work in the Muscle Shoals region was only partially successful, and river traffic presently

began its last stage of decline, the old demand for improvement of the Tennessee remained steady and kept enough momentum to bring about further changes at difficult points. In 1911 the Colbert Shoals Canal was opened. It eliminated the obstacles at Colbert and Bee Tree Shoals, and steamboats no longer had to halt their upstream progress at Riverton. Not far ahead, too, was Hales Bar Dam, which would tame the Narrows of the Tennessee at last, and beyond that would come other and bigger improvements: low navigation dams at Bellefonte Island and Widow's Bar; and finally Wilson Dam.

But all this time steamboat traffic was falling off. The better the navigation facilities became, the fewer the steamboats. By the nineteen-twenties steamboat traffic had almost reached the vanishing point, at least on the Upper Tennessee.

Before the packets surrendered, however, they had one champion that triumphed over her snub-nosed, ungenteel rival, the towboat, and triumphed most devastatingly. The race between the *John A. Patten* and the *Parker* is remembered by old rivermen, perhaps for what it symbolizes no less than for the sheer and tragic excitement of the event.

The *John A. Patten*, called "perhaps the finest and handsomest packet ever operated on the Tennessee," was built at Jeffersonville, Indiana, in 1906. The *Parker* was a powerful towboat operated by a sand and gravel company. The rivalry between the two boats was partly, it would seem, a rivalry of brothers. Will Thompson was pilot of the *Patten*; Bob Allison was her engineer. The brothers of these men held the same positions, respectively, on the *Parker*, which had Jim Thompson as pilot and Jess Allison for engineer. The two boats began their race on leaving Chattanooga for a run downriver, the *Patten* with her usual load of freight and passengers, the *Parker* with a tow of empty barges. For more efficient operation, the crew of the *Parker* had pulled the bow of their boat up with chain tongs fastened securely to the barges. Thus, when the full power of the engines was applied, the bow would not be driven under the water.

The two boats raced on about even terms until they drew near the tip of Williams Island. At that point the *Parker* began to move ahead. Farmers who saw the occurrence from the shore said that the *Parker* at this moment was "literally jumping through the water." Jess Allison, the engineer, without telling his pilot, had tied down the *Parker's* "pop valve" to generate an extra head of steam. As the *Parker* began to draw ahead of her rival, Jess Allison stood in the door of his engine room and gestured tauntingly with a rope, as if to offer a tow to the rival boat. But the next moment, when he threw in his large pump to supply more water to his red-hot and overtaxed boilers, the *Parker* blew up. Allison was blown through his engine room and into the water. He swam to safety, but he had not a tooth left in his mouth. Jim Thompson, the pilot, landed senseless on a plank, from which the crew of the *Patten* rescued him, just as he was about to sink. Three members of the crew were killed outright. Two of the bodies were discovered, months later, but the body of the Negro fireman, pinned underneath the heavy ashpan in the shallows could not be retrieved, and his skeleton, cleaned by the tides, is said to lie there still. One boiler was blown on to Williams Island itself, another into the water. The *Parker* was a wreck, but its powerful engines were salvaged and today are doing service on a modern towboat.

The *John A. Patten*, which had seen her rival perish utterly, the victim of her own impudent trifling with the power of steam, did not survive to experience the humiliation that was visited ultimately upon most packets. The snub-nosed towboats would finally rule the waters, but the *Patten* would not be converted into a wharfboat, as some packets were, or into a covered barge or towboat, as others were. The *Patten* caught fire while lying at Bridgeport in

1910. She burned completely, and was a total loss, to the amount of $22,500.

Other packets might as well have burned. Their fight against towboats was hopeless. But all river shipping gradually declined, as time went on, and the great cause of the decline was the competition of railroads. While the river people worried about navigating conditions, the railroads captured the trade, and people in general got used to a new pattern of transportation. In the first stages of the fight between steamboats and railroads, it seemed at times that the steamboats had some advantage. They could offer cheap rates for the shipment of heavy goods that did not have to move speedily. But the railroads found ways of nipping off steamboat competition. They bought into steamboat lines, got control of waterfronts and terminal facilities, and manipulated their tariffs so as to offer very low rates at points where there was steamboat competition and relatively high rates at intermediate points where there was no such competition.

The mortal results of the battle between the two forms of transportation are suggested in the history of the various navigation companies that hopefully started up at Chattanooga during the heyday of the packets in the late nineties. Of half a dozen or more companies organized between 1888 and 1902, only one, the Tennessee River Navigation Company, survived into the modern period, and in the end it became a rather puny survivor.

The Kingdom, so many times promised, so many times almost realized, was not coming after all, it seemed. Not for the people who were fond of river transport and believed in it. True, there was something in the towboat idea—especially if the government ever got around to finishing the job at Little Muscle Shoals, Nance's Reef, and such points. Even that possibility at times seemed like a very faint hope. But the Chattanoogans, the Tri-Cities people at Florence, Tuscumbia, and Sheffield, the Knoxville people, the Decatur people, kept protesting that the problems of the Tennessee River must be solved, and, God and the federal government assisting them, would sometime be solved.

The frogs of Aesop's fable asked for a king, and Jupiter sent them a log. Discontented still, they hopped upon that useless log and croaked that they deserved a better king. Whereupon Jupiter sent them King Stork.

A King was about to arrive in the Tennessee Valley, but his name was not Stork. The name was Kilowatt.

CHAPTER XI

# The Uneasy Reign of King Kilowatt I

THE TALE OF HOW Kilowatt became king of the Tennessee is no wonder tale of modern science, but it might be called a saga if the term is used as in Galsworthy's *Forsyte Saga*. Those who sought to enthrone Kilowatt were southern Forsytes—promoters of the "New South" persuasion. Electricity was becoming a salable article. To make a light by turning a switch on a glass bulb was deemed an act of virtue and progress, just as, earlier, it had seemed admirable to ascend from candles to coal oil, and from coal oil to gas. The mysterious current, which Mr. Thomas A. Edison had taught to glow in the incandescent lamp, was being made to run streetcars, too, and it would undoubtedly develop other uses.

Now, in a burst of revelation, it was perceived that the great nuisance, Muscle Shoals, was really a kind of waterfall and would generate electricity if properly improved. The very thing that made Muscle Shoals irritating and dangerous to steamboat people endowed it with interesting possibilities to other people. Why not, they said, persuade the federal government to allow power production facilities to be incorporated in a dam that, from the legal standpoint, would be an orthodox navigation improvement? This thought was something that even a Republican Congress during the McKinley administration might hearken to. Therefore the old

Confederate cavalry leader, Joe Wheeler, representing Alabama in Congress, introduced a bill on March 21, 1898, which asked consent for the erection and operation, by an Alabama company, of a hydroelectric project at Muscle Shoals. Nothing came of this effort, although the bill passed Congress; but the history of the Tennessee Valley Authority must, in principle, be dated from this moment. From 1898 until the passage of the TVA Act in 1933 every session of Congress had before it, in some form or other, legislation dealing with Muscle Shoals, and the most consistent sponsors of this legislation were the Alabama delegation in Congress.

Meanwhile, at Chattanooga, persons of similar mind remembered that they had a famous navigation obstacle to overcome—the still unconquered Narrows of the Tennessee. They, too, proposed to combine navigation improvement and power. Their plea was successful, and in 1903 Congress authorized a dam to be built. In 1905 the Hales Bar site, thirty-three river miles below Chattanooga, was selected, and construction began. It was a high dam by the standards of that day. It had a lock lift of 33 feet, and the lock chamber was 60 by 267 feet, dimensions which seemed ample at the time. By agreement, the Tennessee Electric Power Company erected the dam under the supervision of the army engineers. The federal government retained title to the dam, lock, and reservoir, and received certain other concessions. In return the company received a 99-year franchise for the generation of power. Thus Hales Bar Dam, completed in 1913, became the first combined navigation-and-power improvement on the Tennessee River system. It ended the ancient perils of the Suck, Boiling Pot, Skillet, and Pan—though the fog, the winding channel, and the tricky currents remained. Since it inundated only a relatively worthless mountain ravine and made it possible for people in greater numbers to turn on Mr. Edison's incandescent bulb, everybody who took notice of the event was quietly happy. Nobody bothered to think of the Tennessee Electric Power Company as endowed with more malevolence than any other corporation. Rather, in the fashion of the times, it was viewed as a public benefactor. Nobody bothered, either, to notice that few boats were left to use the thirty-three miles of good slackwater.

If Europe had not gone to war in 1914, it is possible that the pattern of the Hales Bar project would have been followed at Muscle Shoals and elsewhere on the Tennessee. There would have been more navigation-and-power dams, but they would have been isolated, conservative improvements of the Hales Bar type—joint projects of government and private interests, or government subsidies of private interests if one prefers to take that view.

In North Alabama certain people, especially in the Tri-Cities area, were bent on such development, and they applied a quiet, insistent pressure where pressure would do good. The Tennessee River Improvement Association, an organization of frankly promotional character, had long been one of the instruments for applying pressure. John A. Patten of Chattanooga was its president, and it embodied the joint interests of Chattanooga and North Alabama, with some elements from up and down the river. The driving force of the movement, however, came from the Tri-Cities and centered in the efforts of the Muscle Shoals Hydroelectric Company to secure Congressional approval of a joint development by the government and the company at Muscle Shoals.

Behind the drive was a guiding genius, a man of extraordinary resourcefulness and insight who made the improvement of Muscle Shoals the passion of his life, yet who stayed so consistently away from the spotlight of publicity that in 1947 no sketch of his life, and hardly any notice of his activities, appeared in the common sources of information.

This genius was J. W. Worthington, a native Alabamian, who at the age of forty-six came to Sheffield to share in and promote its rising industrial hopes. His local connection was with the Sheffield Company, a northern-owned utility that operated light, power, and streetcar facilities at Sheffield, and he had other business interests; but it was in his role as promoter of the Muscle Shoals project that Worthington influenced the course of history. If from one point of view Senator Norris was entitled to be called "Father of TVA," then, from another point of view, Worthington was certainly TVA's grandfather; and although not one of the great TVA dams was named for Worthington, all were, in a sense, memorials to his endeavors.

By 1906 the Muscle Shoals Hydroelectric Company, of which Worthington at that time was vice-president, had entered the field with a proposal that predicted later developments and was in all respects farsighted and ambitious. The new plan called for *three* navigation-and-power dams in the Muscle Shoals area, to be undertaken as a joint investment of the government and the company. The plan was not accepted, but it set forth the essentials of the design followed in a long series of later proposals. There is every reason to believe that Worthington's capacity for adapting the first design to new engineering possibilities, no less than his political adroitness and his determination, kept the Muscle Shoals project alive.

Worthington was involved in a web of interests, which political opponents later held against him, but somehow he made all contribute to the Muscle Shoals development. His friend, Frank Washburn, was president of the Muscle Shoals Company up to 1912, after which Worthington was president until 1920. Both men were interested, for a period, in the Alabama Power Company, which finally absorbed the Muscle Shoals Company. But Washburn's chief concern was with the American Cyanamid Company, of which he was president, and he was interested in Muscle Shoals for its electrochemical and metallurgical possibilities. By 1920 both men had quarreled with the Alabama Power Company and had severed their connection with it. Up to the building of Wilson Dam, Worthington's contribution to the Muscle Shoals project had three main features: he had broadened the engineering plan, in terms of navigation and power; he had figured out a plausible financial basis for joint investment; and he finally added, to navigation and power, the possibility of manufacturing nitrates.

Prior to 1916, however, all the proposals advanced fell through for one reason or another. There was opposition in Congress, especially from Republicans of the conservationist school, led by Theodore Burton of Ohio. The army engineers, being navigation-minded, were slow to approve the sweeping new plans. Worthington, it would seem, was gradually able to persuade the engineers to his view. The surveys and reports of the engineers during the years preceding the entrance of the United States into World War I indicate the change. The Rivers and Harbors Act of 1915, for example, directed that the Muscle Shoals section of the river be studied for the purpose of combining navigation improvement with power development, with the understanding that plans be prepared in collaboration with the engineers of the Muscle Shoals Hydroelectric Company. Major H. Burgess, in his report of March, 1916, recommended approval of the Muscle Shoals project and stated, as an assumed principle, "that the radical improvement of this river appears to rest on the economic practicability of co-operation between the power interests and the navigation interests."

At this point the Muscle Shoals Company, despite continued opposition in Congress, was seemingly within reach of its goal. But the Imperial German Navy decided otherwise. German submarines scared Washington into wondering whether, if the United States should go to war, the country might be cut off from its supply of Chilean nitrates. This lamentable contingency offered a new talking point for the Muscle Shoals project. In May, 1915, the Tennessee River Improvement Association entertained a large delegation of congressmen and other dignitaries. The three-day junket included a barbecue and a steamboat trip through the Muscle Shoals area, and tours to Chattanooga and Knoxville. The visitors were presented with a handsomely illustrated souvenir booklet which emphasized, along with navigation and power, the adaptability of the Muscle Shoals project to the production of nitrates and ammonium phosphate.

The National Defense Act of 1916, however, ended the hopes of the Muscle Shoals Company. Section 124 of that act provided that the president, after investigation, should select whatever site or sites within the United States might best be utilized "for the production of nitrates or other products needed for munitions of war and useful in the manufacture of fertilizers . . ." But it added, forbiddingly: "The plant or plants . . . shall be constructed and operated solely by the Government and not in conjunction with any other industry or enterprise carried on by private capital." In view of the latter clause, the chief of engineers recommended that action on the proposed contract with the Muscle Shoals Company be postponed. Section 124 represented an embodiment in the act of a surprise bill for government ownership introduced by Senator Ellison D. Smith of South Carolina.

But the hopes of Worthington and his friends, who were now about to break with the Alabama Power Company, shifted to a new basis. When the United States entered the war, any very elaborate consideration of the choice of a "site or sites" was cut short. Worthington learned that President Wilson had asked Secretary Newton D. Baker to make an immediate recommendation and that Baker was inclining toward a North Chattanooga site. He prevailed upon Senator Oscar Underwood of Alabama to go directly to the president. Underwood visited the White House promptly, in company with Kenneth D. McKellar, newly elected senator from Tennessee. Shortly afterwards, President Wilson sent Baker the following memorandum: "Advise Chief of Staff I have selected Sheffield."

So the decision was made, and the great Muscle Shoals project, out of which TVA grew, began, under government responsibility, as a defense measure. Doubtless Senators Underwood and McKellar, in urging the "Sheffield site," did not fail to point out that Muscle Shoals, where so much water power could be developed, was deep in the interior of the continent, with a mountain barrier to the east, and was far from any harm that could be wrought by any enemy then conceivable. The great project would assist navigation, develop power, and manufacture nitrates for explosives or fertilizer.

The plan of the engineers, much like the earlier plans of the Muscle Shoals Company, called for a group of three dams. The main dam—called Dam No. 2 by the engineers and afterwards named Wilson Dam—would be a massive structure 137 feet high. Hugh L. Cooper, the designer, gave its architecture a restrained touch of the classic, for not yet was it thought that function and mass alone could impart beauty to a public enterprise. Its arches, like a graceful colonnade, would span the river for a length of 4,860 feet at the lower end of Big Muscle Shoals. It would have two locks in tandem, with a doublelift of 90 feet. The lock chambers would be 60 by 300 feet—ample dimensions for such river traffic as could be visualized. Along the great embankment a highway would run from shore to shore. Wilson Dam would be the grandest thing in the United States.

Fifteen miles above Wilson Dam the engineers planned Dam No. 3, to drown out old obstacles and generate more power. Below Wilson Dam they aimed to build a canal with a low-lift navigation lock to end the old trouble at Little Muscle Shoals.

There were to be two of the indispensable nitrate plants and they were supposed to achieve fixation of atmospheric nitrogen by two different processes. Plant No. 1, an experimental plant, was designed for the production of ammonium nitrate by the Haber process. Plant No. 2 was to use the cyanamid process. Despite the expenditure of $13,000,000 at Plant No. 1, it never got into continuous operation, never completed but one of its units, and was in fact obsolete all along. Plant No. 2 was not ready to produce ammonium nitrate until after the war was over. It made a test run in 1919 and was then held in stand-by condition. Plant No. 2, with the two auxiliary steam-power plants and other properties, cost $69,000,000 in all. Wilson Dam was not finished when the war was over. It was only thirty-five per cent finished by 1921, when the moneys previously appropriated by Congress were exhausted, and work was stopped. It stood there, incomplete, an obstruction instead of a help.

The great Muscle Shoals project looked very sick. Its contribution to the war effort had been just about zero. It was an embarrassing moment for North Alabama and for the congressmen who had sponsored Muscle Shoals development. King Kilowatt I was tottering on his throne.

In preparation for the presidential campaign of 1920, Republican congressmen assailed the project, charged that the nitrate program was a costly failure, and made political capital out of the connections of Worthington and Washburn. Once in power, the Harding administration took the position that the Muscle Shoals project was a white elephant and had better be sold. In March, 1921, Secretary of War John W. Weeks invited buyers to make their offers. Silence followed. There were no offers. The chief of engineers advertised for bids. Still, for a while, there were no bids.

Then, to the accompaniment of crackling newspaper headlines, Henry Ford came forward and on July 8, 1921, made his historic offer. The great industrialist would pay the government $5,000,000 for the nitrate plants, the steam-power facilities, and other miscellaneous property. He offered to finish Wilson Dam and Dam No. 3 for the government at cost, provided dams and power plants were leased to him for a hundred years. He promised, more vaguely, to manufacture nitrogenous fertilizer.

Exactly what Henry Ford planned ultimately to do in the Muscle Shoals region was never fully disclosed. But he spoke a gospel that North Alabama ears were wide open to receive, and his antipathy to Wall Street and his works-in-general made him popular with farmers and little businessmen everywhere. What the country did not know was that J. W. Worthington was now fighting the Alabama Power Company, which hoped to buy the Muscle Shoals project for a song; that he had persuaded Henry Ford to enter the field; and that he had devised the terms of the Ford offer. These terms, especially in the provisions for repayment of costs over a 100-year period, followed closely the terms of a proposal made by Worthington for the Muscle Shoals Hydroelectric Company in 1913, and in certain features foreshadowed the cost-allocation plan later adopted by Congress for TVA.

The Ford offer brought the Muscle Shoals question into the full glare of national publicity as nothing else could have done. Almost immediately Senator Norris secured an appropriation to resume construction, and so Wilson Dam was finished in 1926, powerhouse and all, at a cost of about $47,000,000. In the Muscle Shoals area itself there was tremendous excitement. The Ford offer was like commutation of a death sentence. It offered new life, in terms that the Alabama people had been teaching themselves to hold productive of good. The Tri-Cities, never backward in such matters, developed a boom, which was quickly and ruthlessly exploited by speculative interests in New York and elsewhere. God's infinite blessings, the Alabama people felt, were about to be showered upon them. The great industrialist would create a great industrial metropolis. At long last southern enterprise would compete with northern or eastern enterprise on something like equal terms. They had hardly dared hope for such bliss. Country singers caught up the theme and added a crudely eloquent stanza to the song, "On the Dixie Bee Line":

> Henry Ford went to Muscle Shoals
> To bring to the people of the South pure gold.
> Let him have it, says O my Lord!
> The Lord's ridin' in Heaven on a Henry Ford.

But enthusiasm slowly ebbed as a bitter fight developed in Congress over the Ford offer. Ford advocates were caught in a tangle of complications and delays.

The private power companies, especially the Alabama Power Company, which had been circling cautiously in the hope that the government property would be dumped like worthless carrion, were compelled to end their watchful waiting. They flapped down from on high and made their own offers. They had hoped to get Muscle Shoals for its power facilities without promising to manufacture fertilizer. Now, since Ford had promised fertilizer, they had to.

Discussion of the Muscle Shoals problem dragged on and on. The Ford offer had tremendous popular support, and it was only one of various offers. In March, 1924, the Ford offer passed the House, but it failed of acceptance in the Senate, and Ford then withdrew.

The rejection was largely the work of Senator George W. Norris of Nebraska, a progressive Republican who was chairman of the Senate Committee on Agriculture and Forestry. This committee's report on the Ford offer, evidently the handiwork of Norris, charged Ford with pettiness and shrewd calculation in the terms of his bid. It also removed the Muscle Shoals question into a field of new consideration.

Norris pleaded that the Muscle Shoals property be kept in government hands, if only as a resource in time of war. He pointed out that Nitrate Plant No. 2 was like a battleship. "It must be kept in order ready for any unfortunate emergency." To dispose of the Muscle Shoals property to a private agency, with the risk of having to buy it back when need arose, was absurd. "It would be as reasonable to put our battleships up for sale . . . or to dispose at scrap value of the guns and munitions in our forts and arsenals."

The senator from Nebraska pictured the massive nature of the government's work at Muscle Shoals and the hugeness of its investment, in contrast with the small sum offered. He argued that Henry Ford could get back his $5,000,000 by selling the miscellaneous government furniture, lumber, buildings, machines, and other scattered property left over from wartime operations. He frowned upon the speculative enthusiasm of the Tri-Cities and deplored the general willingness to furnish a multimillionaire the opportunity, at public expense, of multiplying his millions still further.

They have platted the country for miles around [said the report]. If their propaganda is anywhere near true, there will be, if Mr. Ford gets this property, a city spring up there which will make New York look like a country village. Why a warranty deed to the Capitol at Washington was not included in this great transfer of government property to this wonderful corporation has never been explained . . .

Gloom and bitterness descended on the Tri-Cities and other points on the Tennessee when the Ford offer was refused. The metropolitan dreams once more had failed. Now weeds and brush would grow along the concrete sidewalks, pushed for miles into the country around Florence, Sheffield, and Tuscumbia. These despondent relics would long mark the wistfulness of their belief in the wonder-working genius of Henry Ford. The prestige of Senator Norris in the Tennessee Valley at that moment was correspondingly nil. A miracle had been about to happen, and the man from Nebraska had addled it. With righteous wrath they noted that the great liberal, Norris, had joined forces with the reactionary Alabama Power Company (a British-owned affair), which was also working to defeat the Ford offer, and they asked what kind of liberalism was that. But they did not surrender. Delegations of Alabama petitioners and lobbyists kept beseeching Congress, and the great debate continued.

The situation had its peculiar features. The advocates of Muscle Shoals were inured by long experience to the reluctance of Republican majorities to spend government money south of the Ohio. But they were not used to having an ally in the Republican camp. Senator Norris, despite his addling of the Ford miracle, was in a sense their ally. But what an ally!

The fertilizer issue was gradually dropping into the background, and power was coming forward as a main issue. Senator Norris was very intent on that issue. Actually he was becoming the leader of a fight to develop Muscle Shoals as not only a government-owned but perhaps also a government-operated project. Much later, in his book, *Uncle Sam's Billion Dollar Baby*, Frederick L. Collins charged that Norris's plans and ideas at this stage derived from the agitation of a Socialist group who believed, with Lenin, that government-owned power offered a short cut to state socialism. At any rate, Norris held on relentlessly to the conception of government ownership. Although during the Ford debate he had been political bedfellow with the Alabama Power Company, he, like other progressives, viewed the private utility companies with great suspicion. Their charges were too high, it was said, and their profits too lush. They were making too free with the public resources and were using their influence too often with lack of scruple. Norris seemed to believe that the utility companies could be restrained if Muscle Shoals were developed entirely as a government affair and were used as a "yardstick" to measure what private companies should charge for power.

On this point the southern and midwestern minds did not meet. The Southerners found it difficult to agree that the government ought to exercise an economic function through an official agency set up in the field reserved, by their thinking, for private enterprise. In the politics of business they carried over, rightly or wrongly, the Jeffersonian notions that they had derived from the customs and philosophy of an agricultural society. The great length and tediousness of the Muscle Shoals debate, which fairly wore out Congress and the country during the nineteen-twenties, were caused by this conflict of ideas. It seemed impossible to draw up a bill which would pass both houses of Congress and also secure executive approval. In the twelve years between 1921 and 1933, no less than 138 Muscle Shoals bills were presented in Congress.

As the question was argued, it continued to develop new aspects which added new complications. The great Mississippi floods of the nineteen-twenties compelled national attention to the problem of flood control, and so it became necessary to ask how much the Tennessee contributed to flood damage both in its own valley and along the Ohio and Mississippi. Could the Muscle Shoals development be so planned as to serve the threefold purpose of improving navigation, generating electric power, and aiding flood control, with production of explosives in war and of fertilizer in peace as a necessary adjunct?

A fresh study by the army engineers was an evident necessity. Congress ordered such a survey in 1922, before Wilson Dam was completed, and further authorizations were added in later years. Preliminary reports were made during the progress of this work, but the final report was not ready until 1930.

It was really one continuous study and from the beginning developed the features that were eventually to mark it as especially distinguished. In 1922, when the first survey was authorized, it happened that the army engineer in charge at Wilson Dam was Lytle Brown of Williamson County, Tennessee. He was a native Tennessean, well aware of the long tale of trouble connected with the Tennessee River. During his previous experience on the Ohio, Wabash, and other rivers, he had noticed that engineers' surveys were generally too limited in scope. Their tradition inclined them to put navigation requirements first, with small heed to other factors. In this attitude they reflected the government and the law. But modern river problems required something more ambitious than data for low navigation dams. Accordingly, Brown suggested that the Tennessee survey be broadened to include all related possibilities of river use. The new survey should "go to the foot of the hills." This suggestion was followed.

Soon after this, Brown was ordered to duty in Panama. Strangely enough, the survey came under the direction of another native Tennessean, the district engineer, Major Lewis H. Watkins, and he was also from Williamson County. Watkins was an unusually thorough man, with a genius for rounding out to the last degree of elaboration and polish the exact kind of survey that Brown had conceived. He was not a man to rush, and was doubtless pleased that the long Congressional debates gave him time to carry out an exhaustive study.

Meanwhile the secretary of war was selling electric power at Muscle Shoals on short-term contracts, but there was only one customer—the Alabama Power Company. The Alabama congressmen, though by no means adherents of the Alabama Power Company, were friendly to the notion that such arrangements as existed might offer a basis for a permanent policy. Senator Underwood argued strongly for the sale of government-generated power "at the switchboard" to private concerns.

With Senator Norris in opposition to that idea, and with the whole question greatly complicated, the progress of Muscle Shoals legislation was very slow indeed. After some preliminary attempts that came to nothing, Norris came forward in 1928 with a new and ambitious proposal which included the erection of a large storage dam at the Cove Creek site on Clinch River. The function of this dam would be to equalize the flow of water in the Tennessee River and to assist in flood control. To Norris's proposal the House added a provision for operation of both power and fertilizer facilities by a government corporation. This bill passed Congress and went to the White House. President Calvin Coolidge gave it a pocket veto, and all was to do over again.

In 1931 a bill embodying many of the features of Norris's 1928 proposal, but returning to the theory of private operation of the Muscle Shoals plant passed both houses of Congress. President Herbert Hoover vetoed it, and the veto was sustained. But Congress, at President Hoover's suggestion, appointed a Muscle Shoals Commission to advise it. The recommendations of the commission also passed into the bottomless gulf.

During this troublesome battle Senator Norris was by no means the only active figure. Among others, Senator McKellar of Tennessee was fertile in suggestions. Between March, 1925, and January, 1929, McKellar introduced seven Muscle Shoals bills, all of which, however, failed of action. His most notable suggestion was his proposal to establish a Muscle Shoals Commission which, like the later TVA, would be a government corporation administered by three commissioners. Senator McKellar also pointed out that the vast inundation caused by the proposed Cove Creek Dam would withdraw an enormous amount of property from taxation. State and county revenues would suffer, and just what did Norris intend to do about that? Norris, in his preoccupation with government ownership, had not been disposed to make any provision, but in the end he agreed that state, though not county, revenues ought to be replaced by the federal government.

And still, after more than a decade of jockeying and quarreling, nothing tangible had been accomplished except the completion of Wilson Dam and its modest supplement, the low dam and canal at Little Muscle Shoals. It had taken a world war to get Wilson Dam started. What would it take to get the Muscle Shoals project completed? The Tennessee River seemed to be a hoodoo. It had caused more anguish in Congress than any other river in American history. It was defying the ingenious and massive approaches of the twentieth century almost as effectively as it had defied the cruder attacks of the nineteenth century. But while Congress quarreled, the army engineers were busy. When they finally spoke, it was the beginning of the end for the old wild river of the Cherokees and the pioneers.

In 1929 Lytle Brown, now a major general, was made chief of engineers of the United States Army. On assuming command, he asked about the Tennessee River survey for which he had made certain initial suggestions. He learned that it had been carried out, but the report was not yet ready for Congress. It was still in Lewis Watkins's hands, and doubtless he was lovingly polishing up the details. Lytle Brown knew what to say to his fellow Tennessean. Besides, he was commanding officer. The report came through and was published in March, 1930, in a 734-page volume entitled *Tennessee River and Tributaries.*

This amazingly comprehensive document put the old hard question once more in the way of solution. Although the major interest of the engineers was still in navigation, they now treated in exhaustive detail not only the navigation problem but also power development and flood control. For the first time it was made clear that these questions, where the Tennessee system was concerned, were interdependent and that ideal results could possibly be obtained by a unified development that would deal with the entire Tennessee system, not merely with the notable obstacles of the main stream. The engineers presented a scheme under which every project undertaken in the future would fit into a broad plan.

Earlier, it is true, Norris, in a Senate report, had emphasized the need of a unified plan. "It is . . . apparent," he said, "that to develop the maximum hydroelectric energy the entire stream and all its tributaries should be considered as a whole." But the 1930 report showed that this plan was not only conceivable but possible. It indicated precisely the arrangements that would achieve the desired results. It showed what a skillful engineer would do with the Tennessee River if he had an endless supply of money and permission to erect whatever structures he, as a technologist, would deem adequate for combined purposes.

On the main stream the engineers showed that a 9-foot channel, the year around, could be secured by adding seven high dams to the two high dams already existing. These dams could be built so as to meet related requirements and fit into the unified system. The sites recommended were: Aurora Landing, 43 miles above the mouth of the Tennessee; Pickwick Landing, 206 miles upriver; Dam No. 3, already provided for in the old Muscle Shoals plan, later erected and named Wheeler Dam; Guntersville, 354 miles upriver; Chickamauga, 472 miles upriver, just above Chattanooga; White Creek, 543 miles upriver and 13 miles above TVA's Watts Bar Dam; Coulter Shoals, 605 miles upriver at approximately the site of TVA's Fort Loudoun Dam.

As for flood control, the engineers planned storage on the tributaries and "surcharge pondage" for the main river pools. The main river dams, they noted, would have relatively little effect in controlling floods. Flood control could be achieved only by a delicate and careful planning of storage reservoirs on tributaries and surcharge on main river reservoirs, and all these had to be adjusted to power requirements.

They plotted sites for 149 hydroelectric developments which could be operated as a single system and which, they figured, could produce three and a half million to four million kilowatts of firm power if storage plans were carried out and auxiliary steam plants maintained. They figured that the entire system could produce a total of about twenty-five billion kilowatt-hours annually. The power could be produced at a price of about 4.33 mills, and they estimated what the probable market for it would be. They also contemplated "interchange of power and storage" between parts of the system and mentioned the need of a central agency to manage all this, but added, "There appears to be no legal means for establishing such an agency by the United States."

On the other hand, while the 1930 report foreshadowed TVA in its physical plan, it adhered to the policy followed by the army engineers during the previous decade or more in assuming that the government would co-operate with private companies in navigation-and-power enterprises and would divide costs with them in return for power franchises. A number of applications had already been made by private companies under the provisions of the Federal Water Power Act.

The engineers thought of their plan, apparently, as capable of being carried out only by gradual stages over a long period of time. It would be completed only at some far-off day, if ever. If it were ever completed, the total cost would be $1,200,000,000. It was inconceivable in 1930 that any administration, Democratic or Republican, would ever lavish so much of the people's money on a single river project.

Therefore they gave systematic attention to alternative plans—to ways and means of combining public works and private enterprise so as to reduce the cost to the government. The most conservative possibility—not recommended, however, by the district engineer, except as a standard for judging costs to the government in other schemes—was to abandon the high-dam system and return to low dams for navigation only, as on the Ohio. A 9-foot channel could be obtained on the Tennessee by adding thirty-two low navigation dams to existing improvements. This conservative plan would cost only $75,000,000. But as a further suggestion it was recommended that, if a private company should enter a joint investment with the government, a high dam might be substituted for any two or more of the low dams, under certain conditions. Another plan, among the four suggested, would be to build only the seven high dams on the main stream for the sake of navigation and power benefits alone. This project would cost about $250,000,000. But it was open to the objection that it would have little flood-control value and would involve, instead, "the purchase and permanent flooding of much land in the Tennessee Valley which is now subject only to occasional flood damage."

The chief of engineers, General Brown, concurred for

the most part in the recommendations of the district engineer, Major Watkins, but emphasized the view that the sum mentioned for the ultimate or ideal plan, $1,200,000,000, must not be thought of as something that the engineers were proposing for the United States to spend. "It is a vast plan," he wrote, "possible to a proper combination of private enterprise and public works. The total cost is of no special interest in this report since only a minor part of it enters into prospective operations by the General Government."

Finally, General Brown added, with a hint of firmness and a suggestion of pride, that no good would be done by leaving the project "in the air." "The project," said the general, "should be definite and final, and it is possible to make it so in this case, if ever, because there never has been presented to Congress a more thorough and exhaustive study."

The report became the basis of Congressional policy toward the Tennessee River. Yet in 1932 the outlook was still bleak in the Tennessee realm of King Kilowatt. In the matter of Muscle Shoals, a point of tedium and futility had seemingly been reached. Furthermore, there were other elements involved, hardly to be calculated by an engineer. There was a climate of public opinion. By 1932 public opinion had become grotesquely uncharitable and hostile toward Tennessee and the Tennessee Valley.

CHAPTER XII

# Trials by Jury and Otherwise

NOTHING in the quarter of a century preceding the Dayton trial could have prepared the people of the Tennessee Valley for the painful indignities heaped upon them by that cause célèbre. A few years later the Scottsboro case deepened the injury and added threats more ominous than had been known since Reconstruction days.

It could not have been predicted. As the conquered Cherokees in their time had learned to follow the white man's path, so the Southerners of the valley, during the intersectional truce that began about 1900, had accepted the counsel of "New South" leaders and in steadily increasing numbers had imitated the ways of the North. At the cost of junking their excellent private schools, they had established and persistently expanded a modern system of free public schools and had built up a state university and teachers' colleges. To make sure that the imitative system was exactly right they had invited northern experts to instruct them, even to govern them, in the accepted educational procedures. Similar educational facilities, under the biracial and segregative plan followed throughout the South, were open to Negroes on a legally equal basis, although the shortage of qualified Negro teachers and the general lack of funds made complete equality in education unattainable for the time being. Race relations were good and had been steadily improving. The whites in general accepted the new liberal leadership. The Negroes, for their part, inclined without much visible dissent to the Booker T. Washington school of Negro thought: they believed in gradual improvement under established conditions rather than in bitter strife for impossible goals.

The region, too, had fully demonstrated its loyalty to the Union. The older generation, volunteering in large numbers for the Spanish-American War, had worn the federal blue and had fought under the Stars and Stripes in Cuba and the Philippines. The younger generation, many as draftees, but very many, again, as volunteers, had carried the same flag to the Rhine in World War I. The great individual soldier hero of that war was Alvin York, an uneducated but devout Tennessee mountaineer, a dead shot with rifle and pistol, who almost singlehanded captured an entire machine-gun battalion of German soldiers, after killing more than twenty-five of them.

It was a shock for the people of the valley to discover, during the nineteen-twenties, that all this was as nothing to the North and West. Although there were other troubles of similar kind, it was the two internationally famous affairs at Dayton and Scottsboro that brought down upon the unsuspecting valley, in a peculiarly intense and derisive form, the organized wrath of the outside world. The wrath was so condescending and purposeful that it seemed to have the character of deliberate attack. It reopened the breach between North and South that everybody had thought long closed, and was so uncompromising that it seemed to confront the valley with the old demand for "unconditional surrender" in a new form.

Ironically, the passage of Tennessee's anti-evolution statute, or "Monkey law," was linked with Governor Austin Peay's legislative program for strengthening the state educational system by extending the school term and increasing appropriations for the state university and teachers' colleges. A strategic bloc of rural legislators held out against the governor's educational bill. Their support, it seemed, would be assured only if the governor would sign the Butler anti-evolution statute, which was certain to pass. A veto would mean a fight in the legislature and possibly a defeat or an emasculation of the educational bill. Both the governor and his supporters viewed the Butler bill as a freak law, of trivial importance. Governor Peay noted that there was "nothing of consequence in the books being taught in our schools with which this bill will interfere in the slightest manner—probably the law will never be applied."

John Washington Butler of Macon County, author of the statute, was a solid, quiet-speaking farmer. Apparently he had been touched by the Fundamentalist agitation which, with other postwar disturbances, had swept over many states. He was no unlettered ignoramus. Of his own initiative he had read, it later appeared, Darwin's *Origin of Species* and *Descent of Man*, and he would not, he said, mind having his children read them as he had done. Butler was not conscious of, or at least did not accept, the intellectual refinements by which modern churches had hallowed materialistic science and admitted it into working partnership with religion. He did not realize that he was a solid century behind the times—that he had revived the controversy which in Victorian England had brought Thomas Huxley into debate with prominent clerics and men of letters. Butler had no thought of implanting any general proscription of freethinking or modern science. He did object to and wish to prohibit the teaching of what he conceived to be antireligious doctrines in schools maintained by the state—schools which, in most communities, were now the only schools available and which Tennessee children, under the new system, were compelled by law to attend. Unfortunately his statute applied not only to the secondary schools but to the state university and other institutions maintained by the state. It provided—

> That it shall be unlawful for any teacher in any of the Universities, Normals and all other public schools of the State which are supported in whole or in part by the public school funds

of the State, to teach any theory that denies the story of the Divine Creation of man as taught in the Bible, and to teach instead that man has descended from a lower order of animals.

Governor's Peay's expectation that the law would become a dead letter was quickly proved folly. Before the Civil War the town of Dayton—a step away from the Tennessee River—had been a quiet village. Now it was a modern town, and it had certain misguided citizens who would go to any lengths to advertise Dayton.

So one day at a Dayton drugstore, over the Coca-Colas and ice-cream sodas, it was agreed among a group of ardent booster spirits that they would contrive to bring a test case under the anti-evolution law. George W. Rappleyea of Dayton would assume the role of prosecutor, and John Thomas Scopes, a young man from the North who was biology instructor at Dayton High School, agreed to take the role of offender. The ardent spirits were out for fun. No doubt they also wanted, as it was later said, to "see whether the law would stick." But their test case was essentially a publicity stunt. They hurried their plans because they had learned that a test case was being prepared at Chattanooga, and they wanted to get ahead of Chattanooga.

Before anybody could say Jack Robinson the "Monkey Trial" was making the front page all over the country—all over the world. John Randolph Neal of Tennessee, professional liberal, perennial and always defeated candidate for high office, enlisted as attorney for Scopes. The American Civil Liberties Union offered its services, and Arthur Garfield Hays was added as counsel for defense. In June, a month before the trial, Scopes visited New York. The New York *Times* carried an interview which impressed upon the public the modesty and sincerity of the young teacher and, by implied contrast, the alleged intolerance of Tennessee. Rapidly the Scopes case became the focus of a holy war in behalf of science and liberalism. Other notables joined up as defense counsel: Dudley Field Malone, who would not have missed it for anything; and, above all, the famous criminal lawyer and skeptic, Clarence Darrow, who not long before had defended the youthful murderers, the notorious Leopold and Loeb.

To the amazement of the country, William Jennings Bryan announced that he would offer his services on behalf of the state of Tennessee and what he believed to be the right. The Great Commoner had made the defense of religion the sacred cause of his later years. He wished now to defend religion in Tennessee against what he deemed to be a wanton assault by the forces of mischief. At once it was evident that the battle between Bryan, champion of religion, and Clarence Darrow, the skeptical advocate of science and materialism, would overshadow the real issues in the Scopes case.

The trial began with the town of Dayton arrayed as if for a carnival—"half circus, half revival meeting," said a reporter. Notables of the religious and scientific world, star journalists, famous writers, wandering revivalists, freaks, and souvenir vendors mixed with the citizens of Rhea County—with the plain countrymen and townsmen invariably described by metropolitan newspapers as "hill folk." Opposing counsel thundered preliminary challenges for the benefit of the press. Darrow declared that he was going to breach the "Chinese wall" that Bryan was trying to build around Tennessee. Bryan led religious services on the mountaintop and issued a statement objecting to the use of scientists as expert witnesses. "If a law like this were passed in New York," he said, "and witnesses were called from Tennessee to assure the people of New York that they were unduly alarmed . . . their testimony would be objected to as offensive as well as improper. . . . The people of Tennessee have a right to protect the Bible as they understand it. They are not compelled to consider the interpretations placed upon it by people of other states, whether Christians or scientists, or both."

American newspapers raucously whooped on the fracas and kept the Dayton trial in front-page headlines for the better part of a month. Gleefully, the New York papers culled out and published samples of world opinion which uniformly deplored the barbarousness of Tennesseans. The Bishop of Birmingham, England, contributed an ecclesiastical sniff. George Bernard Shaw, interviewed, declared that the "Monkey law" would make Tennessee into "a mere reservation of morons." EUROPE IS AMAZED was the headline in the New York *Times*.

The trial began on July 10, 1925. The weather was hot, and the eminent attorneys, gratefully following the example of Judge J. T. Raulston, shed their coats. The actual courtroom proceedings consisted almost entirely of arguments between opposing counsel on points of law and verbal combats in which the clash between religion and science, rather than the guilt or innocence of Scopes, was the issue. The jury, excluded during the wrangles, heard little of these sublimities. The presentation of evidence occupied but a small part of the trial.

Early in the trial Darrow emphasized his theme: "This is as brazen and bold an attempt to destroy liberty as was ever seen in the Middle Ages. . . . Not a single line of any constitution can withstand bigotry and ignorance when it seeks to destroy the rights of the individual." He objected to Judge Raulston's procedure of opening court with prayer and in this connection engaged in an angry exchange of words with Attorney General A. T. Stewart, who was conducting the case for the state. Judge Raulston ruled that to open with prayer was within the discretion of the court, but, in answer to a petition offered by Arthur Garfield Hays, to the effect that the prayers ought to be offered by preachers, priests, or rabbis of all sects in rotation, the judge said that he would accept whomever the Rhea County Pastors Association would designate. To the discomfiture of the visitors, the Pastors Association promptly designated a Unitarian, Rev. Charles Francis Potter of New York, to say the next prayer.

The defense sought to introduce a formidable array of

scientists who presumably would testify that modern science could not be taught without acceptance of the theory of evolution. One of the experts, Maynard Metcalf of Oberlin, took the stand, but the state immediately objected. After prolonged argument Judge Raulston ruled out the testimony of the experts, but permitted Darrow to enter their prepared statements in the court record.

On July 20, after the eminent attorneys had battered one another for ten days, the judge transferred the trial from the hot courtroom to the courthouse lawn, where a platform and bleachers had been erected. There Bryan agreed to take the witness stand himself, as a Bible expert. Then, under what the New York *Times* called "the most remarkable circumstances ever known in court proceedings," Darrow harried the Great Commoner for nearly two hours. In blue shirt and suspenders, leaning against a table, with a Bible in his hand, Darrow pounded away on his favorite subject, the folly of a literal interpretation of the Bible. Did Bryan believe that the whale swallowed Jonah? Did he think Eve was made from Adam's rib? Did he believe the serpent had always crawled on its belly because it had tempted Eve to sin? The grotesque inquisition mounted to a climax in an almost violent exchange during which fists were brandished:

*Bryan.* The only purpose Mr. Darrow has is to slur at the Bible, but I will answer his questions. I will answer it all at once, and I have no objection in the world. I want the world to know that this man, who does not believe in a God, is trying to use a court in Tennessee—

*Darrow.* I object to that—

*Bryan.* To slur at it . . . and while it will require time, I am willing to take it.

*Darrow.* I object to your statement. I am examining you on your fool ideas that no intelligent Christian on earth believes.

At this point Judge Raulston hastily adjourned court. Later he ruled that Bryan's testimony should be expunged.

Attorney General Stewart, anxious lest Bryan's overenthusiastic efforts should injure the state's case, pressed for a conclusion of proceedings. The trial ended July 21. Scopes was found guilty, and Judge Raulston fined him $100. The defense attorneys, who had expected the result, prepared for an appeal. Their legal purpose was to destroy the Tennessee law on grounds of unconstitutionality. They probably hoped that occasion might offer for bringing the case to the Supreme Court of the United States, but first they had to face the Supreme Court of Tennessee. Their general purpose—which was no less Bryan's—was to use the Dayton trial as a sounding board. In this both they and Bryan had succeeded perfectly. The case was tried in the newspapers and periodicals of the world, and continued to be tried there. Bryan's advocacy, far from helping the state of Tennessee, was cleverly turned against both him and the state. Bryan and Tennessee, overwhelmed by the incredible outcry, lay deep in the pit of humiliation dug by Messrs. Scopes, Rappleyea, and their eminent coadjutors.

On July 25, Bryan, already exhausted and overwrought, made a speech at Winchester in the course of which he said: "When a Christian wants to teach Christianity, he has to build his own college, but the atheist expects to usurp public colleges and schools." Coming back by train, he made a brief rear-platform speech at Cowan. At Dayton the next day he died in his sleep at the home of Richard Rodgers. The Unitarian visitor, Rev. Charles Francis Potter, said what was in many a mind: "He was sincere in his beliefs. The Dayton trial was his death-blow."

The Supreme Court of Tennessee prepared to hear the appeal. While the court waited, it was deluged by uninvited instruction from all over the country. The public battle went on. Scientific associations passed resolutions condemning the Tennessee statute. University presidents, cocking an eye at northern philanthropists, hinted that Fundamentalism could best be confounded by a provision of larger endowments for scientific departments. The Tennessee Academy of Science, with Messrs. Waller, Stokes, Carden, and Colton as attorneys, prepared to enter the case as *amicus curiae*.

The appeal was heard at Nashville, in the September, 1925, term of the court, but this time without the "half-circus, half-revival" trimmings. Before Tennessee's distinguished court, in the stately surroundings of the capitol, Darrow no longer seemed an effective advocate. His fire was gone, or there was no place for it. He was eclipsed by members of the Tennessee bar—by Frank M. Thompson, attorney general, and attorneys Seay and McConnico and others who joined in the state's strong brief; and by Thomas H. Malone, who appearing as *amicus curiae*, sharply and skillfully attacked the vague language of the statute. The Scopes defense argued vigorously that the statute violated the constitutions of both Tennessee and of the United States.

The court, with one judge dissenting, decided that the law was constitutional, though in the opinions of Chief Justice Grafton Green and of Judge Chambliss different reasons for so ruling were given—reasons that suggested that the court had by implication found the statute ambiguous in terms. However, the court also found that Judge Raulston had erred in assessing a $100 fine. Under the law, the jury should have fixed the punishment. The judgment of the lower court was therefore reversed.

At the same time, with what seemed to the suffering people of Tennessee a stroke of genius, Chief Justice Green added a recommendation. "The Court is informed," he said, "that the plaintiff in error is no longer in the service of the State. We see nothing to be gained by prolonging the life of this bizarre case. On the contrary we think that the peace and dignity of the State, which all criminal prosecutions are brought to redress, will be better preserved by the entry of a *nolle prosequi* herein. Such a course is suggested to the Attorney General."

The attorney general at once "nolle prossed" the case.

So it was all over. There could be no appeal to the Supreme Court of the United States. The "Monkey law" remained on the statute books of Tennessee, despite attempts at repeal, for the legislature, now that Tennessee had been ridiculed and attacked, was more stubborn than ever. The law was of course now a dead letter, like many other freak laws throughout the country.

But irreparable damage had been done. Publicity seekers, extremists, and character assassins of both sides had wrought deadly injury to the good will that should have existed between Tennessee and her sister states of the North and West. The discredit that fell upon Tennessee was extended to the South in general and embittered sectional relations. The clamor obscured the real issues. Now it was virtually impossible for Tennessee to face the real educational question that had been raised and to seek a dispassionate answer. The state was under a peculiarly irritating kind of surveillance which it could neither effectively resent nor abjectly accept. The result was that there was no discussion at all of the hard question of what state control of education might mean and how it ought to be applied. The subject was taboo. The state could not make the first approach to defining an educational policy in terms of its actual situation, its true needs, its native genius. Under the old system of private responsibility there might have been less education in terms of quantity, but the new difficulty could not have arisen. Now, being under pressure, about all Tennessee could do was to try to get up money to buy a kind of education trade-marked "progressive." If it did not like the brand, it could hold its nose, shut its eyes, and swallow.

Soon enough it was Alabama's turn to be in the soup, and it was very hot soup. The Scottsboro case was the grimmest episode in southern experience during the years between two world wars. The whole thing began, appropriately enough, near the point where Rosecrans's army crossed the Tennessee for the Chickamauga campaign.

The persons involved in the Scottsboro case, white and Negro, were of such low degree and were so ignorant that it seems possible they never understood the meaning of the eminent noises made over them from all quarters of the earth. Two white girls, Victoria Price and Ruby Bates, spent the night of March 25, 1931, at Chattanooga, and it was alleged that their bivouac was a hobo "jungle." Next day, dressed in overalls, with hair bobbed, they hopped a freight train for Memphis where they said they were going to seek work. They rode in an open freight car, a gondola, two-thirds full of gravel. There was a group of white boys in this car, also hoboing. When the train crossed the Tennessee River and stopped at Stevenson, Alabama, about twenty Negroes (men and boys) got on. Some of the Negroes abusively challenged the white boys. A fight followed, in which the Negroes sought to chase the white boys off the train. The more numerous Negroes prevailed. They put the white boys off—all but one hapless wretch. He was about to fall to certain death between the cars, and a Negro, relenting, saved him. This white boy remained in the gondola, a helpless witness to what happened next. One of the white boys who had been put off, bleeding and angry, telephoned the railroad station about what had happened, and the telegraph operator notified Paint Rock, on the line ahead, that there was trouble on the train. At Paint Rock the county sheriff and a posse of deputies met the train and searched it. They arrested nine Negroes. The other eleven escaped. The Negroes were put in jail at Paint Rock and were charged with rape. Word of the trouble quickly passed around the country, and a mob gathered, intent on a lynching. The Negroes were removed to Gadsden, and the lynching was prevented. The trial was set for April 6, 1931, at Scottsboro, county seat of Jackson County, where these incidents had occurred.

Even in normal times such an affair would have stirred the countryside. But the war of nerves that had beaten upon southern sensibilities since the Dayton trial or before, had brought the South to a condition of semibelligerence, aggravated by the disorder of the economic depression that began in 1929. The uplanders of Jackson County, like uplanders elsewhere in the South, had an entrenched dislike of Negroes. They took the affair very personally and buzzed like hornets. Scottsboro, when the trial opened, did not repeat the carnival effects of Dayton. The Alabama National Guard was on duty. Ten thousand people, reporters estimated, crowded into town. There were few outsiders among them, and no dignitaries from far away.

The accused Negroes had difficulty in obtaining counsel. Only Milo C. Moody of the Jackson County bar would touch the case. A Negro preacher named Stephens, who had gone to work on behalf of the accused, procured the services of a young Chattanooga lawyer, Stephen Roddy. Communist groups, already working in the South, were interested, but were slow in coming into effective action. At the trial, Victoria Price and Ruby Bates testified that they had been raped by the Negroes. Their testimony was supported by the white boy who had stayed on the train. Three of the Negroes also said that they had seen other Negroes attack the girls. The jury found eight of the Negroes guilty, and they were sentenced to death. One Negro, a fourteen-year-old boy, got off with a mistrial.

The verdict was welcomed locally as if some battle had been won. There was open jubilation and even—or so it was reported—triumphant playing by a band. But the Alabama people were much mistaken if they thought it was all over.

A Communist group, working from Chattanooga, began a determined campaign on behalf of the Negroes, who speedily became "the Scottsboro boys" in the national press. The Communists were following the general instructions of the Seventh National Convention of the Communist party of the United States, which had said: "Protest against the special oppression to which Negroes are subjected must take the form of intensive political campaigns and mass organization to fight against lynching. Negro workers and farmers persecuted on the basis of discrimination must be accepted and treated as class-struggle victims." The campaign for the Scottsboro boys followed this pattern skillfully. The trial was represented as a "legal lynching," and the Scottsboro boys were pictured as being "persecuted." The Communists persuaded another Chattanooga lawyer, George W. Chamlee, to join the defense. Much more important, however, was the entry of the International Labor Defense, which began its work by sending Judge Hawkins, then sitting on the case, a threatening telegram, in which the senders called the case a "legal lynching" and declared that they would "hold him responsible." At this stage, Joseph Brodsky was the I.L.D.'s attorney.

Mr. Roddy, displeased with the attitude of the I.L.D., finally retired from the case. Preacher Stephens became alarmed and solicited aid from the conservative National Association for the Advancement of Colored People. Forthwith the radical I.L.D. and the conservative N.A.A.C.P. began to compete for the privilege of defending the Scottsboro boys. The bewildered prisoners and their relatives were heavily importuned by the two groups. Both the I.L.D. and the N.A.A.C.P. also campaigned in the South for Negro support and in the North for support at large. The campaign reached curious heights when the mothers of the Scottsboro boys were transported about the nation to appear at rallies. There were not enough mothers to supply the demand, but the Communist group did not hesitate to employ spurious "mothers" on occasion. The Communists organized parades, demonstrated in Harlem with such vehemence that the New York police had to be called out, and even carried their agitation into foreign capitals.

Motion for a new trial was denied, and the Scottsboro case went up to the Alabama Supreme Court, which affirmed the lower court's decision. Appeal to the United States Supreme Court resulted in an order for a new trial, on the ground that the defendants had not had adequate opportunity to secure counsel and prepare their case. This was only the beginning of a tedious series of retrials and appeals to the higher courts. A change of venue to Decatur, Alabama, was allowed for the retrials. W. W. Callahan finally supplanted James E. Horton as trial judge.

Meanwhile, the burden of the defense of the Scottsboro boys passed to Samuel S. Leibowitz of New York, and he became, in the phrase of *Time* magazine, the "Scottsboro hero." In the courtroom proceedings, Leibowitz devoted himself systematically to breaking down the evidence brought by the prosecution. The long continuance of the case, the successive trials which went over and over the same evidence, and the tremendous public pressure brought for the accused and against Alabama worked in his favor. The oftener the witnesses testified, the more confused and contradictory they became. Ruby Bates finally repudiated her sworn testimony.

Outside the courtroom, and even to some extent within it, Lawyer Leibowitz did not hesitate to make it clear, through various provocative utterances, that he had contempt for the courts and people of Alabama and of the South and that he deemed himself a missionary appointed to rescue the persecuted from the baneful clutch of the heathen. In Decatur and New York, Leibowitz had a way of using such terms as "lantern jawed morons and lynchers" when he referred to the people of Alabama. They and their fellow Southerners were, in his outspoken language, "boll-weevil bigots" . . . "creatures whose mouths are slits . . . whose eyes pop out at you like frogs, whose chins drip tobacco juice, bewhiskered and filthy." "One can never tell," he said, "when one of those hill-billies will pump a six-gun at him."

The Alabama courts tolerated Leibowitz's impudence, and the "boll-weevil bigots" pumped no six-guns at him. Though under extreme provocation, they proceeded with the forms of justice as they understood those forms. Except in one case in which Judge Horton declared a mistrial, the Ala-

# TRIALS BY JURY AND OTHERWISE 209

bama juries repeatedly found the defendants guilty and the Alabama Supreme Court steadily upheld the lower courts.

The United States Supreme Court refused to hear Lawyer Leibowitz's last appeal. In August, 1937, the case reached its end so far as courts were concerned. The state of Alabama, evidently tired of the long agitation, "nolle prossed" the indictments against four of the Scottsboro boys and released them on condition that they leave the state. One defendant, Ozie Powell, was tried and found guilty on a new charge—attacking a deputy. Two others were held in prison under what amounted to a life sentence. Another was still under a death sentence, but he was not executed.

Meanwhile, off and on during the years of the Scottsboro case, and especially during the period following the first trial, race relations passed from a state of high tension into open and widespread disorder. Negroes split into two camps, one radical, one conservative. In an article published in *Harper's Magazine* Walter White, secretary of the N.A.A.C.P., described the activities of Communist groups among the Negroes and bewailed their violent tactics, which threatened, he indicated, to destroy the careful work done by his own organization. The admonition was needed. Exploiting the frenzy worked up by the Scottsboro case, the Communists had brought Alabama to the point of a race war. White vigilantes watched the movements of Negro groups, and vice versa. Negro meetings were fired into and broken up, and the violence and intimidation of Reconstruction days threatened to return, full scale.

In the end calmer counsels prevailed, or the more abundant promises of the New Deal distracted the attention of the belligerents. But again, as in the Dayton episode, permanent harm had been done. A way had been found, despite Edmund Burke's old pronouncement, to draw up an indictment against a whole people. The outside world denied Tennessee the right to govern its educational system in accordance with what was the evident will of its legislature and the probable desire of a heavy proportion of its people. The reason given was, in effect, that the legislature and the people were too ignorant to know what was good for them. To Alabama that same outside world had said, by its clamors and insults, that the courts and the people of Alabama could not be trusted to execute justice for the Negro race. To lynch offending Negroes was damnable, as Alabamians and Southerners in impressive numbers were more than ready to agree. Could it be that it was also damnable to submit Negroes to due process of law in the regularly constituted courts of Alabama? The nation's verdict in the Scottsboro case and other cases seemed to indicate that such action also was damnable. They were damned if they did, and damned if they didn't, and just what were they expected to do?

The specific attitudes engendered in the outside world by the exploitation of these cases might change, as time dulled the memory of the public and other sensations were provided by newspaper, radio, and movie. But there would remain, and did remain, an impression of Tennessee and Alabama and the Tennessee Valley that put the outside world in a condescending relation to them. The residue left by the Dayton trial and the Scottsboro case was the picture of valley residents as ignorant, bigoted, backward, moronic, degenerate caricatures of humanity, who might in their better moments be quaint or picturesque but could not be thought of as counting for much.

Thus were decades of painful upward striving canceled at a blow. The reaction of valley citizens toward their condition of pariahship was various. The more liberal group became more trenchantly liberal; they demanded more and bigger and more progressive colleges and schools, more industries, more labor unions, a general relaxation of old attitudes. The conservative group, less vocal, began to wonder whether they had been wise in making as great concessions as had already been made. They remembered the tales of their grandfathers, reread the history books, and began to resent the entire modern regime.

But both groups were relatively impotent to control the trend of events within the valley. To the new legend of the social depravity of the region was soon added the newer legend that all their ills and their sins were due to economic bad habits. The New Deal emphasized the latter legend in its open pronouncements and offered its services as uplifter. If the Muscle Shoals project could have been devised and finished in the early nineteen-twenties, it would have been a plain river improvement project, promising nothing but navigation, power, and nitrates, with whatever good might come of them. The Tennessee Valley Authority, riding on the wave of the economic uplift, promised through economics to wipe all sins away. Behind its mechanical provisions for taming the Tennessee River was the open hint that social goodness would be substituted for supposed social depravity through the distribution of government-controlled electric power. In its general motivation as well as more specifically in the planning sections of the TVA Act, the authority owed much to the trials by jury and otherwise that plagued Tennessee and Alabama during the years preceding 1933.

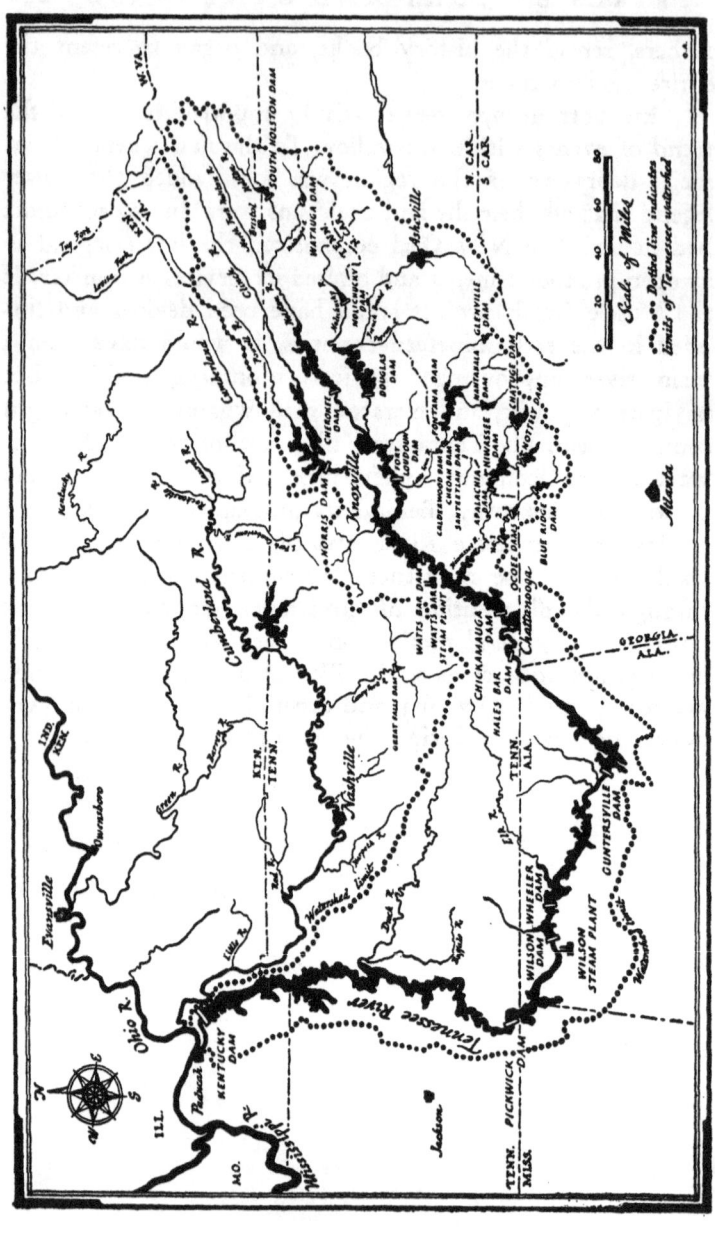

CHAPTER XIII

# At Last! The Kingdom Really Comes!

THUS matters stood when Franklin D. Roosevelt and the New Deal arrived on the national scene. The sweeping Democratic victory of 1932 allayed, for the time being, the harsh sectional animosities that had been reawakened by the events of the preceding years. Once more it was reasonable to hope that the inherited stigmas and handicaps of Civil War and Reconstruction might be removed and that the states of the valley, with other parts of the South, might enjoy the privileges of full membership in the Union rather than merely to be dragged along as an unprivileged appendix. Such hopes were even more important to the valley than the hope, general throughout the United States, that the new administration would restore the tottering national economy, but the people of the valley, though accustomed to ruin, were glad to be rid of it and they joined in that general hope, too. The fall of the Hoover administration might seem a tragic event to the Republican parts of the valley, but it was soon evident that the Great White Father at Washington would wipe away their tears. The East Tennessee Republicans were about to receive from the Democratic pork barrel more generous hunks of favor than any Republican dispenser, from Lincoln on down, had been able to offer.

After the Coolidge and Hoover vetoes of Muscle Shoals legislation, the development of the Tennessee River had seemed to be indefinitely postponed. Now it was in immediate prospect; it was indeed a "must" item on the agenda of the new Democratic administration. It competed for priority with other must items that had national and international importance. This was an entirely new phenomenon. With an amazement that was almost incredulity the valley saw Omega miraculously becoming Alpha. If at that moment Gabriel had blown his trumpet from the dome of the Capitol, few would have been surprised.

In his campaign speeches Mr. Roosevelt had emphasized the "yardstick" theory of electric power rates. People knew, too, that he had actually been in the Tennessee Valley and had looked at it with his own eyes. They were told that, back in the nineteen-twenties, the ex-assistant secretary of the navy and defeated candidate for vice-president had traveled through East Tennessee on his way to the healing waters of Warm Springs, Georgia, and that, even then, he had highly resolved somehow, someday, to restore the land of the pioneers to its ancient good health.

Furthermore, one of Mr. Roosevelt's first acts after his election was to visit the Muscle Shoals area with Senator Norris and there publicly promise that the Muscle Shoals development would indeed be put on the map. During the same tour, in a speech at Montgomery, the president-elect also pronounced the magic word "planning" and forecast something more ambitious than a mere Muscle Shoals development. The development, declared Mr. Roosevelt, would be more than "a kind turn for the people in one small section of a couple of states."

> Muscle Shoals [he said] gives us the opportunity to accomplish a great purpose for the people of many States and, indeed, for the whole Union. Because there we have an opportunity of setting an example of planning, not just for ourselves but for generations to come, tying in industry and agriculture and flood prevention, tying them all into a unified whole over a distance of a thousand miles so that we can afford better opportunities and better places for living for millions yet unborn in the days to come.

## AT LAST! KINGDOM REALLY COMES! 215

All this might have been only a politician's big talk—such big talk as had been heard in the valley, from time to time, for a century or more. But it was not just big talk. It was the real thing at last. The Kingdom was coming, sure enough.

Something more was in the air than the Muscle Shoals power development—something more, even, than the ideal unified development of the Tennessee River visualized as a dim possibility by the army engineers. On April 10, 1933, a little over a month after his inauguration, when the economic crisis was still a formidable and urgent fact, the president sent a notable message to Congress in which he recommended passage of the Muscle Shoals legislation. In this message, however, the Muscle Shoals development itself dropped into a minor position, and a grand design emerged:

> It is clear that the Muscle Shoals development is but a small part of the potential public usefulness of the entire Tennessee River. Such use, if envisioned in its entirety, transcends mere power development; it enters the wide fields of flood control, soil erosion, afforestation, elimination from agricultural use of marginal lands, and distribution and diversification of industry. In short, this power development of war days leads logically to national planning for a complete river watershed involving many States and the future lives and welfare of millions. It touches and gives life to all forms of human concerns.
>
> I, therefore, suggest to the Congress legislation to create a Tennessee Valley Authority—a corporation clothed with the power of government but possessed of the flexibility and initiative of a private enterprise. It should be charged with the broadest duty of planning for the proper use, conservation, and development of the natural resources of the Tennessee River drainage basin and its adjoining territory for the general social and economic welfare of the Nation. This authority should also be clothed with the necessary power to carry those plans into effect. Its duty should be the rehabilitation of the Muscle Shoals development and the coordination of it with the wider plan.

Action on the president's suggestion came swiftly, but the statute that created the Tennessee Valley Authority was not written at the White House end of Pennsylvania Avenue. It was not the creation of some group of "brain trusters." The bright young men of the New Deal were already devising laws and sending them to Congress to be passed, but they did not write this particular law.

The act that created the Tennessee Valley Authority, like other Muscle Shoals bills which had been before Congress, was a compromise between the views of Norris, in the Senate, and of certain southern congressmen in the house, notably the congressmen from Alabama. Even before Congress had received Mr. Roosevelt's message, Representative John J. McSwain of North Carolina, chairman of the House Military Affairs Committee, had introduced a Muscle Shoals bill which made reference to a Tennessee Valley Authority. After the receipt of the president's message, Senator Norris and certain interested congressmen conferred with Mr. Roosevelt at the White House. In this conference the president said, according to Congressmen McSwain: "You gentlemen draw the bills that you think represent our collective views that we have been expressing here." Thereupon Norris introduced a bill in the Senate, which was immediately reported favorably by the Committee on Agriculture and Forestry; and in the House, bills were introduced by Lister Hill of Alabama, then a member of the House, and by E. B. Almon of Alabama, long a faithful promoter of Muscle Shoals; and McSwain himself introduced a second bill of his own. Of the House bills, it was H. R. 5081, introduced by Hill, that was reported out. The chief difference between the Hill and Norris bills, as claimed by Hill himself, was that his House resolution was "on a much better business basis," in that it included arrangements for amortizing the cost of the dams to the government. In the Senate, Norris's bill was substituted for Hill's, but in the end the bill that passed Congress, after the usual process of adjustment between Senate and House views, was numbered H.R. 5081. This statute, as well as the very similar proposals that it eventually displaced, represented in a

## AT LAST! KINGDOM REALLY COMES! 217

fairly well-defined way the joint views of Congress and the White House.

So, on May 18, 1933, the act creating the Tennessee Valley Authority was passed by Congress, and promptly received the president's signature.

The law went through with very little debate. It was as if twelve years of discussion had used up the available supply of words relative to this old subject. The congressmen from Alabama and Tennessee spoke mostly for the record and in glowing generalities. They were on the bandwagon at last and proposed to have a good ride. Senator Vandenberg of Michigan objected to the provision—included as a result of Senator McKellar's earlier insistance—that five per cent of the authority's receipts for power sales be allocated to Tennessee and Alabama as a reimbursement for tax losses. Senator Metcalf of Rhode Island, arguing against the bill, improvised a sarcastic bit of doggerel:

> Oh, Shade of Jefferson, where were you that day
> When Muscle Shoals was built to stay?

In the House there was some passing mention of the high-dam program of construction suggested by the army engineers report of 1930.

But in general, to the southern congressmen at least, the TVA bill was simply another Muscle Shoals bill in a somewhat altered form. Furthermore, Congressman Hill and Congressman Almon had both taken great pains to see that the law carried a provision requiring that "The Corporation shall maintain its principal office in the immediate vicinity of Muscle Shoals, Alabama." Senator Norris did not object to this provision, nor did anybody else. In fact, when Senator Logan of Kentucky expressed some doubt as to whether the salaries provided for the directors would be adequate to attract men of high caliber, it was Norris himself who pointed out that the law provided that each member of the board, in addition to his salary, would be entitled to occupy as his residence, rent-free, one of the houses owned by the government at Muscle Shoals.

In general, too, despite the language of the president's message and certain clauses of the act itself, the remarks of the southern congressmen clearly revealed their expectation that the old Underwood principle of sale of power at the switchboard would prevail and that the TVA would not engage in competition with private utility companies, as the northern congressmen were prophesying. They must have looked upon certain features of the act as rhetorical flourishes —nice, resounding words that in practice would mean little. They had little conception of how far-reaching the plans of the authority itself might turn out to be. In short, they did not know exactly what they were voting for, and neither did the constituencies they represented in Congress.

If they had known—if they could have visualized the TVA that would emerge instead of the TVA they had in mind—they might have insisted upon certain modifications of the act, for they had schooled themselves to think in terms of private enterprise which might to some extent be subsidized by government, and did not, like Norris, think in terms of government replacing private enterprise. But if they had any doubts, such doubts are not revealed in the record of debate. The southern congressmen had the votes at last, they believed in the Muscle Shoals dream as they conceived it, and they were behind the president one hundred per cent. They put the legislation through in a hurry. Thus was TVA born. That prodigious birth signified—at least to all urbanminded dwellers in the Tennessee Valley—that the dynasty of Kilowatt at long last was securely seated and established.

Yet somehow between the earlier Congressional acceptance of the Tennessee River problem as one requiring "unified development" and the actual formulation and adoption of the TVA statute, a new and revolutionary conception had intervened. The law creating the TVA was by official title a

## AT LAST! KINGDOM REALLY COMES! 219

Muscle Shoals bill, and it embodied various provisions which had earlier failed of enactment. Specifically, it provided for construction of Dam No. 3 of the old Muscle Shoals project and for the Cove Creek storage dam on the Clinch River; it reasserted the old provisions for the use of the nitrate plants for the manufacture of fertilizer in peace and for explosives in time of war. It also authorized the TVA to "sell the surplus power not used in its operations," with preference to states, counties, municipalities, and co-operatives; and it provided that the TVA could construct, purchase, or lease transmission lines by which to dispose of its power.

At the same time, in Sections 22 and 23 of the act, there was much reference to planning on a very broad regional scale. A. E. Morgan, it seemed, had a hand in writing these sections. Section 22 provided that the president, within the limits of appropriations made by Congress, might order "surveys of and general plans for" the entire drainage basin of the Tennessee River (and maybe some adjoining territory) with a view to developing its resources and looking after "the general welfare of the citizens." This would be done with the general purpose of "fostering an orderly and proper physical, economic, and social development" of the region, in conjunction with the states affected and their subdivisions and agencies or "with co-operative or other organizations." Section 23, after emphasizing flood control, navigation, and electric power as among the purposes of the authority, added specific reference to proper use of marginal lands, reforestation, and economic and social well-being, and included them among the concerns of the authority to which the president himself would give particular attention from time to time, through his recommendations to Congress. The president at once, through executive order, made TVA responsible for carrying out the "surveys and general plans" referred to.

Thus the principle of unified development went beyond

any mere adjustment of navigation, flood control, and power production in a single engineering plan. The Tennessee Valley Authority, under Sections 22 and 23, became, in the sociological language of the day, a very ambitious "multiple purpose project" which seemingly would be geared and authorized to take notice of any item of valley life that could be included under the term "general welfare" or "physical, economic, and social development."

What did these clauses of the act mean? Just how broad would the authority's powers be over the lives, property, and miscellaneous concerns of the valley people? Nobody really knew, as yet, but nobody seemed much bothered, unless it was the private utility companies and their attorneys, already anxiously bestirring themselves.

Furthermore, the TVA was not an ordinary bureau or agency of the federal government. It was set up as a government corporation. Political scientists knew what a government corporation was, and so did such financiers and businessmen as had already had dealings with the Reconstruction Finance Corporation. But such government corporations had been few in number and had worked in limited and rather special spheres. The public in general did not know what a government corporation was, or had only such acquaintance with the device as might be gained from the sketchy notices given in newspapers and news-weeklies.

The sphere in which the TVA might move was, in its farthest possible limits, not well defined. During the period when its dams and power plants were being built, it would have to depend upon Congress for moneys and was to that extent subject to scrutiny and check. Congress also had power, under the terms of the act, to remove the directors by concurrent resolution and to require annual reports and accountings. The TVA was allowed a limited power to issue bonds; and it had no capital.

On the other hand, the TVA was accorded striking liberties. It was exempt from civil service requirements, and the law specifically provided that "in the appointment of officials and the selection of employees . . . no political test or qualification shall be permitted or given consideration." Thus the TVA personnel was entirely removed from the controls, partly federal and direct, partly local and indirect, to which most government agencies were subject. It could retain and use, subject to certain limitations, the revenues that it might derive from the sale of power. Seemingly, too, in some indeterminate fashion, the business operations and accounts of the TVA were not under the specific control of the General Accounting Office and the Bureau of the Budget, and thus it escaped the routine supervision that slowed up government bureaus. Accordingly, the TVA was not clogged by "red tape." It could go about its business with a speed and efficiency unknown among governmental agencies. When its building program was finished, it would not need to ask Congress for appropriations, it would be self-sufficient, it would run like a regular business enterprise. Congress could, of course, investigate the affairs of TVA, or abolish it (though not its works, once these were complete); but it was entirely free of state or local controls. The people of the valley, although ruled in certain ways by its three directors, could not elect them. They were appointed by the president, and TVA was seemingly responsible directly to the president, as well as to Congress, for it was outside the normal departmental system of the federal government. Nor could the people of the valley and their several states in any way control or influence the policies of TVA, except through the roundabout process of federal legislation. It was always a difficult matter to invoke that process against well-established government agencies of any sort, and in the case of TVA the difficulty was magnified by the regional character of the authority. For if the people of the valley should object at any time, through their representatives in Congress, to TVA policies or administration, they would be in the position of bringing before the representatives of forty-eight states what might seem to be an entirely local plea of a few states. Just how would such problems work out in the end?

At the moment, nobody seemed to care. The Tennessee Valley received its savior in a holiday mood. The Muscle Shoals problem was going to be laid to rest forever. More than that, something tremendous and magnificent was in the making, something that even the wildest optimist could hardly have pictured. During more than threescore years of almost unbroken Republican domination the federal government, generally speaking, had been about as distant from the local concerns of the Tennessee Valley as the old government of King George III, and no more helpful. There had been a break during the Wilson administration, but the high hopes of those days had evaporated. Now everything would be different.

President Roosevelt's appointments to the Board of Directors of TVA were generally approved. The chairman, Arthur E. Morgan, was already a famous engineer, and, furthermore, as president of Antioch College, in Ohio, he was known as something of an idealist and a sage, a thinker as much concerned about people as about dams. He was a leader of a kind rarely produced in an industrialized civilization—an expert and a specialist who had overleaped the bounds of his science and had come to think and act in terms of the general interest. Grim he seemed to some people, more than a little grim, and certainly not suave. Yet one could feel, when he spoke to valley audiences, that though there was austerity in Arthur Morgan's manner, one was undeniably in the presence of intellect and dignity.

As representative of the valley on the board, President Roosevelt appointed Harcourt A. Morgan, then president of the University of Tennessee. He was, however, not a native of the valley, or of the South, or of the United States. Canadian born, he had not been naturalized as an American citizen until 1920, but he had lived long in Tennessee and was well acquainted with all the basic problems of life in his adopted region. Originally an entomologist, Harcourt Morgan had become interested in agriculture in general, and he knew, as well as an administrative expert could, the good and the evil of the farmer's estate in the Tennessee Valley. Inevitably, he would have much to do with whatever agricultural policy TVA might develop under its apparently very broad responsibility. He was a quiet, retiring man who avoided controversy and publicity. During the hubbub of the Dayton trial, he had preserved a discreet silence.

The third, and youngest, member of the board was David E. Lilienthal, a brilliant attorney who had distinguished himself in Wisconsin's fight to regulate private power companies. Lilienthal was a graduate of the Harvard Law School and a member of Donald Richberg's law firm. Much more than the other two members of the board, he represented the type of young administrator that the New Deal was already calling into public service. From his background, it seemed entirely probable that the power program of TVA would be his foremost concern, and his public activity soon made evident the reason for his appointment. Of the three men, Lilienthal was farthest removed from the ancient, indigenous life of the valley; in fact, in comparison with the other two men, he seemed much more definitely an "outsider." But Lilienthal was suave, as the two Morgans were not; he had obvious gifts of personal attraction that bound followers to him. He was essentially an advocate, and a skillful one, full of passionate conviction about the benefits of electric power and the great possibilities of TVA.

In the hands of these three men, endowed by Congress with extraordinarily broad administrative authority, rested the future of the Tennessee River, its valley, and its people. These three had powers that kings might have envied, and that no king or political officer had ever enjoyed in the Tennessee region except in the days when federal authority meant federal bayonets. They had the resources of the federal treasury to draw upon in a time when a pliant Congress approved the philosophy of spending freely from the public purse. They could change the natural environment to such an extent that the natural order might be deeply and even permanently affected; and in changing the natural order they might change the course of human life in the seven states of the Tennessee Valley. Their engineering decisions would result in engineering works of unprecedented mass and intricacy, and were therefore unlike political decisions, which can be amended or annulled. One cannot repeal a great dam, once it has been built, much less a system of great dams controlling a watershed of more than forty thousand square miles. If they achieved good, as was expected, it would be the good that they and their staff of experts had pondered and blueprinted, not the good that might emerge from the various assemblies, nonexpert, discursively democratic, of the people of the valley. If they made a mistake, it would be made on a gigantic scale and could not be easily rectified. It would leave a scar forever. *They could not afford to make a mistake.* They were in the position, as one of their own supporters afterwards said, of playing God to the Tennessee Valley.

If the three members of the board trembled at the prospect of exercising such power, they gave no public evidence of it. On the whole, they seemed to take it as a matter of course that the official union of the Indian river with his Majesty Kilowatt II was but the obvious climax of a mission foreordained to be consummated under their auspices. As they took their posts and began without the slightest hesitation to enlist their cohorts, give their orders, and issue the expected news releases, pamphlets, and government documents, the celestial dome resounded with their praise, and from coast to coast the press of the nation, with almost unanimous voice, announced the coming of the Kingdom. It was a moment which seemed to require the voice of some exultant poet like Percy Bysshe Shelley, who ended his imaginary drama of a rather similar occasion with the words—

> This, like thy glory, Titan, is to be
> Good, great and joyous, beautiful and free;
> This is alone Life, Joy, Empire, and Victory!

For indeed, the regime of Hoover, now cast down, seemed to parallel the dominion of Jupiter, overthrown in Shelley's *Prometheus Unbound;* and the wedding of the Tennessee and Kilowatt was expected to produce about the same utopian results as Shelley's symbolic union of Prometheus and the nymph Asia. None of the practicing American or British poets, however, seemed prepared for the occasion, and so, while Hoover-as-Jupiter was dragged off the scene by the Furies, the TVA got along very well with the tumult of trucks, bulldozers, and cement mixers and with such hymeneal noises as the press and the radio could produce.

CHAPTER XIV

# The TVA Makes a New River

THE FIRST TASK of the TVA was to round out the unfinished business of the Muscle Shoals project, to which, as the prime cause of its being, it owed both legal and filial duty. The authority had to maintain and operate Wilson Dam and its power plant, together with the old nitrate plants. Almost immediately, too, the authority found itself charged with building the Cove Creek Dam, for which the army engineers had already made preliminary surveys. This project, located far to the east on the Clinch River, just below the confluence of the Clinch and the Powell, had come to be viewed as an essential part of the Muscle Shoals scheme. The rather vaguely worded statute, while authorizing TVA to build dams and other works, seemed to leave construction itself to the army engineers, under the secretary of war or the secretary of the interior, but the president quickly straightened out that knot by directing TVA to proceed with the Cove Creek Dam. Shortly afterwards he asked that TVA also begin work on Dam No. 3, or Wheeler Dam, where the army engineers were already constructing a navigation lock. Thus at an early stage TVA had two large construction jobs on its hands, and furthermore it was obliged to build without delay a transmission line from the Cove Creek Dam to Muscle Shoals in order to unite the power facilities of the widely separated projects.

For the first year or more of its existence, TVA made

no very definite motions toward putting any grand scheme under way. It was, indeed, necessarily preoccupied with the two massive construction jobs already on hand; it was also marshaling its forces, getting acquainted with its terrain, and determining its strategy. To assemble a force of competent administrators, engineers, and experts for all its multiple purposes while simultaneously pushing ahead two enormous tasks of construction was in itself a tremendous accomplishment, which might have daunted or defeated lesser men. Yet, with really amazing expeditiousness, the two Morgans and Lilienthal were able to organize and to execute, to plan and to build, to desire and to consummate in one single administrative motion, as if thought and deed were inseparable and continuous. Never before in the Tennessee country, and probably never anywhere else in the world, had so great an enterprise gone so rapidly into action. It seemed to be governed by a genius, zeal, and experience of a high order, and it also seemed to borrow momentum from the enthusiastic upsurge of the first Roosevelt administration.

The general public, though it knew little of the authority's tasks of organization and its painful awareness of difficulties ahead, seemed to feel that some new principle of vitality had been released by TVA to redeem an ailing world. What the people heard and read, came as messages and pronouncements from A. E. Morgan and Lilienthal, and less often from Harcourt Morgan; these gave the public an inspiring, if as yet somewhat generalized, anticipation of great things ahead. What people saw, as the Cove Creek Dam rose to view, with its adjacent embellishments, confirmed the interpretation that the authority had prompted.

The Cove Creek Dam was named Norris Dam in honor of Senator Norris. Senator Norris was, the newspapers said, the "Father of TVA." Most certainly he was its most influential friend and sponsor, outside of the White House. He had triumphed after many defeats, and he was a beloved public personage.

The very naming of the dam attracted enormous and favorable attention to the great project, and TVA and the friends of TVA took care that none of this attention was wasted. Evidently someone in high place knew how to focus this attention so that it would count, but the name, the physical situation, the magnitude of the work, and the fact that Norris Dam seemed to symbolize the new hope represented by TVA—all this was something worth focusing on, as the most carping critic would have to admit. The combination was irresistible. It could not fail to impress. For years to come millions of Americans, after visiting the spot, would define TVA as what they saw at Norris Dam, on some fine happy day of a Tennessee spring or summer or autumn.

The engineers pitched the dam across the gorge of the Clinch at a point where the impounded waters sent back long, tranquil bays between wooded ridges into the blue distance. Looking at it there, with a green bank and wooded hill on one side and a rugged cliff on the other, a gazer thought it aptly fitted where it belonged, if one were going to build a dam, and one neglected to think about its great height —265 feet—or its length of 1,860 feet, or its massiveness that overlooked the large powerhouse at its base, or the fact that its barrier could flood about 37,000 acres of Tennessee land for a distance of sixty or seventy miles up the twin valleys of the Clinch and the Powell.* The visitors' house, unobtrusively modern in design, and the parking spaces and drives that curved between plots of green, were toned gently into the pattern. The woods were all around. One could feel at peace.

But that was not all. One came to Norris Dam from

---

\* This figure of 37,000 acres, with the corresponding figure for Kentucky Reservoir, is arrived at by subtracting the original river bed area from the supposed maximum lake area. The figures given in the earlier annual reports of TVA (in 1940, for example) are sometimes at variance with the latest available figures. TVA from time to time has also altered slightly its statistical terminology. The author is not responsible for discrepancies arising from such causes.

Knoxville and after following a state highway turned on to the Norris Freeway. The freeway led the motorist along a pleasant narrow valley. On either side, as the road wound among the ridges, the motorist could see, or begin to see, neatly fostered illustrations of the forest conservation and proper land use which the authority was committed to sponsor. The nearer he came to Norris Dam, the more the countryside took on the appearance of an amiable wild park which told him, without words, how Tennessee ought to look if it were benevolently protected from man's foolishness. At a neat filling station—also designed to illustrate how very pleasant a filling station might be—he found signs directing him to Norris Village, which of course he had heard much about and was bound to visit. For Norris Village was the model town, or ideal town, of the Tennessee Valley, as the authority conceived a rural town. It had grown out of Chairman Morgan's belief that money ought not to be wasted on ugly temporary shacks of the "shotgun" type that usually housed a construction force. Why not make the workers' village into something permament that would serve the community when the dam building was over—something like a "resettlement" or a "subsistence homestead" project? So there was Norris Village, with its modest houses that represented attractive sublimations of the local domestic architecture of Tennessee, and its community center with stores, school, and chapel as ideally spick-and-span as anything in the Williamsburg Restoration. With its curving drives along which houses were tastefully scattered, it was as fine as anything could be. It was, in fact, despite its air of modesty, a little too fine to become a resettlement project. For country folks could not live in a park, away from means of subsistence. And anyway, in those rather small houses, just what would you do with a pack of children and a lot of kinfolks? But Norris Village did very well for people who had few children and perhaps no nearby kinfolks—namely, the staff and office force of TVA itself. It speedily became, therefore, their suburban residence, and served very well for that. To Westbrook Pegler's sarcastic eye, Norris Village was "Camp Fauntleroy." One could laugh, without malice, at this typically American quip, and still, in one's heart, commend the pleasantness of Norris Village and the principle behind it. For, like the Williamsburg Restoration, it seemed to tell the visitor that modern America on the whole had done rather poorly with its resources, and it reminded him what might have been, if only . . . if only! It was a lesson in something or other that Americans ought to learn.

The average motorist, however, made a simpler speculation. He unconsciously assumed a general dispensation of blessings that TVA was providing throughout the valley, and, with an illustrated TVA pamphlet in his hand, picked up at the Norris drugstore, he motored on over the hill and presently coming up the narrow valley of the Clinch caught in the distance his first entrancing view of the wonder, Norris Dam.

All along the freeway, down almost to the banks of the river, TVA had made plantings of native shrubs and trees which told the visitor how beautifully the country could come alive under TVA's care; and the statistics in his clutched pamphlet told him, furthermore, how many eroded acres TVA had restored in Norris basin and how many trees it had set out for reforestation. He stopped, perhaps, at the foot of a little ravine and bought a sack of water-ground corn meal at the eighteenth century grist mill—a restoration, perfectly equipped with authentic millrace, millwheel, wooden machinery, and millstones, which TVA had thoughtfully assembled at that point. The contrast between the slow-turning, old-fashioned water wheel and the turbines of Norris Dam was too obvious to miss. It was the difference between the land of the pioneers and the planned society of the New Deal. The exhibit seemed to say that, although now Norris Dam represented the proper modern thing and you had to accept it because it was modern, TVA was still by no means heedless of what the gristmill stood for. TVA would, apparently, promote Norris Dam and likewise cherish with fond care the individualism, the homeliness, the folkways, the crafts of the old time in Tennessee. It could do both.

After this lesson the motorist would go on up the slope toward Norris Dam itself, pausing now and then, as view after view unfolded. He would look his fill at every level of vision and receive polite, discreet instruction from the highly trained and evidently well-bred attendants who were, like Chairman A. E. Morgan himself, employees of the mighty government, the United States of America. If the motorist happened to be lucky, he might stay overnight at one of the tourist cottages tucked away in the woods. It would be an experience that Mom and the children and Grandma or Auntie would take back with them to keep at Sauk Center, or Peoria, or Akron, or Brooklyn, or Pittsburgh. There would be millions of such pops, moms, grandmas, and aunties, and their young ones, for Norris Dam, thus connected intimately with Knoxville, was most conveniently located to tap the great tourist stream that flowed annually through the nearby Great Smoky Mountains National Park, and so on to Florida or the Valley of Virginia or elsewhere.

Meanwhile, in the Great Bend, where Wheeler Dam was going up, it was also nice, yet not so nice as at Norris. The fervors of North Alabama subsided into a mixture of satisfaction and disappointment. There was satisfaction that the Muscle Shoals project (for so the Alabamians thought of it still) was rounding out at last. But there was cold horror, followed by anger, when the Alabamians realized that the center of gravity of the vast enterprise had been shifted from the Great Bend to the Upper Tennessee—to Knoxville itself, in fact. The Alabamians pinched themselves and wondered if they were having nightmares. The law said quite plainly in Section 8 of the TVA Act: "The corporation shall maintain its principal office in the immediate vicinity of Muscle Shoals, Alabama." Nevertheless, the authority, in seeming disregard of statutory requirements, was renting whole buildings and moving into a vast amount of office space at Knoxville, which was not in the vicinity of Muscle Shoals, but was three hundred miles away. To be sure, the authority had caused a puny sign to be put up on a building at Muscle Shoals: but that was adding insult to injury, since no business of importance was transacted in that building, whereas the board sat at Knoxville, did its managing from that point, crowded the city with its numerous employees, and filled all East Tennessee with its bustle.

It was generally felt in North Alabama that Chairman A. E. Morgan was somehow personally hostile to their country, and maybe the other directors were, too. Chairman Morgan had spoken in a slurring and depreciatory manner about their school facilities and seemed in general to disapprove of their arrangements. He also seemed to think that North Alabama was just looking for a chance to launch a grand real estate boom, and he proposed to quash it. The Alabama people knew—as A. E. Morgan knew—that the new Muscle Shoals boom was being inflated by New York City promoters, not by Alabamians. But in any case, why should the Muscle Shoals people be punished—if the policy was intended as punishment? And how was any corporation, even a government corporation, entitled to violate the law that created it?

The policy met with quick reproof and protest from Alabama sources. Hugo L. Black, then senator from Alabama, at once raised the issue in a series of letters to Chairman Morgan. He was, he said, a friend to TVA, but he could not "defend a plain, palpable, and open violation of the statute."

The authority answered such tart criticisms rather evasively at first. Its official position was finally stated in a letter by A. E. Morgan, August 15, 1934, in which he took refuge in the old dodge often practiced by corporations—what might be called the Delaware dodge. The language of the statute, said Chairman Morgan, referred to a "legal headquarters," and that was not necessarily a working headquarters. The "legal domicile" of TVA was, truly, at Muscle Shoals. But, he went on to say, "There are hundreds of corporations in America . . . of which the principal offices are located at one point and the business and working offices at another."

This official answer to complaint was not accepted with very good grace, but the tumult died away for the time being. As the vast scale of TVA operations became more evident, the North Alabama people became more placid, if not yet reconciled. They nursed a sense of injury, however, and it was to some degree allied with party feeling and the old sectionalism. As loyal Democrats, they felt that they were entitled to the big plum, TVA headquarters; and it irked them grievously that the plum fell into the lap of Republican East Tennessee, which, they felt, had been at best rather tepid toward the long-promoted development of the Tennessee River. They could not help feeling that TVA was antipathetic toward them; that it rather hoped, through the location of its headquarters in East Tennessee, to erase the memory of its true progenitor, Muscle Shoals; and that furthermore, A. E. Morgan and his northern friends preferred the balmier mountain climate of the Knoxville region to the hotter, cotton-and-corn climate of the Great Bend.

Meanwhile the authority, having quashed these local expostulations, was busy with its great affairs. It had early become evident that, if the full aims of the multiple-purpose project were to be realized, it must apply its corporate brains to a fundamental problem. Exactly what system of "unified development" would TVA use for the Tennessee River and its tributaries? Would it supplement Wilson, Wheeler, and Norris dams (and the old Hales Bar Dam) with a system of low dams, for navigation purposes only, such as had been suggested in the 1930 report of the army engineers as representing the most conservative treatment of the problem?

Would it choose the high-dam system also described as feasible, but extremely costly, by the army engineers? Or would it find some compromise between a conservative and a radical approach?

The low-dam system would make the river navigable, would be inexpensive, and would not necessitate large inundations of rich valley land. But the low-dam system would slow up transportation by requiring a large number of lockages. It would contribute nothing to flood control. And the Muscle Shoals arrangements, with Wheeler Dam and Norris Dam added, would certainly not give the maximum power development.

Quite evidently TVA was inclined from the start to favor the high-dam system, as is indicated from the authorization by the board of the Pickwick Landing project in November, 1934, of the Guntersville project in November, 1935, and of the Chickamauga project in December, 1935.

The high-dam system would be very expensive indeed. It would cost many times as much as the most conservative plan; the engineers' estimates, for the whole Tennessee system, had run far over a billion dollars for this plan. But the TVA tended to believe that the enormous immediate expense and damage of the high-dam system would be more than offset by ultimate benefits. To develop the maximum electric power would increase TVA revenues and could eventually serve to liquidate, through an amortization plan, the large construction costs. The people of the valley, especially the farmers and others of modest estate, would benefit greatly by the availability of cheap electric power. The same high dams that developed the maximum power could be built so as to afford a salutory degree of flood control. Reconciliation of the demands of power production and flood control—which might easily come into conflict—could be worked out if the high dams of the main river were properly supplemented by storage dams on the tributary rivers, with the system arranged so as to be operated as a single vast unit.

And the high dams would expedite navigation by reducing the number of lockages to a minimum and by converting the Tennessee River into a chain of quiet lakes.

The lure of maximum possibilities was irresistible. Before the calculating eyes of the TVA directors and their staff of experts rose the vision of a river valley uniquely adapted to a far-reaching development which they could achieve through great engineering works, with whatever might be added of social engineering. The land itself, they deemed, was crying out for just the kind of economic and social improvement that their great design would bring. It was too bad, of course, that the inundations of the high-dam system would retire from cultivation large areas of fertile soil—the very soil that farmers of Tennessee and Alabama cherished most highly.

It was also too bad that, in order to achieve flood control, they would have to create a permanent flood in the valley itself—a permanent flood that would put the main river always beyond its banks in the wide reservoir stretches and that would back far up into smaller rivers and creeks—a permanent flood locked up under watchful eyes and instruments and held, or raised, or lowered according to the seasonal needs of the multiple-purpose project. Because of its encroachments, there would be removals of many a family from homes where, in symbol or in fact, the Revolutionary sword or the pioneer rifle still hung above the mantel. Hearth fires would be extinguished that were as old as the Republic itself. Old landmarks would vanish; old graveyards would be obliterated; the ancient mounds of the Indian, which had resisted both the plow of the farmer and the pick of the curiosity seeker, would go under the water. There would be tears, and gnashing of teeth, and lawsuits. There might even be feud and bloodshed. Yet these harms, inflicted upon a sizable and innocent minority, weighed less in the TVA scales than the benefits that would accrue, in terms of industrial and social engineering, to the nearby or the distant majority who sacrificed only tax money.

The Tennessee Valley, once it was viewed in engineering terms, indeed did offer unique possibilities. All the historic causes that had worked against the people of the valley now worked for the TVA and the high-dam system. The Indian wars that had diverted population movements and stamped the pioneer pattern deep upon the valley culture; the terrible destruction of the Civil War and the cruel bleeding of its aftermath; the old hindrances to navigation in the river itself; the impoverishment and economic disadvantage of the people under the modern regime—all these had left the valley unimproved and thinly populated in the areas to be inundated by the high-dam system. Luckily for TVA, few railroads and few major highways would be seriously affected. Said the authority itself in one of its official statements: "Of the major streams east of the Mississippi, the Tennessee River is one of the few, the banks of which are not continuously occupied by principal railroad and highway systems. One of the chief limitations upon a system of high dams is therefore absent."

Few towns of any size and no important urban areas would be subject to inundation. Few industrial establishments would be affected. The earlier agrarian preference of the valley people, the effects of the Civil War, the great industrial pre-eminence of the North had combined to check industrial development, and there were no important industrial establishments to endanger. No mineral deposits, except a few relatively valueless marble claims, would be covered up.

So the way was clear for TVA to make its decision. Since Chairman Arthur Morgan, who was both a civil engineer and a social engineer, was the member of the board chiefly responsible for engineering decisions, it may be assumed that the brunt of the responsibility for the great decision lay with him. If his fellow members of the board had any different ideas, they did not appear in the voluminous public records of TVA. Harcourt Morgan and David Lilienthal would hardly have opposed a high-dam system; it was not in conflict with their hopes and wishes. Besides, there was the great outline already laid down by the army engineers as an ideal, though probably unattainable, possibility. TVA could now get what the army engineers could not—unlimited funds. TVA could attain the unattainable.

Yet before the authority announced its official decision and sent it to Congress, there was a very strange period of hesitation.

Although the TVA board had authorized Pickwick, Guntersville, and Chickamauga dams by December, 1935, it seemed hesitant in asking for the Congressional authorizations and appropriations that alone would enable the construction program to be pushed forward. In 1934 the authority received an allocation of fifty million dollars from funds appropriated for the National Industrial Recovery Act, and in the following year received a similar allocation of twenty-five million dollars. Its first direct appropriation, made in 1935, was a sum of thirty-six million dollars. During this year, however, the friends of TVA in Congress became aware that the authority for some reason was holding back. It had not presented a definite plan of development or a schedule of construction, and its somewhat indefinite suggestions of a building program were not being supported by explicit requests for Congressional approval.

In later years, when arguments about TVA policies began to acquire a sharper edge, and it became convenient for the more fanatical partisans of the authority to develop the fiction that Senator Kenneth D. McKellar of Tennessee was "an enemy of TVA," the senator turned on his detractors with a surprising countercharge. Far from being an "enemy" of TVA, he pointed out, he had advocated the building of Pickwick, Guntersville, Chickamauga, Gilbertsville, Watts Bar, and Loudoun dams over the opposition of A. E. Morgan and other directors. "All of those dams," said Senator McKellar, in a hearing before a Senate committee, "were built not only over the opposition of the TVA, and members of the TVA, but against the opposition of A. E. Morgan . . . We got no recommendation of the TVA to build any of these others dams except the Norris and Wheeler Dams." Not only that, he declared, but while Chairman Morgan was "lobbying" against the construction of the dams, he, Senator McKellar, had intervened to see that the dams were authorized and that adequate appropriations were made. He pointed out that through his intervention, the Second Deficiency Act of 1935 was amended to authorize and direct "the continued construction of Norris Dam, Wheeler Dam, Pickwick Landing Dam," together with the beginning of construction of the Guntersville, Chickamauga, and Fowlers Bend dams, and investigations for the construction of dams at or near Aurora Landing and White's Creek.

The answer of the authority to Senator McKellar's statement was merely to present a detailed record which left much unexplained. In 1938, during the investigation of TVA by a Congressional committee, the testimony of both A. E. Morgan and Lilienthal indicated that in 1935 the members of the board were not only hesitant as to their ultimate construction program, but were having considerable difficulty in agreeing about important features of TVA policy. In fact, the breach between A. E. Morgan and the two other board members was by that time rather pronounced. From the testimony of the two directors, it would seem that Morgan was not yet satisfied as to the foundation conditions at the site of Chickamauga Dam, and he had unresolved doubts as to the function and practicality of that and other dams. Lilienthal, for his part, was concerned lest the authority overreach itself by undertaking too much too soon, and, more particularly, he was afraid that the authority might develop power production facilities more rapidly than it could find a market for power.

## TVA MAKES A NEW RIVER

Whatever the causes for the authority's hesitation, Congress was unmoved by those causes and called for action. In 1935 Congress amended the original TVA Act so as to eliminate its former vagueness and to make TVA's powers more broad and more definite. It now gave TVA specific authority to construct such dams as, in addition to those already in progress, would provide a 9-foot channel from Knoxville to the mouth of the Tennessee, with due provision also for flood control. This cleared the way for a high-dam system. Furthermore, Congress directed the TVA to report to Congress, not later than April 1, 1936, its recommendations for the unified development of the Tennessee River system.

The decision now had to be made. TVA rushed its surveys and studies and came forth at last, three years after it had been created, with its plan for subduing the Tennessee River. The plan was presented in a handsome, book-size publication, equipped with maps, charts, and photographs, entitled *The Unified Development of the Tennessee River System*. It proposed a completely radical treatment of the old problem—a thoroughgoing high-dam system. The plan was immediately approved by Congress. An overwhelming conquest of the old river and its wide-flung tributaries was at last assured. The Tennessee and its branches were to be obliterated by their own waters.

On the main river, the Tennessee itself, the new plan provided for nine high dams, including those previously erected or at the moment in progress. To Wilson, Wheeler, and Hales Bar dams the authority would add six magnificent structures approximately where the army engineers had already calculated they might be put, and these dams would create six great reservoir lakes.

Below Muscle Shoals there was first of all Pickwick Landing Dam, which by 1936 was already authorized and under construction. Its name preserved a local tradition, harking back to the days when the postmaster at the landing, a Dickens enthusiast, waited eagerly for the boat to bring him the latest installment of *Pickwick Papers*. The new dam would submerge the Colbert Shoals Canal, and Riverton Lock, which Goethals had designed. Between its location, a little above the battlefield of Shiloh, and Florence, about fifty miles upstream, it would lay down a broad sheet of sparkling water—a deep lake that would drown out most of Riverton, a good deal of old Waterloo, and much bottom land. It would turn Bear Creek and Yellow Creek into tremendous fresh-water versions of the firths and fjords of Europe. It would retire from use approximately sixty thousand acres of land, would uproot over four hundred families, and would cause highway readjustments of eighty-one miles. The dam structure would be 113 feet high, and the length of its embankments of concrete and earth would be 7,715 feet. The navigation lock would have a chamber of standard Mississippi size, 110 feet wide by 600 feet long. It would be a single-lift lock, and would raise and lower boats a maximum of 63 feet. Its power facilities, when completed, would generate 216,000 kilowatts. It would be provided with one of TVA's characteristically neat construction camps which could later be transformed into a permanent recreation center. It was scheduled for completion by 1939, but was brought into operation well ahead of schedule, in 1938.

Between Pickwick Landing Dam and Paducah only one dam was planned. This gigantic affair, the most startling of all the TVA projects, would be placed near Gilbertsville, Kentucky, at a point where the Tennessee and the Cumberland almost, but do not quite, meet. In anticipation of this construction Chairman Morgan had seen to it that the rights to the Aurora Landing project, which had been acquired by a private company, were taken over by TVA immediately after passage of the TVA Act. But the authority finally rejected the Aurora site and chose the Gilbertsville site instead, about twenty miles farther downstream. After the project was authorized, in 1937, and construction began, it became the Kentucky project, and the dam was named the Kentucky Dam.

And Kentucky Dam was to be a mighty affair. Paducah, twenty-three miles downriver, would repose nervously in its shadow. Behind its wall, which was 206 feet high and over a mile and a half long, the waters of the Tennessee

PICKWICK LANDING DAM

would be backed up for 184 miles, all the way to Pickwick Landing Dam. Its vast lake would stand, almost like the lagoon of geological ages past, on a straight north-and-south line across the width of Kentucky and Tennessee. Its reservoir would permanently retire from use 134,000 acres of land (not to speak of at least 100,000 more acres to be occasionally invaded for flood control), would cause the removal of some 3,500 families, and would completely drown out such Kentucky river towns as Birmingham and Newburg, and would vitally affect the arrangements of such places in Tennessee as

Stribling, Danville, Johnsonville, Trotter's Ferry, Cuba Landing.

These were all, of course, just little river villages, crossroads, or shipping points, beloved enough to their inhabitants, but lacking in industrial installations and therefore inexpensive to buy up. On the other hand, some very expensive readjustments of railroads and of railroad bridges would be necessary at Gilbertsville, Danville, and Johnsonville. The Big Sandy River and Duck River would become fresh-water estuaries, and Duck River bottoms, long famous for their corn crops, and other good bottom land along the Tennessee, would be invaded by water; and you could not grow good corn, in that country, except in the bottoms. The reservoir area would measure 256,000 acres of water. The navigation lock, like the one at Pickwick, would be of standard Ohio-Mississippi size, and would be a single-lift lock of 73 feet. The power facilities would eventually provide 160,000 kilowatts. The TVA scheduled Kentucky Dam for completion in 1944.

In the Great Bend the TVA, following the lead given by the army engineers, decided to erect a high dam at a site a little below Guntersville, Alabama. It was not such a majestic dam, quite, as some others, since it was only 94 feet high and 3,979 feet long, but its reservoir would back up the Tennessee for about eighty miles, all the way to Dragging Canoe's old citadel at Running Water, and would drown out the almost brand-new conservative improvements at Widow's Bar Dam. It would submerge, too, some of the historic islands of the river, and a great deal more corn land and cotton land. It would not drown out any towns, but it would leave Guntersville on an elevated peninsula, with a fresh-water lake almost all around it, and would transform life at Guntersville to a considerable degree. Decatur also would be affected, but it was luckily on the high side of the river. The Guntersville project would bring about 1,182 removals of families, and it would cause the TVA no little

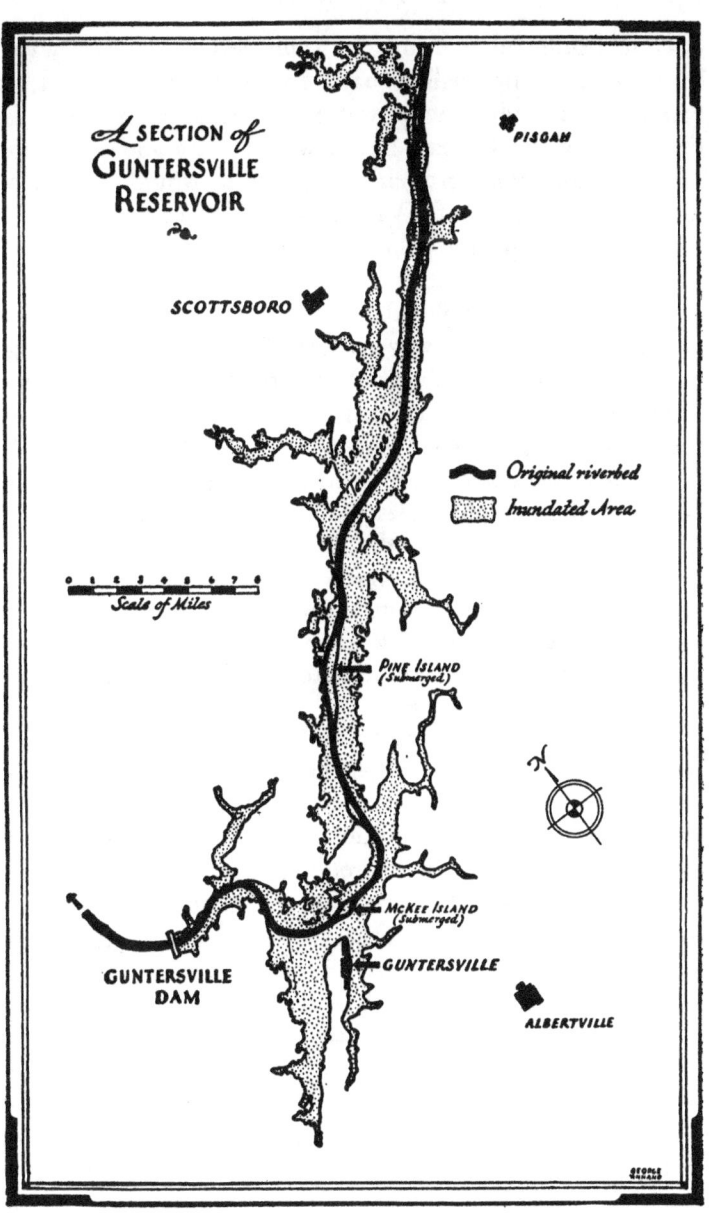

grief in bridge adjustments. It would send Tennessee water backing up, along shallow bays, for many miles inland, at various points where wide water had never been before in the times known to man, and it would retire about 110,000 acres of land from ordinary use; but it would be one of the most spectacular of TVA's lakes, and the power facilities would generate 97,200 kilowatts of the royal juice.

On the Upper Tennessee, the authority planned Chickamauga Dam, seven miles above Chattanooga; the Watts Bar Dam, a little over halfway between Chattanooga and Kingston; and the Coulter Shoals Dam, later named Fort Loudoun Dam, which would be erected near Lenoir City, just above the mouth of the Little Tennessee.

These new dams on the main river, together with Wilson, Wheeler, and the old Hales Bar Dam, would create the desired 9-foot channel on the Tennessee River all the way from Kentucky Dam to Knoxville, except in certain short stretches where minor improvements would eventually be necessary. Below Kentucky Dam, the 9-foot channel was already secured, from Paducah to the TVA dam, by Dam No. 52 on the Ohio River.

In their general character and function, the Upper Tennessee dams would not differ much from the dams lower down. As parts of the unified system, they would make their proportionate contribution to navigation improvement, flood control, and power production, and their reservoirs would bring about the same kind of inundations, removals, and readjustments as the other dams. In respect to navigation, however, they differed in one important way: their navigation locks, without exception, were only about half the standard Ohio-Mississippi size: that is, they were 60 by 360 feet instead of being 110 by 600. In this the authority seemed to be following the precedent set at Wilson, Wheeler, and Hales Bar dams, all of which had small locks. There still seemed to be an expectation that, as of old, there would be less river traffic above Muscle Shoals than below it, despite

## TVA MAKES A NEW RIVER 247

the boon of the 9-foot channel and the drowning of all obstacles.

Since the upper river was in the mountain section of the Tennessee Valley, the lakes formed by the high dams would be much more irregular in their contours than the lagoon-like reservoirs of the lower river and the Muscle Shoals region. The gathered waters would push up into ravines where forests came down to the lake's edge; they would curl here and there in unexpected arcs to follow valleys gouged out by the rush of primeval floods, ages past; or, at other points, they would lap over cultivated valley land, bringing fish to the farmer's doorstep and floods or marshy shallows where water had rarely, if ever, been seen. Chickamauga reservoir, pushing up into the Hiwassee, would make Charleston-on-the-Hiwassee a genuine river port; and it would also put underwater a large part of Hiwassee Island, at the mouth of Hiwassee, where Sam Houston, during one of his rages against civilization, had once lived with his Cherokee friends. Dayton, formerly off the river, would find the Tennessee creeping up within its town limits, to cause the removal of a grammar school, several business establishments, and many families. So it would go, all the way from Paducah to Knoxville, until the 9-foot channel and all other multiple purposes were achieved.

The location of the upper river dams was, of course, in some part predetermined by the earlier building of Hales Bar Dam and by the presence on the river of its only two cities of real size, Chattanooga and Knoxville. Chickamauga Dam, of necessity, had to be situated at the head or near the head of Hales Bar pool, but it could not be placed as near the head as the authority might have wished, because the nearer site would have devastated Chattanooga. TVA was caught in something of a predicament, since the eligible foundation sites above Chattanooga, after being explored, presented real difficulties to high-dam builders. It finally had to select a site, faute de mieux, where the foundation overlay certain mixed and faulty rock structures, and these had to receive special treatment. Fort Loudoun Dam, also, had to be placed so as not to cause grief to the city of Knoxville.

There was another difficulty at the other end of the river. Kentucky Dam was in the New Madrid earthquake zone, where great natural convulsions had occurred early in the nineteenth century. There, again, the TVA had to take special precautions. But it had plenty of money and all the engineering skill it needed. It had very able consulting geologists; it made the dams conform to their recommendations and went ahead.

And still that was not all. In its 1936 plan for unified development the authority also recommended a storage dam at Fowler's Bend on the Hiwassee, about 75 miles above the mouth of the river. This, the Hiwassee Dam, completed in 1940, extended the operations of TVA into Georgia. It also proposed to acquire the Fontana site, high up on the Little Tennessee River, although this site was owned by the Aluminum Company of America, which had already built its Calderwood, Cheoah, and Santeetlah dams on this historic branch of the Tennessee. Not until many years later, however, did TVA carry out its plans and build at last its Fontana Dam—a structure 480 feet high, the most astonishing of its mountain valley projects.

As time went on, and the position of TVA became more securely established, it went far beyond the rather hasty and incomplete design of 1936. As the threat of war grew in the nineteen-forties, the Chatuge, Apalachia, Nottely, and Ocoee No. 3 projects, all in the Hiwassee basin, were ordered to be built. Cherokee Dam went up on the Holston, just above Knoxville. On the French Broad, Douglas Dam was authorized and built, although not until earnest local protests had been overridden and Senator Kenneth McKellar of Tennessee had led a vigorous fight against the inundation of another rich valley. As its power widened, TVA acquired other dam properties through purchase, such as the Tennessee Electric Power Company's dams on the Ocoee and the Great Falls development on the Caney Fork, which was outside the Tennessee Valley. It had added, too, a steam-power plant to the Watts Bar project. By 1946 it possessed, or in one way or another controlled, twenty-six dams, finished or in the latter stages of completion. In its dossier, too, were still more plans, including one for a dam near the mouth of the Little Tennessee which would send water lapping around the ruins of old Fort Loudoun and would inundate the pleasant fields and weather-worn mounds where the Cherokees had lived of old.

What the total cost of all this work would be was still not definitely known in 1946. By the end of 1945 about $678,000,000 had been appropriated by Congress, and more appropriations were in prospect. In one public statement Mr. Lilienthal estimated the ultimate cost at a billion dollars. Of the authority's earnings, it reported, in 1947, that it had returned $23,000,000 to the federal treasury within two years; the earnings previous to that return had been "plowed back" into the business.

Clearly, this grand proliferation of the original Muscle Shoals improvement plan was not a result of any initiating impulse or will of those most immediately affected, the general public of the valley region itself. It was true that Lytle Brown, the army engineer from Tennessee, had contributed to the predesign of TVA and that Lewis Watkins, also from Tennessee, had guided the survey that resulted in the 1930 engineers' report. Yet to these men the Tennessee was a physical problem rather than a social cause. The TVA, on the other hand, had grown by what it fed on, in response to the logic of its own being or to policies not indigenous to the Tennessee Valley. The decision to follow the high-dam system for the entire river basin was an engineering decision, or a kind of engineering decision, in which the people of the valley had had no effective part. The experts could say that the issues were too complex for the people to comprehend and too technical to be argued in any popular forum. Furthermore, the major decision and all subsequent decisions arising out of it had been submitted to and approved by Congress. The advocates of TVA could and did argue that the great enterprise had a national meaning. The temper of Congress supported the TVA. It was a favored child of the Roosevelt administration. To be sure, the temper of Congress might change after a while. There would someday be a new administration. But by that time the dams would be built and the whole project would be in operation. Not even the Supreme Court would order TVA to take down its high dams or junk its transmission lines.

TVA could, and it would, and it did, make a new river, and not only a new river but a new river system. The supporters of TVA had reason to exult in that. The transformation was marvelous. Still, it was not exactly the transformation that Tennessee and Alabama might have thought up.

CHAPTER XV

# The Workings of TVA

A S THE GREAT LEVIATHAN rushed its physical works to completion and developed its numerous co-ordinated applications of physical and social science, it became evident that here in the Tennessee Valley, of all places, was emerging one of the marvels of the modern world. The event was as unimaginable and surprising as the rise of a Marxist socialist state in backward Czarist Russia, of all places, had been earlier. It was something nobody would have predicted for the Tennessee Valley. Nevertheless, this unprophesied technological eruption made happy not only the immediate recipients of TVA blessings but also many anxious Americans who had begun to wonder whether the United States could adapt its political mechanisms to modern needs. Abroad, the totalitarian regimes were boasting about their efficiency. Theirs seemed to Americans a cruel efficiency, gained at the cost of liberty. The TVA, it was now said with pride, answered the totalitarian challenge by proving that a democratic government could be even more efficient than a totalitarian regime, and yet be kind and good and not in any way oppressive.

The TVA people went ahead as if, all their lives, they had been training to demonstrate such a thesis. Within a brief decade nearly every important engineering enterprise was either finished or well under way. Once it developed its methods, assembled its machinery, and instructed its personnel, TVA could move from project to project without loss of time or momentum. It could keep several projects under construction at different stages and could switch its corps of specialists and workers from point to point like a general maneuvering armies at different stages of a modern battle. Where sheer construction was involved, it was an engineers' paradise.

But since it was a multiple-purpose project, warmly humanitarian in bias, and was charged under the law with fostering social and economic welfare, TVA had responsibilities of a kind that engineers rarely worry about. For its own legal security TVA must see that the demands of navigation, flood control, power, fertilizer, national defense, and conservation were duly satisfied. Then, in harmony with the spirit of its foundation, it was also bound to alleviate the harsh or tragic dislocations that its program necessitated.

TVA took forethought of everything. Its check list of things to do was encyclopedic, but it let no item go unchecked. TVA had a carefully framed labor policy, designed to use local manpower in the areas of construction. It did not let jobs out to contract, but hired and trained its own labor force, with careful respect for union standards and with some regard for regional peculiarities. It forestalled trouble on the race question by employing Negro workmen in proportion to the amount of Negro population in a given area, and gave them white folks' wages. There was still some complaint from Negro leaders in the North about the "white-collar" worker problem, but TVA managed to explain itself out of trouble.

Avoiding repetition of its early and costly mistake at Norris Village, TVA built neat temporary villages to house its workers at the various projects, and then converted the residue of these villages into recreation centers when the construction work was over. It provided technical schools for its workers and arranged its schedule of operations so that the ax and saw men of the reservoir clearance gangs could take up the slack of unemployment and fill the gaps in seasonal farm labor.

It hearkened to the plaints of archaeologists who were alarmed that the mounds and village sites of the Indians, especially the island sites, would so soon be immersed, fathoms deep, and, utilizing the services of the archaeologists of Kentucky, Tennessee, and Alabama, arranged for them to go into every reservoir area, with funds and labor at their command, and to dig, survey, photograph, and tabulate to their hearts' content. So for every new inundation there was a new archaeological study, published or in prospect.

More in line with its own purposes, however, were the careful studies of physical resources, of agricultural and industrial phenomena, and of all conceivably related matters which TVA either undertook with its own staff or wheedled federal, state, county, and community agencies into undertaking. In part these grew out of TVA's responsibility for making the principle of "unified development" actually work; and in part out of the vaguer, ill-defined "planning sections" of the TVA Act. As these studies accumulated, the bibliography of TVA publications swelled to stupendous bulk. The Office of Information, directed by T. L. Sturdevant, not only provided expert service for the TVA staff but was also a willing and courteous bureau of information for the valley and the country at large.

By the very nature of its enterprises TVA was almost forced into the role of consultant and adviser. In the course of its dam building TVA had to relocate stretches of highways, build new bridges, and readjust the waterworks and sewerage systems of towns and cities along its reservoirs. All this, a gigantic labor in itself, might have been only a straight engineering job but for the fact that the law had equipped the corporation with a soul, or at least with a social consciousness. Therefore its relationship to the communities affected was not that of a purely professional adviser. In return for the damage inflicted, TVA felt obliged to offer more than money. It wanted to show that good might be brought out of evil; that new arrangements, better than the old arrangements, might be put into effect. As it showed how this might be done, TVA found itself drawn into planning and zoning. It began to be sought out for such ends, for in some instances it could offer an advisory service more adequate than states and municipalities.

At one time, early in TVA history, Chairman Morgan tinkered with the idea of promoting the consolidation and reorganization of counties, especially those which were split in twain or sliced off by the great reservoirs. To its surprise, the authority found itself sharply rebuffed. The sundered parts of Union County were not to be wooed into marriage with adjoining counties. They cared nothing for the social and economic gains to be achieved by such consolidation. Long, long had they been Union County and, poor though they might be, they would remain parts of Union County even if oceans roared between. Hastily the authority dropped that subject. Nevertheless, as planner for all and sundry matters, it benignly continued to make or to sponsor extensive studies in county government and administration, in community planning, in rural economics, and it was eternally busy—no one knew exactly why—with adult education, library service, and such miscellaneous endeavors.

The most delicate problem of all came under some such technical heading as "reservoir clearance" and had to do with the purchase of land and other property in the reservoir areas and the removal of valley inhabitants out of the way of the rising waters. By June, 1946, in the sixteen areas where it had erected high dams, TVA had acquired, with easements and certain special purchases included, over 1,129,000 acres of land, or approximately one twenty-third of the valley area. In the reservoir areas proper the authority purchased not only the land that would be inundated, but also a protective belt, varying in width in the different reservoirs, around the margins of its vast lakes.

By June, 1946, the authority had removed 13,449 families from sixteen reservoir areas, and there were still about one thousand families to be removed. Of the 13,449 families, 4,578 were owners of their land and 8,871 were tenants. The authority reported no figures showing the number of *persons* removed. But if an average of five persons could be counted to a family—a conservative figure for rural areas—then the sum total of persons removed, when all was done, could be estimated as no less than 72,000. This was perhaps three or four times as many persons as had been forced to go west at the time of the Cherokee Removal; or, in modern terms, the equivalent of half the population of a city like Nashville. If the 72,000 had been removed in one lump, the exodus would have seemed sensational. Fortunately for TVA, it was achieved by gradual stages over a period of years and was handled without public friction.

After a slow start at land purchasing in the early years, TVA found that its construction program so far outpaced its land purchasing that new measures were necessary. It therefore set up a brand-new land acquisition division and put at the head of it John I. Snyder, a young New York attorney, who had trained for this job by purchasing blocks of urban property for big city real estate interests.

Under Snyder, the urban expert, a speedy system was developed. The authority adopted what it called a "nontrading" policy, which was aimed, on the one hand, at closing out purchases at a fair price and without untoward delays and, on the other, at eliminating speculative collusion. After mapping and studying a reservoir area, the authority sent out field appraisers who estimated the value of the land with its timber and improvements. The reports of the field appraisers went to a nonpartisan committee which determined, subject to approval by TVA's board of appraisal and review, what price the authority would offer. There was a separate committee for each reservoir area. The members were supposed to be persons acquainted with land values in that area.

When once the price was set and the title had been examined, the authority made its offer. The owner could not "trade." He could only take it or leave it. If he rejected the offer, condemnation proceedings would follow—ultimately. But condemnation was generally the last stage in reservoir clearance. When condemnation became necessary, the property was reappraised by three commissioners appointed by the United States District Court, and this commission, after a hearing, made an award on the basis of all the evidence offered. The case might be appealed to the District Court and to the Circuit Court of Appeals.

The policy was successful, at least in statistical terms. As of 1946 the TVA could report that only 5.4 per cent of its land acquisitions (exclusive of certain special purchases) had had to be argued in court against a contesting landowner. TVA interpreted the figures to mean that the population in general considered TVA's appraisal methods fair.

Certainly, although the removals were in the last analysis forcible evictions, they were so adroitly managed that the refugees may often have felt that a great favor was being done them. Nowhere was it necessary to use the armed forces of the United States, as in the Cherokee Removal. Only in rare instances was it necessary to send the marshal with a court order. The rising waters gave TVA an argument that General Winfield Scott did not have in 1838. One may take arms against a sea of troubles, no doubt, but one cannot take down a rifle to fight an actual, practical flood. When TVA surveyors came through the valley and put bold marks on trees and barns to show where the water would come, the argument was really over. Tears might be shed, and angry words might be passed, but the only questions worth discussion were: How much will you pay? Where do we go next?

TVA felt that its appraisal methods answered the first question. The second was more difficult, but was not beyond answer. In developing its relocation service, TVA was careful to maintain an advisory rather than a supervisory role.

For this delicate business it enlisted the aid of all public organizations that could and would help; but the really effective agent in relocating the displaced persons was likely to be the hard-working local assistant county agent, who was a valley dweller himself, and knew the people, and understood their problems, and could tell them where they might find another farm suitable to their needs. TVA figures, in 1946, indicated that most of the displaced persons located in communities or on farms near to their old neighborhood; that 29 per cent left their old counties, and only 5 per cent left the state. TVA held that, under its wise guidance, many of the displaced families, if not most, were suitably or even prosperously re-established, even though they might have moved from bottom land to highland; and in a complex statistical analysis it furthermore argued that not nearly as much arable land was removed from cultivation by its floods as might be thought. However, by TVA's own figures, furnished in 1947, out of the total of 467,000 acres inundated at normal pool levels, 298,000 were crop and pasture lands, and of these latter 90,000 were flooded "initially and solely by TVA reservoirs."

Although no very specific facts as to the state of mind of the displaced persons were available, it seemed that, in general, probably half of them were ready to make an adventure of it, and were content; out of the remaining fifty per cent at least half were easily persuadable. The majority of the willing folks were the young folks who still had their destiny in the making. The worst tragedy of the removal was in the fate of the older folks. They were genuinely reluctant to let the waters take the acres where they had spent their lives. They could not bear to think of living elsewhere. For many of these, death was hastened by the removal.

Tenants, although they were often resentful, were used to moving. Little landowners might be surly, but they had no means of fighting back. Absentee landowners—persons who, for one reason or another, had left the old farm but retained ownership for sentiment or profit—these often harbored deep resentment. They might have the means to take the condemnation proceedings to the last lap and might make a point of doing so. TVA treated that merely as a matter of law.

It was different when the TVA men encountered some unconvinced old grandmother who told them that never, in all her life, had the river risen above that-air sycamore yonder, even in the biggest freshets. She just downright didn't believe it ever would, and it was her land and her place, and she wasn't goin' to move, and even the gover'ment couldn't make her. Or they might run across some lonely Negro fisherman, who had bought or inherited a few acres of his own—acres that might have come down to him from slave times, when ol' marster give 'em to his pappy for taking keer of him endurin' the war. He above all others would be surly and suspicious. They better keep off his land if they didn't want git shot. He didn't mess in nobody else's business, and he didn't want no white folks comin' round' messin' in his business.

It was better to avoid a ruckus with such people. A ruckus would bring, alas, some sensational public dramatization of TVA's doings. Of course they could send the marshal and his deputies, but it was better to refrain if possible. TVA could contrive no greater insult than to imply, somehow, that Wiley Beene, or Old Man Jim Scoggs, or Widow Llewellyn was but an insignificant straw in the designs of an all-wise, all-planning government. Such folks still carried the Revolutionary banner, DON'T TREAD ON ME! Like the happy man of Wotton's poem, they were lords of themselves, though not of lands, and having nothing, yet had all. They did not even want to receive favors against their will. The very thought of it might send them into a fit of contrariness and feuding.

Therefore TVA walked carefully, or officially it did so, and sought gradually to accustom such folks to the dispensations of progress. It catered to them and in certain ways made much of them. It worked out decent and considerate arrangements for the relocation of old cemeteries, many of them small family graveyards, that dotted the reservoir lands. The TVA people, or their assistants, traced down, where it was possible, the relatives of the deceased and consulted their wishes. It provided new cemetery sites, new caskets for the bones, and transportation to the new grave. It arranged for a preacher and a reinterment ceremony. It set up the old tombstone or provided a new one of a standard model. Since many of the cemeteries were old and neglected, the task of identification of bodies and location of relatives was a large and tedious undertaking. In the Norris reservoir, 5,000 graves were moved; in the Watts Bar reservoir, 2,500; in the Kentucky reservoir, 2,000. As this work went on, old memories and stray bits of history were exhumed along with the moldering bones and old caskets. Chattanooga could sigh a reminiscent sigh over the exploration and removal of the old Harrison cemetery, which went back to pioneer times. In that cemetery TVA brought to light the cast-iron coffins of the Bell boys—Granville and David Newton Bell—both of whom died in their teens. Each coffin was provided with a plate-glass window, and one could look in and see Granville and David perfectly preserved, not a hair disarranged. There was a certain gruesome comfort in all this, and TVA got the credit for it.

Also under the heading "reservoir clearance" came the matter of cutting away trees and brush. It was necessary to denude each vast area before the waters rose, and to know exactly where stumps might be left and where they should be cut off flush with the ground. Since stumps, particularly cypress stumps, have remarkable powers of endurance when submerged, they should never be left at the edges of navigation channels. No person is more entitled to righteous wrath than a river captain who has snagged his boat on a hidden cypress stump. TVA was not well coached at first in the matter of stumps, and some were left, to the peril of navigators. It took heed to correct the error in later clearances.

The annoying and vital problem of malaria had to be solved. If it were not solved, the great lakes of the Tennessee would become a utopia for the anopheles mosquito, and the human inhabitants would cease to care whether they had electricity or not. At some sacrifice of its power program, with which malaria control by no means perfectly harmonized, the health division of TVA, under Dr. Eugene L. Bishop, a Tennessean, worked out a scheme for discouraging mosquito breeding by raising and lowering pool levels at times ingeniously calculated to cause the greatest amount of infant mortality among the mosquito tribes. It also used larvicides and other control measures, backed up by constant field study.

But while it contrived death to mosquitoes, TVA gave the fish, the wild ducks, the geese, and other waterfowl a hearty welcome to its watery domain and bade them be fruitful and multiply. Nothing loath, they did just that. In addition, gulls, newcomers to the region, appeared on the vast lakes, and young herons, white feathered, stalked in the shallows near forsaken cotton fields.

Since, of course, the game birds and fish could not read newspapers and pamphlets, they were not aware that TVA was advertising their numerous presence and was inviting the hunters and fishers of the nation to descend upon them with lures, decoys, flies, hooks, and shotguns. Accordingly, this part of the TVA program was among its undebatable successes. To their astonishment, TVA biologists discovered by 1946 that they no longer needed to institute closed seasons for fishing on TVA lakes and could abandon their restocking arrangements. The more fish were caught, the more were left to be caught. Even mussel fishing, it was said, was not entirely put out of business as had been feared. Furthermore, TVA developed scientific methods to forecast the depths at which game fish could best be caught, and the

## THE WORKINGS OF TVA

fisherman's task was made easy—if that was a gain. So the fish business zoomed. In 1946 commercial fishermen alone took over a million pounds of fish from TVA lakes.

All this, of course, was a part of TVA's carefully devised recreation program, which was designed to foster public enjoyment of the facilities for boating, swimming, and camping that the permanent flood had created. Early in its history the authority drew up a remarkable prospectus which showed how, when all was done, the Tennessee Valley might become a tourists' paradise. This prospectus, *The Scenic Resources of the Tennessee Valley*, was a little alarming. It tempted a reader to wonder whether the TVA would leave anything in the valley but scenery, tourist cottages, and antique shops. But the public asked no questions, and the program was a smashing popular success. It became evident that bigger facilities would have to be provided to meet the public demand, and TVA began to work out plans for leasing spots in its domain to commercial-minded apostles of the great out-of-doors. Meanwhile TVA multiplied parks, sold a little land here and there for summer cabins, and gave the come-on signal at various points to the Boy Scouts and the Girl Scouts and to modern church groups who had come to think that bathing suits and camp fires stimulated a Christian attitude toward the problems of life.

Such undertakings, however, were but incidental to TVA's fundamental task, which called for the utmost ingenuity and resourcefulness. The primary duties of TVA in their accepted order of importance were to provide a 9-foot channel from Paducah to Knoxville and to do whatever else was needed for navigation; to provide the maximum degree of flood control and the maximum degree of power development under the co-ordinated, unified development plan; and to experiment with fertilizer production in close conjunction with soil conservation and reforestation. The high-dam system must do all those things together.

The navigation problem was easiest. The high dams, with a few added improvements, would without question establish a 9-foot controlling depth from Paducah to Knoxville, and much more than nine feet in many stretches.

The flood-control problem was far more difficult. There were good engineers who held that flood control and power production could not be reconciled, but were in fundamental conflict. The army engineers, however, took a different view in their 1930 report, and the TVA engineers in general followed their lead. In the Great Bend TVA inherited the beginnings of a high-dam system at Wilson and Wheeler dams, which were in the old plan. There was also Hales Bar Dam. These high dams, as they stood, already took up some of the "natural storage" afforded by the river bed in the middle region. If a flood coming from above should reach them at a time when their reservoirs were full, it could not spread out; it would rush on down, with a damaging result below. But if those reservoirs were kept low, to catch the flood, then power production would fall off. The more high dams were built on the main river, the greater the flood danger would be—unless other provision against floods were made—because the reservoirs would take up more of the "natural storage" afforded under unimproved conditions. Elimination of "natural storage" on the main river, though good for power production and navigation, was bad for flood control. In fact it would not do. As Chairman Morgan at one time pointed out, Chattanooga citizens could not afford to dream that Chickamauga Dam, just above the city, would of itself give protection. Under certain conditions its presence might only magnify flood danger.

Chattanooga was the great danger point on the river. Its business section and part of its residential area were on low ground. Below Chattanooga the ravine of the Narrows partially dammed any large flood. The waters therefore backed up and spread out where the city was. The more prosperous Chattanooga became, the greater the flood damage would be.

## THE WORKINGS OF TVA

It was in a bad spot, and there was no getting it out of the spot.

The great source of the danger was far above Chattanooga in the mountainous region of East Tennessee and North Carolina, where the annual rainfall was eighty inches. From that country, along the gorges of the tributaries, especially the Hiwassee, but not from it alone, the great floods came. They came with a good deal of seasonal regularity, generally at some time from December to May—which was, of old, the season when flatboatmen rode the "tide." The key to flood control was in the wide ramifications of the Upper Tennessee, but safety measures must be taken at other points too —especially if TVA was determined to achieve both maximum power production and maximum flood control. Maximum flood control meant, among other things, that TVA must be prepared to handle what engineers called a "500-year flood," like the flood of 1867, which reached a stage of 57.9 feet at Chattanooga. Statistically, such a flood would appear, on the average, once in five hundred years, but actually it might come unexpectedly in any year. TVA engineers said they were building not only for a 500-year flood but for a 1,000-year flood—which would theoretically reach 77 feet at Chattanooga under unimproved conditions.

TVA solved the problem by building, not only high dams, but very high dams—superdams—and by providing "tributary storage" on the Upper Tennessee system and "surcharge" both on the main river and on the tributaries. In other words, the multiple purposes, piled one on top of another and translated into feet, ascended vertically from the point, low on the dam structure, where the "head" of water was carried against the turbines, to the much higher point where flood control was provided. Each main river dam was constructed to provide surcharge—that is, a certain number of acre-feet above and beyond what would give the desired head for power—and so to hold back a certain volume of floodwater even though, at the time of flood, the reservoir might be operating at normal pool level for power purposes. But the tributary dams were not pure flood-control projects, either. They had a certain height for power and a height above that for flood control. But during the approach of the flood season their reservoirs could *not* be held at a level good for power. They must be drawn down to receive and hold the winter floods, which would afterwards be let out gradually.

The reservoirs also had to be fluctuated for malaria control during the warm months. And at all times during the dangerous rainy months it was to be supposed that power was duly adjusted to the needs of flood control and could not take precedence over flood control. "These reservoir operation plans," said Sherman M. Woodward, TVA's chief water-control planning engineer, in 1938, "have been based primarily on flood control. The power calculations . . . are based on the amount of water that will result from these flood control operations." It was also true that, under the unified plan, the water let out from a tributary dam, like Fontana, was not released from kilowatt duty until it had hit the turbines of every powerhouse between Fontana and the mouth of the Tennessee.

Such at any rate was the principle of the scheme. It was a very expensive scheme, and it required an extraordinary delicacy of adjustment throughout the complex, multiple purpose system. Perhaps TVA held its breath in certain winters to see whether the scheme would really work. Up to 1946, it worked. A heavy rain in January, 1946, for example, above Chattanooga, might have produced the fifth largest flood in Chattanooga history. TVA tributary dams, said the authority, held the flood to a crest of 35.7 feet. This was still flood stage, but without the tributary dams the flood might have reached 45.8 feet. Although the flood problem at Chattanooga was still not fully solved, even with all TVA dams functioning, and would require levees or other local works of some sort, TVA felt certain that it had greatly reduced extreme danger at Chattanooga and elsewhere. TVA also reported that its control system was capable of reducing Ohio flood crests at Cairo by 2½ to 4 feet and therefore also exerted beneficent influence on Mississippi floods.

Meanwhile TVA was busy experimenting with production of new types of phosphatic fertilizer for use in its great scheme for restoring soil vitality and preventing erosion. Its "test demonstration" program, carried on under an agreement with the land-grant colleges, gained steadily as the years went on. There was little debate even among TVA critics as to the merits of this program. It plodded along quietly enough.

But there was nothing quiet about TVA's power program. Of all TVA's multifarious concerns, the power program was most dramatic in its impact upon the public. Already, in the "yardstick" slogan, it had been politically dramatized, and for many years it furnished the most definitely political angle of the multiple-purpose project and was most frequently in the news.

The law did not talk about yardsticks. Instead it authorized TVA to sell electric energy "in order to avoid the waste of water power" and spoke of this sale as intended "so far as may be practicable, to assist in liquidating the cost or aid in the maintenance of the projects of the Authority." It directed that TVA give preference in the sale of power to states, counties, municipalities, and nonprofit-making cooperatives, and it furthermore provided that TVA should control resale rates. It emphasized the obligation of TVA to engage in experiments and studies in the interest of wider use of power for the general welfare of the region and, more specifically, "for agricultural and domestic use, or for small or local industries." It spoke of the power that was to be sold as "surplus power" and in unequivocal language declared that direct sale to industries was to be considered a "secondary purpose, to be utilized principally to secure a high load factor and revenue returns which will permit domestic and rural use at the lowest possible rates." As amended in 1935, the TVA Act more explicitly than ever declared navigation and flood control to be primary purposes to which the sale of power was subsidiary.

As a first step, TVA announced that it would operate the Wilson Dam plant and would erect transmission lines to connect it with Norris Dam. It declared that it would serve the region in proximity to these points, but later on, when the market developed, it would serve the entire Tennessee basin. It might go outside that area, as the law allowed, if occasion should so justify. It did not wish to duplicate physical facilities and enter into "wasteful competitive practices," and therefore it would buy private systems where purchase seemed advisable. Injury to private utilities would be "a matter for serious consideration," but not a determining factor.

Under this policy TVA looked for customers. Tupelo, Mississippi, was the first municipal customer. There were not many more at first, although Mr. Lilienthal's ability as promoter set the valley and much of the United States ringing with praise.

Citizens were much taken with the yardstick metaphor. They were hardly prepared to scrutinize closely the elaborate calculations by which a power rate was determined—calculations which in fact TVA itself, as was later revealed, had not explored to the last depth of arithmetical mystery. But the citizens got the general idea. If they could get some PWA money or somehow arrange to buy out the local private utility and set up a municipally owned company of the TVA model, they could get a contract with TVA. Then their monthly bills would be less, much less, than the bills they were receiving from, say, the Tennessee Electric Power Company, a subsidiary of the great Commonwealth and Southern Company—of which, they presently learned, a Mr. Wendell Willkie was president. With the issue thus simplified, they naturally concluded that Mr. Lilienthal and TVA were on the side of the angels and that the private utilities were down,

## THE WORKINGS OF TVA

far down, among the powers of darkness. A clamor arose for towns and cities to follow the shining light of Tupelo. Rural co-operatives began to form—after some coaching as to how one went about it to co-operate. Crusading newspapers took up the theme. Congressmen got on the bandwagon.

But the powers of darkness, rearing their huge frames amid the sulphureous murk, vowed that, though the field was lost, all was not lost. They, too, had once had angelic pretensions—had in their day been hailed as redeemers and agents of progress. They would not surrender without a fight. They might now be thought powers of darkness, but they were also corporations with a large and profitable business, about to incur damage. Among the owners of their securities were some very high-class colleges and universities and other respectable identities, as well as the usual array of widows and orphans, who after all really existed and whose investment must be protected. Although the corporations were "persons" according to the Fourteenth Amendment, as interpreted by the Supreme Court, the law had unfortunately not equipped them with souls as it had so thoughtfully equipped TVA. They were therefore under some disadvantage in the political arena. It was not so in the courts. The law said that TVA could sue and be sued. They would sue.

Therefore when TVA began to invade their service areas and absorb electric properties and when towns and cities made motions to buy or build municipally owned plants, the private companies got to work with injunctions and pleas of damage, or their stockholders did so. For a brief period there was a possibility that TVA and the private companies might agree to divide the sales territory in some kind of co-operative scheme, but that was soon over. The legal battle began. Its long continuance kept TVA short of customers, and although TVA was rapidly constructing power facilities and preaching its gospel of low rates and wide use of electric energy, it did not at once make progress with the power development set forth by Congress.

If the great contestants could have fought with physical weapons instead of briefs, the battles between TVA and the private utilities might have been like those in Homer, full of earthquakes, conflagrations, and the tramp of armed hosts, and might have ended with Achilles TVA triumphantly dragging the corpse of Hector TEP up and down the Norris Freeway. But the arguments in the Ashwander case and the Eighteen Power Companies case were too obstruse for epic dramatization. By 1939 the United States Supreme Court had decided that TVA was not to be legally interfered with on the grounds urged.

The private companies then quit the field. Mr. Wendell Willkie offered to sell the entire holdings of Commonwealth and Southern in the valley area—the chief part being, of course, the properties of the Tennessee Electric Power Company. He did not want to sell it piecemeal but to sell it all and get out. After hot debate Congress amended the TVA Act to permit the authority to acquire, through bond issues, not only the transmission lines and water-power properties of Commonwealth and Southern, but its steam-power plants also. The deal was consummated for a basic price of about $78,000,000. With other purchases made here and there by TVA and its contracting associates, about $110,000,000 had gone into such acquisitions by August, 1939, and soon afterwards TVA held a practical monopoly on the distribution of electric power in its "natural service area."

Its position was now vastly altered. In 1935 TVA had sold—in round numbers—only about 13 million KWH to municipalities, 4 million to rural co-operatives, 3 million to electric utilities, and none to industries by direct sale. By 1942 it was selling 2 *billion* KWH to municipalities, 282 million to co-operatives, 679 million to electric utilities, and about 2½ *billion* direct to industries.

Sales enlarged rapidly as construction rushed on to completion and TVA prices won customers. For the fiscal year ending in 1944 TVA reported that it had produced—and had

THE WORKINGS OF TVA 269

sold or disposed of—a total of 10 billion KWH. In 1945 the production total leaped to 12.4 billion under war conditions. In 1946, with the war over, it was still 12.3 billion. The distribution of this energy production, as of 1946, was as follows: 3,264,560,756 KWH to municipal and county systems (with Knoxville, Chattanooga, Nashville, and Memphis taking about two-thirds of the amount); 445,596,591 to co-operatives, mostly rural; 4,167,789,274 to industries and federal agencies; 728,649,157 to utilities; 421,646,529 in interdepartmental sales; and the small remainder in temporary direct service and small contracts. The total power *sales* in this year of expected postwar decline was still over 9 billion KWH. The revenues for power for the year amounted to $16,783,000 in net income returned to the federal treasury—but not returned under any accepted amortization scheme, for TVA in 1946 still had no such official plan. The average rates charged for TVA power were: to municipal and county systems, 4.19 mills per kilowatt-hour; to co-operatives, 5.49; to industrials and federal agencies, 3.43; to electric utilities, 4.01; interdepartmental, 2.93. The average rate for all sales was 3.85.

The high proportion of direct sales to industry might seem surprising to any who were aware of the low priority given to such sales in the TVA Act. This fact subjected TVA to criticism. But no quibbles regarding that disposition were in order during the anxious years of World War II, when American productive facilities were everywhere being strained to the utmost. It was then a cause for gratitude, no doubt, that TVA dams and turbines had trebled the available valley power between 1940 and 1945; that TVA had provided energy for the great atomic plant at Oak Ridge, Tennessee, and for the vast increase in aluminum production necessitated by the demands of the air forces; and that TVA had also, in its character as defense plant, converted the Muscle Shoals arrangements for producing fertilizer and had gone into the production of incendiary bombs, tracer bullets, and other weapons of combat, meanwhile aiding through its facilities the manufacture of small naval craft at Decatur and engaging in sundry other activities pertaining both to war and to peace.

With peace of a sort at last arrived, and its construction task almost done, TVA might have to face other questions, but it was firmly seated, regnant in its established domain, aware of its might, and aware, too, that the world was looking at it, now with applause, now with doubt, but on the whole with more applause than doubt.

TVA was fulfilling, or was in a way to fulfill, all its multiple purposes. It had finished up the centuries-old Muscle Shoals problem. It had tamed the Tennessee River, and in so doing had made the name of that river, the world over, a symbol of what technology might accomplish for man's material good. It had made a new river; and what had been in many ways a nuisance, a deplorable trick of nature, had become something to admire, to use, or to play with. TVA had modernized a region scolded for its backwardness—had greened its fields, put money in its pocket, taught it to fix itself up and behave. In the massiveness of its dams and their auxiliary structures it had shown that government buildings need not be merely efficient or pretentiously monstrous, but could be modern works of art, adapted both to function and to site. For this it got much praise. It had brought an able personnel to its many tasks and had proved that government, big government, need not be dilatory or dull or callous or just fatly bureaucratic. It had shown, if David Lilienthal's interpretation of TVA policy could be accepted as final, that democracy could be made to function at the "grass roots," even though its government might be leviathan in size and principle. It had developed—or at least TVA so reported—good relationships with the people of the valley and their local governments and had shown that all could work together in their spheres. It had repaired some of the damage that its great works had caused. Even the sore matter of tax replacements, incompletely decided in the early years of TVA, was alleviated by the Norris-Sparkman amendment of 1940, which, with certain limitations, arranged for payments to be made in lieu of taxes to injured counties and extended the earlier tax replacement provisions to all the valley states. Although it had obliterated its local rivals, the private utility companies, it could argue that the TVA preachment of the doctrine of low-rates-and-increased-use had improved the position of all other power companies. It could claim, and did claim in one of its annual reports, that it had brought "a new kind of pioneering" to the old land of the pioneers.

CHAPTER XVI

# Navigation, New Style

BUT WHAT IS a river for if not for navigation? From pioneer times, the people of the Valley had thought of their river as primarily a waterway. TVA owed its existence in large measure to their determination to conquer Muscle Shoals. Now Muscle Shoals was conquered, and all other obstacles were drowned out. Then where were the boats? When would the Tennessee become again "an artery of commerce"?

To these questions TVA answered that performance was good and prospects were still-better. Between 1933 and 1939, with only part of the 9-foot channel available, traffic had trebled. By 1944 the 9-foot channel was available all the way to Knoxville. On February 14 of that year, TVA celebrated the arrival at Knoxville of the first modern tow to navigate the entire length of the improved river. It was the *Muscatine* with a tow of grain barges. Captain Paul Underwood, a Tennessean, was the master pilot in charge, journalists and dignitaries were on hand, and it was an occasion somewhat comparable to the famous arrival of the steamboat *Atlas* in 1828. If the celebration did not quite have the festive exuberance that marked the arrival of the first steamboat, one hundred sixteen years before, that was no fault of TVA's. There was snow on the ground, and it was a war year.

The optimism of TVA was evident in certain new arrangements for the accommodation of traffic. There had never been any good river "terminals" on the Tennessee. Passengers and freight had been loaded or unloaded, any old way, on crude wharves or cruder landings or at best on wharf boats. There were no good storage or loading arrangements. Out of its funds TVA therefore provided four new "public use terminals," located at Decatur, Guntersville, Chattanooga, and Knoxville. War shortages caused the originally ambitious plans to be modified, and TVA fell back like other builders on cinder-block and timber construction and stiff-leg timber derricks. Now miscellaneous freight shipments to or from the four ports involved at last had places to load or unload, with immediate access to railroad tracks and highways.

But the most important thing was the 9-foot channel, which by 1946 was complete almost to the last detail of minor improvement, and was better than a 9-foot channel. Actually there was a depth of 11 feet or better and a width of 300 feet in the navigation channels of the great reservoirs, and much more than that at the lower ends of the reservoirs.

If traffic did not develop, one should not blame TVA. It was providing something like ideal navigating conditions. The chain of lakes would make possible "the most efficient waterway operation in the world." A towboat pushing its string of barges on the Tennessee would have slackwater under its keel all the time. There would be no great struggle with the current, as in a natural river. In the wide, well-marked channel, a boat would have none of the problems of maneuver that it would find in a river canalized by a low-dam system. These conditions were very favorable to modern tows, which might draw from seven to nine feet of water. For the first time in Tennessee River history, traffic could keep a schedule, because the rate of speed could be fairly uniform over the whole chain of lakes. The high dams meant few lockages and therefore few delays. There were only ten lockages—for the nine high dams and the one low dam—in 652 river miles from Paducah to the French Broad. Even if a towboat had to "break" a big tow, it could still make better speed on the Tennessee than, say, on the Ohio.

As TVA pondered upon the navigable reaches of its kingdom—which now extended beyond the main river and up the tributaries—some of the crusading enthusiasm that had marked its fight with the power companies began to flow into its discourses on navigation. Perceptibly, it was becoming a regional champion and was beginning to talk like a native resident. The railroads were now given some of the bad eminence formerly applied to the power companies. After much patient research TVA emerged with studies arguing that the interterritorial discriminations visited upon the South in freight rate charges were disadvantageous. It also rediscovered and proclaimed that river transportation suffered from no such embarrassments. For "bulk commodities" especially, the inland rivers offered a cheaper form of transportation than railroads or trucks. The old dream of the men of the western waters was, in a fashion, on the point of realization. Within the Mississippi Valley lay the domain of the inland waterways, of which the great lakes of the Tennessee were at last an integral part. Goods could go and come from Milwaukee to Knoxville, from Knoxville to New Orleans or Pittsburgh, with cheapness and ease. Thus the economy of the interior could float itself free from some of the trammels imposed upon it by the railroading and imperialistic East.

Statistical reports on Tennessee River traffic were good. In 1946 TVA reported 256,465,000 ton-miles of freight haulage in its domain for the calendar year of 1945. This was 61 per cent above the total for 1944 and 31 per cent better than for the previous record year, 1943. In tonnage totals (rather than ton-miles) the figures were not quite so good. In 1943 the river carried about 2,800,000 tons of traffic and in 1945 (by estimate of February, 1946) about 2,250,000 tons. The latter figure was about 400,000 tons short of the 2,647,509 figure predicted by TVA, four years earlier, for 1945. Yet it was fair to point out that the earlier figures represented a great quantity of sand and gravel hauled for short distances for construction work. The ton-mile figures for 1945 represented a greater diversity of freight, much of it "high value" freight, and much less sand and gravel. Coal shipments had assumed prominence, along with grain, forest products, and petroleum products. Some of the coal went down the river and on to midwestern ports. On the other hand, especially during the war years, many thousands of tons of coal were monthly barged up the Tennessee for use at TVA's Watts Bar steam plant—a strange contradiction.

All the same, the ton-mile figures, which were the only valid mathematical representation of the true volume of river use, meant that towboats with their barges were using long stretches of the river—the entire length of it, when they wished. At last there was real "through traffic" all the way. The high dams of TVA had accomplished what canals and channel improvements had failed to do. The "through traffic" could go and come at any time of year. There might still be fog or storms, but there were none of the old seasonal delays. There was no more waiting for a "tide" to get over the shallow parts. There was no need for light-draft auxiliary vessels to fill out the links of the navigation chain, and no more worry about the Suck or Muscle Shoals or any other shoals.

The possibilities were splendid, and during the hard years of World War II they became blessed reality. The oilless East, far from its source of supplies and at times all but cut off by German submarine attacks upon seagoing tankers, shivered and despaired during the bad winter of 1942-43; but oil barges came up the Tennessee on schedule, safe from submarine attacks, free from the congestion of railroads. For the first time since the Civil War, too, there was building of warships above Muscle Shoals—at the Decatur works of the Ingalls Company.

Since ton-mile figures showed a consistent increase as one lake after another was opened to traffic, TVA became more and more optimistic. In its 1941 prediction as to "prospective commerce"—based upon interviews with 3,700 firms in 191 cities and towns—the authority calculated that by 1960 the river might carry six million tons of traffic per year. By 1946 it revised the figure upward. In another fifteen years or so the annual total might reach seven million tons.

An analytical breakdown of TVA estimates and reports and a comparison with former years made a somewhat less encouraging picture. In 1923, for example, with Wilson Dam still incomplete, the traffic was over a million and a half tons, which was better than TVA could show for 1937, 1938, or 1939. And in that year, 1923, 12.5 per cent of the total was miscellaneous freight, and 24 per cent was forest products—which was better than the new river had done in those categories up to 1946. The reports seemed to indicate that short-haul traffic would decrease and that long-haul traffic would swell in importance; that river traffic between Knoxville and Chattanooga, or between Chattanooga and Florence, might become negligible, but that traffic between Minneapolis or Pittsburgh and Tennessee ports would thrive.

The picture took on other colors and aspects if the statistical reports were laid aside for a look at navigation.

The usefulness of any river for modern transportation is conditioned by the dimensions of the locks provided in its dams. A lock 60 feet wide and 360 feet long would accommodate, rivermen said, a towboat and three barges. A towboat with six barges, encountering such a lock, must break its tow and make two lockages. As the science of towboat construction and towing developed, tows of eight, ten, twelve barges, or more, had become common on the Ohio and Mississippi. Accordingly, locks 110 feet wide and 600 feet long had become standard on rivers with a large volume of traffic. Auxiliary locks were needed, too, and these were frequently 60 by 360 feet.

Unfortunately for TVA, the double-lift lock at Wilson Dam was only 60 feet by 300 feet. The Wheeler lock, already under construction by the army engineers when TVA took over, was 60 by 360.

TVA did not undertake to change these lock dimensions at the two Muscle Shoals dams or at Hales Bar Dam, which had a lock 60 by 267 feet. Nor did it construct any auxiliary locks, although it drew these into its blueprints and thus allowed for future changes. At the new dams above Muscle Shoals—Guntersville, Chickamauga, Watts Bar, Fort Loudoun—TVA built locks of the 60 by 360 size. Only at Pickwick Landing Dam and at Kentucky Dam, both below Muscle Shoals, did it provide locks of the "standard" 110 by 600 size.

In the eyes of rivermen, therefore, TVA had limited navigation possibilities from Muscle Shoals to Knoxville by erecting permanent structures with locks whose width did not exceed 60 feet. The *Waterways Journal* indicated what this limitation meant when it reported that the *Muscatine*, on its 1944 trip to Knoxville, "took three lockages and two hours and forty-five minutes" to lock through Chickamauga Dam. It did not seem that TVA really expected traffic of the Ohio-Mississippi type to flourish on the Upper Tennessee. Either that, or TVA had partly fumbled its job of providing for modern navigation. Why spend so much money without providing for maximum possibilities?

Rivermen had other doubts and qualms. The immensity of Kentucky Dam rather shocked them. "Never before in the history of the world, so far as I know, did the human race plan to slackwater for navigation, by one dam alone, 185 miles of any river large or small," testified Captain Donald T. Wright, of the *Waterways Journal*, at a hearing of the Rivers and Harbors Committee in 1937. The Lower Tennessee, he pointed out, could be rendered more navigable by ordinary channel improvements plus a few low dams.

And the great lakes of the Tennessee, enchanting and easily navigable, had certain dangers. In time of storms the lakes worked up waves that created difficulties for the low-lying craft of the inland rivers. Locks and lock machinery were not adequately protected, it was said, against such waves. Lock attendants could not stand on the locks and serve them at such times, and lock motors got drowned out. Driftwood washed in. At Wheeler Dam in April, 1937, such a storm stopped navigation for six days. Waves, dashing above the lock walls, smashed the wooden bulkheads improvised to protect the machinery pits, and navigation had to stop until the lock motors were dried out.

There might be trouble even when all was calm. The channel was plainly marked, and a pilot knew that in the part of any reservoir just above the dam he was in deep water and had easy going. In the uppermost part of a reservoir, too, it was easy, for there the Tennessee was much like any other river. You followed the channel, and where the river widened in the slackwater you could still see on either side of the boat the old banks, converted into island fringes with some tree growth on them. The real danger came in the middle part of a reservoir, where you had a deep channel in front, but on either side the old banks, submerged and indistinguishable, stretched out in shallows. If in any way you miscalculated—when passing another boat or in making a turn—you might catch the hull on a stump that had been left on the edge of the old bank. If the stump snagged the boat badly, then you were wrecked on the edge of deep water, with a long stretch of water between the boat and the distant new banks. In such fashion the *Jayhawker* was wrecked in 1939 and went to the bottom of Pickwick Lake. In the spring of 1944, a mile and a half below Decatur, the *Elizabeth Smith* snagged her hull on stumps and sank quickly.

It might seem that such troubles could be avoided in a channel 300 feet wide and perhaps 11 feet deep, but a string of barges with a towboat at the end took up a lot of space, lengthwise. It had a wide radius of swing and could not be maneuvered like an old-style steamboat. Channel

## NAVIGATION, NEW STYLE 279

markings—the buoys and daymarks—were widely spaced at some points in the big pools. There was also a continual, though unadvertised, conflict between navigation people and malaria-control people. Pilots preferred that willows and bushes be left growing on the old banks and elsewhere. Such growth made landmarks and helped them to steer. But malaria-control people wanted to cut the growth back in order to discourage mosquitoes.

And what if there was engine trouble while a boat was navigating the great lakes, or what if a storm came up, or if for any other reason you needed to get to the bank and tie up? Just where—asked the rivermen—in all that enormous reach of water, did you steer your boat to tie up?

TVA had answers to some of these questions. Stumps were cut off sheer with the ground at the danger points in reservoirs prepared after TVA took notice of the enmity between pilots and stumps. TVA also built safety harbors. It made navigation charts to guide boatmen, and by 1946 these were available to all who might need them.

The navigation charts were drawn on a scale of one inch to the half mile. The sailing line was marked as a bold red line with every successive mile point entered where it belonged. On that line and at every point indicated by white space there was always nine feet of water, or more. The secondary channel, used for approach to safety harbors and landings, was indicated. Shadings of blue denoted the varying depths of less than nine feet. At all needful points, lake depths were entered on contour lines. Submerged stumps and other obstacles appeared as clumps of dots. All types of buoys, daymarks, lights, bridges, towns, landings, even houses near the bank, were shown on the chart, and, with them, the important features of the neighboring country for some miles on either side of the river.

With such a chart the pilot would know, say, as soon as he approached Mile 58 on Kentucky Lake, that there was a safety harbor, first class, at the mouth of Hughes Creek, on the right bank, and another safety harbor, second class, just above Hughes Creek. Between Mile 57.8 and Mile 69.3 his chart would show two safety harbors, first class, and four safety harbors, second class, on the right (east) bank, and two safety harbors, first class, on the left (west) bank. At the heads of pools the chart would not be needed, but at such point as Mile 67 and Mile 68 on Kentucky Lake, where the new Tennessee sprawled over an area approximately 5½ miles wide, a pilot might well be thankful for a TVA chart. The great stretch of water, much of it shallow, was now the Tennessee National Migratory Wildlife Refuge. It might be wonderful for ducks, but it was not wonderful for a pilot if he had to make a quick landing or if by some mistake he turned up the mouth of Big Sandy instead of continuing up the Tennessee. The *Waterways Journal*, reporting a trip on the Fort Loudoun pool, spoke about "how easy it is to become confused, even lost, in a river that has become overnight a vast expanse of water in volume far greater than at record flood stage."

But with navigation charts, and the Coast Guard *Light List*, and channel markings, and such knowledge as a pilot ought to have, TVA felt that there should be no particular trouble about navigating the lakes. Danger could not be completely eliminated, of course. There was hazard in any kind of navigation.

As for waves and storms, there were waves and storms on all rivers. They were inescapable. On other matters the TVA had nothing in particular to say. It believed thoroughly in its high dams, including Kentucky Dam, and it emphasized the fact that traffic was steadily increasing. From its relative silence on the matter of lock dimensions, one did not know what to suppose.

It might be that TVA, despite all the big speeches made by Mr. Lilienthal, accepted the possibility that for a long time to come river traffic on the Tennessee could not aspire to the volume attained on the Ohio and Mississippi and that the really big tows of twelve, fifteen, or twenty barges would rarely, if ever, be seen above Wilson Dam. The TVA figures of 256,465,000 ton-miles of traffic in 1945 did not look so impressive if they were compared with figures for other inland waterways. In 1947 the owners of the *Irene Chotin* boasted that that boat alone towed over two billion ton-miles of freight on the Ohio-Mississippi system between January and June. In the prewar year of 1938, traffic on the entire Mississippi system totaled 9,978,987,000 ton-miles. For the Ohio in 1946, a total of 4,999,559,560 ton-miles was reported.

The new-style traffic, nevertheless, was something to be reckoned with. Modern towboats and barges were being built with steel hulls. Since they no longer had to be able, like the old flat-bottomed packets, to float "on the morning dew," they could be built for deep water, with more freeboard. The Diesel engines of the towboats were built to develop as much as 3,000 horsepower. A single tow of five or six 1,000-ton barges, pushed by these monsters, could carry as much freight as one or two freight trains, and so on beyond that, according to the size of the tow, which might be, in effect, a whole flotilla of boats lashed together with metal ratchets and patented steel barge connectors.

Such tows moved over very long distances. They had covered barges for commodities that might be injured by weather and open barges for coal, rock, or iron. Miscellaneous "package freight" such as the old steamboats carried would not be much in evidence. TVA could report only 13,300 tons of miscellaneous freight as having passed through its terminals in the year ending June, 1946. Still, the barges could and did carry some package freight too.

Now instead of flatboat, keelboat, or steamboat "lines" it was "barge lines." There were private carriers like the great oil companies that built their own tanks at the ports they served; grain and milling interests that put up their own elevators at Chattanooga, Decatur, and elsewhere; and coal companies with tipples at Soddy or South Pittsburg. And there were common carriers: the well-established barge lines on the Ohio and Mississippi and a few lines doing business from Tennessee ports, like Igert of Paducah, Clifton Towing Company of Clifton, and Tennessee Barge Line of Chattanooga. Along with such towboats and their barges, there were Coast Guard boats, a few small TVA boats used for special tasks like studying mosquitoes and fish, and, in increasing numbers, the miscellaneous small pleasure craft that congregated near cities and towns.

But the traffic of other days had vanished. There were still the ugly, familiar dredges, the N.C. & St.L. Railroad ferry between Hobbs Island and Guntersville, and small ferryboats at other points. No packet steamboats operated any more from Tennessee ports. The *Gordon C. Greene* of Cincinnati and the *Golden Eagle* of St. Louis came up the Tennessee at intervals. They had been built, long before, for the older type of river trade and had miraculously survived into the day of the towboat-and-barge. They were beautiful boats, all complete with cabin deck, texas deck, paddle wheel, and melodious steam whistle. But they were no longer packets. They were tourist steamers. There was an occasional "excursion" boat, like the *Idlewild* and, more rarely, a dejected showboat.

Steamboat days were over. Although towboats carried a heavy volume of freight in a single trip, they did not make many trips. So the new Tennessee could hardly be said to be teeming with traffic. For days on end you might see nothing on the Tennessee but a Coast Guard boat, a lugubrious dredge, a noisy speed boat or so, and a solitary mussel boat. The well-tamed, new model river of TVA was a beautiful river still and was wide open to navigation, but there was not much navigation. The river was lonesomer than it had been at any time, perhaps, since the days of the early steamboats. No speeches, no researches, no predictions altered that baldly obvious fact.

No more, at the old river ports, could you see several

steamboats tied up or anything resembling the traditional "busy scene" of loading and unloading. The cursing mate and the roustabouts were gone. There was no singing any more, for one does not sing while handling a derrick and a clam-shell scoop. There were no cotton bales and wagons, no ladies with parasols, no attentive gentlemen handing them up or down the landing stage—or even a modern equivalent of such phenomena.

The waterfront of Chattanooga was the most unfrequented spot in the city. At the old wharf, most likely, you would see only a few stolid Negro fisherwomen, their backs indifferently presented to the observer. Wordless and motionless, they smoked their pipes and waited for the fish to bite. Somewhere up or down the river were the great cylindrical tanks of Gulf or Texaco. Somewhere else were tipples, conveyor belts, or other loading apparatus, and the U.S. Engineers boatyard, and the docks or boathouses of the little pleasure craft. But these were dispersed over miles of riverfront. At the wharf there was nothing to see except the quiet river. and the distant mountains, and the highway bridge over which automobiles streamed on the real business of life.

But what about the new TVA public use terminal, and where was it, anyhow? Well, it was not anywhere around Chattanooga wharf. It was quite hard to find. But if you were persistent, and adventured far enough along Water Street among Negro shacks and factories, and asked enough questions of bewildered passers-by, and took enough wrong turns, you would eventually discover a sign pointing down a new and evidently not much used road. At the end of the road, there it was, nicely located on the bend with a fine view toward Lookout Mountain. It was a neat building, with that air of being modern, yet not *too* modern, found in all TVA architecture. Across the front of the building a handsomely lettered sign said PORT OF CHATTANOOGA. A newly built spur of railroad, coming along the river, bisected the loading pier, and at one end of the pier was a derrick, a pile of unsalvaged scrap at its foot. All was deserted. The superintendent of the port was not there. Everything was closed up. The heavy planks of the pier—poor lumber, no doubt, hastily assembled during the war—were already rotting badly and in some places were broken through. It was not safe to walk on the pier. Despite the newness there was an astonishing air of disuse about the place. One suspected that it was seldom busy. Even if a tow were going to arrive, the superintendent of the port could check its slow progress by telephone. He could dictate many letters and prepare many dossiers and reports before that tow would arrive.

At Knoxville it was much the same. There, in 1946, the TVA terminal was in good order. The planks were not rotting. Freight cars were on the spur track, and heavy machinery was being jostled around. The superintendent of the Port of Knoxville was readying a clam-shell scoop and the port in general for the expected arrival of grain barges from the Midwest. But upriver, in the shadow of Gay Street Bridge, the remains of Chisholm Tavern moldered away on the slope of the old landing. There were busy factories and oil tanks, and there were also ramshackle tenements and weeds. Knoxville had a plan for improving the waterfront. Someday it might be turned into a kind of park. Yet though, in its casual disarray, it was an interesting spot on a sunny morning, one knew that the real business of Knoxville was on the heights where the modern city towered, not in the semislum where the steamboats and keelboats once tied up.

Paducah was different of course. It had always been different, with its Marine Ways, its throng of boats of all descriptions, its consciousness of being a true river city. Paducah was the heaven of retired or otherwise unemployed captains, pilots, mates, as well as of the active rivermen. Although, in the November 3, 1945, issue of the *Waterways Journal*, Forrest Crutchfield could report that, for the first time in its river history, Paducah was without a steamboat belonging to its own harbor, it still had plenty of steamboat men, and plenty of towboats, docks, ways, shops, whatever went with fresh-water navigation. Fred G. Neuman's column in the Paducah *Sun-Democrat* carried river news and old lore as matters of current interest. It was the last stronghold of the old tradition. In its native son, Irvin S. Cobb, Paducah had produced the only eloquent literary spokesman of that tradition who had appeared on the Tennessee River. But the stories and sketches of his books were the swan song of the tradition, which was dying even as he wrote about it. Paducah owed its modern liveliness, not to the Tennessee River in particular, but to its fortunate position at the junction of the Tennessee and the Ohio, with the Cumberland close by and the Mississippi not far away. The Tennessee river towns and cities were not like Paducah.

In fact, everywhere the movement, the stir of excitement, the sense of unpredictability and struggle with odds that had marked the old river were gone from the Tennessee. The managed river, though not without its hidden perils, had taken on the dullness that inevitably attends a reduction to a state of pure economic function. The seven million tons of "prospective commerce," taken as a statement of value, were relevant to something or other, but one could hear the statement without a quickening of interest. It was not like saying, "I'm coming home on the *Joe Wheeler*," or "The flatboatmen are in town," or "The *Lookout* came through the Suck without laying a line."

Old rivermen felt this, although they did not put it that way. No doubt the new generation would be different. The old generation did not talk much about TVA, and rarely praised it. If TVA was mentioned, they changed the subject and talked about the past. . . .

It is a bright September afternoon near Chattanooga, and close to the Suck Creek road, on a porch facing the Tennessee River and almost overlooking the Suck itself, a man lounges in a rocking chair. A hound dog sleeps at his feet. On the road between house and river, automobiles flash by continually, and the roar of trucks often drowns conversation. S. L. Massengale is an easy-talking man, and he talks well, in a country twang that has flavor to it but no crudeness. You would hardly think he was ever a mate on the old steamboats. He wears an old-style mustache, and it is white. The dark eyes above have a lively twinkle. The voice runs along, easy and gentle. . . .

Yes, he was arunning his trot-lines out there, when we come by in the morning—that's why he wasn't at home—but he didn't get a bite. No, he wasn't "captain." He served as mate. He had followed the river since he was twenty. He was on the *Chattanooga,* the *Trigg,* the *Joe Wheeler,* and many other boats . . . the *Forrest,* the *Lucy Coker.* Served under Captain Wilkey, too, who was his boss when he worked for the Tennessee River Navigation Company.

Best work he did, though, was for the government. The *John Ross* was a government boat. "That was my mistake," he said, "not staying with the gover'ment. If I'd 'a' stayed with the gover'ment, I'd 'a' had $75 a month. I'd be amakin' $75 a month, but it would be free money, a pension."

Well, the reason was, he left the gover'ment when his uncle took sick. He saw his uncle was mighty sick, was goin' to die, and he left the gover'ment boat. His uncle told him not to do it. "If you stay with the gover'ment, Si," his uncle said, "you'll have a pension in your old age, and that's what you better do." But he said, "No, Uncle, I jest *cain't* do it!" So he left the gover'ment, but it was a mistake, and he ought to 'a' done what his uncle said.

Now, he'd been asettin' there thinking about all they had done to the river, with the dams and improvements and all, and they had a 9-foot channel, and navigation was no trouble a-tall. In the old days he and his crews would get out and push a boat through with poles—lever it over the shoals. And they carried all kinds of freight, high water or low water—corn, hay, cows, hogs, cotton, chickens, ever' kind of thing. Now they had a 9-foot channel, and, Lord, they didn't carry a sack of corn, or a kag of molasses, or a cow or hog—not even a chicken. He laughed and repeated with gusto, "*Not even a chicken!*"

Did he know the story about the flatboat caught in the Pot? Oh, yes, he knew that story, but it wasn't a flatboat, it was a raft, a log raft. And it all really happened, it happened to a cousin of his named Brown. They used to run logs in those days down the river to South Pittsburg. Didn't try to haul 'em overland, but run 'em down the river. And his cousin Brown, that night, they got caught in the eddy of the Pot. It made a back-current, "a whirl about as long as from here to yan side of the river." And they saw the folks in the cabin fiddlin' and dancin', and then another cabin with fiddlin' and dancin', and then another, and another. But it was the same cabin all the time.

He remembered a lady once, who came on board his boat late at night, and heard him talking to the deck hands when they unloaded. It was a lot of grocery boxes and barrels, and it happened to be convenient to put them right near the engines. During the night they unloaded, upriver, and that lady heard him shouting to the rousters, "Knock it, roll it, knock it in the head—but keep away from that doctor!" Next morning she asked the captain, "Who was that cruel man that knocked somebody in the head and wouldn't let him go to the doctor?" The captain said, "You just wait a minute, and he'll be coming in." So when Si Massengale came in, the captain introduced him, and he had to explain that the doctor was the doctor pump. For hours that lady watched him work the hands, and then she wrote a piece about him and put it in a book.

And there was the story about the pilot who called the captain one night and said, "Captain, there's a log out yonder, and I can't get ahead of it." Come to find out, the log was the end of the long stogy he kept in his mouth. Sticking out there in the dark, at an angle, it looked like a log in the channel.

Oh, they had boats for high water and low water, in the old days. The low-water boats, unloaded, drew about 1½ feet. And of course they had to warp. The fixed capstan on the bank was called a "crab." His own father kept the one in the Suck. If a boat, coming up, got out of the "canal," then it had to lay a line, and it might take two days and nights to get it up the Suck. He remembered the *Joe Wheeler*, being taken up for repairs, had to lay a line, but there was a knot in the line, and it broke. The wind carried her against the bank, and they tied up to the bank. They were pulling up to an anchor when the line broke, and that old anchor is in the river yet.

He used to give a whisky ration to his roustabouts at the end of a trip. Had the whisky in a bucket and gave each hand a dipperful. Then he'd always throw out some coins for them to scramble after. But that was extra. He always paid ever' man what was owin' to him, but he expected 'em to work, and do what he said, and they knew it. He never had to tell 'em twice. . . .

The sun slanted low. The river was dark out there by Tumbling Shoals. The shadows of the mountains deepened and lengthened as we took our leave, going north over Suck Creek Mountain, going back into a world where too many people had to be told twice.

CHAPTER XVII

# Green Lands and Great Waters

THE TVA AGRICULTURAL PROGRAM got under way with far less hullabaloo than any other of the authority's multiple purposes. The changes it promised were slower of attainment than dam building and generation of power, and they could not be as vividly dramatized in metropolitan newspapers. Yet those changes were far-reaching. If they came to realization, the farm economy of the valley would be something very different from what the valley had known in the past. The very landscape, at least in its surface features, would be gradually remodeled. Perhaps the people would be much changed, too.

It was hard to say how much the TVA agricultural program owed to engineering decisions and to the fertilizer clauses of the act, and how much to the "planning sections." The law charged the authority with a duty toward "marginal lands," but that term, like the "yardstick," became obsolete. The authority had to be concerned with all lands, marginal or otherwise, that drained into the Tennessee River. It had to think, not only of its own huge structures, but of the billions of little dams that forest, grassy sod, and small grains might provide.

At an incautious moment TVA made the mistake of declaring, or implying, that prevention of soil erosion was an important part of flood control. It sponsored a moving picture, *The River,* that seemed to tell the public that floods were provoked or augmented by unwise denudation of land. A paragraph in the 1936 report, *The Unified Development of the Tennessee*, repeated the error by talking too rashly about the absorptive capacity of well-covered soil. Later, when Congress was investigating TVA, Arthur Morgan testified that such talk about the storage capacity of well-covered soil was "true in fact but . . . misleading in inference." He attributed the mistake to Harcourt Morgan's enthusiasm for beginning water control at the place "where the rain falls."

To prevent soil erosion was in itself a good thing, and was necessary, but such prevention, in truth, had little relationship to flood control. There had been floods in the Tennessee Valley when all the land was green wilderness. There had always been floods, except when there were drouths. In the great rainy seasons, when the bottom fell out of the sky, the soil was soon saturated, and the ground storage was used up; then, if the rain continued, the water ran off everywhere, over good farms and bad farms without discrimination. The thickly forested slopes of the Smoky Mountains sent forth freshets, under certain conditions, with as much enthusiasm as unforested slopes. Soil coverage would not stop the great floods. The only hope was to catch them in storage reservoirs.

The engineers had a different reason for wanting to prevent soil erosion. They did not want their reservoirs to fill up with silt. Although the army engineers in 1930 had reported that there was no very marked erosion in the valley, TVA did not accept this view. There was erosion. In some areas it was serious, and it caused siltage. The effect of siltage on reservoirs was to reduce their efficiency. The authority estimated, in 1936, that about one third of the storage capacity of the Hales Bar Reservoir had been lost to siltage in twenty-three years. At that rate, what would happen to Norris Lake and all the other lakes over a period of fifty or a hundred years?

TVA instituted scientific studies of the rate of siltage. First reports were optimistic and seemed to indicate that siltage was, after all, not as bad as had been feared. Norris Lake was pronounced good for centuries of performance, by statistical estimates. Nevertheless, the engineers knew that the farmer's plow was a great enemy of TVA. TVA's enthusiasm for saving the soil was in some definite measure an engineering necessity. Or it was a hedge against the fallibility of statistical predictions.

The ideal agricultural situation, from the pure engineering point of view, would be a kind of farming in which the naked earth would be nowhere exposed. It would be, in a sense, not farming at all, but a combination of a pastoral culture with as much of forested wilderness as the inhabitants would tolerate. The artificial lakes must have a natural environment as much like the green country of Indian times as TVA could make it. This would be a far cry from the existing agricultural economy, which, though well diversified in most of the valley and by no means as "backward" as the nation had been taught to think, still relied extensively on tillage. What could the engineer do with the stubborn independent farmers of the Tennessee Valley who, like their English and Scottish forebears, were ever ready to sing "God speed the plow!" Could he just *make* them stop plowing?

It was not necessary to *make* them stop. There was Harcourt Morgan, ex-president of the University of Tennessee and member of the TVA board. Harcourt Morgan, with others of his view, had a philosophy of agriculture that suited the engineer's needs. The bad plight of the southern farmer, reasoned these philosophers, came from his addiction to the great cash crops—cotton, corn, tobacco—which exhausted his land and left him at an economic disadvantage. Land planted in those staple crops, always intertilled, was subject to erosion. It was heavy erosion if the land was sloping or hilly and if the farmer was unskillful and careless. So the valley farmer must be weaned away from his preoccupation with cash crops. He must be put on a different economic base.

Then, too, the soil was not only eroded or eroding. It

was tired. It had lost much vitality through leaching and agricultural abuse, and farmers had tried to make up for the loss by stuffing it with nitrogenous fertilizer. It needed a restorative rather than a stimulant, and the only true restorative was phosphate.

If phosphate were applied in the right manner, in association with lime and a long-time program of legumes and cover crops, the soil would gradually recover its vitality, erosion would be stopped, and the agricultural cycle which requires that you put back into the soil as much as you take out could be re-established. Contour plowing, terracing, and strip cropping should be used where needed. Much of the land should go into pasture, and some into woodland. A balanced farming program and reforestation naturally went together.

If this program could be put under way, the valley would change over from a cash-crop, row-crop farming to dairying, cattle and sheep raising, poultry, small grains, and truck and fruit crops of the conservationist type. Farm families, it was argued, would then live "on" not "off of" the land. TVA's recreation program would bring tourists, whose spending would provide cash money to make up for the surrender of staple crops. Iudustry would have to be encouraged, too, in order to secure a more "balanced" general economy, and there might be various others ways of making everything modern and nice.

Perhaps—though nobody knew this for certain—the authority had the power simply to order that these things be done. Apparently navigation and flood control could be stretched, as sanctions, to almost any legal limit, and the authority's authority might therefore conceivably begin at the place "where the rain falls." But to act on that assumption would be untactful and unwise. It was better for the change to come gradually and, as it were, spontaneously. Try to force the farmers or lay down the law to them, and they might do just the opposite of what you wished, just to prove that they feared no man.

TVA's agricultural program began with experiments in the manufacture of phosphatic fertilizer at Muscle Shoals. The arrangements at Nitrate Plant No. 2 were adapted to this purpose. Almost immediately, too, the authority began to purchase neighboring Middle Tennessee lands that contained rich phosphate deposits. Simultaneously it made arrangements to work out a co-operative agricultural scheme with the land-grant universities and colleges of the valley states and with the United States Department of Agriculture. After general provision had been made in a three-way memorandum of understanding, more particular provision was worked out through identical contracts with the various land-grant institutions.

The arrangement was highly complex. It meant, in effect, that TVA depended in some considerable measure upon the agricultural experiment stations of the land-grant colleges to do much laboratory work and to give advice, while TVA tinkered with phosphate, furnished certain subsidies, and supplied a good deal of motive power. The ticklish work of persuading the farmers was passed over largely to the county agents and assistant county agents. Accordingly, although TVA conducted experiments of its own, had its own agricultural organization, was perpetually busy with agricultural suggestions, and touched the farmers directly at many points, nevertheless the land-grant colleges, the agricultural extension service, and the soil conservation organizations carried the burden of seeing that TVA's agricultural (or pastoral) wishes were made effective. The plan was always described by TVA as a "co-operative" arrangement or a "joint regional program," and the authority was careful in its reports to give basic credit to its allies. At the same time, it was not easy to distinguish between the sphere of actual TVA performance and the spheres of operation of its intermingled and somewhat confused allies. The public of the nation, which read newspapers and magazines rather than technical reports, somehow or other tended to conclude that TVA was doing the whole job.

Very soon the authority evolved new processes for the manufacture of phosphatic fertilizers. These processes were the more valuable because they utilized even the lower grades of phosphate rock. By 1946 TVA was distributing not only triple superphosphate and calcium metaphosphate, but had added a new plant nutrient which it called fused tricalcium phosphate. An experimental plant at Columbia, Tennessee, near the great phosphate deposits of Maury and Williamson counties, was established for production of the new plant food. TVA developed another phosphate plant at Mobile, Alabama, and, as need became great, both at home and abroad, it also went into the production of ammonium nitrate.

The planned distribution of these fertilizers was handled through the scheme of "test demonstration" farms which TVA instituted with and through its allies, the land-grant colleges and other organizations. Under this scheme the farmers of the valley—and many other farmers scattered throughout the nation—began to undertake the shift toward a more pastoral type of farm economy. By 1946 nearly seven thousand farms in the valley itself had enlisted in this great experiment, and approximately 1,150,000 acres of farm land in the Tennessee watershed wore the green of TVA.

All of it was on a co-operative basis, and it was very far from being just an abstract plan. It was the only part of the authority's program that rested on the voluntary acceptance of thousands of individual persons, and for this reason, of all the authority's multifarious activities, it was the nearest to being "democratic." To many Southerners of rural bias it was the most hopeful and least debatable part of the great enterprise. In part it compensated for the permanent loss and destruction brought about by the engineering works of TVA.

Under the test demonstration scheme, the county agent or some other representative of the agricultural extension service arranged for a meeting of farmers in some selected community. It might be, and often was, a meeting of some already existing farm organization. The test demonstration program was explained, and the farmers were asked to nominate one of their number to undertake the program. If he consented, he then signed an agreement to embark on a five-year plan of land use and soil conservation. He agreed to provide—or to have provided for him—a map showing his fields and their present use. He had to take an inventory of his situation and to plan, under guidance, what use he would make of his farm for the next five years. He had to agree, of course, to use TVA phosphate. TVA furnished the necessary amount of phosphatic fertilizer. There was no charge for the fertilizer itself, and to that extent the farmer was subsidized. But the farmer paid the expenses of shipment from Muscle Shoals. He also furnished the lime rock that had to be applied with the phosphate, and he had to bear other expenses. He was not free, under the agreement, to do anything he pleased with his farm; he had to stay within the limits of the approved program. But on him lay the chief responsibility of working out his land-use program within the framework that had been explained to him. He had to exercise initiative and be his own boss. At the same time, he could get all the advice he wanted from the finest experts, who were ready to analyze his soil for him, to estimate with scientific exactitude its requirements and possibilities, and to keep him posted on all the latest developments in agronomy.

Thus the laboratory and production work of TVA and its allies was continuously tested in varied local situations; and the farm where the phosphate was applied served to demonstrate to neighboring farmers the visible benefits of the general scheme.

For communities where there had been in past years a

great deal of agricultural damage—as, for example, in the badly eroded old Cherokee lands of North Georgia—the agents of restoration sponsored large-scale demonstrations which sought to control small watersheds as a whole. These projects were called "area test demonstrations." They enlisted whole communities in a five-year program of land use. Between 1936 and 1946 a total of 658 communities joined up in this particular kind of co-operative effort.

And just how well did the program work? In TVA reports, news releases, and pamphlets it worked very well—it always worked. The excellent files of the agricultural relations department of TVA were crowded with interesting case histories that told the story, and told it most convincingly, with exact and minute statistics to back up the attractive photographs. It was always a well-dramatized story of "before" and "after," with the shadows in the "before" part and the happy sunshine of agricultural prosperity streaming over the "after" part.

Invariably, after TVA phosphate was applied and all the other things were done in due order, the yield of the test demonstration farm was increased, and was of better quality. The yield was greater, always, even though the acreage devoted to row crops was sharply reduced. The farm animals, feeding on pastures to which vitality had been restored, thrived greatly. The whole place cast off the weedy, rundown appearance characteristic of southern farms in the long years of agrarian defeat. On pastures where briers and iron weeds had previously flourished, the grass and clover came back. Sometimes they sprang up anew of their own accord where the phosphate treatment was applied. It was as if the soil had been sick and had been made well.

The new vitality of the land was reflected in the spirits and energy of the farmer. He had less of row crops planted than before—perhaps he had abandoned them altogether, except for what he grew as animal feed—but he discovered that he was in better economic health and was able to make some of the improvements that he and his wife had longed for but had despaired of achieving. He painted the house, repaired the barn, maybe added a new barn or a creamery or a good chicken house or a little building for storage of fruit and vegetables. He put up fences. He went in for electrification and perhaps bought a tractor and other farm machinery. Still he found that, with all the outlay, which may have been expensive, the value of his farm had increased and that also, since he was more definitely "living at home," his cash surplus was real cash and not paper. He had larger, better ordered fields, and fewer meaningless patches. His farm had taken on a pattern; it had come alive.

Meanwhile the neighbors saw with their own eyes what was happening. There was an interchange of ideas, both from person to person and in meetings. Other farmers, big and little, emulated the practices of the test demonstration farm, and the situation of the whole community improved. Perhaps it became once more a community—under the disintegrating impact of modern forces it had almost forgotten how to be one.

Meanwhile, too, soil erosion was stopped, the forests extended their bounds, there was much more land in grass and woodland pasture and cover crops. There was more terracing of slopes, more strip cropping and general protection against rain, and less gullying and waste. The idle lands, the poor lands, were either returned to the silent curatorship of the forest or were built up and restored to right use.

TVA could cite many an example to back up its broad statistics of gain. It liked particularly to dwell on the "hard cases" of farmers who had lost good bottom land to a reservoir project. In 1942, for example, it could report that R. L. Parham of Rhea County, who had lost 136 acres of his farm, near Dayton, to the Chickamauga reservoir, was making a greater profit on his 120-acre upland farm than he had formerly made on his whole farm of 256 acres. What Parham did was to terrace his hill land, apply 9,200 pounds of calcium metaphosphate and 200 tons of lime in four years, and go into pasture land, beef cattle, and small grains.

J. W. Davis, of the Birchwood community, lost 300 acres of his farm to TVA. "I thought we would starve to death," TVA quoted him as saying. "I started to leave, and I would have, too, if I could have found the land I wanted. Now I am glad I didn't." He was glad he didn't because, when the Birchwood community, steered by the assistant county agent, took up the TVA program, conditions im-

proved. In 1941 Davis had a larger herd of dairy cattle than before he lost his land, and he had been able to adapt himself to woodland farming.

There were also convincing examples of area test demonstrations that built up run-down communities. Such a one was the Young Cane community of North Georgia. It had been, in the words of one of its citizens, "probably one of the poorest, least productive, and least attractive" of the communities of Union County, Georgia. By 1942 it was growing fifteen or twenty varied crops for the commercial market. With less acreage in corn, it was getting 30 bushels to the acre where it formerly got 10. It had fine pastures, fine cattle, electrified homes (30 to 40 per cent of which had been painted), and was feeling good. The farm lands had increased from an estimated value of $175,000 to $350,000.

As the test demonstration scheme took root in the valley, TVA added numerous helps, ingeniously calculated to assist the farmer who would follow its program, and of course it continued to work through federal, state, and county agencies in promoting these helps. TVA wanted to encourage the growing of barley, oats, rye, and wheat, for these afforded useful ground cover in winter and early spring, when the cycle of freeze-thaw-rain characteristic of valley weather inflicted terrible damage upon unprotected land. Accordingly TVA developed and promoted a small "trailer thresher"— a simple, inexpensive, two-wheel affair which could be used in the small-farm areas. It promoted a furrow seeder which enabled a farmer to plant small grains in contour furrows directly in lespedeza sod. It developed hay driers. It helped to sponsor community refrigerator plants for storage. It experimented with quick-freezing of strawberries and other marketable fruits and vegetables. It built an experimental quick-freezing laboratory, mounted on barges, which could be towed from point to point on the river. The purpose was to test quick-freezing methods and to determine what varieties of fruits and vegetables were best adapted to those methods.

TVA did countless other things to aid its agricultural program. It encouraged, or at least gave approving fatherly nods to, the growth of co-operatives, like the Lauderdale County Cooperative of North Alabama. Other co-operatives, both of the producer and of the consumer type, sprang up. TVA made continuous studies of past performance and built up voluminous research that looked to the future. It thought of everything and apparently did almost everything it thought of.

The reforestation program, TVA reported, was well under way. From its own nurseries TVA had provided millions of seedling trees by 1946 and had reforested, it said, 123,000 acres. It promoted farm woodlands, good forestry, timber "harvesting" of the approved type. It tried to prevent forest fires. It worked up forest management demonstrations in areas where timber companies, coal companies, and other large owners had extensive holdings. It made a start toward redeeming the famous "desert" of Copper Hill in the extreme southeastern part of Tennessee. There, many decades before TVA was thought of, the Ducktown copper plant had ineptly and heartlessly spread noxious fumes over the countryside. Practically all vegetable life vanished over an area of 23,000 acres, and the region looked worse, and was worse, than the "bad lands" of the West. This was a hard problem, and by 1946 TVA could claim that only five per cent of the Copper Basin had been reforested.

As the century approached its mid-mark, one could begin to reckon results. The statistical reports from state and county agencies were encouraging. The agricultural transformation of the Tennessee Valley was visibly advanced, although perhaps it was going a little more slowly than TVA wished or its most ardent supporters claimed. In the eastern parts of the valley, where the grass-and-woodland farm was already an accepted type, the world was surely getting greener, and there was less red soil showing than of old. In the cotton country of the Great Bend, less acreage was going into cotton and other row crops, and hayfields and pastures appeared where they had not been seen before. Along the Lower Tennessee the gains were less apparent. The late completion of Kentucky Dam and the demands of World War II may have delayed progress. Certainly the Tennessee and Kentucky farmers of that area, long at a tragic disadvantage, had hardly begun to make their country green. Although TVA could draw from its files interesting case histories to show that scattered individuals in this area had joined up with the cause, nevertheless the smell of burning woods in springtime, the pale stalks of shriveled corn in summer, and the gullied earth told the traveler all too surely that the test demonstration program was not yet widely accepted.

There were other spots of dissent or failure that any passing eye could see. Even in East Tennessee, less than fifty miles from the buzzing office of TVA itself, one could find, near historic Fort Loudoun, unco-operative farmers who still insisted on hanging their corn fields on a 45-degree mountain slope. Perhaps such spots were proof that TVA was not forcing the issue, as it possibly had the power to do. Harcourt Morgan and his corps of assistants did not, after all, propose to liquidate, Soviet fashion, the man with the nonco-operative cornfield.

The coming of World War II was in many ways disastrous, for the time being, to the TVA program, even though the nation at large derived great immediate benefits from TVA works. The war renewed the demand for staple crops, it drafted farm labor or lured it away to factories, it was in every way disturbing to the slow-working voluntary plan for valley agriculture. One of its worst features was that the shortage of farm labor intensified and accelerated the process of mechanizing the farms. This could mean only that more farm capital was going into expendible materiel, that the small farmer was being put at renewed disadvantage, and that small farmers and large farmers alike were taking financial risks which the future might not justify. But as for TVA, the multiple-purpose project now found how grossly one of its purposes might conflict with others. TVA had plumed itself on its merits as a decentralized, regional agency, better disposed than bureaucratic Washington to hearken to local needs. But in the years of war the regional agency became a national weapon. The needs of war, which in 1917 had created Wilson Dam and the nitrate plants, now largely diverted the fertilizer factories of TVA to the manufacture of explosives and incendiaries. The plight of England required that a large part of TVA phosphates be shipped abroad to make up for the loss of the North African phosphates. In all TVA supplied 114,000 tons of fertilizers for export to the allies of the United States, while it simultaneously produced chemicals and explosives for the military needs of American forces. The minerals thus used up made a dent in TVA resources. They were gone forever, and the available supply of nutrient for restoring farm land was lessened by that much.

Nor was the general agricultural picture in all respects as beautiful or as favorable to the TVA program as the publications of the authority and the claims of its friends argued. TVA pamphlets, case histories, news releases pictured happy farmers who unvaryingly succeeded under the TVA program and grinned with pleasure and approval. TVA never told, of course, about the dour, gloomy, resentful people who did not like TVA plans, or those who accepted because they had no other choice.

No TVA blurb said anything whatever, for example, about Uncle Bob, whose bottom lands were extensively inundated by TVA. The appraisers viewed his land when the water was already over the corn bottoms. It "looked bad" when they came along, and they offered him an indecently low price for the place. Uncle Bob forced condemnation proceedings, and the court gave him some thousands of dollars more than the appraisers had offered. Now there he was, on higher ground, with a 400-acre farm close to his old place that lay under the waters he could see from his window. Did he like his new place? Yes, he liked it all right, and he had no hard feelings against TVA. Did TVA treat him all right? Well, he reckoned so, except for that appraisal, but the TVA folks didn't always do what they should. Would he follow the TVA program, if he were left to do so, of his own accord and entirely at his own expense? Well, Uncle Bob didn't know. He was doubtful. Probably he wouldn't. Not that the program wasn't good. It was good, and he liked ridge farming all right. But probably he just wouldn't take the trouble to do all that planning and keep all those records. More than likely he would grow more cash crops than TVA would like to see grown.

Nor did TVA news releases say anything about the old storekeeper who stood looking at the river not far from the sites of Fort Heiman and Fort Henry one day in May, 1942. To the north, along the west bank, the reservoir clearance gangs had been stripping the earth of trees, and the distance was filled with the smoke of their burnings. The people were being moved out, and the little cluster of rude buildings would soon go too. The old storekeeper's eyes were gloomy as he spoke of the removals. Where were the folks going? Why, back on the poor land, of course, and the landowners would get some money, but the tenants, they would get nothing, and there were a lot of tenants.

He couldn't understand it, he said sadly. He thought there was something mysterious behind it all. Surely TVA wasn't doing it just to make electricity. There must be some strange unknown purpose. They couldn't be doing it for navigation. Why, he had lived right thar on the river for thirty years, and all that time boats had navigated the river without any trouble, right on up to Chattanoogy. It was wasteful. And it was costly, too costly. What were the poor folks going to do? Where were even the landowners going to go? That land down thar in the bottoms was the best land. It was the only good land in Henry County, and pretty soon the water would lie over it. What about all those logs, or were they logs that were burning? Yes, they were logs. TVA was cutting off all the timber. Folks could have it if they could get a way to haul it off, but who could get wood hauled these days? He spat contemptuously in the dust.

On the general, more impersonal front, large questions loomed. It was quite uncertain, in the first place, whether TVA was entitled to take as much credit as it was claiming for the improved estate of agriculture in the valley. Much of the improvement might have happened anyway, under the soil conservation program of the United States Department of Agriculture, which, under New Deal direction, was affectionately subsidizing and indoctrinating farmers throughout the nation. Much credit should go to federal agencies in general, and some, surely, ought to go to the states and to farmers' organizations. Federal and state programs did not necessarily require the stimulation or assistance of a TVA.

Development of phosphatic fertilizer was a good thing, and TVA had a real point there; yet it seemed entirely possible that that same phosphatic fertilizer, with all its benefits, might have been obtained without drowning the whole Tennessee Valley and spending what promised to be, in the end, perhaps a billion dollars.

As for TVA figures that showed economic betterment on test demonstration farms, why, farmers everywhere were making money. Federal subsidies, price fixing, quick war prosperity would have done that, or could have done it, though not precisely according to the approved TVA pattern. The Department of Agriculture and the state agencies were out to prevent soil erosion and to promote reforestation. Those were valuable purposes, but they were being accomplished elsewhere without benefit of TVA. They really had to be accomplished, TVA or no TVA. Maybe the voluntary TVA program was in fact a little too voluntary, a little too slow. Maybe more urgent measures were needed, for the land could not wait indefinitely for TVA's program of democratic co-operation to catch on. There was some discontent among TVA's allies, who were bothered by overlapping and confusion of jurisdiction. Although outwardly all official relationships were amiable, there were signs that state conservation authorities were restless and critical. They were not perfectly happy about all parts of the TVA program, and might become quarrelsome and difficult.

But if, in the long run, the TVA program succeeded, the transformation of the land would certainly take place. The effect on the landscape of the Tennessee Valley, combined with other tendencies of similar kind, would be much like the effect of the enclosures of Henry VIII's time, and later, upon the England of Elizabeth and succeeding monarchs; and it might have some of the social effects which accompanied those great dispossessions and which later made acid for the pen of Karl Marx. Green fields would be many, and tillage would be small. The Tennessee farmer would become a cattle raiser, a dairyman enslaved to the aching, compulsive teats of a herd of cows and to the trucks and price scale of Borden, Pet, Carnation. And then he might also become—though in 1946 he still detested the idea—a forester, a mountain guide, an operator of tourist homes and hot-dog stands, a tipped purveyor and professional friend to tippling fishermen, hunters of ducks unlimited, abstracting artists, tired neurotics, and vacation seekers of all sorts. Under the TVA agricultural plan it might even turn out, eventually, that the various rural dialects of the valley would acquire a marketable value and could be entered among farm assets, along with the blooded bulls, hogs, alfalfa, and refrigerators.

## CHAPTER XVIII

# The Battles of TVA

DESPITE the heavy political support and the highly favorable publicity that it received, there was hardly a year when TVA was not under attack from some quarter or in trouble of some kind. The sunshiny confidence of its official utterances was an instrument of defense. Directly or indirectly, TVA was always arguing its case. Even its Annual Reports to Congress were as much arguments as accountings. In them the heavy factual material was relegated to the back of the book. The front part, enlivened by striking photographs and neat topical slogans, became more and more a skillfully dramatized story of TVA's accomplishments and plans. Its appealing pamphlets were widely distributed. They even found their way into schoolrooms.

At first, before the need of caution became evident, spokesmen of the authority committed occasional indiscretions. There was a tendency to overemphasize the "power" and "planning" phases of TVA activities. Mr. Lilienthal spoke with sweeping enthusiasm about the authority's "yardstick" program. The wholesale electric rates of the authority, he declared, "while strikingly low, cover all costs of furnishing service." On one occasion he was quoted as saying, "We are expending, and expect to expend millions upon millions of dollars in construction activities, all looking toward the development of more and more power."

When danger began to loom, such utterances were toned

down. There was no use in furnishing free ammunition to enemies who would like to prove that TVA was a socialistic affair or that it was violating the law. So TVA became more and more a navigation and flood-control project which only incidentally or perhaps inadvertently produced billions of kilowatt-hours annually. A TVA engineer, if queried as to the function of Norris Dam (which had no navigation lock), would carefully explain that it was for navigation and flood-control primarily. Even such precautions did not keep TVA out of trouble.

The legal battles, of course, would have come anyhow. They were severe. Mr. Lilienthal and other members of TVA complained that they could not get their regular work done for having to face the numerous lawsuits—over fifty in all —that were directed at the authority during its quarrel with the private companies. The most notable of these were the Ashwander case and the Nineteen Power Companies case.

In the hard-fought Ashwander case the complainants, who were stockholders in the Alabama Power Company, brought suit to prevent the company from carrying out a contract made with TVA for the sale of certain properties. Their attorneys chose to attack the central issue. They charged that TVA, both in the contract involved and in its general performance, was acting without constitutional authority. In the Federal District Court TVA suffered a devastating defeat. Judge William I. Grubb ruled that TVA arrangements for disposal of power were "illegal proprietary operations," declared it was exceeding its constitutional limits, annulled the contract, and tied up TVA with injunctions.

This judgment was reversed in the Circuit Court of Appeals. The case went up to the United States Supreme Court, which in February, 1936, handed down an opinion favoring TVA.

Yet the Supreme Court decision in the Ashwander case, although it was a defeat for the complainants, was far from being a clear victory for TVA. The attorneys for the stockholders argued that the program of TVA was "a *coup d'état* that would commit the Government permanently to the manufacture and distribution of electricity." This coup, they held, if admitted to legal standing, "would open every essential industry and service to direct . . . governmental competition." TVA, they declared, was invading a field reserved to the states and their citizens. It had sought no com-

pact among the valley states, but had "silenced the state administrations with a revocable stipend [payments in lieu of taxes]." They charged that TVA was using navigation as a fiction to disguise unconstitutional acts.

The TVA attorneys skillfully directed the attention of the court to Wilson Dam and based their argument largely upon the accepted authority of the federal government to build that dam and the nitrate plants as a war measure and to dispose of the surplus power there generated.

Chief Justice Hughes, who read the opinion of the court,

accepted the view of TVA. He upheld the right of the government to dispose of all the electric energy generated, not only to the extent that it might be a surplus necessarily created in operating navigation and defense works, but beyond that point. Any other view would lead to "absurd consequences." At the same time the chief justice made it clear that the court was limiting its consideration to the Wilson Dam plant. It ignored, it forbore to rule upon, the works and policies of TVA in general. "We express no opinion," he said, ". . . as to the validity of any other dam or power development in the Tennessee Valley . . . or as to the validity of the TVA act . . ."

This refusal to pass on the constitutional question was disconcerting to TVA supporters. If the Supreme Court in some later case should sway toward the view of Justice McReynolds, TVA might find its hands tied. In his strongly worded dissenting opinion in the Ashwander case, Justice McReynolds upheld the claims of the stockholders and asserted the relevancy of their attorneys' charges against the general TVA program. An enterprise like TVA, he said, "may dispose of water power or electricity, honestly developed in connection with permissible improvement of navigable waters." "But," he added, "the means employed . . . must be reasonably appropriate to the circumstances. Under the pretense of exercising granted power, they may not in fact undertake something not intrusted to them." He did not adhere to the narrow view that the Wilson Dam project must be considered in isolation from the general performance of TVA. The court should consider "the deliberately announced purpose of Directors clothed with extraordinary discretion and supplied with enormous sums of money." The TVA program, he noted, was not confined to the Muscle Shoals area, and if its plans were carried out, with the approval of the court, then "an easy way has been found for breaking down the limitations heretofore supposed to guarantee protection against aggression."

The private companies, seeing that opportunity was still open, pressed a new attack. In May, 1936, the Tennessee Electric Power Company and eighteen other companies brought suit against TVA, claiming damage and pointing to unconstitutional acts. After a long spell of legal jockeying the case was finally brought to trial at Chattanooga, in November, 1937, before a special three-judge court over which Judge Florence Allen presided. The extensive charges of the complainants held, among other things, that TVA had engaged in "coercion and fraud" to push its power program and that it had conspired with Harold L. Ickes, public works administrator and secretary of the interior, to force municipalities to accept TVA power. The instrument of compulsion was the public funds, controlled by Ickes, which, it was alleged, he threatened to withhold from municipalities that refused to join up with TVA.

The court ruled in favor of TVA. It held that TVA and Ickes had not engaged in fraud and conspiracy; the co-operation of public officials could not be so regarded. Nor had the complainants suffered damage, as averred, though they might so suffer in the future. That would be, however, *damnum absque injuria* [damage without injury], "unless sales of power by TVA are unlawful." The court held that the sales were not unlawful; that constitutional authority had not been exceeded; and that, furthermore, the contention of the complainants that the doings of TVA violated state rights was of no force, since the states concerned, by their legislative "enabling acts" had conceded TVA the right to do just what it was doing. (No valley state appeared in court to support the complainants, but Vermont filed a brief as *amicus curiae*.)

The case went up to the Supreme Court, as it happened, after the president had launched his campaign to reform or "unpack" the Supreme Court. Again the court warily avoided any rulings as to constitutionality. The appellants argued that TVA was not a bona fide navigation and flood-control

## THE BATTLES OF TVA

project; it sought, "under the euphonious title of a 'multiple purpose project' to yoke together constitutional and unconstitutional enterprises." The court wiped out this argument by ignoring it—by simply declaring that the companies had no standing in the court. The "vice of their position," said Justice Roberts, was "that neither their charters nor their local franchises involve the grant of a monopoly or render competition illegal." They had no ground for action. Again, however, there was a strong dissenting opinion. Justice Butler, much like Justice McReynolds, held that the navigation and flood-control clauses of the TVA statute were "mere pretexts" to cover unlawful acts; that TVA had inflicted upon the private companies "direct and special injury"; and that the TVA act was unconstitutional.

But it was the majority opinion that decided the case. TVA was free to "develop its service area" by whatever means it chose. True, the issue of constitutionality remained undecided, but the decision of the court made it unlikely that the issue would be raised in the future, except in the improbable event that some state or municipality might bring suit against TVA.

On the other hand, the great trials had a jarring effect and boded possible ill, if not to TVA, then to the conception represented in TVA. The TVA lawyers had won the cases, but it was possible that their opponents, in a broad sense, had won the cause. The evidence and the arguments presented in the trials did heavy damage to TVA's "yardstick" slogan. It lost its political value and passed out of currency.

Furthermore, TVA had been revealed as indulging in some of the very practices for which TVA officials and partisans had upbraided private corporations. It had "strong-armed" its rivals, had used various forms of pressure to gain its ends, and had propagandized without too nice a regard for facts. It had even entered into an "interlocking directorate" with the Electric Home and Farm Authority, a government enterprise which subsidized the sale of electric appliances (and from which TVA later, somewhat shamefacedly, withdrew). To crown the process, it had been as glad as any private company to seek refuge in legal technicalities. Now it had legality, but how much virtue was left? What had happened to the soul of the corporation? The court record was there, a record which included the dissenting opinions of Justices McReynolds and Butler; and dissenting opinions, for all their lack of immediate force, could have considerable long-range philosophic and political effect. The Supreme Court had saved TVA and had also opened the door, perhaps, to putting the government into any kind of business. But that prospect, once foreseen, might receive attention from later political regimes.

In the valley itself, too, TVA had generated a certain amount of ill will that might prove someday to be annoying. North Alabama had been cold-shouldered in the matter of the location of the principal offices of the authority. It decided that TVA was not above twisting the law to suit its convenience. Other instances of cold-shouldering were observed and might be treasured up in remembrance.

It was quite impossible, the valley learned, to get a TVA job through a recommendation from one's senator or representative. That, perhaps, was as it should be, since TVA was such a peculiarly high-souled affair. At the same time it was very odd that so few valley natives, or for that matter Southerners, seemed eligible for the higher positions in TVA. The key men of TVA were almost uniformly unknown to the inhabitants of Tennessee and Alabama and had neither cousins nor grandparents south of the Ohio. Of course TVA was hiring its labor force in the local area and was admitting valley people to minor jobs like typist or file clerk. But that only made things look worse.

The large city newspapers of the valley, which had "gone all out" for TVA improvements, looked the other way when this hot topic was discussed. But the small papers took down their squirrel guns. The Florence *Tribune* said: "The Authority, its spokesmen claim, eliminated all politics from its make-up; its sole aim was efficiency. Nevertheless, in the opinion of many living within its jurisdiction, it has played the narrowest kind of politics, almost a carpetbag brand. . . . Asked to explain its policy, officers of the TVA intimated that the section in which its work centered was a section of backward people, that needed new blood."

The Rossville *Open Gate*, speaking to the same point, said: "If the TVA directors persist in this policy they will either destroy themselves or seriously damage the valley program of President Roosevelt." Individual citizens wrote letters denouncing "the yellow-bellied scoundrels from north of the Mason and Dixon line" or called TVA "a colonization scheme for the benefit of Yankee Republicans."

The TVA seemed unruffled by this spatter of guerrilla bullets. Like the Yankee gunboats of other days, it was happily armor-plated, and it chugged stolidly on. The Congressional investigation of 1938 revealed that after five years of domicile in the valley, the authority was still rather heavily northern in its top personnel. Out of a list of thirty-nine "major staff members" furnished by Gordon R. Clapp, it could be discovered that five were residents of valley states. Thirty of the thirty-nine were from the North.

The authority brushed off niggling complaints about such matters, however. It pointed to its "merit system" and its nonpolitical character. It felt that it had succeeded in attracting an unusually competent, even a distinguished personnel. Indeed, it was perfectly true that the work sponsored by TVA and its comparative freedom from red tape attracted a type of administrator and technologist that could not ordinarily be lured into government service. Once in office, they quite frequently stayed.

Other difficulties could not exactly be brushed off.

While the Tennessee Electric Power Company case was still pending, the Berry marble claims suddenly emerged as an issue of disagreeable importance. There were signs of a breach between Chairman Morgan and his fellow directors. Soon the astounded public witnessed a battle of Titans. Titan Arthur Morgan hurled mountains of complaint at his two associates, which Titans Lilienthal and Harcourt Morgan promptly hurled back. The Grand Titan, Roosevelt, intervened and, failing to quell the strife, tossed Titan Arthur Morgan out of office. But Titan Morgan, bouncing up like Antaeus, demanded a Congressional investigation. It was an exciting but unedifying spectacle.

The matter of the Berry claims was as ticklish a problem as a high-minded TVA expert would want to encounter. Major George L. Berry, an East Tennessean, was a labor leader, a high union official. For a time he was senator from Tennessee, and he had been co-ordinator of industrial co-operation under the NRA. With certain associates—but not in his own name—Major Berry had acquired, beginning in 1932, extensive mineral rights in the area subject to inundation by Norris Dam.

In April, 1935, with inundation not far off, Major Berry politely but firmly asked for a settlement of his claims, about which the authority had done singularly little. However, the TVA geologists and their consultants had examined the claims and had reported them not commercially valuable. The Berry claims thus became a hot issue in TVA board meetings. Chairman Morgan was suspicious of "bad faith," but TVA's legal department had not uncovered any substantial evidence of bad faith. Lilienthal and Harcourt Morgan favored a conciliation agreement, under which the Berry claims might be settled out of court. They wanted to get Dr. John W. Finch, of the Bureau of Mines, to act as conciliator under an arrangement that would not bind either TVA or Berry. Major Berry was agreeable to this plan, but Chairman Morgan did not like it. He called on Major Berry to declare precisely the nature of his interest in the marble claims. Major Berry, standing on his legal rights, refused to give the information requested.

In the arguments among board members, Lilienthal and Harcourt Morgan took the position that bad faith was not an issue. The sole question was the value of the claims; but they apparently wished to avoid condemnation proceedings. Chairman Morgan, aware of Berry's political influence, felt that he was applying "unseemly pressure." Overruling Chairman Morgan, the two other directors voted that the chairman should ask Secretary Ickes to loan Dr. Finch as conciliator. Chairman Morgan sent in the official request, but coupled with it a statement of his views. Ickes found it convenient to report that Dr. Finch would not be available—was otherwise engaged. So condemnation proceedings became inevitable.

Then, in the fall of 1937, after tedious prowling through courthouse records, TVA investigators at last found some evidence of bad faith. They uncovered certain powers of attorney executed by landowners to Berry and his associates. About this time, also, one of the persons involved decided to tell what he knew. Evans Dunn, who was handling the condemnation proceedings for TVA, produced the powers of attorney in court. In answer to Berry's statement that he did not know of the existence of the powers of attorney, TVA put in evidence certain contracts, signed by Berry and associates, in which the powers of attorney were mentioned. The commission which heard the case, however, passed over the bad faith charges and restricted its judgment to the question of value. Major Berry and associates, who had apparently hoped to get as much as $5,000,000 for their claims, were completely routed.

Chairman Morgan had been uneasy lest the Berry case should not be pressed severely enough. To the consternation of TVA attorneys, he insisted on appearing as a witness—just as he had done, against their wishes, in the case of the nineteen power companies. His testimony, it was said, added nothing substantial. Seemingly Morgan was determined to make up for what he felt to be a certain slackness on the part of his fellow directors and would have preferred that Berry and associates be prosecuted on serious charges. In a letter to Representative Maury Maverick, he called the Berry claims "an effort at a deliberate, bare-faced steal." Elsewhere he held that the policy of Lilienthal and Harcourt Morgan "did not show frank, disinterested public service." In March, 1938, he charged that his colleagues had not supported him in his wish for "honesty, openness, decency, and fairness" in government. He called for a Congressional investigation of TVA.

Charges and countercharges came thick and fast. The White House released a memorandum of January 18, in which Lilienthal and Harcourt Morgan suggested that the chairman either cease to "obstruct the carrying out of determined policies" or resign. They complained against his "rule or ruin" attitude. They said he was nonco-operative and had sought, by means which they deplored, to subvert board decisions.

In reply Chairman Morgan released the text of his extensive letter to Representative Maverick, written previously, in which he reviewed the differences between himself and his fellow directors. Since the early days of TVA, he said, Lilienthal and Harcourt Morgan had combined against him. He had carried the burden of TVA's construction program, but had been impotent in determining power and fertilizer policies. "My vote," he declared, "does not count."

The gist of his charges was that Lilienthal and Harcourt Morgan had reached an understanding by which the one would have a free hand in power policy, the other in agricultural matters, and that, by always voting together, they made it appear that their individual policies were board policies. They had hemmed him in with restrictions and intrigued against him. "There is," he said, "a practice of evasion, intrigue, and sharp strategy with remarkable skill in alibi and

## THE BATTLES OF TVA

the habit of avoiding direct responsibility, which makes Machiavelli seem open and candid."

Apparently President Roosevelt thought he could talk the quarreling Titans into agreement. He summoned the directors into conference. Chairman Morgan refused to participate. Only after the president's request had been twice repeated did he reluctantly agree to attend. Then followed an unprecedented hearing—called by some critics "a star chamber trial"—before the president. Reporters, in an adjoining room, were furnished with a quick stenographic transcript of the proceedings. The "build-up" of the press had prepared the country for sensational disclosures, but this build-up proved to be a gross misrepresentation of Chairman Morgan's purpose. Challenged by the president to give evidence of dishonesty or misfeasance on the part of his codirectors, Chairman Morgan ignored the question. He declared the proceedings useless, refused to answer the president's questions, and repeated his demand for a Congressional inquiry. The other directors replied at length to the chairman's accusations and renewed their counteraccusations.

At first the president suggested that the directors either compose their differences or else all resign, for the good of the country. Not one offered his resignation. Continuance of the hearings only brought the same result as at the first hearing. Finally President Roosevelt read a statement in which he rebuked the chairman for refusing to answer questions. This refusal, said Mr. Roosevelt, "gives credence to the charge that he has been unwilling to co-operate with his fellow directors and that he is temperamentally unfitted to exercise a divided authority." Messrs. Lilienthal and Harcourt Morgan had supported their charges, but Arthur Morgan had not. Therefore, unless the chairman either withdrew his charges or resigned, he, the president, would act upon the evidence. Chairman Morgan refused to do either. "I challenge the suggestion and deny the right and the power to remove or suspend me," he said. Whereupon the president, as of March 23, 1938, removed Arthur Morgan from office, both as chairman and as director, on the ground of "contumacy."

By this extraordinary series of events, Arthur E. Morgan, the man who above all others was responsible for the physical creation of TVA as an engineering enterprise, and who had shaped its early organization and given it much of its initial force, was dismissed from office by the president who had appointed him. The directors whom he had accused were retained. Thus the weight of presidential authority and with it all the power of the New Deal were thrown to the support of the accused directors. The same act marked Arthur Morgan for destruction.

Arthur Morgan carried to the courts his bold challenge of the president's power to remove him, but in the subsequent litigation failed to establish his view. In Congress it was different. There it was clear that Senator Norris's effort to secure a "friendly" investigation by the Federal Trade Commission would fail. Norris's proposal was denounced by Senator H. Styles Bridges as the kind of thing that might be expected from a "rubber-stamp, machine-led partisan," but hardly from the great liberal Norris. Congress voted for a full-scale investigation by a joint committee of Senate and House. TVA had to face the music.

The music would be by no means a death march, since the Democrats controlled Congress and could in large measure determine the committee appointments. The investigating committee consisted of six Democrats and four Republicans. The chairman, Senator Vic Donahey, former governor of Ohio, occupied himself mainly with calling the committee to order and with watching the clock for the hours of recess or adjournment to arrive. At one fervent but somewhat incoherent moment, however, Senator Donahey burst forth with the words: "I will resist with all of the power at my command to keep from putting in the hands of the big utilities of this country any information that will help them wreck TVA."

Throughout much of the investigation the burden of questioning witnesses fell upon Francis Biddle, general counsel for the committee and later attorney general of the United States, and upon Representatives Charles A. Wolverton of New Jersey and Thomas A. Jenkins of Ohio. Biddle was on the whole a gentle questioner. His purpose seemed to be to steer the various witnesses, especially TVA staff members, along the easier, more obvious paths. He did not open trails into the bushes. Wolverton and Jenkins, who as Republicans had no desire merely to take a pleasant woodland walk, were forever breaking away and treeing the game in secluded spots. Their sharp questions gave TVA dignitaries some bad moments.

The angry vigor of the contest that preceded the investigation led the public to expect odorous revelations, and the press exaggerated this expectation by treating the TVA trouble as the common garden variety of political scandal. Newspapers apparently assumed that Arthur Morgan's charges of "dishonesty" could mean only that somebody had carried off millions of dollars in a little black bag. The investigation, therefore—although it was inherently a far more serious affair than the Dayton trial—"flopped," from a journalistic standpoint, when Arthur Morgan, on the witness stand, declared: "I have not charged that any director of the TVA has taken bribes or stolen money; nor have I charged that any director has profited financially through any transactions of the Authority. There are other and more subtle forms of failure to meet a public trust which are no less a menace to good government."

Upon second thought, furthermore, the deposed chairman retracted some of his charges and admitted error. And so, although his substantiation of other charges was detailed, specific, and lengthy, the majority report of the committee, when finally published, asserted that "Dr. A. E. Morgan's charges of dishonesty . . . are without foundation, not supported by the evidence, and made without due consideration of the available facts." The majority report praised Lilienthal and Harcourt Morgan for their "forbearance and dignity."

By such assertions and by their wholehearted unwillingness to find anything wrong with TVA, the majority of the committee thus achieved what was, in common parlance, a "whitewash" of TVA. The minority report took a very different view, but the minority were Republicans and at the time did not matter politically.

The printed record of the hearings of the committee, which filled four tremendous volumes and contained over six thousand pages of testimony, did not altogether support the majority view. Much of the committee's time, it was true, was used in hearing the directors and major staff members, and in one sense the investigation simply provided a forum in which the contending directors could defend their positions and review their acts and policies at great length.

TVA staff members, of the higher levels, had much the same privilege, but were more closely questioned by Wolverton and Jenkins. Relatively few witnesses of non-TVA connections were summoned, and in general the investigation did not go far beyond the opinions of the experts who were ready to talk about power, flood control, navigation, fertilizer, personnel, or such particular spots of interest as the Berry claims.

All the same, the story of TVA from its beginnings was there in rather full detail, and at times, through accident or through prompting from unknown sources, the committee uncovered some surprising odds and ends of information.

Early in the investigation the committee was astounded to hear from Arthur Morgan that he could not produce certain evidence because he was not being allowed to confer with TVA engineers. He had a certain limited access to TVA records, but he had been informed by Mr. Biddle that "I must not talk to any TVA employee . . . except in the presence of counsel [i.e., Biddle]." This statement caused a flurry in the committee room. Hastily, James L. Fly, general counsel for TVA, interrupted and explained that Dr. Morgan was not, of course, being placed incommunicado, but that the conferences had to be arranged "in an orderly administrative manner." The board, he declared, "feels that if Mr. Arthur Morgan, or any other person, is permitted to go secretly and underground and maintain and continue repeated contacts with a great number of TVA employees, it will result in utter demoralization of the staff."

At this brash explanation Representative Jenkins boiled over. TVA employees, he vowed, had a right as American ctizens to talk to whomever they pleased. Turning to Biddle, he charged that worthy with relaying to Fly whatever the TVA employees said in the officially arranged conferences. Then the top blew off.

After a heated wrangle, the committee finally voted, upon motion of Jenkins, that TVA employees need not report to any official either before or after conferring with a witness.

Before the committee had recovered from this upsetting experience, further testimony disclosed that TVA officials, especially Fly, had earlier carried to great lengths their mistrustful surveillance of Arthur Morgan. Charles A. Hoffman, assistant secretary of TVA—whose activities were supervised by Fly, as official secretary—testified that during the Berry condemnation proceedings Fly had upbraided him for furnishing Dr. Morgan with certified copies of certain board minutes, even though these were called for in court, and that Fly had ordered him not to furnish certified minutes for Dr. Morgan in the future except by his, Fly's, permission. The prohibition, apparently, did not extend to the other two board members.

Later, in June, 1938, shortly before the committee transferred its hearings from Washington to Knoxville, certain extraordinary incidents occurred. With the zeal of a Soviet commissar, the redoubtable Fly all but kidnaped Hoffman upon his return from an innocent holiday visit to Dayton, Ohio, where, Fly seemed to think, he was engaged in secretly conspiring with Arthur Morgan. Fly sent a messenger with a TVA car to meet Hoffman at the train upon his return and gave instructions to bring him at once, "baggage and all," to Fly's office. There Fly, in the presence of Herbert Marks and a stenographer, put Hoffman through a lengthy inquisition. The object was to discover whether Hoffman was in league with Morgan and also what had happened to a certain file containing minutes of the board, which file, Fly rashly inferred, had been slipped out for Morgan's use.

The file was, in truth, something for Fly to be concerned about since it contained, not minutes approved at official board meetings, but the "changed minutes" as altered and approved by individual directors in a fashion so peculiar and devious that the committee had great difficulty in understanding it. Startled and amazed, the committee learned that for years the directors had made a practice of altering board minutes and that nearly all the alterations were made by Mr. Lilienthal or by his order.

The changes had to do mainly with such matters as his negotiations with Wendell Willkie and with various features of power operations. Profoundly impressed by Hoffman's testimony, the committee ordered the minutes of the board and other records to be impounded, and later questioned the directors, especially Lilienthal, about this matter, for which no sensible explanation was ever offered.

Such evidence suggested that in too many instances the personal loyalties of TVA employees had eclipsed devotion to the public welfare. Some blame might attach to Arthur Morgan for his difficult temperament, his readiness to detect evil by the mere pricking of his thumbs. Yet it was also clear that Lilienthal and Harcourt Morgan had controlled TVA decisions in whatever spheres interested them and that they were responsible for much obscurantism. Their blandness was too miraculous to be true. By their own account these paragons of virtue had not, in five years of TVA history, made a single mistake—well, hardly any. Their remarkably perfect explanations explained everything but the obvious fact that they had fallen out with their distinguished chairman, and, not being able to persuade him, they had overridden him and then, with the aid of the president, destroyed him.

As for Arthur Morgan, stiff-necked and unamiable though he might be, he was at least more prone to admit error and to retract unwise statements, even at the cost of weakening his case. Although some of his charges were in the "not proved" category, his analysis of the costs, putative and hidden, of TVA power was destructive to the "yardstick" conception, which, as publicly advertised, now seemed to be Lilienthal's conception and not his.

Arthur Morgan's meticulous and thorough analysis of a group of Mississippi "yardstick communities" seemed to support his claim that those power enterprises showed a profit only because various costs were not accounted for; they were hidden subsidies—services supplied free by TVA and other government agencies and not available to private companies.

To this charge the answer of Lilienthal and of the chief power engineer, J. A. Krug, was that TVA wholesale rates really covered all costs. They minimized, they pooh-poohed as unimportant any hidden subsidies that had to be admitted. But ex-Chairman Morgan made a point against Lilienthal when he revealed that Lilienthal had really favored the "by-product" theory, which would have greatly reduced the costs chargeable to power, and was reluctant to accept the cost-allocation scheme finally required by Congress.

It was doubtful whether history could very soon do justice to such arguments, which only economic specialists could thoroughly unravel. Yet the main issue was not so obscured by technicalities as to bar the plain citizen from making a judgment.

The main issue was whether a public enterprise like TVA ought to be guided by the conscience of an Arthur Morgan or the conscience of a Lilienthal and a Harcourt Morgan. The two consciences represented different philosophies of public duty. Both favored the broad conception represented in TVA—the conception that, under modern conditions, the full resources of big government ought to be employed paternalistically for the public benefit in order that the fruits of technological progress might be distributed widely and equitably. This was a socialistic conception.

But Arthur Morgan believed, apparently, that the socialistic conception required of administrators a moral scrupulousness far above the common average in American affairs. He would not tolerate in himself or others any taint of politics or expediency. The public business must be an open book. He would not obscure issues or suppress facts—not even to win a victory over a power company or to appease an influential politician. He would not even *seem* to do so.

Complex TVA could not be explained in everyday words, but he did not think that fact entitled an administrator to hide behind a screen of experts and to tell the people only what it was thought good for them to know. Nor would he argue that TVA was anything but what it was. In a speech in Chattanooga, April 20, 1934, Morgan openly implied that TVA might indeed be "undemocratic," as critics had charged. But what of it? "In a perfect government," he said, "there would be some elements of communism, some of democracy, some of technocracy, and some of dictatorship." The important thing was not theory, but "to achieve sincerity towards oneself and others . . . and to nurture a strong and passionate commitment to serve the common good."

To David E. Lilienthal—with Harcourt Morgan seemingly in agreement—this attitude represented a hopeless lack of realism. It was "puritanical," as some TVA supporters openly said. The important thing was to get TVA well established before it could be destroyed by its opponents or by the changing currents of politics. They had a cause to promulgate and would not sit around deciding nice ethical points while the cause waited. They had no trouble in transferring to a vast, modern, technological, socialistic undertaking the cheery motivations of the nonsocialistic, untechnological past. They were careful not to say that the people were "too damned dumb to understand," but they knew that if folks received cheap electric current and certain other popular material improvements, no ugly questions would be asked. They chose the path of expediency and glorified it with romantic talk in which they perhaps believed. The end, which they thought good, justified the means, which did not seem too bad.

So David Lilienthal announced yardstick rates and signed twenty-year contracts for industrial power before the true cost of TVA power could be calculated. What of it? The public good was being served in many ways. There was no need to proclaim from the housetops that TVA was socialistic, when such admission was politically injurious. One could argue, moreover, that socialism was a kind of democracy, and one was therefore justified in saying that TVA was democratic. So, to Arthur Morgan's challenge, Lilienthal in good conscience could say: "The real objection of our critics is not that the basis for our rates is hidden. . . . The fact is that TVA's opponents do not like those rates." And "No business in this country has submitted cost data and estimates to the general public with the frequency and detail that TVA has done. . . . TVA has lived in a goldfish bowl." These were political utterances, and they were winners in 1938 and later.

Victorious on all fronts, but not without scars, TVA returned to work, but took good care to set its house in order at some points. It gave renewed attention to its accounting system, which even the friendly majority of the congressional investigating committee had termed "extremely unsatisfactory" and which the brand-new comptroller of TVA admitted was "appalling."

TVA also tackled, more earnestly than before, the brain-befuddling theory of cost allocation which was to determine how much of its investment should be charged to power. As of November, 1940, TVA decided to allocate 36 per cent of its "joint investment" to navigation, 24 per cent to flood control, and 40 per cent to power for the seven-dam system then in use. The layman, noting that of the $210,000,000 *total* investment at that stage, 66 per cent was attributed to power, 22 per cent to navigation, and 12 per cent to flood control, might be thunderstruck that only 40 per cent was allocated to power for the purpose of determining power costs. The answer to him, of course, was that he simply did not understand how to calculate "joint cost allocation" according to the "alternative justifiable expenditure" theory, which was the most reasonable of several possible theories including the fantastic and utterly repugnant notion that all should be charged to power.

There were certain changes in the board. Harcourt Morgan became chairman and ex-Senator James P. Pope of Idaho was appointed to fill the vacancy left by the deposing of Arthur Morgan. After three years Harcourt Morgan stepped gracefully aside and, in 1941, David E. Lilienthal became chairman of TVA.

It was a very popular appointment. Mr. Lilienthal was urbane and friendly. He could explain everything down to the last acre-foot, ton-mile, and kilowatt-hour, and was not bashful about doing so. In 1944 he published a little book, *TVA: Democracy on the March*, in which he gathered up all his explanations and restated them with his usual success. Reading it, you were bound to feel that everything was hunkydory in the Tennessee Valley. Tramp, tramp, tramp the boys were marching, though not to the old tune or in the same uniforms. All over the country people said what a wonderful thing it was that Mr. Lilienthal was doing for those poor fellows in Tennessee and Alabama.

But all the genius of Lilienthal could not keep TVA out of trouble. In the autumn of 1941, with the nation already on a war footing, Senator Kenneth D. McKellar of Tennessee suddenly spoke out in opposition to the proposed building of Douglas Dam on the French Broad River and launched a caustic personal attack upon Mr. Lilienthal. The senator accused Chairman Lilienthal and J. A. Krug of "indefensible and vindictive obstinacy" and declared that both men ought to resign.

Behind the senator stood a powerful section of East Tennessee opinion, armed with hot and specific protests. Not only would Douglas Dam flood, it was said, 31,000 acres of the finest farm land in East Tennessee, dispossess more than 3,000 persons, invade historic Dandridge, and cause the removal of prosperous canning plants and flour mills; but it would add another almost unbearable inundation to the inundations wrought by Chickamauga, Fort Loudoun, Norris, Cherokee, Watts Bar, and Hales Bar dams, whose reservoirs retired from use 172,960 acres of East Tennessee soil. Should East Tennessee be asked to give up still more?

In an eloquent public letter President James D. Hoskins of the University of Tennessee called attention to the harm done to rural life by the TVA removals:

> Good soil exists elsewhere, and for a price it may be had. When a home is destroyed, however, the loss may be irretrievable. . . . Farm homes thrust their roots deep within the soil. . . . East Tennessee and its culture, and its political institutions, are built upon the family, and the family is rooted in the soil.
>
> What provision can be made for these dispossessed? Is a Government check or ready cash any solution of their problem or of the community problem? What wounds will this money heal? Even if the Government should survey America from one end to the other in search of a whole area to be carefully planned as a community it would achieve only a poor substitute for a commu-

nity of growth and tradition. . . . There is more than damage here. There is destruction, irreparable destruction, irretrievable loss for some 3,000 persons.

In the first stages of the battle, at least, the senator had all the better of the argument. He conceded the need of additional power for the great aluminum plants of the valley, already engaged in the production of war materials, but argued that just as much power, or more, could be generated from two dams on the upper Cumberland, which the army engineers were ready to build, and from the dams on the Holston and Watauga, which TVA itself had earlier proposed. What had made the TVA suddenly change its mind? Why was it substituting the Douglas Dam project, which was bitterly opposed in Tennessee itself?

The answer of TVA was in strict engineering terms. Its construction crews and machinery were ready and could be transferred at once from one of the main river dams, just being completed, to the Douglas site. Douglas Dam could be built more quickly and economically than any other dam in view. It was too bad to inundate more farm land, but this was a "national emergency." The property, of course, was unavoidably local. Besides, TVA noted coldly, the value of the power generated would be greater, in money terms, than the value of the property inundated.

But though TVA and the New Deal mustered all their forces, the arguments of the senator from Tennessee prevailed, and the project failed of approval in the United States Senate.

Then came Pearl Harbor and the war. Although Senator McKellar and others remained unconvinced as to the special merits of Douglas Dam, the objections could no longer be pressed. It *was* a national emergency. The Douglas Dam project was revived. The dam was built upon the order of the War Production Board and was completed in record time.

Senator McKellar was not through fighting. In 1928, more than a decade previous, during the Senate debate on the Cove Creek Dam and in connection with the argument over tax replacements, he had confronted Senator Norris with a question. The people of Alabama, he conceded, had asked the federal government to develop Muscle Shoals and had not bothered about the inundation of their lands. They could do so if they wanted to. But in Tennessee there had been no such demand.

> Certainly the State, by its legislature, by its governmental authority, has never been here demanding it. They have made no request for it; and why, without their consent, should this be done? Is that the way the Federal government is going to treat one of its States—to come here and take, without its consent, and over its protest, its property in this fashion? . . . You have got to have the valleys, and you take them all.

Now, in truth, the valleys had been taken. As a matter of fact, Senator McKellar had not ultimately objected to that seizure, but had promoted it. The *Congressional Record* showed that his vote, on various occasions, had saved TVA appropriations in committee and that his great influence had expedited TVA business on the floor of the Senate. Now, for reasons that nobody could adequately explain, the senator was fiercely at odds with Chairman Lilienthal of TVA. Pro-TVA newspapers and commentators quickly stigmatized McKellar as an "enemy of TVA" and turned upon him their full powers of vituperation and ridicule.

As time went on, these attacks became more intense and systematic, but they had absolutely no deterring effect upon the senator from Tennessee. Senator McKellar was apparently determined not only to wage war upon Chairman Lilienthal, but also to bring TVA itself more closely within the direct supervision of Congress. He introduced various bills designed to limit TVA's financial autonomy. He argued that the authority should pay in funds and ask for appropriations like any other department of government. When his proposals failed, he reintroduced them, over and over. Among Senator McKellar's bills was one that would require federal administrative appointments, above a certain salary figure, to be approved by the Senate. This was greatly feared by TVA and was blocked only after arduous political exertions.

Undiscouraged, Senator McKellar renewed his legislative attempts, and he continued to fight Chairman Lilienthal. In 1946, when President Truman sought to transfer Mr. Lilienthal to the chairmanship of the new atomic commission and to appoint Gordon R. Clapp to the chairmanship of TVA, Senator McKellar made a very strong fight against both appointments. This time he charged that both men sympathized with or were tolerant of Communist doctrines. He produced witnesses who declared that a Communist cell had been allowed to flourish in TVA. After a prolonged and bitter struggle, both appointments were confirmed, but Clapp squeaked through by the narrowest of margins.

TVA survived. It survived its greatest peril, the peril of democracy. For although TVA and its advocates proclaimed ceaselessly that the authority was the finest flower of democratic tradition, it obviously dreaded and disliked the practical application of the tradition as it was represented in Kenneth D. McKellar, senator from Tennessee and president pro tempore of the Senate. Tennessee, the state upon which the authority's operations had the greatest physical effect, was not disposed to rebuke the aged but doughty fighter who had represented it for more than thirty years. In 1946, when McKellar was up for re-election, his opponent for the Democratic nomination, Edward Carmack, based his campaign principally on the charge that McKellar had been hostile to TVA. Carmack was supported by prominent newspapers and was aided by a large-scale propaganda, conducted on a Southwide basis and aimed at retiring from Congress the "reactionary" southern bloc. But the pro-TVA man made a miserable showing against his veteran opponent. Senator McKellar was renominated, and re-elected by one of the largest majorities of his career.

Although TVA had a perfect score in all its major battles, there were other rumbles of dissent. Many people, including a great many valley people, steadfastly believed that it was an act of impiety to doubt the goodness of TVA and would have been less shocked by a denial of God's existence than by assertion of the mildest flaw in the blessed authority.

Yet the human tendency to be heretical would not altogether down. There was a growing tendency to question TVA practices. Farmers whose lands had been sliced off by reservoirs were profoundly disgusted when TVA, changing its mind, began to sell off some of the "protective belt" of noninundated land at public auction. In 1939 Representative Jenkins, in his special minority view, criticized the "reckless abandon" with which TVA was purchasing land and said: "The record is full of disclosures of harsh practices of dealing with land-owners and of complaints of land-owners at treatment received...." TVA prestige suffered, and complaints multiplied, during the nineteen-forties when, in the Kentucky reservoir area, impelled perhaps by wartime haste, TVA agents seemed on occasion to behave like despoilers.

There was, for example, the Tishel farm, known as the Eagle Hill farm, on the right bank of the river at the Kentucky line, but on the Tennessee side. The farm was settled in the mid-nineteenth century by Frank Tishel, a young Bohemian immigrant who had left his native country to escape compulsory military service in the Austrian army. Tishel set up a tannery, but his son, Joe Tishel, forsook the tanyard and developed the farm. When TVA came along in the nineteen-forties, the farm was still in possession of the Tishel heirs, who had retained it as their beloved old home place, even though there was no longer a farmer in the family and the place had to be run by a tenant. It was a farm of nearly 600 acres, much of it in bottom land, and it also contained a large stand of virgin timber of high quality.

TVA flooded 435 acres of the Tishel place, including the valuable timber tract, and obtained an easement on 184 acres in addition. After an apparently hasty appraisal, TVA offered $15,765.78 for the tract needed as reservoir land. Since the heirs valued the place at $30,000 or more, they refused the offer. Condemnation proceedings followed and attracted unusual attention in the region. After hearing the evidence, the commission judged that TVA should pay $26,740 or almost double the appraisal price. The case went up to the Federal District Court and the Circuit Court of Appeals—but TVA lost.

TVA not only lost, but was revealed as having sadly misbehaved. The Tishel case hinged, in the end, on the value of the timber, the appraisal and disposal of which had been most negligently handled by TVA agents. Part of it was hastily cut and sawed under contract, as a rush job. The rest, including valuable walnut and cherry logs, was piled and burned.

Cases like this made a deep impression upon rural communities along the Lower Tennessee, particularly in the area where the Tennessee and the Cumberland run close together. People in that area feared that TVA might take over the Cumberland River too, in which case a tier of counties in Kentucky and Tennessee would suffer new losses. They would be flooded on two sides. A silent resistance gathered head. When Representative Percy Priest began, as was expected, to press his bill to TVA-ize the Cumberland, there was open, vocal, and well-organized opposition, and the proposal was beaten.

Within its own domain, however, TVA was established and seemingly impregnable. What the nation might think about TVA or the TVA idea was for the nation to decide. That was a privilege that the Tennessee Valley had not had with respect to TVA. The agitations of a few men and the long deliberations of Congress had decided all. Outside of a handful of responsible parties, the most ardent enthusiast for TVA within the valley had as little to do with its origin, maintenance, and continuance as had TVA's most bitter opponent. Whether TVA's power program, or any other of its programs, was right or wrong, cheap or costly, fair or unfair, it had to be accepted in the valley. One might hold that TVA as a power enterprise existed primarily for the benefit of urban areas and big industry and that therefore, in principle, it had violated the law and deceived the people. Or one might hold the opposite. It made no difference. It was nothing that either critic or defender could do anything about.

Accordingly, when Mr. Clapp moved up into Mr. Lilienthal's place, there was about the same amount of concern in the valley as when, during the Middle Ages, the peasant learned that a new king had been crowned at a distant city. All that anybody could do was to hope and pray that Mr. Clapp would be a good king and would behave kindly toward his subjects. If he should turn out to be a bad king, there was still not much that anybody could do. In other days, if you were discontented with a power company, you could appeal to the government. If you were discontented with TVA, to whom did you appeal? TVA was the government. In the Tennessee Valley there was nothing above it.

CHAPTER XIX

# Journal of a Voyage from Chattanooga to Paducah on the Good Steamboat *Gordon C. Greene*

*June 5, 1942.* Luxurious modern steamboats, or for that matter steamboats of any kind, are a rarity on the Upper Tennessee. The average Tennessean hardly ever thinks about such possibilities, but if he should want to go voyaging on the great river, it is not easy for him to find out what boat to take, or when, or where, or even if there is a boat. But, a few days ago, a little paragraph in the *Waterways Journal* announced that the *Gordon C. Greene,* of the Cincinnati Greene Line, would be at Chattanooga on June 5, 1942, and would leave on the following day for her return trip down the Tennessee. It would be the first trip she had ever made to Chattanooga. For a Tennessean, it was obviously the chance of a lifetime, and, with a global war going on, it might not come again soon. Until the TVA could bring in Watts Bar Dam and Fort Loudoun Dam, no steamboat trip would be possible above Chattanooga. But the *Gordon C. Greene* would take you from Chattanooga to Paducah—464 miles out of the total river length of 652 miles. Then away to Chattanooga and the *Gordon C. Greene.* . . .

The afternoon of June 5 is hot, and there is no relief from the heat at the Chattanooga waterfront, where the cobblestones of the old wharf slope down to the river, just below the Market Street bridge. There is no trouble in picking out the *Gordon C. Greene.* She is the biggest thing in view—and the only boat tied up there, except the *Dixie Queen,* a showboat that has fallen on hard times and is not at the moment in operation. The *Gordon C. Greene* is a true river packet of the old, familiar type, but she has been specially fitted out for the tourist trade. Above the cabin deck, which is of the regular kind, the owners have added an unusually elaborate texas deck, with a glassed-in front. Above that, and beneath the pilothouse, is still another deck with accommodations for the boat's officers and the pilots. The hull is steel, and so is much of the superstructure. There are stainless steel deck chairs, cushioned in bright colors; there are games for the passengers and space to promenade and sunbathe. The *Gordon C. Greene* carries no freight, of course. She takes folks for pleasure trips on the Ohio, the Mississippi, and the Tennessee; and the Chattanooga cruise, a fourteen-day trip, is in the nature of an experiment. Until the TVA built its dams above Muscle Shoals, the *Gordon C. Greene* never came higher than Florence. Now her master, Captain Tom R. Greene, wants to see how a cruise on "the Great Lakes of the South" will work out. With him is his mother, Captain Mary B. Greene, the famous woman pilot. On their boat, a passenger feels that he is enjoying the hospitality of a peculiarly gracious, appropriately old-fashioned family. There are Ohio-Mississippi pilots on board, too, anxious to learn the new river—among them Captain Jesse Hughes of the Greene Line and Captain Lawrence Allen. The Tennessee River pilots in charge are Captains Paul H. and Harris D. Underwood. They are sons of Captain Ambrose Underwood, a veteran pilot of the Upper Tennessee who, though past eighty, is still in service.

It is really an occasion for everybody concerned. The evening before, when the *Gordon C. Greene* tied up at the Chattanooga wharf, the Chattanoogans were ready with a special reception. As the landing stage was being lowered, the visitors were greeted with old southern airs, sung by a choir of Negroes, and a Chattanooga delegation welcomed the new arrival as the largest steamer ever to come to the city. Now as the hot afternoon verges toward evening, there is a bustle at the landing stage. Captain Stephen S. Yeandle, district commander of the Coast Guard, is coming on board with his wife. Other eminent persons appear: TVA officials, Chattanooga river enthusiasts, officials of barge lines, and visiting pilots, among the latter a tall Kentuckian, Captain William C. Dugan. The passengers drift back in groups from their excursions to Lookout Mountain and Chickamauga Park. They are mostly people from the East who are forced by the war to find some substitute for their usual Caribbean cruise or their Bermuda trip, but among them are some Ohioans and Middle Westerners, devotees of river travel.

Late in the afternoon a gust of wind sweeps down the river, and with it a quick, cooling shower. A little excursion boat, weak-powered and clumsy, with her wide upper deck fitted up as a dance floor, is caught broadside by the squall and cannot make her landing on the other side of the Tennessee. The current and the wind take her downstream out of sight. But when the rain stops, here she comes back, under control once more. The wharf at twilight is deserted, but you can still make out the old sign, "The Tennessee River Navigation Co.," across the end of a warehouse. An engine whines and rattles in a nearby factory—it must be war work. Negro men and women are fishing at the far end of the wharf, their backs silhouetted against the still water. The circling mountains gradually melt into the dark. The passengers are playing bridge, or just lounging. But there are also groups of talkers. In one of them, the most interesting of all to a traveler, there is Captain Donald Wright, the alert editor of the *Waterways Journal*, ready with cordial talk, and with him are some of the pilots and officers. What goes on here is in the western and southern tradition—the good-humored banter flung back and forth, the tales, the jokes. When Captain Jesse Hughes was coming through the Suck yesterday, did he try to see those old ring bolts, once used for warping, and didn't he know they were all under TVA water? But they might as well have been warping the *Gordon Greene* upstream, for all the speed they made. They were ahead of time, it was such easy traveling in slackwater, and they had to hold back, almost to drift back at times, in order to be at the Chattanooga wharf at 7 P.M., for the official reception. Had they heard the story about how old Captain So-and-so took soundings on the Big Sandy? He made a boy jump overboard, and the boy would call out, as he waded ahead, "Calf—calf—less than a calf—calf—calf—calf and a half!" And then the captain would yell, "Jump on, boy, I'll drive her through!" Or the story about the captain who lifted his boat off a sand bar by an unusual method. He had a load of turkeys on board. He nailed their feet to the deck, and then blew the whistle. The turkeys flew up, and the boat came clear. But more seriously, the question was whether they would have to lower the *Gordon Greene*'s smokestacks when they came to Scottsboro Bridge on the return trip. Coming up, they had lowered the stacks, but Captain Tom Greene thought they could clear the bridge without lowering, and they might try. As for bridge clearances in general, that was a subject to be serious about. The TVA, apparently, had not been too keenly alive to such little problems when it took over from the army engineers. How could it build dams so fast and be so slow about changing the various bridges? As the pools filled and their levels rose, many bridges, constructed for earlier river conditions, would certainly have to be raised. Otherwise, Mississippi River steamboats could not use the Tennessee with satisfaction.

*June 6, 1942.* We cast off at five o'clock in the morning. Not a soul to wave us good-bye, and the passengers nearly all asleep. It is done swiftly. In a few moments we are in midstream. Ahead, in the pale light of early dawn, the top of

Lookout Mountain is deep blue, and below it a belt of gray fog stands thick. The vapors rise from the river and cluster on high, until Lookout seems not the end of a ridge, but a cloud-encircled peak. Behind us, the darker factory smoke hovers in Chattanooga valley. At first real daylight we are rounding Moccasin Bend. The river here is not too wide to imagine how it happened that Mr. Payne, of the Donelson party, was killed by an Indian's rifle, firing from the thickets on Moccasin Bend. Brown's Ferry used to be along here, but it is not needed now. As we pass the great wedge of Williams Island, the sun is beginning to rise, and river and sky take on some color. The Tennessee is smooth as glass, and you would never know that we are sliding over what used to be the Tumbling Shoals, a boulder-strewn, tumultuous stretch; hardly anybody even remembers the name, these days. But a few large boulders are still visible at the water's edge.

It is good daylight when we steam toward the entrance of the Suck. It begins where Suck Creek comes in at the right, its mouth hardly discernible among the trees. In the mild June dawnlight the encircling mountain walls stand in clear relief, a green, slow-turning cyclorama. Signal Mountain is on the east, its abrupt cliffs set far back from the river. On the other side are the wild masses of Raccoon Mountain. These wooded steeps, so near a modern city, yet so inaccessible and unfrequented, are still, as in Indian times, the home of eagles, falcons, and the rare American raven; and Raccoon Mountain, in particular, is known to the forest-wise as a favorite haunt of rattlesnakes.

The sunlight strikes the mountaintops now, and we can see the characteristic shape of the rugged escarpment that forms the walls of the deep valley, really a great winding ravine, through which the Tennessee flows in this region. On the top, outlined against the sky, there is always a thin line of trees, the individual trees straggling and distinct; below, a belt of bare rock; gray, almost perpendicular cliffs running at the same level for miles; then the long, curving slopes of the mountain shoulders, thickly forested, running down, with deep valleys between them, to make a sharp angle with the river. As the boat swings to enter the Suck, the lofty promontories of Walden's Ridge line up in parallel juttings on our right, above the green of the descending slopes, and the dark, almost black-green sides of the nearer steeps overlie them, making overlapping geometrical patterns in the foreground, and almost meeting, it would seem, at the narrow passage of the river. And, at the lowest level, the perfectly quiet water, unrippled except by our passage, reflects in reverse order the layered, overlapping bulk of the mountain walls.

We round the point, turning abruptly to the left, and the same design is repeated, and so for many miles, as wooded point juts beyond wooded point. We know our direction only from the changing position of the sun. It was on the right when we entered the Suck. Now it stands squarely on the left.

The completion of Hales Bar Dam backed up the Tennessee in this mountain region and gave it this canallike smoothness. The building of Hales Bar Dam for a private company created no such inundation as the TVA has engaged in, but it made the Suck easily navigable. One can hardly believe that Untsaiyi ever waylaid travelers here, or that Untiguhi clutched boats in his whirl. The mountains are lonely. For thirty miles we see hardly a sign of human presence. A cabin or two, tucked away in a cove. A straggling patch of corn by a riverbank. Two mountaineers, surprised at our presence, turn to wave. They are the only persons we see in the thirty-odd miles between Chattanooga and Hales Bar Dam. After passing Kelly's Ferry (where there is no ferry now) the Tennessee takes us north again, and then almost straight west as we take the deep stretch above the dam.

There is a slight crackling noise from the cabin deck, and suddenly the voice of the purser, Roy Barkhau, comes over the loud-speaker, inviting us to breakfast at seven o'clock. We are also cautioned, and indeed are sternly admonished, to bring all cameras and deposit them in the purser's office. By government wartime orders, it is strictly forbidden to take pictures in the neighborhood of any dam. The *Gordon C. Greene*, we are informed, will be stopped and inspected by the Coast Guard before we can enter the lock, to make sure that no one among us is capable of achieving harm to lock or dam. On the jack staff flies the quarantine flag— a black ball on a yellow ground—to signify that the *Gordon C. Greene* was thoroughly inspected when she started on her trip. But an additional inspection is to be made at every dam.

Sure enough, as we approach the dam, a neat cabin cruiser comes up to challenge us, young men in sailors' uniforms standing on the gunwale and clinging to the cabin roof. We stop, and the Coast Guard detail swings smartly aboard. The swing looks easy, but we note that the young men wear life preservers. Snappy and spruce, the Coast Guardmen walk among the passengers and look us over as we lock through. The *Gordon C. Greene* is a large boat, and the Hales Bar Lock makes a fairly tight fit. By 7:45 we have locked through, and pass another Coast Guard boat, waiting for upstream traffic.

Below Hales Bar Dam is a shining new bridge for the new highway that goes over Raccoon Mountain to Chattanooga. There is nothing at all to remind one that Dragging Canoe's old capital, Running Water, once stood in this valley; but the great cliff where Major Ore's men, coming up from Nickajack, met and routed Dragging Canoe's tribesmen almost overhangs our passage. As we approach Shellmound and the region of Nickajack Cave the river gradually widens, and the mountains are away from the river in the near background. We are entering the Great Bend of the Tennessee and the corn-and-cotton lands of North Alabama. Behind us, the promontories of Walden's Ridge fade away. But it still seems an almost unpeopled country near the river. Except for South Pittsburg, where the houses stand out and the ferry is busy, we see few habitations, few people. There is the upper end of Long Island, and somewhere, buried among the trees on the right, is Bridgeport, the main crossing place for the Federal army in 1863. We take the left side of Long Island, and pass through the turnbridge. At noon we approach Scottsboro Bridge, and the *Gordon C. Greene*, moving very slowly, goes under the bridge without lowering smokestacks, indeed, with a few feet to spare.

Now we are far into the middle section of Guntersville pool, and the river is vastly wider. Widow's Bar Dam, well submerged, lies somewhere under the water. And there, too, impossible to distinguish now, is the old site of Crow Town. A piece of Bellefonte Island remains. We must be near Bellefonte Landing. The mountains have shrunken into hills and ridges, covered with scrub oak and occasional patches of pine. We meet a dredge or two, but no boats. In the wide channel, well marked by buoys, we move safely and easily, but in the shallows, at a little distance, the stumps raise their black heads, like old, neglected expanses of piling for some piers that never were built. Islets dot the river, green knolls of islands or of old river banks now submerged.

We are in the region of the permanent flood by which the TVA intends to prevent occasional floods, as well as achieve other multiple purposes. Here, the Tennessee is no longer a river, but an inland sea lapping the distant ridges. The new name, "Great Lakes of the Tennessee," has romantic merit in it, but really, the effect is like that of the Finger Lakes of upper New York, for the river fills the wooded valleys in curving, irregular hooks and quiet, narrow bays. Nevertheless, there is a certain immensity about it.

In the valleys of North Sauty and South Sauty creeks, which once entered the Tennessee from Jackson County on the north and Marshall County on the south, there are no longer any creeks, but only great bays that reach far inland from the old river channel. By rough measurement on a TVA map, the pool from the tip of North Sauty to the tip of

South Sauty must be at least twelve miles wide, perhaps as much as fifteen. And this Sauty Bay—as yet unnamed, but it might be called that—hooks one of its arms around a part of Jackson County and turns it into an island which is two or three miles wide and three or four miles long. Then, uniting with the valley of Roseberry Creek to the east, it reaches a prong toward Scottsboro, and makes a peninsula of the land between Scottsboro and the Tennessee.

Below, Pine Island is all gone, completely submerged. We are getting into the real lake now, above Guntersville. Gone is McKee Island, gone Henry Island. Pine Island was the old Creek Crossing Place, famous in pioneer times, but there is no crossing here now. Here was probably the Indian town of Coste, where De Soto's men, marauding foolishly, almost got into a battle; and on McKee Island was the Tali, the main town of the Indian province, near which De Soto camped.

On Buck Island, nearby, was enacted one of the tragedies of the last year of the Civil War. Thither, as Dr. W. A. Wyeth tells, five men, all noncombatants, fled for safety during the confusion of the great invasion. They hid in the cane, with their cattle and belongings, and were joined by a Confederate soldier, who had been wounded and was on furlough. But a notorious bushwhacker named Ben Harris found them out and followed them with his band. Harris lined up the five men and the Confederate soldier and gave them five minutes for a last prayer. Then he went down the line and with his six-shooter put bullets through the hearts of the five men. The Confederate soldier dropped just as Harris shot, and so the bullet did not pierce his heart. He feigned death, and was flung into the river with the five dead men. Fully conscious, holding his breath, he floated underneath some driftwood and hid behind a log while the marauders rounded up the cattle. When they had gone, he hid again in the cane and examined his wound. The bullet had struck a rib and glanced off without injuring him seriously.

The river-lake widens into two great prongs, and between the prongs the unflooded part of Guntersville, its waterfront remodeled by the TVA, perches on a hill. We make toward the long highway bridge that crosses the northern prong of the immense lake. That bridge was a headache to the TVA because it had to be raised to provide clearance for steamboats above the new level of the pool. It is a long bridge, more than a half mile long. Where we pass under it, Guntersville seems distant. And on the west side the river-lake also surrounds Guntersville. It has new docks, and a boat harbor, but is no more just a river town, it looks more like a seaport. Cabin cruisers and the N.C. & St.L. Railroad ferry tie up on what used to be the side of a hill, and far beneath the water is the old landing—the landing where the flatboats crowded, and from which many Cherokees, among them Will Rogers's great-grandmother, were shepherded into boats for their forced journey to the west.

At Guntersville Dam, again the warning from the loud-speaker, the rush to deposit cameras, the slow locking through. Inside the lock walls, it is stifling hot, but soon we are out again on the broad reaches of Wheeler Lake, and the motion of the boat cools us off. The texas deck, and the hurricane deck above, are like Lido or Atlantic City or Miami Beach, with passengers lolling or strolling in weirdly colored slacks and shorts. Some young women in scant bathing suits sprawl and improve their sun-tan. One diversion of the afternoon is a kind of automatic racing machine, with tiny painted ponies loping jerkily along wires, while C. W. Stoll of Louisville calls the races and announces results on the loudspeaker. The passengers bet on the numbered, jerking dummies. But on the river, which was almost a natural river again at the head of the pool, the bends widen as we pass the mouth of Paint Rock River and the bold bluffs on either side known as Paint Rock Bluffs. Did the Indians, perhaps, once paint great effigies of bird and beast on those cliffs? Water, oozing between the rock strata, stains the cliffs with colored drippings that take grotesque shapes, where romantic fancy can almost trace out the snake, bear, deer, and thunderbird of Indian times.

It is a rugged country, on the north side, but still no people or habitations. The only river traffic is the busy railroad ferry—the *Huntsville* and the *Guntersville* pushing great flats with freight cars aboard. In late afternoon we pass Hobbs Island, not much changed probably, with old trees and heavy undergrowth on its long spine. But neither here nor anywhere else do we see the thick cane of pioneer times. At Whitesburg, there is only a green point of land, no town at all, but another enormous highway bridge flings glittering arches across the river. On the point where a little creek enters, a dinky railroad brings dump cars loaded with clay which is carried on barges to a Decatur brickyard. An old Tennessee pilot, who knew the river in other days, supervises the loading. Ditto's Landing is truly almost as lonely as when Old Man Ditto first came here. Strangely enough, the great chemical arsenal that stretches for many miles along the river between Ditto's Landing and Huntsville is commanded by a Colonel Rollo Ditto. It covers one of the TVA's most cherished and beautiful area test demonstration projects. The army, like the TVA, always wants the best land.

We are getting into the real lake again, and it is hard to get oriented without studying the maps, old and new, and consulting the Coast Guard's *Light List*. Almost without knowing it, we pass old Triana, which was so ambitious once to become the Piraeus of Huntsville—Athens itself lies inland, farther west. Indian Creek, according to TVA maps, is backed up for many a mile, and Huntsville almost has access to the main river.

Straight ahead down the great lake, with steady throb-throb of engines, we steam for Decatur. From behind summer rain clouds the sinking sun throws a golden line of light along the water from which the Decatur sky line gradually emerges. The first sky line of a city that we have seen since leaving Chattanooga, about 160 miles upriver! It is 7:15 P.M., and we will tie up at Decatur for the night. There, on the south bank, are the lofty modernistic cylinders of a brand-new grain elevator. Wheat is brought here in grain barges, direct from the Upper Mississippi, by the company that manufactures Mother's Best Flour. Which doesn't harmonize, somehow, with the TVA's promotion of the culture of small grains in the Great Bend.

We bear over to the Decatur side of the river and make for the old landing, at the foot of Bank Street, near the railroad bridge. On the other side, the widened river stretches away in endless flats crossed by another new highway bridge with a viaduct and a long fill. The TVA spent close to two million dollars in this general area for highway adjustments alone. On the north side of the river, where Swan Lake used to be, there is still a large expanse of stump-infested shallows. How lucky for Decatur that it was on the high side of the river! How lucky, too, for the TVA!

The landing at Bank Street is badly neglected. Although the Ingalls Shipyard has excellent marine ways just around the bend, where barge building and shipbuilding are going on at a tremendous rate, and although the oil companies and the grain company have their own private terminals, there is nothing here for the general public. This sad condition, fortunately, the TVA proposes soon to remedy, with its terminal-building program.

Now there is nothing resembling a wharf—just rubble, dirt, and rank weeds at the sloping end of Bank Street, and the back ends of various unsavory-looking shacks and houses. The *Gordon C. Greene* must do considerable maneuvering to find a decent place to tie up. A TVA floating laboratory impertinently occupies the only good place where the landing stage can be put out. The engines back and come again as the donkey engine lowers the stage. The mate is in a bad temper, and hard to please, but at last the stage is down, and the passengers descend, picking their way through the weeds and trash. It is Saturday night. The imagination has to stretch a good deal to imagine what it was like here in the old days, when Decatur was a bustling transfer point for whatever had to go overland, around Muscle Shoals. Nothing is here now except the *Gordon C. Greene* and the TVA boat.

*June 7, 1942.* Sunday morning. We sleep late. The Catholics on board go to early mass. It is 9:30 when we put off into the wide part of Wheeler Lake. It is good farming country here, on the level south side, with a trend toward big plantations and mechanized farms. Nothing, not all the persuasions of TVA, seems to lessen enthusiasm for cotton. In Colbert County, it is said of a certain landed family: "They don't want all the land in the county; they just want what lies next to theirs." If you get out at dawn on a workday, and drive along the Decatur-Tuscumbia road, you can see trucks picking up the gangs of cotton choppers or cotton pickers, according to the season; or tractors busily intertilling the vast level fields, TVA or no TVA.

A curious-looking steel tower stands right in the middle of the lake, a little to one side of the main channel. It is a wave-measuring machine, which automatically records (and graphs) for the TVA the height and force of waves. TVA set it up after the discussion arose about the trouble that river traffic might have with waves on the new lake. Even on the natural river, there were dangers aplenty, of this sort. Irvin Cobb has not colored the picture too highly in his *All Aboard*. Big rivers are always dangerous.

The pilots talk of storms, which are common in the Tennessee region and very severe at certain seasons. Captain Paul Underwood says that, for his part, he always likes to tie up to the bank during a storm. But his father, Captain Ambrose Underwood, preferred to keep to the open river, because he reasoned the boat would "give" more to the wind in such a location, and there was less danger that the pilothouse might blow away. Moreover, he always opened wide the windows of the pilothouse, and let the wind come through. Still, Captain Paul Underwood feels better near the bank, and does not follow his father's example. And Captain Allen chimes in, "Yes, give me a good tree in a storm." In a mild, easy voice, his dark eyes casually reflective, Captain Underwood goes on, as if storms, after all, were a perfectly commonplace phenomenon, no worse than sand bars and shoals. The very first trip he took as a licensed pilot, a twister hit his boat. Though it lasted only a few minutes, it wrecked the pilothouse, tore a man's clothes completely off him, and upset things generally. He knew of a pilot who, after such a storm, found his pilot's license was missing. Luckily he recovered it, in a nearby field, wrapped around a cornstalk.

A tall, gray-haired man comes into the circle. He is Captain Conway Graden, navigation inspector of the Tennessee Valley Authority, and he used to be a Tennessee River pilot. In his time, before Wilson Dam came in or TVA was imagined, the rivermen could predict the stages of the river according to the weather cycle. For instance, at a certain time in early autumn, after the river had fallen very low, there would always be a slight rise—just a few inches maybe. This was the "leaf rise"—so called because it came at the time of the first fall of leaf. Soon afterwards, probably, would come a real rise, when the autumn rains sets in. And so on. But now the river has changed, and the weather has changed too, and what can be predicted?

He walks away, a commanding figure, with a little of the easy lankness of the woodsman about his shoulders and arms. They all belong to the country, the real country, these Tennessee pilots do. And the Ohio and Mississippi pilots are the same sort. They stand quite apart from the urbanized passengers. They belong to the world of Mark Twain and Mr. Bixby.

Island-spits appear, remnants of the old banks. We ought to be near Brown's Island, which of old gave warning that you were approaching Elk River Shoals and the long, bad stretch. But Brown's Island is gone. At high noon we pass the mouth of Elk River, another great bay leading north. Gone are Elk River Shoals. Gone is that old nuisance, Nance's Reef. At this point you can hardly tell which is Elk and which is Tennessee River, and besides, there is a southward bay, too. The pilot quickly picks up the daymark and goes ahead. It is really so easy. Or it looks easy.

We pass the Coast Guard inspection again and lock through Wheeler Dam. Beyond is the famous region of Big Muscle Shoals, but it's just Wilson Lake now, and no excitement whatever. The river is beautiful here, of course, but a little dull. The kind of made-over beauty that Hollywood prefers. Who cares now that we are, actually, slanting down, with the river falling 133 feet in 37 miles? The old flinty rocks are deep underneath our even keel. On the right you can follow, if you look close, the almost submerged remains of the old Muscle Shoals canal. The towpath, where the government-owned railroad used to run, barely sticks out of the water. Trees and bushes grow on it. A solitary cow, munching the fresh grass in the shallows near the bank, raises her head to stare at us. How narrow that canal was, how very conservatively it hugged that low bluff on the north bank! How narrow, how conservative, in comparison with this radical ocean-stretch of lake water before us, smooth and featureless!

Now the great double-lift locks of Wilson Dam, ninety feet altogether. There is hardly anything else like it on the inland rivers. But you can't see the majesty of Wilson Dam from the locks. Mostly you see a rush of water, and the cluttered masses of rock and drift at the tips of Jackson and Patton islands. The once-difficult channel between Patton Island and the north bank is now a canal. We coast almost noiselessly. It is a quiet shaded passage for a few moments, with great trees close around us, and cows grazing in the narrow meadows. Lock No. 1, below, is a very low lift, just an entrance to the canal. Then under the Florence bridge.

There is hardly anything in sight that looks like a wharf or a landing. We are at the back of Florence, and we are far from Tuscumbia. We slip downriver to Sheffield Landing, where a large Coast Guard boat and sundry barges are tied up, close to the overhanging trees. Here we too tie up for a while, and taxis are ready to take the passengers and some of the boat's officers and guests to Sheffield for an hour's visit. At 5:00 P.M. we are off again, passing Seven Mile Island, which is still much as it used to be because it is near the head of Pickwick Lake and is therefore not inundated. Ancient trees, matted with vines, stand close to the water's edge.

The island is being farmed still, there is a big cornfield, there are barns. Great water birds flap up from the timbered banks—blue herons they must be, though the rivermen call them cranes. Wild roses bloom profusely, flinging their sprays right above the water. A late afternoon shower comes, and passes, leaving long streamers of rain in the distance. The lake is an iridescent blue-green. All around, as it widens, we see the island-spits left from the old banks, covered with a fresh green of young sprouts, and on the south side, as we come near it, the sloughs and deepened creek mouths characteristic of a great reservoir area. As we approach the deep part of Pickwick Lake in the cool of evening, all is wild, lonely, deserted. Narrow arms of deep water enter the low wooded ridges. Colbert Shoals and old troubles lie fathoms deep, and where the Colberts used to ferry pioneer travelers on the Natchez Trace, all is a miles-wide expanse of calm lake water. A government signal light marks the point where Colbert Shoals Lock used to be. Far off, the remains of Riverton show on one distant hill, and soon, on another distant hill across the river, the remains of Waterloo, its farm bottoms all gone, a gash on the high north bank marking the relocated road.

Bear Creek, coming in from the left, is enormous. It looks as big as the Tennessee River itself. Eastport, Mississippi, was somewhere along here in the old times, but Eastport is long gone, long forgotten, covered up by time and the river.

But an old theme comes into the conversation of the modern rivermen—the haunting, frustrated wish of flatboat and early steamboat days, when men wanted to turn south for New Orleans, but at this point had to turn north with the Tennessee, and go the long way around. If there were only a canal! And a canal is still talked about, says Captain Wright. If Bear Creek, now already backed up far inland, could be joined with the Tombigbee River, say, and if you could thus get slackwater navigation all the way to Mobile, two great benefits would result. The Upper Tennessee would connect directly with the Gulf of Mexico; and shipping that came down the Mississippi could return by way of the Bear Creek canal, without having to struggle against the current and the devious windings of the Father of Waters.

In the twilight the swollen mouth of Yellow Creek is just visible. Here Sherman made his first dash against the Confederacy in 1862, and, failing miserably, steamed back to Pittsburg Landing and such fame as he got there. He would not know the place now.

Somewhere below Yellow Creek we tie up to the trees of the south bank. We are back in Tennessee, just across the boundary from Mississippi, almost at the corner where three states meet. Frogs croak. All is quiet and lonesome around us. Beyond the circle of light made by the *Gordon C. Greene*, the woods stand impenetrable and hostile. Within our company it is time for merrymaking. At one end of the long, ornate cabin the dining tables and chairs have been pushed aside. A little orchestra strikes up, and we have dancing, both "round" and "square." Captain Tom Greene himself calls the figures for the square dances, and he leads the Virginia reel with his mother, Captain Mary Greene. His version of the Virginia reel differs a little from the familiar southern one: the first gentleman and first lady don't "cross over," but the first couple lead, and there is less of standing still in line for the other dancers. Also there is singing. Captain Dugan, resplendent and handsome in a white tuxedo, gives several solos, in a fine tenor. The best of all, and the most popular with the passengers, is "Ol' Man River." There is a "mind reader" among the passengers, who mystifies us pleasantly by reading off, without seeing them, the things we write on slips of paper. He simply puts them to his forehead, and the matter comes through by magic. More music, more chatter, and a long quiet time afterwards on the silent, unfrequented river.

*June 8, 1942.* At daylight we are steaming across the wide, lonely reaches of Pickwick Lake, the deepest part, and almost immediately go through the great lock of Pickwick Landing Dam. We enter now the wild, natural river, which cannot be very different from what it was when the Donelson party came down it or when the Linkum gunboats moved up it in 1862. It is deeper, however, and has a more even flow, because the regulated release of water from the TVA dams has its effect. Before the TVA developments occurred, the controlling depth on the lower Tennessee was 5½ feet. Now it is 7½ feet.

And so, without noticing, we pass Big Bend Shoals, an old obstacle, and by breakfasttime are tying up at Pittsburg Landing, where automobiles are already arriving from Savannah to take passengers for a tour of Shiloh National Park.

Pittsburg Landing looks about like any ordinary ferryboat or country landing on the Tennessee—a strip of gravel and sand at the water's edge, and big trees overhanging the curving road that slants steeply up to the top of the bluff. The road follows the side of a short ravine or gulch. Along this ravine, probably, and on the steep banks and the narrow beach, the Federal soldiers crowded on the first day of Shiloh, glad to find a space defiladed from Confederate fire.

A few mussel boats are moored on the little beach, and their masters lounge nearby in the shade. A mussel boat is a small, homemade skiff, with boards fixed upright at bow and stern on each side. The boards are notched at the tops to hold two iron bars, placed lengthwise of the boat. From these

bars strings of small grapnels dangle in even festoons. A mussel fisherman takes his boat into the stream to show the passengers how the fishing is done. He drops the iron bar into the water, retaining it by a line fastened to the boat and puts out something that looks like a small sheet anchor. It both steadies and propels his little craft. The boat moves with the current, and the hooks drag across the mussel bed. Presently he hauls in, and returns the bar to the notched uprights. Mussels of all sizes now hang on the strings, often several on one string. When their open valves felt the hook, they shut tight, and now there they are. He throws in the other drag. It is lazy, easy fishing, but one has to know where to find the mussel beds. The little boat, outlined against the shadowed water, has a curiously primitive, archaic look.

Mussel fishing is indeed the oldest occupation on the river, but the prehistoric Indians who began it had no such boats or hooks. When Kentucky Dam comes in, mussel fishing, some think, will be ended on the Lower Tennessee, because the mussels can live only in water of a certain depth, where there is a good current, and a minimum of silt. In the changed environment of deep, slow-moving slackwater, they will not get the right food, the sediment will cover them, their larvae will not find the right hosts to cling to. The pearl-button industry, which depends so largely on mussels, will suffer a great loss, and the mussel fishers of the Lower Tennessee will lose occupation and income.

The mussel fisherman comes close, and opens a shell to reveal the pale flesh within, and the rich color of the concave. How much does he get for his shell? "Thirty-two dollars a ton," he answers. And of course there are the freshwater pearls, too, which bring something.

On the bluff above, the passengers return from their tour among the planted cannon and monuments of Shiloh Park, and gather at Park Headquarters for a lecture, given by an attendant, on the battle itself. His long pointer moves over a big wall map, tracing the stages of the battle. Some of his audience drift away and visit the museum, where there are Indian relics as well as rusty swords, muskets, and Minié balls. In one of the cases is a ceremonial pipe, beautifully carved out of catlinite—a piece that is sometimes loaned for special exhibits, for it is truly one of the great works of Indian antiquity. It was taken from a cone-shaped Indian mound near Dill Branch, the point of the farthest Confederate advance, where in very ancient times some unknown tribe of Indians had a fortified city on the lofty bank of the river. The figure is of a male Indian, completely nude. The perfectly muscled body is relaxed in a half-kneeling, half-crouching position that might be the posture of worship or submission, or he might be only waiting and listening. The inscrutable primitive face is tilted up a little. The figure is so placed that we must bend over to look at it closely, and we unconsciously assume his pose, half-kneeling, half-crouching, as if to harken to some whisper, to receive some oracular word, from the old gods of these woods and this river.

But no word comes. We issue into hot noon sunshine and see the tablets, the silent cannon, the stilted granite monuments among the trees, and walk past the ivy-covered walls where the Federal dead are buried, through the cultivated shrubbery, and down the road to the landing. Already the *Gordon C. Greene* is blowing her whistle.

Off again, down the old river. Not a great many more people will see the river exactly as we do now, with its wall of trees above banks of clay and gravel, gently curving in broad bends. Nothing is disturbed here. Driftwood, piles of brush, sometimes whole trees, naked of bark, lie where the current has lodged them. Herons flap lazily by. Sometimes they cross in front of us—"without whistling," as the rivermen say. Occasionally there is a buzzard, or a hawk, or a kingfisher with gaudy blue feathers and rattling cry. There is more wild life here than on the lakes. The islands—Diamond Island, Wolf Island, and others—are densely forested, just as Irvin Cobb says in his *All Aboard*: "Weeds and sedges and willows along the marges; pawpaws and sassafras and other stuff high upon its gentle slopes; a line of big trees like soldiers marching, going down its center from almost its upper tip to almost its lower tip." Through the trees lining the banks we get rare glimpses of cultivated fields, but it is a wild country—wild as when deer and turkey and Indian roamed here. And there are no people anywhere, except an occasional mussel fisherman.

Crump's Landing. The loud-speaker reminds us that here was posted General Lew Wallace's division. The Savannah bridge, and the old ferry, and the lofty façade of the Cherry House on the bluff. The loud-speaker calls attention to the Cherry House. But the passengers, relaxed and inert, hardly seem interested. They thumb no guidebooks and seek no lore of the country. Possibly they are not too clear in their minds about the Civil War—who was fighting whom, and about what.

The steamboat runs differently now. As we take the chutes around the islands, the water seems almost bumpy underneath. Paddle wheel and engines labor momentarily; the whole boat vibrates. That is a sign of shoal water, where the paddle wheel has little to bite into. But the *Gordon C. Greene* is a regular packet, shallow bottomed, easy floating, and she has good pilots. We go right on.

At Cerro Gordo the Tennessee bends sharply where the stream hits a bluff on the right bank. Perched high among trees and rocks is a huge brick building—one of the few remaining "general stores" of the old-fashioned kind, a famous place in its way. There is little else to be seen from the river at Cerro Gordo. And nothing is visible at Saltillo, farther down. The names tell part of the story of this region —of the days when the young men took the long trip by keelboat and steamboat and went off to war in Mexico, to follow the banner of Sam Houston, to remember the Alamo and Davy Crockett.

At Petticoat Riffle, just above Saltillo, the boat labors.

There are dikes on one side to deepen the channel. The pilot hugs the east bank, almost brushing a large sand bar. There will be no sand bars when the TVA takes over completely.

We pass into long, calm reaches of water. The placid stream reflects the tree shapes and the clouds. And there is Swallow Bluff, an ancient landmark. Shelving limestone rocks project, their levels slightly tilted, and make a cliff, curiously eroded. In the holes of this cliff the swallows have made their nests for thousands of generations. The whistle blows, and out they come from their hiding place, a cloud of swallows wheeling and twittering over the water. Underneath those shelving rocks, too, are what the pioneers called "rock houses" —sheltered places where hunters could camp, where Indians camped long before them. When Kentucky Dam comes in, and the waters rise, Swallow Bluff will be covered, and the ancient tribe of swallows, like the Indians, the farmers, the sharecroppers, will have to seek new homes. Since TVA will hardly provide for them, they will have to make shift for themselves. Perhaps they can lodge their cornucopia-shaped nests of mud on the concrete of Pickwick Dam.

Eagle's Nest Island, and a swift current in the chute. We go through fast. Somebody is firing a shotgun among the oaks and poplars of the island. Big birds rise up, and circle, but they are not eagles. They look like hawks.

Clifton stands high on the right bank, an old river town, scene of many Civil War troubles. From the river, Clifton does not look inviting. A street comes down to the edge of the bluff. There are stores and a hotel. But the landing, if it could be called a landing, is brushy, gullied, unkempt. There is a sawmill, with crossties and lumber piled near. Since World War II started, millions of board feet of lumber have been sawed in this country. Before, it was mainly crossties for the railroad, cut from these endless oak forests. No warehouses, no wharf, no boats at Clifton.

Hillier country now. A great rock bluff on the river. More sand bars, more islands, a narrow channel. At Beach

Creek Island we stop to let a large tow pass upstream. Two towboats—the *James H.* and the *Little Eddie*—are pushing five gasoline barges. Probably they dropped off the sixth at Perryville Landing. In the three days of our cruise, this is the one big tow we have seen.

Passing Perryville Landing, hardly noticeable, we turn and twist for a while, taking the chutes swiftly, seeming almost to be borne by the current. The river straightens out, and all is placid and dreamy again. This must be one of the favorite fishing grounds of the mussel boats. We see them far ahead, in groups of two or three, poised in silhouette on the blue water. As we come near, they take up their drags and scurry to the bank. We are in a drowsy world where time has stopped and life is simple. Utter wilderness. A rough country, with ridges of the plateaus east and west of the river appearing now and then above the banks. On a sunny sand bar, dark-colored birds are hopping to and fro. A throng of them, black and a little awkward, yet strangely agile in a grotesque way. They are buzzards, a whole colony. Overhead, more buzzards wheel in majestic circles, their broad wings never moving. Near Cuba Landing, a shower overtakes us. On the high east bank there is a log cabin with a dog-run, almost the only one we have seen near the river, out of all the thousands of pioneer cabins in this country. No other houses. No people. For a long stretch, trees are blown down—the track of a tornado that visited here during the spring.

Duck River comes in unobtrusively, but it makes a series of dangerous shoals. The *Gordon C. Greene* follows the curve of the west bank here. Duck River Suck is a tricky place. Here Ellett's Marine Brigade got in trouble with Confederate guerrillas. It was a favorite spot for Indian attacks, too. But in two years more, the river will widen enormously. There will be a great expanse of lake, and Duck River will become a broad estuary, curving deep into Humphreys County.

The sun is setting. We are coming into the region where the reservoir clearance gangs of the TVA have been at work. They have denuded the landscape within the area where the water will come. You can see what a river valley is like without trees in it. The timber gone. The earth in its bare skin. The *Gordon C. Greene*, on the river, is in a big winding ditch, full of water, which is the actual river bed. That big ditch traverses a still bigger one, an enormous trough scooped out between the rims of the highlands east and west. Fine cornfields checker the rich bottom lands now, but the water will cover all these. Beyond them, above the reservoir line, is the poor soil of the highland, where the scrub oaks grow. The timber crews have been lately busy and logs and brush are piled, to be hauled away or burned. Some are evidently not to be hauled. They are burning. The pungent smoke drifts across the river. Smokes go up all around as from a forest fire or the campfires of an army of Civil War times. It is not all just brush burning. Some of those burning piles look like good logs. They *are* logs.

Near the ferry landing, not far from the blazing piles, stands a little house. It must go, too. It is in the way of the water and will be wrecked or burned. The house of some sharecropper or mussel fisher, perhaps. If it were a mansion, its fate would be the same. They are burning up the country again, along the Tennessee River—to make way for rising water. To make way for the Tennessee Valley Authority. For President Franklin D. Roosevelt and the shining New Deal. For Senator Norris of Nebraska, father of the TVA. For Mr. David Lilienthal and "decentralized" government. General Progress is marching up the river. General Progress is marching through Old Kentucky and Tennessee.

In Knoxville, at this quiet moment of evening, the offices of the TVA are vacant, and the economists, the agricultural experts, the power engineers, the planners, the authorities have all gone to dinner, in excellently serviced homes on the Kingston Pike or in Norris Village. But the letter files wait, the dossier is ready on the desk, the blueprints are in precise order, and tomorrow inexorable calculation will resume its plotted course, filling in, bit by bit, the enormous design; and the axmen and tractors of the clearance gangs also will resume, while below, at Kentucky Dam, the concrete mixers and pourers, the steam cranes and steam shovels, the swarming, orderly trucks will fulfill decisions of yesterday.

In twilight we pass the railroad bridge at Johnsonville, and Johnsonville itself. Gravel barges and a dredge on the east bank. The roof of the ancient, decaying hotel, where travelers used to wait for the steamboat. Nothing else.

Darkness is falling on the Tennessee. Where is Reynoldsburg Island in this darkness? Or Danville, or the mouth of Big Sandy? Or what used to be Paris Landing? Or Fort Henry and Panther Island? Across the river lie the arches of highway bridge and railroad bridge, for still, as of old, the lines of men's going and coming cross the river and do not follow it. Bridges on the Lower Tennessee are poorly lighted. The pilot must go carefully. On one great bridge there is just one dim red lamp. Our pilot turns on a searchlight. The beam goes probing ahead, feeling through the darkness, swinging right and left to pick up the buoys and daymarks. The deforestation of the banks by the TVA has made night navigation difficult, for the time being, even for good Tennessee River pilots. Familiar landmarks are gone. The banks look different. But the searchlight probes and swings, resting a moment on one bank, then flashing to the other.

Again we pass an area where fires have been set. Their numerous blazings mingle with the distant lights of the channel, far ahead. The *Gordon C. Greene* moves on. She will not tie up tonight, for we are due in Paducah at early morning. We are in Kentucky now. Between here and Gilbertsville will be the deepest part of the reservoir lake made by Kentucky Dam. There are little Kentucky towns that will be blotted out beneath the advancing waters. Newburg, for example; one of the oldest shipping points on the river, a haunt of guerrilla bands in wartimes—near it is an old graveyard called "the guerrilla graveyard." The "home guard" of Newburg hid in the bushes and shot the guerrillas as, with their horses, they swam the river. The town was shelled by gunboats, and it knew the night riders of later days. Now it must be drowned out.

Past midnight, and more dancing fires along the bank. The smoke settles on the river. It gets in your eyes. There is nothing more to see along here.

*June 9, 1942.* Coming into Paducah at early daylight. From C. W. Stoll we learn that at three o'clock in the morning, when nearly everybody was asleep, we passed the *Golden Eagle,* a famous old Mississippi boat, the only other packet that makes regular cruises on the Tennessee. She was going up, for her regular trip to Sheffield. Captain Buck Leyhe shouted greetings as the two boats passed, a little above Gilbertsville. As we come near the mouth of the Tennessee we meet, at last, numerous boats, mostly government craft and towboats. Many more are tied up in what is called the Duck's Nest, between Owens Island and the Paducah side. It is a famous winter harbor, for the Tennessee seldom freezes, and many boats from the Ohio and Mississippi seek shelter here from the ice that jams the Ohio. Beyond, you can trace a distinct line where the blue water of the Tennessee meets the yellow water of the Ohio. Paducah is a real river city, indeed is the only place in 464 miles of voyaging where you can see a river front crowded with shipping, some boats tied up and waiting for business, others being overhauled, some being loaded, others putting out. It is a long riverfront, but presently the Koppers Marine Ways comes in sight, and here we are at Paducah wharf—a real wharf, with plenty of room and a good place to tie up. It is time to say good-bye. Good-bye to Captain Donald Wright, who is off for the city at once, on an editorial errand. Good-bye to Captain Tom Greene, master, and to his mother, Captain Mary Greene, the best of hosts. And to Purser Roy L. Barkhau, who has so helpfully furnished bus and train schedules, to Mate Carr, and Second Mate Fenton, and a special good-bye to the pilots who brought us down the great river. Good-bye, Captain Hughes, Captain Allen, Captain Harris Underwood—but not yet good-bye to Captain Paul Underwood, for he is getting off, and we will seek the Nashville bus together. Good-bye to Mr. Stoll and to the engineers. And another special good-bye to Watchman John M. Wolfe, who knocked on the cabin door at dawn, three days running.

A step on the deck, and a hearty handshake. It is Fred Neuman, of the Paducah *Sun-Democrat*, the historian of Paducah. He has his car ready, and we must by all means join him until bustime.

Later, over our coffee, we hear a whistle blowing and a bell ringing. Captain Underwood looks at his watch. The *Gordon C. Greene* is bound for Cincinnati, but she should have left long before. She is blowing her whistle again. The deep sound comes up the street, dominating traffic noises and small talk. Must be for some latecomer, and he had better come on. Could it be for Captain Wright? Might well be.

It is time to go.

Farewell, Paducah. Farewell to the Tennessee. We are back in the difficult hurry of modern roads and ways, but we will not forget that mighty river bending in the valley where God put it, the most controlled of rivers now, but once so uncontrollable. Farewell, for a long, long time to the Indian river, to the river of the pioneers, of the steamboats and gunboats and mussel boats. New times, new customs have made you look new, but you are very old. What dove will fly over your deluge, bringing word of still newer change, we cannot know.

Fare you well, Tennessee.

# Acknowledgments

**M**Y INDEBTEDNESS to various individuals and institutions has been previously indicated in the acknowledgments appended to *The Tennessee, Volume I;* to these benefactors I renew my earlier expression of thanks. I am deeply obliged also to the following persons who have kindly furnished information or made suggestions during the course of the work on Volume II: Stanley F. Horn, Nashville; F. A. Scott, Mentor, Ohio; Andrew N. Lytle of Tennessee; J. Bodine Henslee, "Admiral of the Tennessee," Murray, Kentucky; Gilbert Govan and J. W. Livingood, University of Chattanooga; Captain Joe Holland, Paducah; Captain Paul Underwood and Captain Harris Underwood of Tennessee; Captain Jesse P. Hughes, Cincinnati; Captain Donald T. Wright, St. Louis; S. L. Massengale and Iley M. Thompson, Chattanooga; J. N. Winn, Florence; Clopper Almon, Sheffield; General Lytle Brown, Franklin, Tennessee; Dr. George R. Mayfield, Vanderbilt University; Professor John Van Sickle, Wabash College; Professor Dan M. Robison, Vanderbilt University; Mrs. Newman Brandon, Nashville; Edgar Graham, Nashville; Harvey Broome, Knoxville.

T. L. Sturdevant, Director of Information for the Tennessee Valley Authority, was most generous and prompt in answering questions, in supplying data, and in facilitating my inquiries by arranging interviews with the TVA personnel of various departments. I am indeed grateful to Mr. Sturdevant and his staff and to the members of the TVA staff who patiently heard my questions and gave me much

## ACKNOWLEDGMENTS 363

valuable technical information and instruction. The interpretation of TVA activities that I give is, however, my own, except where otherwise indicated.

I wish to thank Thomas B. Alexander of Clemson College for permitting me to read his valuable unpublished study, *The Political Reconstruction of Tennessee*.

# A Selected Bibliography

**BOOKS**

AMBLER, CHARLES H., *A History of Transportation in the Ohio Valley.* Glendale, Calif., 1932.
ARMSTRONG, ZELLA, *The History of Hamilton County and Chattanooga, Tennessee.* Chattanooga, 1931, 1940.
BELKNAP, CHARLES E. (ed.), *History of the Michigan Organizations at Chickamauga, Chattanooga, and Missionary Ridge* (2nd ed.). Lansing, Mich., 1899.
BISHOP, JOSEPH BUCKLIN, and BISHOP, FARNHAM, *Goethals, Genius of the Panama Canal.* New York and London, 1930.
BOKUM, HERMANN, *The Tennessee Handbook and Immigrant's Guide.* Philadelphia, 1868.
BRAZELTON, B. G., *A History of Hardin County, Tennessee.* Nashville, 1885.
BROWNLOW, WILLIAM G., *Sketches of the Rise, Progress, and Decline of Secession, with a Narrative of Personal Adventures among the Rebels.* Philadelphia, 1862.
CAMPBELL, T. J., *The Upper Tennessee.* Chattanooga, 1932.
CIST, HENRY M., *The Army of the Cumberland.* New York, 1882.
COBB, IRVIN S., *All Aboard.* New York, 1928.
COLLINS, FREDERICK L., *Uncle Sam's Billion Dollar Baby.* New York, 1945.
COULTER, E. MERTON, *The Civil War and Readjustment in Kentucky.* Chapel Hill, 1926.
———, *William G. Brownlow, Fighting Parson of the Southern Highlands.* Chapel Hill, 1937.
DANA, CHARLES A., *Recollections of the Civil War.* New York, 1898.
DAVIS, ELMER, *History of the New York Times, 1851-1921.* New York, 1921.
DRAKE, EDWIN L., *The Annals of the Army of Tennessee and Early Western History.* Vol. I, April-December, 1878. Nashville, 1878.

## A SELECTED BIBLIOGRAPHY 365

FLEMING, WALTER L., *Civil War and Reconstruction in Alabama*. New York, 1905.
———, *The Sequel of Appomattox: a Chronicle of the Reunion of the States*. New Haven, 1919.
FITCH, JOHN, *Annals of the Army of the Cumberland*. Philadelphia, 1864.
GRACIE, ARCHIBALD, *The Truth About Chickamauga*. Boston, 1911.
GRANT, U. S., *Personal Memoirs of U. S. Grant* (2 vols.). New York, 1885.
HENRY, ROBERT SELPH, *"First with the Most" Forrest*. Indianapolis, 1944.
HORN, STANLEY F., *Invisible Empire: The Story of the Ku Klux Klan, 1866-1871*. Boston, 1939.
———, *The Army of Tennessee; A Military History*. Indianapolis, 1941.
JOHNSON, ROBERT UNDERWOOD, and BUEL, CLARENCE C. (eds.), *Battles and Leaders of the Civil War* (4 vols.). New York, 1884-1887.
KILLEBREW, J. B., *Introduction to the Resources of Tennessee*. Nashville, 1874.
LESTER, J. C., and WILSON, D. L., *Ku Klux Klan: Its Origin, Growth, and Disbandment*. Nashville, 1884.
LILIENTHAL, DAVID E., *TVA—Democracy on the March*. New York, 1944.
LYTLE, ANDREW NELSON, *Bedford Forrest and His Critter Company*. New York, 1931.
MAHAN, A. T., *The Gulf and Inland Waters (The Navy in the Civil War*, Vol. 3). New York, 1883.
MOORE, A. B., *History of Alabama*. University, Ala., 1935.
MORTON, JOHN WATSON, *The Artillery of Nathan Bedford Forrest's Cavalry*. Nashville and Dallas, 1909.
NEUMAN, FRED G., *The Story of Paducah*. Paducah, 1927.
PARKS, EDD WINFIELD, "Sawney Webb: Tennessee's Schoolmaster," in *Segments of Southern Thought*. Athens, Ga., 1938.
PORTER, ADMIRAL DAVID D., *Naval History of the Civil War*. New York, 1886.
PRITCHETT, C. HERMAN, *The Tennessee Valley Authority: A Study in Public Administration*. Chapel Hill, 1943.
RANSMEIER, JOSEPH S., *The Tennessee Valley Authority: A Case in the Economics of Multiple Purpose Stream Planning*. Nashville, 1942.
RIDLEY, BROMFIELD L., *Battles and Sketches of the Army of Tennessee*. Mexico, Missouri, 1906.

Rothrock, Mary U. (ed.), *The French Broad-Holston Country: A History of Knox County, Tennessee*. East Tennessee Historical Society, Knoxville, 1946.
Scharf, J. Thomas, *History of the Confederate States Navy*. New York, 1887.
Scopes Case (Appeal). *Briefs and Arguments of Thomas H. Malone, Amicus Curiae; Tennessee Academy of Science, Amicus Curiae; John Randolph Neal, Clarence Darrow, and others, for the Appellant; Frank M. Thompson, Attorney General, and others for the State of Tennessee*. Supreme Court of Tennessee, September session, 1925.
Sheridan, P. H., *Personal Memoirs*. New York, 1888.
Sherman, W. T., *Personal Memoirs* (4th ed.). New York, 1891.
Sorrel, G. Moxley, *Recollections of a Confederate Staff Officer*. Washington, 1905.
Spence, W. Jerome, and Spence, David L., *A History of Hickman County, Tennessee*. Nashville, 1900.
Temple, Oliver P., *East Tennessee and the Civil War*. Cincinnati, 1899.
*Visit to the Tennessee River, A: On the Invitation of the Tennessee River Improvement Association*. Illustrated Souvenir Booklet, 1915.
Walke, Rear Admiral H., *Naval Scenes and Reminiscences of the Civil War in the United States, on the Southern and Western Waters*. New York, 1877.
Wallace, Lew, *An Autobiography* (2 vols.). New York, 1906.
Williams, Samuel C., *General John T. Wilder, Commander of the Lightning Brigade*. Bloomington, Ind., 1936.
Wyeth, John Allan, *Life of General Nathan Bedford Forrest*. New York, 1904.
———, *With Sabre and Scalpel: The Autobiography of a Soldier and Surgeon*. New York, 1914.

GOVERNMENT PUBLICATIONS AND OTHER PUBLIC DOCUMENTS

General:

*Congressional Record*.
*Official Records of the Union and Confederate Armies in the War of the Rebellion*.
*Official Records of the Union and Confederate Navies in the War of the Rebellion*. Series I, Vols. 22-27.
*U.S. Statutes at Large*, vol. 48, p. 58. (Provisions of the Tennessee Valley Authority Act of 1933.)

# A SELECTED BIBLIOGRAPHY 367

Hearings of Committees:

*Investigation of the Tennessee Valley Authority.* Hearings of the Joint Committee. 75th Cong., 3rd Sess. 14 parts, 4 vols. Washington, 1939.
*Hearings before a Subcommittee of the Committee on Agriculture and Forestry of the U.S. Senate.* 77th Cong., 2nd Sess., March 16-19, 1942. (On Senator McKellar's proposed amendment to TVA Act.)

Legal:

*Ashwander et al. v. Tennessee Valley Authority et al.,* 297 U.S. 288 (Feb. 17, 1936).
*John Thomas Scopes v. the State.* 154 Tenn. 105. (The Scopes appeal.)
*Tennessee Electric Power Co. et al. v. Tennessee Valley Authority et al.,* 306 U.S. 118 (Jan. 30, 1939).
*Tennessee Electric Power Co. et al. v. Tennessee Valley Authority et al.,* 21 F. Supp. 947 (1938).

Reports:

*Annual Reports of the Chief of Engineers.*
*Annual Reports of the Tennessee Valley Authority, 1934-1946.*

Congressional Committees (in chronological order):

*Report of the Joint Committee on Reconstruction.* 39th Cong., 1st Sess. Washington, 1866.
*Ku Klux Conspiracy. Report of the Joint Select Committee to Inquire into the Condition of Affairs in the Late Insurrectionary States.* Feb. 19, 1872. (Especially Vol. I.)
*House Report 998,* 66th Cong., 2nd Sess., 1920. (Charges of waste, etc., in construction of Wilson Dam.)
*Senate Report 831.* 67th Cong., 2nd Sess., 1922. Report of the Committee on Agriculture and Forestry on Henry Ford's offer.
*Majority and Minority Reports of the Muscle Shoals Inquiry.* Appointed on March 26, 1925. 69th Cong., 1st Sess., H. Doc. 119.
*Report of the Joint Committee on the Investigation of the Tennessee Valley Authority.* 76th Cong., 1st Sess. Sen. Doc. 56. Washington, 1939.

Surveys (in chronological order):

*Survey of Tennessee River from Chattanooga to Paducah.* William B. Gaw, 1868. 40th Cong., 2nd Sess., H. Ex. Doc. 271.
*Survey of Tennessee River at the "Suck", or Mountain Section, below Chattanooga.* G. T. Nelles, 1900. 56th Cong., 1st Sess., H. Doc. 461. (Recommends lock and dam at Scott Point.)
*Survey of the Tennessee River from Scott Point to Lock A.* Maj. Dan C. Kingman, 1901. 57th Cong., 1st Sess., H. Doc. 170.
*Tennessee River, Tenn., Ala., and Ky.* Maj. William W. Harts, 1910. 62nd Cong., 2nd Sess., H. Doc. 360.
*Tennessee River between Brown's Island and Florence, Ala.* Maj. H. Burgess, 1916. 64th Cong., 1st Sess., H. Doc. 1262.
*Tennessee River and Tributaries. North Carolina, Tennessee, Alabama, and Kentucky.* Major Lewis H. Watkins, 1930. 71st Cong., 2nd Sess., H. Doc. 328.

Tennessee Valley Authority—Technical Reports and Pamphlets:

BALL, CARLETON R., *A Study of the Work of the Land-Grant Colleges in the Tennessee Valley Area in Cooperation with the Tennessee Valley Authority.* Knoxville, 1939.
*Chattanooga Flood Control Problem, The.* 76th Cong., 1st Sess., January, 1939. H. Doc. 91.
*Cheaper Transportation via the Tennessee River.* Tennessee Valley Authority Commerce Dept. Knoxville, 1946.
ELLIOTT, JOE A., *Test Demonstration Communities.* Publication 271, Agricultural Extension Service, University of Tennessee.
*Farming for Victory and Peace: Some Lessons from Tennessee Unit Test Demonstration Farms.* University of Tennessee Agricultural Extension Service, Knoxville, 1942.
FERRIS, JOHN P., *Engineering and Social Progress in the South.* Georgia School of Technology, Experiment Station Bulletin, No. 6, December, 1938.
*Forests and Human Welfare.* Washington, 1940.
*How Cheap Electricity Pays Its Way.* TVA pamphlet.
*Malaria and Its Control in the Tennessee Valley.* Chattanooga, 1942.
MORGAN, HARCOURT A., *Rural Electrification: A Promise to American Life.* Washington, 1938.
SHEEHAN, W. J., *Prospective Commerce on the Tennessee River.* Knoxville, 1941.
*Recreation Development of the Tennessee River System.* 76th Cong., H. Doc. 565. 1940.

# A SELECTED BIBLIOGRAPHY 369

*Scenic Resources of the Tennessee Valley, The.* A Descriptive and Pictorial Inventory. Washington, 1938.
*Technical Reports:*
   No. 1. *The Norris Project,* 1940.
   No. 2. *The Wheeler Project,* 1940.
   No. 3. *The Pickwick Landing Project,* 1941.
   No. 4. *The Guntersville Project,* 1941.
   No. 6. *The Chickamauga Project,* 1942.
*Tennessee Valley Authority Architecture as Published in the Magazine Pencil Points.* (Reprint from *Pencil Points* of November, 1939.) Knoxville, 1940.
*Unified Development of the Tennessee River System, The.* (Report to Congress of the Tennessee Valley Authority.) Knoxville, 1936.

### PERIODICAL LITERATURE

BISHOP, EUGENE L., "The Health and Safety Services of the Tennessee Valley Authority," *Public Personnel Review,* January, 1943.
CROWELL, CHESTER T., "Tennessee Valley, a Prevision of Utopia," *Literary Digest,* CXVII (March 17, 1934).
FORBES, A. F., "No Monkeying with Evolution in Tennessee," *Literary Digest,* LXXXV (April 18, 1925).
GOVAN, GILBERT E., and LIVINGOOD, J. W., "Adolph S. Ochs: The Boy Publisher." *East Tennessee Historical Society's Publications,* No. 17, 1945.
HURST, T. M., "The Battle of Shiloh," *Tennessee Historical Magazine,* V (July 1919), 87. Contains list of steamboats and gunboats used by Federal army in the Shiloh campaign.
LIVINGOOD, JAMES W., "Chattanooga, Tennessee: Its Economic History in the Years Immediately Following Appomattox," *East Tennessee Historical Society's Publications,* No. 15, 1943.
OWSLEY, FRANK L., "Scottsboro: The Third Crusade," *American Review,* I (June, 1933), 257-285.
"Scottsboro Hero," *Time,* XXX (Aug. 2, 1937), 39.
"Some Remarks on Northern Methodist Missionary Appropriations," *Christian Advocate,* Dec. 19, 1874. Editorial.
WHITE, WALTER, "The Negro and the Communists," *Harper's Magazine,* CLXIV (December, 1931), 62-72.
WILSON, EDMUND, "The Freight-car Case," *New Republic,* LXVIII (Aug. 26, 1931), 38-43.

WRIGHT, DONALD T., "On the Upper Tennessee and Four of Its Tributaries," *Waterways Journal*, LVII (March 4, 1944). Report of first commercial tow to reach Knoxville on the new river.

**NEWSPAPERS**

Chattanooga *Daily Times*
Chattanooga *Evening Tribune*
Florence *Times*
Florence *Tribune*
Knoxville *Journal*
Knoxville *News-Sentinel*
Nashville *Banner*
Nashville *Tennessean*
New York *Times*
Paducah *Sun-Democrat*
Rossville *Open Gate*
Sheffield *Standard*

# Index

## A

Agriculture, TVA program, 289-305
  cash crops, 291-92
Alabama & Chattanooga Railroad, 152-53
Alabama and Muscle Shoals, 233-35
Alabama Power Company, 179, 181, 184-87, 189, 307-09
Aluminum Company of America, 248
American Cyanimid Company, 179
Anderson, Major Charles W., 90
*Annals of Tennessee, The*, by Ramsey, 116
Army of Northern Virginia, 9
Army of Tennessee (Confederate), 16, 42, 43, 45, 49, 52, 69, 70, 74-75, 92, 105, 106
*Army of Tennessee, The*, by Horn, 104
Army of the Cumberland (Union), 41, 43, 47, 71
Army of the Tennessee (Union), 16
Atlanta, Georgia, 104
Atomic plant, Oak Ridge, Tennessee, 269

## B

Ballad, "The Battle of Shiloh," 38-39
Bank of Tennessee, 140
Barge lines, 281-82
Barmore, Seymour, 134-35
"Battle above the Clouds," 74
"Battle of Shiloh," ballad, 38-39
Battles. *See* Names of battles
Bear Creek Canal, proposed, 350
Beauregard, General Pierre G. T., 8, 25, 34, 41
Berry, George L., claim, 313-36
Big Muscle Shoals, 171, 182

Boat building, 156-57
Boats, river, 281-83
Bokum, Hermann, 149
Bragg, General Braxton, 9, 26, 41, 42, 43, 47, 51, 55, 61, 62, 68-70, 73-75
Bridges, 117
Brown, General Lytle, 188-89, 191, 193-94, 249
Brownlow, William G. ("Parson"), and the Ku Klux Klan, 118-36
Brown's Ferry, 68, 69, 71
Bryan, William Jennings, 199, 201-02
  death, 202
Buck Island, 342
Buell, General Don Carlos, 8, 36, 41, 112
Burnside, General Ambrose E., 64, 71
Bushwhackers, 80, 89, 106, 110, 112, 113
Butler, John Worthington, anti-evolution bill, 197-98

## C

Canal, proposed, Bear Creek, 350
Capital, Northern, 148
Carpetbaggers and scalawags, 120, 122
Carriger, Christian, 150
Cavalry, floating, 98-100
Charges against Southerners, 210-12
Charts, river, 279-80
Chattanooga, 48, 49, 50, 55, 59, 62, 63, 64, 114, 151, 152-53, 154, 168, 262-63, 283-84, 334-35
*Chattanooga*, 65-66, 67, 75
Chattanooga, Battle of, 9
Chattanooga Steamboat Company, 171
*Chattanooga Times*, 154-55

*Cherokee*, 158-59
Cherokee Indians, 116, 148, 149
Chickamauga, Battle of, 51-76
Chickamauga Dam, 262, 277
Chickamauga Reservoir, 247
Churches, Tennessee, 147
Civil War, 5-117
   cost of, 107-17
   destruction by, 107-17
Civilians, war upon, 84-85
Clapp, Gordon R., 330, 333
Cleburne, General Patrick R., 73-74
Clinch River, 189, 219
Coal, 153
Cobb, Irvin S., 285
Colbert Shoals, 92, 164, 170
Colbert Shoals Canal, 172, 242
Commonwealth & Southern Company, 266, 268
Communists, 206-07, 209
Conservative Unionists, 121-23
Constitution of Tennessee, 136
Convention (Unionist, 1865), 118-19
Cooper, Hugh L., 182
Corinth, Mississippi, 10, 26, 31, 37, 94
Cost of the Civil War, 107-17
Cost of TVA, 249
Counties, 254
Cove Creek Dam. See Norris Dam
Cracker Line, 65-66
Crops, cash, 291-92
Cumberland River, 6, 8, 10, 15, 81, 98, 242, 328, 332
Cumberland University, 139

D

Dam Number 3. See Wheeler Dam
Dams, 177, 178, 224, 235, 236, 239, 240, 241, 242, 244, 246, 248
   high and low, 236, 238, 239, 241, 247-48
   projected, 192, 193
   superdams, 263-64
   see also names of dams
Dana, Charles A., 58, 59, 67
Darrow, Clarence, 199-203

Davis, Commodore Charles H., 80-81
Davis, Jefferson, 7, 9, 41, 46, 70, 91, 92
Dayton, Tennessee, 247
   evolution trial, 195, 196-204
Decatur, Alabama, 344-46
"Destroying Angels," 113
Destruction in the Civil War, 107-17
Development plan, unified, 191-94, 235-36, 253, 341
Dodge, General Grenville M., 111
Douglas Dam, 327-28
Duck River, Battle of, 82

E

Eads, James B., 13
Earthquake zone, 248
*Eastport*, 12, 23
East Tennessee, 116-17
Education, 196-97, 204
   Negro, 147
   public, in Tennessee, 139-41, 197, 200
Electric Home and Farm Authority, 311-12
Elk River Shoals, 169, 171
Ellet, Brigadier General Alfred, 82
Erosion, soil, 289-90
Evolution trial. See Dayton, Tennessee

F

Farming. See Agriculture
Ferries, 117
Fertilizer. See Nitrates
Fitch, Lieutenant Commander Le Roy, 81, 100
Fleet, Union, on the rivers, 16
Floating cavalry, 98-100
Floods and flood control; inundation, planned, 188, 192, 193, 219, 220, 236, 237, 238, 241, 242, 243-44, 262-65, 289-90
   great flood of 1867, 117, 158-59
Florence, Alabama, 40, 47, 93, 110
Fontana Dam, 248, 264
Foote, Captain Andrew H., 13

# INDEX 373

Ford, Henry, 183-86
Forrest, General Nathan Bedford, 9, 24, 35, 36-37, 42-46, 55-56, 62, 64, 69-70, 84, 87, 90, 91-106, 126, 131-33, 149
Fort Donelson, 8, 9, 22, 24
Fort Henry, 8, 9, 17, 18-22
Fourteenth Amendment, 122
Franklin, Battle of, 105
Freedmen's Bureau, 108, 122
Freight, 274-76
French Broad River, 75, 162
Fundamentalism, 197

## G

Game, increase in Civil War years, 117
"Gaps," mountain, 53-54
Garfield, General James A., 59
Goethals, General George W., 170
*Gordon C. Greene*, voyage of, 334-61
Gordon, General George W., 127
Government ownership, 187-89
Grady, Henry W., 147, 149
Grant, General Ulysses S., 6, 16, 25, 31, 33, 64, 70, 73, 133
Great Bend, 10, 32, 40, 41, 108, 110, 112, 113, 152, 233, 244, 262
"Great Lakes of the Tennessee," 341
Greene, Captain Mary B., 335
Greene, Captain Tom R., 335
Guerrillas and gunboats, 77-90
Gunboats, 12-13, 15, 17-18, 19, 46, 67, 95-100
  at Shiloh, 35

## H

Hales Bar Dam, 177, 247, 262, 277, 339
Halleck, General Henry W., 25, 29, 41
Handicrafts, 150-51
Harris, Governor Isham G., 16-17, 140
Hiawassee Dam, 248
High-dam and low-dam systems, 236, 238, 239, 241, 247-48

Highland Rim, the, 43
Hinson, Jack, 89-90
Hood, General John B., 56, 61, 92, 96, 103-06, 118
Hooker, General Joseph, 64, 73
Horn, Stanley F., *Invisible Empire*, 126
Horseshoe Ridge, 58, 59, 60-61
Hoskins, James D., 327
Huntsville, Alabama, 129-30
Hydroelectric power, 176-94

## I

Improvements, river, 168-72
Indians, 148, 149
Industry, development of, 152-54
*Introduction to the Resources of Tennessee*, 137, 138
Inundations. *See* Floods and flood control
Investments, Northern, 148
*Invisible Empire*, by Horn, 126
Iron, 153
Ironclads, 13

## J

"Jayhawkers," 89, 110
*John A. Patten*, 172-74
Johnson, Andrew, 96, 119, 121, 133, 140
Johnsonville, Tennessee, 96, 98, 99, 100, 102, 103, 117
Johnston, General Albert Sidney, 8, 17, 25, 34
Johnston, General Joseph E., 76, 92
Johnston, Colonel William Preston, 32

## K

Kelley, Colonel C. D., 94-95
Kelley's Ferry, 69
Kentucky, Reconstruction in, 120
Kentucky Dam, 243-44, 248, 277
Killebrew, James B., *Resources of Tennessee*, 137, 138, 139-40, 150, 153
Klinck, Leonard G., 85-87

## INDEX

Knoxville, Tennessee, 71, 75, 114, 151, 284
Ku Klux Klan, 118-36
  origin and history, 124

### L

Labor, in Tennessee, 144-45
Lakes formed by dams, 247
Landscaping at Muscle Shoals, 229, 232
Lee, General Robert E., 9
Leibowitz, Samuel S., 208-09
Lilienthal, David E., 223, 227, 239, 240, 266, 270, 280, 306, 307, 314, 316, 326, 329, 333
  dispute with A. E. Morgan, 314, 316-26
  *TVA: Democracy on the March*, 326
Lincoln, Abraham, 8, 25, 91, 92
  plan for Reconstruction, 119, 120
Little Muscle Shoals, 106, 169, 171, 190
Little River, 75
Locks, river, 276-78
Longstreet, General James, 45, 56, 59, 63, 75, 76
Lookout Mountain, 48, 52, 62, 73-74
Low-dam and high-dam systems, 236, 238, 239, 241, 247-48
Lower river, 10, 11, 40, 80, 89, 109, 164
Loyal League (Union League), 125, 128, 132

### M

MacLemore's Cave, 53, 55
Malaria control, 260, 264, 279
March to the sea, Sherman's, 84, 92, 104
Marine Brigade, Ellet's, 82
Massengale, S. L., 285-88
Mate, steamboat, old-time, 285-88
*Mazeppa*, 97
McCook, General Robert L., 110-11
McFarland's Gap, 60

McKellar, Kenneth D., 181, 190, 239-40, 248, 327-31
Memphis & Charleston Railroad, 10, 25, 30, 41, 42, 72, 110, 164
Military Reconstruction Act, 128
Missionary Ridge, Battle of, 62, 71, 73
Mississippi River Brigade, Ellet's, 82
Mississippi Squadron, 13
Mitchel, General Ormsby M., 87, 110
Moccasin Bend, 69
Morgan, Arthur E., 219, 222, 227, 229, 234, 238-40, 254, 262, 290
  dispute with colleagues, 314, 316-26
Morgan, General John H., 42
Morgan, Harcourt A., 22, 227, 239, 290, 301, 314, 316, 326
  dispute with A. E. Morgan, 314, 316-26
Morton, Captain, 98, 101, 102
Mountaineers, 150, 151
Mouth of the river, capture by Unionists, 5, 10
Murfreesboro, Battle of, 43
Muscle Shoals, 11-12, 105, 168, 176, 214
  strategic importance of, 40-50
Muscle Shoals Canal, 168-71
Muscle Shoals Commission, 190
Muscle Shoals Hydroelectric Power Company, 178, 179, 184
Mussel boats, 352-53

### N

Narrows, The, 66, 158, 177
Nashville & Chattanooga Railroad, 47, 48, 93
Nashville & Northwestern Railroad, 96
Natchez Trace, the, 93
Navigation, 246, 272-88, 334-61
Negroes, 120, 122-23
  education, 139-40, 147
  enfranchisement, 122
  labor, in Tennessee, 144-45
  relations with whites, 195-96, 209

# INDEX

Negroes—*Continued*
  social separateness, 145
  TVA workers, 252
  troops, 112-13, 122
New Deal, 209, 211, 213, 223
New Madrid earthquake zone, 248
New South, 147-48, 195
New York *Times*, 154-55
Nitrates (fertilizer), 180, 182-83, 185, 219, 265, 292-97, 301-02
Norris, George W., 179, 184, 185-86, 187, 189, 190, 191, 214, 216, 217, 218, 227
Norris Dam (formerly Cove Creek Dam), 189, 190, 219, 226, 227-29, 232-33, 266, 314
Norris Freeway, 229
Norris Village, 229, 232

## O

Oak Ridge atomic plant, 269
Ochs, Adolph S., 154-55

## P

Packets. *See* Steamboats
Paducah, Kentucky, 5, 109, 284-85, 360
Paine, General E. A., 109
Panther Island, 18
*Parker*, 172-74
Parker's Cross Roads, Battle of, 46
Peabody, George, and the Peabody Fund, 139
Peay, Governor Austin, 196-98
Phelps, Lieutenant, 17, 23, 81
Phosphates. *See* Nitrates
Pickwick Landing Dam, 241-42, 243, 277
Pigeon Mountain, 52-53
Pilot, woman, Mary B. Greene, 335
Pilots, river, 14
Pipe, Indian, 354
Pittsburg Landing, Battle of. *See* Shiloh
Plan, unified, for development, 191-94

Polk, General (Bishop) Leonidas, 6, 17, 56, 58
Poll tax, 141
Pope, James P., 326
Porter, Admiral David D., 71-72, 98
Power, electric, 176-94
  planned amount, and cost, 192
  *See also* Tennessee Valley Authority

## R

Race, steamboat, 172-74
Radical Republicans, 120, 133, 135, 136, 140, 145
Railroads, 164, 168, 174, 274-75
  *See also* Names of railroads
Ramsey, *Annals of Tennessee*, 116
Rankin's Ferry, 66
Rebuilding of Tennessee, 137
Reconciliation, 147-48
Reconstruction, after the Civil War, 109, 113, 118-55
Religion and science, 197, 200
Remaking of the river, by TVA, 226-50
Republicans, Radical, 120
Resources of Tennessee, 137-38
*Resources of Tennessee*, by Killebrew, 137, 138, 139-40, 150, 153
Reynoldsville Island, 100
*River, The* (motion picture), 289-90
Roane Iron Company, 153
Rodgers, Commodore John, 12, 13
Roosevelt, Franklin Delano, 213, 214, 215, 314, 317
Rosecrans, General William S., 41, 43, 47, 51, 54, 58, 59, 63, 64

## S

Scalawags and carpetbaggers, 120, 122
*Scenic Resources of the Tennessee Valley, The*, 261
Schools. *See* Education
Scopes, John Thomas, trial of. *See* Dayton, Tennessee
Scottsboro case, 195, 204-09

Sectional animosities, 209-11, 213
Senter, De Witt C., 135-36
Sequatchie Valley, 64, 113
"Sheffield site," Muscle Shoals, 181-82
Sheridan, General Philip H., 47
Sherman, General William T., 7, 30, 32, 34, 64, 71-73, 82, 84, 91, 92, 93, 103-06, 112, 170
Shiloh, Battle of, 9, 25-37, 353-54
Shipbuilding, 275
Siltage, 290-91
Snipers, Confederate, 14
  See also Guerrillas
Snyder, John I., 255-56
Song, "Kingdom Coming," by Work, 77, 79
Soil erosion, 289-90
Stanton, Colonel J. C., 152-53
Steamboat mate, old-time, 285-88
Steamboat race, 172-74
Steamboats, 11, 65-66, 67, 117, 156-75
  Grant's, 28
"Store boats," 157
Streight, Colonel Abel D., and his raid, 15, 44-45
Suck, The, 69, 158, 177, 338-39

T

Taylor, General Richard, 96
Tennessee, secession, 7
  survey, 137-39
*Tennessee*, 87-89
Tennessee Coal & Iron Company, 153
Tennessee Electric Power Company, 177, 249, 266, 268, 310-11
*Tennessee Handbook and Immigrant's Guide*, 149
Tennessee National Migratory Wildlife Refuge, 280
*Tennessee River and Tributaries*, 191
Tennessee River Improvement Association, 178, 180-81
Tennessee River Navigation Company, 336
Tennessee Valley, destruction in the Civil War, 107-17

Tennessee Valley Authority, 177, 179, 181, 184, 190, 211
  Ashwander case, 307-09
  battles of, 306-33
  cost allocation, 326
  cost of, 249
  criticisms of, 302-04, 306-33
  displaced persons, 255, 257-59
  flood control. See Floods and flood control
  game, fostering of, 260-61
  investigation by Congress, 318-24
  land clearance, 259-60
  land purchases, 255-56
  legal battles, 306-33
  Nineteen Power Companies Case, 307, 310-11
  power production and use, 265-70
  recreation program, 261
  remaking of the river, 226-50
  reservoirs, 254-55
  workings, 251-71
  "yardstick" program, 306, 323, 325
Tennessee Valley Authority Act, 215-22
Terminals, "public use," 273, 283
Thomas, General George H., 49, 53, 55, 58, 60, 64
Tilghman, General Lloyd, 15, 18, 20
*Times*, New York, 154-55
"Tinclads," 80-81
Tishel farm case, 331-32
Tourists, 229, 233
Traffic, river, 274-76
Tri-Cities area, 178, 184, 186
Tupelo, Mississippi, 266-67
Turchin, Colonel, 110
TVA. See Tennessee Valley Authority
*TVA: Democracy on the March*, by Lilienthal, 326

U

*Uncle Sam's Billion-Dollar Baby*, by Collins, 187
*Unified Development of the Tennessee River System, The*, 241, 290

INDEX 377

Union League (Loyal League), 122, 123, 125, 128, 132
Union men in Kentucky and Tennessee, 8
Unionists' convention, 118-19
*Upper Tennessee, The*, by Campbell, 160
Utopias, 145-48
University of the South, 139

V

Valley of the Tennessee, destruction in the Civil War, 107-17
Vanderbilt University, 139
Vicksburg, 9, 40, 41
"Volunteer Companies" (Confederate), 78
Voyage from Chattanooga to Paducah, 334-61

W

*W. D. Terry*, 85-87
Walden's Ridge, 63, 65
Wallace, General Lew, 17-18, 29, 30, 33, 36
Washburn, Frank, 179, 183
Watauga country, 75
Water power, 176-94

Water Power Act, Federal, 193
*Waterways Journal*, 277
Watkins, Lewis H., 189, 191, 194, 249
Wauhatchie Valley, 68
Webb, John, 142
Webb, William R. ("Sawney"; "Old Sawney"), and his school, 141-45
Western & Atlantic Railroad, 52
Western Flotilla, 13
Wheeler Dam (Dam Number 3), 182, 183, 192, 219, 226, 228, 233, 262
"Whisky for the General," 97
Wilder, General John T., 153
Wildlife refuge, 280
Willkie, Wendell, 266, 268
Wilson Dam, 172, 179, 182, 183, 184, 188, 190, 262, 266, 308-09
Woman pilot, Mrs. Mary B. Greene, 335
Work, Henry C., song, "Kingdom Coming," 77, 79
Worthington, J. W., 178-82, 183, 184
Wrecks in new waters, 278
Wyeth, Doctor John A., 87-89, 113-14

Y

Yellow fever, 160
York, Sergeant Alvin, 196

DONALD DAVIDSON (1893–1968), a native Tennessean, pursued the varied career of a man of letters as an editor, journalist, teacher, historian, literary critic, and poet. At Vanderbilt University, Davidson belonged to the Fugitive group of poets, three of whom later joined him in the Agrarian symposium *I'll Take My Stand*, published in 1930. His social criticism includes *The Attack on Leviathan* (1938) and *Still Rebels, Still Yankees* (1957). The two volumes of his history of the Tennessee River were first published in 1946 and 1948.

RUSSELL KIRK, man of letters, who lives at the forgotten village of Mecosta, Michigan, is the president of two educational foundations and editor of the quarterly *University Bookman*. He has written thirty books, published from 1951 to 1992, among them *The Conservative Mind, Eliot and His Age, Enemies of the Permanent Things, Edmund Burke, Beyond the Dreams of Avarice, Roots of American Order,* and *The Conservative Constitution*.

www.ingramcontent.com/pod-product-compliance
Lightning Source LLC
Chambersburg PA
CBHW022059150426
43195CB00008B/192